COMPARATIVE INTERNATIONAL LAW

The modern field of comparative international law emerged in the last century, but it still suffers from a lack of intellectual and methodological foundations. This ambitious collection hopes to fill that gap.

It examines the key concepts of comparative international law, including its historical and critical perspectives. Contributors from a wide geographical range present their diverse and thought-provoking views on international and comparative law. This is a much needed and cutting-edge book on an undervalued yet topical field of research.

Comparative International Law

Foundations and Critique

Edited by
Robert Schütze
and
Mathias Siems

•HART•
OXFORD • LONDON • NEW YORK • NEW DELHI • SYDNEY

HART PUBLISHING
Bloomsbury Publishing Plc
Kemp House, Chawley Park, Cumnor Hill, Oxford, OX2 9PH, UK
1385 Broadway, New York, NY 10018, USA
Bloomsbury Publishing Ireland Limited, 29 Earlsfort Terrace, Dublin 2, D02 AY28, Ireland

HART PUBLISHING, the Hart/Stag logo, BLOOMSBURY and the Diana logo are trademarks of Bloomsbury Publishing Plc

First published in Great Britain 2026

A catalogue record for this book is available from the British Library.

A catalogue record for this book is available from the Library of Congress.

ISBN: HB: 978-1-50997-239-5
ePDF: 978-1-50997-241-8
ePub: 978-1-50997-240-1

Typeset by Compuscript Ltd, Shannon

For product safety related questions contact productsafety@bloomsbury.com

To find out more about our authors and books visit www.hartpublishing.co.uk. Here you will find extracts, author information, details of forthcoming events and the option to sign up for our newsletters.

PREFACE

The view that there is not one but *many* conceptions of international law and that there were and are many distinct international legal order*s* – in the plural – has a long pedigree. During the nineteenth century, for example, international law saw the gradual consolidation of a 'European' conception of international law, and for much of the twentieth century, a distinct socialist conception of international law competed with that of the Western 'First World'. However, with the decline of the 'Second World' after 1989, and despite the rise of 'Third World' approaches to international law, this historic plurality of international law conceptions has been overshadowed by early twenty-first-century claims of ('Western') legal universalism. In the last decade, a small group of scholars have nonetheless 'rediscovered' international law divergences under the banner of 'comparative international law'. The existing literature has thereby mainly focused on national divergences and individual cases studies; yet we still lack a work that critically addresses the intellectual and historical foundations of the idea of comparative international law.

This book aims to fill this gap. It starts from the core question of what, methodologically and substantively, a comparative law lens can contribute to the analysis of international law. This approach has been partly used in the context of the 'comparative foreign relations law' literature as a specific substantive area of comparative constitutional law; yet, unlike the latter, this book applies a comparative lens to international law as such. It is therefore less interested in whether there exist specific national approaches to international law. Instead, it investigates whether different understandings can be grouped into specific 'legal families' and what may explain the differences and similarities between them. It also wishes to explore the mechanisms of – vertical and horizontal – legal transfers through which similarities between different international systems can be created. Finally, the book explores older and newer relationships between the disciplines of international law, international relations, comparative law and global law.

The book is divided into three parts. The chapters in Part I, by the editors, 'set the scene' by exploring the literature and history of comparative international law as a discipline. The chapters in Part II are dedicated to 'historical and comparative perspectives'. They analyse differences and similarities in the most important regional approaches to international law. They also include an immanent element of critique, as they discuss, for example, colonialist influences and transplants when compared to the local or indigenous conceptions of international law. Part III expressly brings these 'critical and analytical perspectives' to the idea of comparative international law. The chapters here explore its relationship to international relations and international decolonisation, but also analyse the roles (international) science and (international) quantitative comparisons play in the conceptual design and content of comparative international law. A chapter on the relationship between 'comparative international law' and 'global law' concludes the book.

The book is a collaborative fruit of a joint project between the Durham Global Policy Institute (GPI) and the European University Institute (EUI), where a conference workshop took place in October 2022. We would like to thank our respective institutions for their funding and organisational support, and Hart Publishing for the professional assistance in producing and printing the final result. In particular, we would like to thank Sinéad Moloney, Sasha Jawed and Verity Stuart from Hart Publishing, Catherine Minahan, Jon Lloyd, Pranav Putcha and Niall O'Shaughnessy for their help with proofreading and editing, Valeria Raso, Andrea Gaiba, Valentina Gorgoni and Louise Haysey for their support in organising the EUI workshop, and Arnulf Becker Lorca, Neha Jain, Sarah Nouwen and Ernst-Ulrich Petersmann for their contributions to the workshop. We would also like to especially thank our patient contributors for updating their chapters up to early 2025.

CONTENTS

LIST OF CONTRIBUTORS

Ge Chen, Associate Professor in Global Media Law and Information Law, Durham University, UK.

Rían Derrig, Assistant Professor, WMU-Sasakawa Global Ocean Institute, World Maritime University, Malmö, Sweden.

Ming Du, Professor of Transnational Law and Co-director of the Global Policy Institute, Durham University, UK.

Saïda El Boudouhi, Professor, Université Paris 8 Vincennes Saint-Denis, France.

Jaakko Husa, Professor in Law and Globalisation, University of Helsinki, Finland.

Marta Infantino, Associate Professor of Comparative Private Law, University of Trieste, Italy.

Max H Mayer, Research Assistant, University of Tübingen, Germany.

Ugo Mattei, Emeritus of International Law at University of California College of the Law, San Francisco, US, and Professor of Civil Law, University of Turin, Italy.

Petra Minnerop, Professor of International Law and Director of the Durham Centre for Sustainable Development Law and Policy, Durham University, UK.

Horatia Muir Watt, Professor at the Law School, Sciences Po, Paris, France.

Kehinde Folake Olaoye, Assistant Professor of Law, Hamad Bin Khalifa University, Doha, Qatar.

Robert Schütze, Professor of European and Global Law, Durham University, UK and Professor, Luiss, Rome, Italy.

Ayesha Shahid, Assistant Professor, Coventry University, UK.

Mathias Siems, Professor of Private Law and Market Regulation, European University Institute (EUI), Florence, Italy.

Avi Singh, Professor, International University College of Turin, Italy, and Senior Advocate, Delhi, India.

PART I

Setting the Scene

1

Comparative International Law

State of the Art

MATHIAS SIEMS

A. Introduction

While the term 'comparative international law' was occasionally used in the twentieth century,[1] today has it come to denote a distinct field of research. In April 2025, a search for 'comparative international law' on Google exceeded 128,000 hits, and on Google Scholar, it also had more than 2,400 hits. Thus, it seems a good point in time to critically review the state of the art of comparative international law.

This is not an easy endeavour. To start with, it may not be clear how far an analysis of the state of the art would need to include older lines of research that dealt with aspects of comparative international law under different names.[2] Yet, as this chapter will discuss, language matters here, as 'comparative international law' goes beyond all possible prior research that connects aspects of comparative law and international law. Thus, this analysis needs to explore which precise topics can and should fall under the heading 'comparative international law'. It also needs to address this field as belonging to both international law and comparative law – not least since research under the heading of 'comparative international law' has so far been mainly pursued by scholars of international law and not comparative law.

The corresponding structure of this chapter is as follows. Section B discusses the origins and contemporary use of the term 'comparative international law'. Section C maps substantive categories of comparative international law. This mapping provides the basis on which section D shows how comparative law can contribute to this field. Section E concludes with thoughts on future developments.

[1] See the citation statistics in section B.
[2] See references in nn 5 and 6, as well as ch 2 by Schütze in this volume.

B. Origins and Use of the Term 'Comparative International Law'

Should it be surprising that international law scholars use comparative ways of thinking? It may well be suggested that this is something natural for any field of research. In the words of Maurice Adams, 'comparing … is a fundamental principle of legal research'.[3] Even more broadly, it is said that 'thinking without comparison is unthinkable. And, in the absence of comparison, so is all scientific thought and scientific research'.[4]

Indeed, there is a long tradition of publications that include both international and comparative law. The *Revue de Droit International et de Législation Comparée* published its first volume in 1869. In the early twentieth century, research by Alejandro Alvarez and Hersch Lauterpacht set some of the intellectual foundations of themes that may fall under the heading of comparative international law today.[5] And, in the second part of the twentieth century, a key point of interest for comparative research in international law was the question of whether there were distinct Soviet and Western conceptions of international law.[6]

However, while such research on, for example, 'international and comparative law' or 'comparative approaches to international law' overlaps with 'comparative international law', it is not the same. To illustrate, consider the following terminologies: 'EU competition law', 'EU property law', 'EU law and property law' and 'EU approaches to property law'. There are many books on 'EU competition law', but none on 'EU property law', given that competition law is to a large extent based on EU law, while property law is almost entirely based on domestic law. Regarding property law, it is therefore more appropriate to write on 'EU law and property law' or 'EU approaches to property law', discussing, for example, how far some elements of EU law play a role in property law or whether future EU

[3] M Adams, 'Doing What Doesn't Come Naturally: On the Distinctiveness of Comparative Law' in M van Hoecke (ed), *Methodologies of Legal Research* (Oxford: Hart Publishing, 2011) 229, 229–30.

[4] GE Swanson, 'Frameworks for Comparative Research: Structural Anthropology and the Theory of Action' in I Vallier (ed), *Comparative Methods in Sociology* (Berkeley, CA: University of California Press, 1997) 141, 145.

[5] A Alvarez, *Le droit international américain. Son fondement, sa nature, d'après l'histoire diplomatique des états du nouveau monde et leur vie politique et economique* (Paris: Pedone, 1910); H Lauterpacht, *Private Law Sources and Analogies of International Law* (London: Longmans, 1927); H Lauterpacht, 'The So-Called Anglo-American and Continental Schools of Thought in International Law' (1931) 12 *British Year Book of International Law* 31.

[6] See, eg, E McWhinney, '"Peaceful Co-existence" and Soviet-Western International Law' (1962) 56 *American Journal of International Law* 951; WE Butler (ed), *International Law in Comparative Perspective* (Alphen aan den Rijn: Sijthoff & Noordhoff, 1980); A Cassese, *International Law in a Divided World* (Oxford: Clarendon Press, 1986).

law harmonisation should take place in this field. In other words, the phrase 'comparative international law' means more than simply saying that there are comparative elements to be considered in international law. Rather, it implies that many parts of international law can be approached from a comparative perspective.

Accordingly, it matters that there is now a growing use of the term 'comparative international law'. A search on Google Scholar shows this trend clearly: prior to 2010, the use of this term was very limited (10 hits prior to 1950; 5 in the 1950s; 15 in the 1960s; 14 in the 1970s; 24 in the 1980s; 60 in the 1990s; 143 in the 2000s), but it rose significantly in the next 15 years (1,047 hits in the 2010s; 771 in the 2020s up to the end of 2023).[7] Moreover, the early publications that contained the term 'comparative international law' did not define it and used it only sporadically in combination with other terms. For example, this can be seen in a 1923 article by Edward Harriman, which seems to be the first to have used the term in English,[8] but also in publications of the second part of the twentieth century.[9] Interestingly, a search for the equivalent French term 'droit international comparé'[10] leads to hits that go back to the nineteenth century;[11] yet here too, there were no further explanations of this term in this early period.

[7] The systemic analysis presented in this section was concluded at the end of the year 2023. Thus, it did not consider more recent publications; eg, DH Rached and CH Mendes, 'Comparative International Law' in M Siems and PJ Yap (eds), *The Cambridge Handbook of Comparative Law* (Cambridge: Cambridge University Press 2024) 561; I de la Rasilla and C Cai (eds), *The Cambridge Handbook of China and International Law* (Cambridge: Cambridge University Press 2024); P-H Verdier, 'Comparative International Law and the Rise of Regional Journals' (2024) 49 *Yale Journal of International Law* 154; A Simonyan, 'International Lawyers in Post-Soviet Eurasia: Decoding Divisibility' (2024) 35 *European Journal of International Law* 63; LL Soares Pereira and F Costa Morosini, 'Textbooks as Markers and Makers of International Law: A Brazilian Case Study' (2024) 35 *European Journal of International Law* 25; M Jorgensen, 'Comparative International Legal Policy: National Political Approaches towards International Legal Order' (MPIL Research Paper No 2024-03), available at https://ssrn.com/abstract=4705207.

[8] EA Harriman, 'The Price of International Law' (1923–24) 10 *Virginia Law Review* 495, 497: 'Now, there is no reason why we should not have books on American international law, English international law, French international law, and comparative international law.'

[9] For example, McWhinney (n 6) 966 ('we are dealing in part with a question of comparative international law, and that the solution of the problem of reconciliation and synthesis of the competing legal systems at the international level'); LC Green, 'Comparative Law as a "Source" of International Law' (1967–68) 42 *Tulane Law Review* 52, 55 ('comparative international lawyers'); WE Butler, 'American Research on Soviet Approaches to Public International Law' (1970) 70 *Columbia Law Review* 218, 224 ('a course in comparative international law is now being offered at the Harvard Law School').

[10] For the analysis of this section, a search was also done for the equivalent terms in German, Italian, Spanish and Portuguese ('vergleichende(s) Völkerrecht' 'diritto internazionale comparato', 'derecho internacional comparado', 'direito internacional comparado').

[11] The first use seems to be by E Glasson in the Preface to F de Schulte, *Histoire du droit et des institutions de l'Allemagne* (Paris: Durand et Pedone, 1882) vi.

Figure 1.1 Google Scholar hits for 'comparative international law'

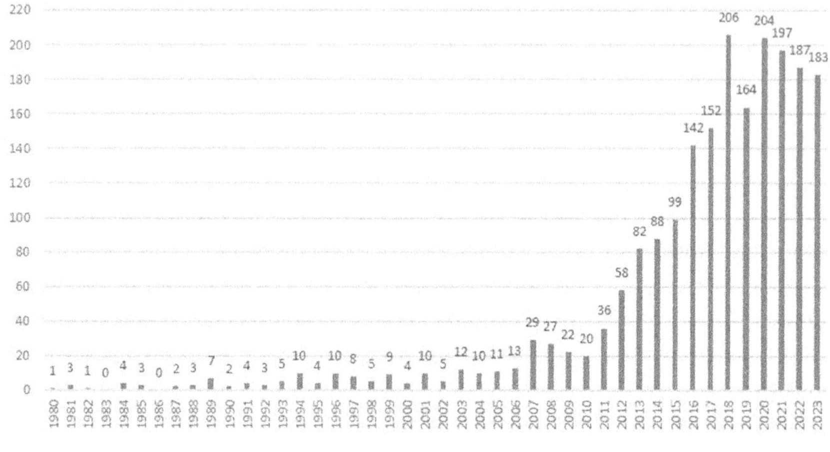

If we consider the time period from 1980 more closely (see Figure 1.1), it can be seen that both in the Cold War period and in the first 15 years afterwards, few publications used the term 'comparative international law'. In 2007, we can see a first rise, and the curve then continues to rise, notably with the highest values in the late 2010s. It should be added, however, that the initial rise in 2007 was again due to publications that did not conceptualise the term 'comparative international law'; rather, this happened, as we will see in the remainder of this section, only a few years later.

Figure 1.2 Key literature on 'comparative international law'

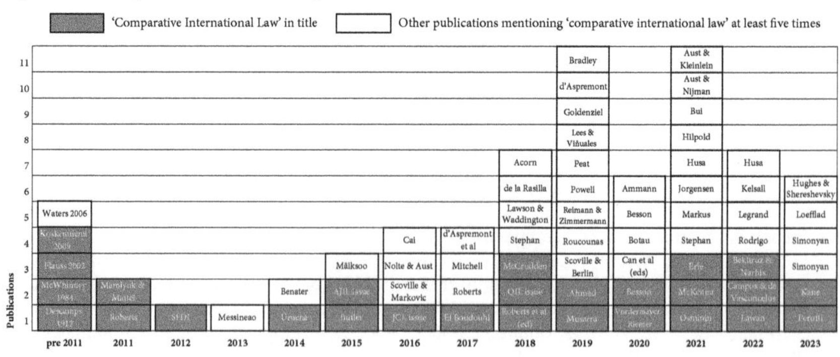

The key literature displayed in Figure 1.2[12] includes two types of publications. First, it shows the books, special issues of journals, book chapters and journal articles that

[12] The names refer to publications cited in the following footnotes. In the columns, publications are always bundled according to the same type (ie, whether they use 'comparative international law' in the

have 'comparative international law' or the equivalent term of another language in the title. Second, it includes further publications that mention the term 'comparative international law' at least five times. This latter search was initially conducted with Westlaw as it provides the search function to require that a particular term be used a certain number of times.[13] Subsequently, other journal publications and books (excluding textbooks) were examined by hand regarding whether they would fulfil this 'five-word threshold' requirement. Of course, imposing such a threshold is not a guarantee that publications will deal with comparative international law in detail, but it presents a useful device to identify publications that can be scrutinised further. In both categories, publications have been excluded that were shorter notes (including book reviews),[14] as well as 'false positives', such as a recent French-language book that used the term 'droit international comparé' in the context of comparing domestic rules of conflict of law (ie, domestic private international law).[15]

The first five publications displayed in Figure 1.2 did not elaborate on the meaning of the term 'comparative international law' in detail, though they already point towards some key themes of this coming field. In the 1912 book by Descamps, the phrase 'droit international comparé' is only used in the title, though in substance it compares, for example, Belgian and Swiss notions of neutrality.[16] The use of the same term by Flauss, 90 years later, is also quite specific, and again without further conceptualisation, namely to explain how the European Court of Human Rights has increasingly considered international norms in its case law (as opposed to strictly following an autonomous interpretation of the European Convention on Human Rights).[17]

title or else mention the term at least five then); then, in the first column, the order is by years; in the following yearly columns, the order is alphabetical.

[13] Specifically: adv: ATLEAST5("comparative international law"). A similar method was applied in M Siems, 'New Directions in Comparative Law' in M Reimann and R Zimmermann (eds), *The Oxford Handbook of Comparative Law*, 2nd edn (Oxford: Oxford University Press, 2019) 852.

[14] This was also applied to a Spanish-language publication on 'Derecho Internacional Comparado' in *Estudios de Derecho* 1963 (available at https://revistas.udea.edu.co/index.php/red/article/view/332962), as it merely outlined the subsequent publications of this issue without mentioning the term another time.

[15] R Sfeir, *Aspects contemporains du renvoi en droit international comparé (conflits de lois et conflits de systèmes)* (Brussels: Bruylant, 2009).

[16] E Descamps, *L'état neutre à titre permanent: étude de droit international comparé* (Paris: Sirey, 1912). Naturally, this was important in the period preceding the First World War. See also F Dhondt, 'La neutralité permanente de la Belgique et l'histoire du droit international: quelques jalons pour la recherche' (2018) 41 *Les C@hiers du CRHiDI*, available at https://popups.uliege.be/1370-2262/index.php?id=614.

[17] J-F Flauss, 'Du droit international comparé dans la jurisprudence de la Cour européenne des droits de l'homme' in Institut suisse de droit comparé (ed), *Le rôle du droit comparé dans l'avènement du droit européen – The Role of Comparative Law in the Emergence of European Law* (Zurich: Schulthess, 2002) 159. The same topic had also been discussed previously without using the terminology of 'comparative international law'; see, eg, PG Carozza, 'Uses and Misuses of Comparative Law in International Human Rights: Some Reflections on the Jurisprudence of the European Court of Human Rights' (1998) 73 *Notre Dame Law Review* 1217.

The earliest English-language publications discuss more general and partly overlapping topics, though with no particular interest in the phrase 'comparative international law' as they often also refer to other phrases, such as 'comparative approaches to international law'. McWhinney, in a 1984 chapter, writes about comparative international law in the context of a discussion to move beyond classical international law towards a 'more representative and pluralistic world public order system'.[18] Waters' introduction to a 2006 book on British and Canadian perspectives on international law identifies the discussion about socialist and Western types of international law as the first stream of comparative international law while noting its re-emergence due to the way in which transnational norms foster the 'horizontal dialogue between actors – courts, administrative agencies, civil society and so forth – across state boundaries'.[19] Koskenniemi's article from 2009 refers to national traditions of publishing and teaching international law as well as the fragmentation of international law as apparently relevant factors – though the article only mentions the term 'comparative international law' once, namely in its title.[20]

If one wanted to choose a birth date for comparative international law, 2011 may be a good candidate as it includes two foundational publications. The first one by Roberts, though, is quite specific as it presents the idea of comparative international law as a means to identify the diverse ways 'international law is domesticated differently by various national courts'.[21] This was subsequently expanded upon by Roberts in her 2017 book, which defined this field as examining 'cross-national similarities and differences in the way that international law is understood, interpreted, applied, and approached by actors in and from different states' (here specifically with a focus on academics and textbooks).[22]

The 2011 article by Mamlyuk and Mattei contains many references to prior publications that had discussed different approaches to international law in the Cold War period by McWhinney, Butler and others. It is also worth noting that Mamlyuk and Mattei refer, in a footnote, to a 2009 call for a conference organised by doctorate students at the University of Toronto which included the theme of exploring the 'possibility of "comparative international law"' through examining 'national "schools" or "traditions"', including 'the place of subjectivity and

[18] E McWhinney, 'Comparative International Law: Regional or Sectorial Inter-systemic Approaches to Contemporary International Law' in R-J Dupuy (ed), *L'Avenir du droit international dans un monde multiculturel; The Future of International Law in a Multicultural World* (The Hague: Martinus Nijhoff Publishers, 1984) 221, 227.

[19] C Waters, 'Introduction' in CPM Waters (ed), *British and Canadian Perspectives on International Law* (Leiden: Martinus Nijhoff Publishers, 2006) 3, 3–4.

[20] M Koskenniemi, 'The Case for Comparative International Law' (2009) 20 *Finnish Yearbook of International Law* 1.

[21] A Roberts, 'Comparative International Law? The Role of National Courts in Creating and Enforcing International Law' (2011) 60 *International & Comparative Law Quarterly* 57.

[22] A Roberts, *Is International Law International?* (Oxford: Oxford University Press, 2017) 2. This book is based on her PhD thesis at the Australian National University, http://hdl.handle.net/1885/124611.

situatedness in international law'.[23] Overall, Mamlyuk and Mattei also state that comparative international law has to be understood in an open way akin to the 'ad hoc muddling through' approach of comparative law.[24]

In the subsequent four years, the publications identified in Figure 1.2 used the term 'comparative international law' usually only in a brief manner. A book deriving from a German-French conference has the term in the title, yet only the Preface briefly indicates that it refers to the way 'domestic institutions [are] involved in affirming and implementing the rules of international law'.[25] Two papers in the *Cambridge Journal of International and Comparative Law*, on the one hand, point towards 'greater attention to be given to the role of national legal culture in the making and practice of international law',[26] while, on the other hand, being sceptical of the way perceived 'national schools' may be 'silencing dissenting voices'.[27] Like Mamlyuk and Mattei, publications by Urueña and Mälksoo emphasise that comparative international law 'echoes some of the themes that have preoccupied the discipline for decades',[28] arguing that 'as an approach [it] has de facto been around for a while already'.[29]

The real breakthrough of 'comparative international law' then happened with edited works by Anthea Roberts, Paul Stephan, Pierre-Hugues Verdier and Mila Versteeg, initially published in the *American Journal of International Law* in 2015 and subsequently expanded upon in an edited book published in 2018.[30] The latter book contains, in 26 chapters, many details on how topics of comparative international law are related to other fields such as comparative politics and foreign relationships law (Part 1); how they interplay with international lawyers and international institutions (Parts 2 and 3); how they relate to domestic legislatures, executives and courts (Part 4 and 5); and how they can be relevant in the areas of human rights, investment and law of the sea (Parts 6 and 7). In both publications, Roberts and colleagues also offer the following 'provisional definition' of

[23] See the call for papers at https://torontogroup.files.wordpress.com/2009/08/toronto-group-2010-call-for-papers.pdf.

[24] BN Mamlyuk and U Mattei, 'Comparative International Law' (2011) 36 *Brooklyn Journal of International Law* 386, 450–51. See also ch 9 by Mattei and Singh in this volume.

[25] Société Française pour le Droit International (ed), *Les pratiques comparées du droit international en France et en Allemagne – Comparative International Law Practice in France & Germany* (Paris: Pedone, 2012) 7.

[26] M Benatar, 'International Law, Domestic Lenses' (2014) 3 *Cambridge Journal of International and Comparative Law* 357, 337 (specifically referring to the 'inner legal culture of international law, which is composed of lawyers, judges and other professionals').

[27] F Messineao, 'Is There an Italian Conception of International Law?' (2013) 2 *Cambridge Journal of International and Comparative Law* 879, 904.

[28] R Urueña, 'Law-Making through Comparative International Law? Rethinking the Role of Domestic Law in the International Legal System' in R Liivoja and J Petman (eds), *International Law-Making: Essays in Honour of Jan Klabbers* (Abingdon: Routledge, 2014) 149, 169.

[29] L Mälksoo, *Russian Approaches to International Law* (Oxford: Oxford University Press, 2015) 15.

[30] Symposium on 'Exploring Comparative International Law' (2015) 109(3) *American Journal of International Law*; A Roberts et al (eds), *Comparative International Law* (Oxford: Oxford University Press, 2018). See also A Roberts et al, 'El caso del Derecho Internacional Comparado' (2021) 9(2) *Revista Facultad de Jurisprudencia* 195.

comparative international law: it 'entails identifying, analyzing, and explaining similarities and differences in how actors in different legal systems understand, interpret, apply, and approach international law'.[31]

In the same period, a number of publications in the *Journal of Comparative Law* presented a possible counter-position to the work by Roberts and colleagues. This line of research also included a special issue on 'Comparative International Law' mainly authored by scholars from Ukraine.[32] In two articles and one book review, William Butler, who had published extensively on the relationship between comparative and international law in the Cold War period, uses but also criticises the term 'comparative international law'. Notably, he refers to the risk of fostering the 'possible fragmentation of general or universal international law' as any 'comparisons … by way of contrast have called into question the existence and viability of international law as law and/or as a legal system'.[33] Yet Butler then also offers his own definition of comparative international law, namely that it:

> [E]ntails, as an integral part of comparative jurisprudence and law in their guises as a method, theory, and instructional discipline, the identification and analysis of similarities and differences within systems of international law, historical and contemporary, and between international legal systems and all other legal systems, and the actors, professions, and doctrines thereof.[34]

Thus, this definition, though similar to that by Roberts and colleagues, emphasises the comparative and historical dimensions of this term.

Further publications of the late 2010s are best understood as specific applications of the concept of comparative international law. Following Roberts' first paper, a number of publications addressed the way in which domestic courts in different jurisdictions interpret and apply international law.[35] Other publications

[31] A Roberts et al, 'Comparative International Law: Framing the Field' (2015) 109 *American Journal of International Law* 467, 469, then quoted in A Roberts et al, 'Conceptualizing Comparative International Law' in Roberts et al (eds) (n 30) 3, 6.

[32] Special issue on 'Comparative International Law' (ed OV Kresin) (2016) 11(1) *Journal of Comparative Law*.

[33] WE Butler, 'Comparative International Law' (2015) 10 *Journal of Comparative Law* 241, 241; WE Butler, 'Some Reflections on Comparative International Law' (2016) 11 *Journal of Comparative Law* 52, 53. For his previous publications, see nn 6 and 9.

[34] WE Butler, 'Comparative International Law: A Review' (2018) 13 *Journal of Comparative Law* 242, 246.

[35] HP Aust and G Nolte (eds), *The Interpretation of International Law by Domestic Courts: Uniformity, Diversity, Convergence* (Oxford: Oxford University Press 2016); C Cai, 'International Law in Chinese Courts During the Rise of China' (2016) 110 *American Journal of International Law* 269; D Peat, *Comparative Reasoning in International Courts and Tribunals* (Cambridge: Cambridge University Press, 2019); N Ahmad, 'Environmental Interests of Women as Human Rights in South Asia and CEDAW: Adjusting to a World of Comparative International Law' (2019) 1 *NHLD Law Review* 1 (analysing case law of domestic courts); O Ammann, *Domestic Courts and the Interpretation of International Law: Methods and Reasoning Based on the Swiss Example* (Leiden: Brill, 2020). See also C Ryngaert, 'Sources of International Law in Domestic Law: Relationship between International and Municipal Law Sources' in J d'Aspremont, S Besson and S Knuchel (eds), *The Oxford Handbook on the Sources of International Law* (Oxford: Oxford University Press, 2017) 1137, 1154 (on the resulting uncertainties,

concentrated on the responsibility of legal academia and education for national differences in international law, often building upon Roberts' interest in these topics.[36] Evaluating such research on the role of actors, it has been said that comparative international law 'implicitly relies upon Realist methodology'.[37] Additionally, publications have dealt with the application of comparative international law across areas of law, given that there may be different dynamics in different areas.[38] A particular point of interest has been human rights law,[39] while other examples are from international anti-bribery law[40] and international environmental law.[41] Furthermore, a book by Vordermayer-Riemer suggests that the application of methods of comparative international law can also be a 'possible means for a systematic reception from one treaty regime (eg, a human rights treaty) into another, related treaty regime (eg, an environmental agreement)'.[42]

Some recent publications have also returned to the definitions and possible shortcomings of comparative international law. A first article suggests that only research that applies comparative law methods to analyse national differences as regards international law is truly 'comparative international law'. By contrast, this is not said to be the case when domestic or international courts use concepts from national law in the application of international law as courts do so with the mere

eg, for determining customary international law); A Nollkaemper et al (eds), *International Law in Domestic Courts: A Casebook* (Oxford: Oxford University Press, 2018).

[36] RM Scoville and M Markovic, 'How Cosmopolitan Are International Law Professors?' (2016) 38 *Michigan Journal of International Law* 119; I de la Rasilla, 'A Very Short History of International Law Journals (1869–2018)' (2018) 29 *European Journal of International Law* 137; R Scoville and M Berlin, 'Who Studies International Law? Explaining Cross-national Variation in Compulsory International Legal Education' (2019) 30 *European Journal of International Law* 481. See also some of the contributions in the category 'specific nations and regions' in the *Oxford Bibliographies in International Law*, available at www.oxfordbibliographies.com/obo/page/international-law.

[37] R Mitchell, 'Sovereignty and Normative Conflict: International Legal Realism as a Theory of Uncertainty' (2017) 58 *Harvard International Law Journal* 421.

[38] A Lawson and L Waddington, 'Setting the Scene' in A Lawson and L Waddington (eds), *The UN Convention on the Rights of Persons with Disabilities in Practice: A Comparative Analysis of the Role of Courts* (Oxford: Oxford University Press, 2018) 1, 2.

[39] C McCrudden, 'Human Rights Theory and Comparative International Law Scholarship' in A Lawson and L Waddington (eds), *The UN Convention on the Rights of Persons with Disabilities in Practice: A Comparative Analysis of the Role of Courts* (Oxford: Oxford University Press, 2018) 594; PB Stephan, 'The Future of Human Rights Scholarship: Lessons from Russia' (2018) 81 *Law and Contemporary Problems* 167; JI Goldenziel, 'Checking Rights at the Border: Migrant Detention in International and Comparative Law' (2019) 60 *Virginia Journal of International Law* 156, 163; S Besson, 'Comparative Law and Human Rights' in Reimann and Zimmermann (eds) (n 13) 1222.

[40] E Acorn, 'Twenty Years of the OECD Anti-Bribery Convention: National Implementation and Hybridization' (2018) 51 *UBC Law Review* 613.

[41] K Morrow, 'Informational Requirements and Environmental Protection' in E Lees and JE Viñuales (eds), *The Oxford Handbook of Comparative Environmental Law* (Oxford: Oxford University Press, 2019) 972, 981 (comparing regional hard laws implementing the Rio Declaration on Environment and Development); RMLM Musarra, 'Comparative International Law: The Scope and Management of Public Participation Rights Related to CCS Activities' (2019) 9 *Journal of Public Administration and Governance* 93.

[42] M Vordermayer-Riemer, *Non-regression in International Environmental Law: Human Rights Doctrine and the Promises of Comparative International Law* (Cambridge: Intersentia, 2020) 463–531.

aim of constructing international law without the desire to engage with comparative methods.[43] A possible response may be that, perhaps, there are different types of comparative international law. Indeed, in two methodological works, we find the brief statements that comparative international law 'either refers to a methodology that consists in studying how domestic legal systems understand and apply international law, or it intends to trace how different cultural traditions influence international normativity'[44] and that 'comparative international law methods contend that abstract rules and principles acquire concrete meaning by the way they are interpreted (and subsequently applied in practice) by international law actors'.[45]

The distinction between method and substance is also apparent in other recent publications. According to Carcano, we should distinguish between comparative international law as a legal methodology and comparative international law as a sociological and political tool. His main focus is on the latter tool, as there is a risk that such sociological reality may be misused to 'justify claims that run contrary to widely accepted communitarian values'.[46] By contrast, Knop and others suggest that critical international law scholars welcome comparative international law;[47] for example, they argue that its emergence may be used to challenge the 'parochialism of US approaches to international law' (and, doing so, also keep it distinct from US foreign relations law);[48] yet, from a critical perspective, d'Aspremont reaches the opposite conclusion as he associates the research by Roberts et al with being a mere modification of a 'modernist idea of international law'.[49]

A number of further publications combine a critical spirit with some constructive advice for the future of the field. Stephan presents the idea of 'comparative international law as a check', meaning that it helps to 'distinguish plausible claims

[43] S El Boudouhi, 'Le droit international comparé. Mythe ou réalité?' (2017) 121 *Revue générale de droit international public* 981. See also ch 8 by El Boudouhi in this volume.

[44] E Roucounas, *A Landscape of Contemporary Theories of International Law* (Leiden: Brill, 2019) 41.

[45] R Deplano and N Tsagourias, 'Introduction' in R Deplano and N Tsagourias (eds), *Research Methods in International Law: A Handbook* (Cheltenham: Edward Elgar, 2021) 1, 3.

[46] A Carcano, 'Uses and Possible Misuses of a Comparative International Law Approach' (2018) 54 *QIL, Zoom-in* 21, 32. For the entire issue, devoted to the proposal by Roberts, see www.qil-qdi.org/category/zoom-in/doctrinal-thoughts-on-a-doctrinal-approach-to-the-problem-of-diversity-in-international-law-revisiting-anthea-roberts-is-international-law-in-ternational-and-comparative-international-law.

[47] K Knop, 'Foreign Relations Law: Comparison as Invention' in CA Bradley (ed), *The Oxford Handbook of Comparative Foreign Relations Law* (Oxford: Oxford University Press, 2019) 45, 49; see also MS Kelsall, 'Disordering International Law' (2022) 33 *European Journal of International Law* 729 ('comparative international law has significant critical purchase').

[48] Knop (n 47). For the relationship between comparative international law and foreign relations law, see also HP Aust and T Kleinlein, 'Introduction: Bridges under Construction and Shifting Boundaries' in HP Aust and T Kleinlein (eds), *Encounters between Foreign Relations Law and International Law: Bridges and Boundaries* (Cambridge: Cambridge University Press, 2021) 1, 7–8; BI Osminin, 'International Law, Foreign Relations Law and a Conception "Comparative International Law"' (2021), published in Russian in *Журнал российского права*. 2021. T. 25. № 2, 145 (English abstract available at https://www.elibrary.ru/item.asp?id=44808570).

[49] J d'Aspremont, 'Comparativism and Colonizing Thinking in International Law' (2019) 57 *Canadian Yearbook of International Law* 89. Similarly, see the critique by P Legrand, *Negative Comparative Law: A Strong Programme for Weak Thought* (Cambridge: Cambridge University Press, 2022) 114–17 ('unfortunate simplifications'; 'under-theorized and unsophisticated theoretical model').

[by states] from invalid ones'; thus, he suggests that it can 'inform the conversation and block off dead ends, keeping alive the possibility of groping toward some kinds of workable rules and principles that might ward off the worst kinds of international misunderstandings and conflicts'.[50] For McKenna too, it is the possible moderation of comparative international law that is an advantage, namely that it 'assumes a fluidity in both the normative structure and material substance of international law' and thus reimagines 'international law as a plural space accompanied by continual and ongoing processes of translation and adaptation between different normative orders through which the substance and structures of international law are made and re-made'.[51] As a comparative lawyer, Husa reaches a somewhat similar conclusion as he advocates the use of a pluralist law-in-context perspective on comparative law to further the (non-normative) understanding of comparative international law.[52] Similarly again, Kane suggests that comparative international law is particularly helpful for a holistic understanding of the role and influence of international law within a certain context.[53]

Finally, the most recent years have seen the growth of the literature of comparative international law beyond the Anglo-Saxon sphere. First, this includes publications on further traditions and jurisdictions. Two books deal with Islamic and Ottoman international law as examples of comparative international law, and a journal article compares the vision of international law by Grotius with that of the eighth-century Islamic scholar Al-Shaybani.[54] Several publications analyse approaches and authors of (comparative) international law in Europe, Latin America, Russia and China.[55] Another article discusses how comparative

[50] PB Stephan, 'Wars of Conquest in the Twenty-First Century and the Lessons of History: Crimea, Panama, and John Bassett Moore' (2021) 62 *Virginia Journal of International Law* 63, 108, 112–13.

[51] MB McKenna, 'Remaking the Law of Encounter: Comparative International Law as Transformative Translation' in ZG Capan et al (eds), *The Politics of Translation in International Relations* (London: Palgrave Macmillan, 2021) 67, 69.

[52] J Husa, 'Merging International Law and Comparative Law: Balancing between Normative and Non-Normative' (2021) 85 *Rabels Zeitschrift für ausländisches und internationales Privatrecht* 745; J Husa, *Interdisciplinary Comparative Law: Rubbing Shoulders with the Neighbours or Standing Alone in a Crowd* (Cheltenham: Edward Elgar, 2022) 177–226.

[53] G Kane, 'Comparative International Law: Enhancing Migration Law Enquiry?' (2023) 7 *International Journal of Migration and Border Studies* 149, 150, 162.

[54] EJ Powell, *Islamic Law and International Law: Peaceful Resolution of Disputes*, (Oxford: Oxford University Press, 2019) 19; L Can et al (eds), *The Subjects of Ottoman International Law* (Bloomington: Indiana University Press, 2020); M Lawan, 'Al-Shaybani and Grotius: An Inquiry into Comparative International Law' (2022) 6 *Asian Yearbook of Human Rights and Humanitarian Law* 148. See also I de la Rasilla del Moral and A Shahid (eds), *International Law and Islam: Historical Explorations* (Leiden: Brill, 2019). See also ch 7 by Sahid in this volume.

[55] P Hilpold (ed), *European International Law Traditions* (Berlin: Springer, 2021); E Loefflad, 'In Search of Paulus Vladimiri: Canon, Reception, and the (In)conceivability of an Eastern European "Founding Father" of International Law' (2023) 36 *Leiden Journal of International Law* 833; A Simonyan, 'Regional International Law Revisited: A Eurasian International Law' (2023) 31 *Michigan State International Law Review* 283; A Simonyan, 'Science of International Law and Regional Orders: A Critical Appraisal of Alejandro Álvarez and Carl Schmitt' (2023) 12/24 *Revista Tribuna Internacional* 19; D Botău, 'Identites du Droit International' (2020) 11 *Romanian Journal of Comparative Law* 257 (China and Russia as 'examples of powers that seek to impose their own version of international law'); M Jorgensen, 'The

international law contributes to the field of law and development by way of understanding how 'developing countries interpret, apply, and approach international law'.[56] Furthermore, two recent publications address cities as sites for the 'localization of international norms', as well as the role of scholars in contributing to formal and informal international law.[57]

Second, a further internationalisation of comparative international law can be seen in a growing number of publications in languages other than English. Some of them are quite specific: for example, two French-language publications address, respectively, possible differences in the national practice of international law's due diligence and how the views of the Italian philosopher Giambattista Vico relate to comparative international law;[58] a Ukrainian-language article considers the case of comparing regional organisations;[59] and a Spanish-language article deals with the international rules on crimes against humanity by the high courts of Argentina and Spain.[60] It is also possible to cite two more general articles published in Spanish and Portuguese,[61] as well as a 500-page German PhD thesis that aims to 'increase the degree of rationality, dogmatic clarity and legitimacy' by way of employing methods of comparative international law.[62]

To conclude, the key publications of comparative international law discussed here show that this term has apparently struck a chord as many authors have applied it to particular examples, but have also discussed its analytical and normative potential. The publications outlined here also point towards some of the key substantive elements of comparative international law. Yet there are at least two

Jurisprudence of the Rules-Based Order: The Power of Rules Consistent with But Not Binding under International Law' (2021) 22 *Melbourne Journal of International Law* 221 (sovereignty-based legal conceptions as articulated prominently by China and Russia as being opposed to rule-based international legal order); MS Erie, 'China and Comparative International Law: Between Social Science and Critique' (2021) 22 *Chicago Journal of International Law* 59.

[56] NS Bùi, 'Vertical Law and Development' (2021) 54 *Cornell International Law Journal* 1.

[57] M Riegner, 'Development Cooperation and the City' in HP Aust and JE Nijman (eds), *Research Handbook on International Law and Cities* (Cheltenham: Edward Elgar, 2021) 251, 259 (especially where development cooperation directly addresses cities and bypasses the national level); D Hughes and Y Shereshevsky, 'State-Academic Lawmaking' (2023) 64 *Harvard International Law Journal* 253.

[58] S Besson, 'La *due diligence* en droit international' (2020) *409 Collected Courses of the Hague Academy of International Law* 153, 208, 245, translated into English as S Besson, *Due Diligence in International Law* (Leiden: Brill, 2023) 60; S Besson, 'L'autorité légitime du droit international comparé: quelques réflexions autour du monde et du droit des gens de Vico' in S Besson and S Jubé (eds), *Concerter les civilisations: Mélanges en l'honneur d'Alain Supiot* (Paris: Seuil, 2020) 49.

[59] KN Bekhruz and M Narhis, 'Comparative International Law and Regionalization of International Law (2022/6) *Juridical scientific and electronic journal* 471, available with an abstract in English at http://dx.doi.org/10.32782/2524-0374/2022-6/106.

[60] IG Perotti Pinciroli, 'Derecho de las relaciones exteriores, derecho internacional comparado y el papel de los tribunales nacionales en la justicia transicional: los casos de Argentina y España' (2023) 16 *Anuario Colombiano de Derecho Internacional* 1.

[61] AJ Rodrigo, 'La ciencia del Derecho internacional', in JM Beneyto Pérez and C Jiménez Piernas (eds), *Concepto y fuentes del Derecho Internacional* (Valencia: Tirant lo Blanch, 2022) 341, 378–79; D Campos and R Carvalho de Vasconcelos, 'Podemos pensar num direito internacional comparado? Viabilidades e obstáculos na fronteira entre direito internacional e direito comparado' (2002) 19/3 *Revista de Direito Internacional* 373, available at https://www.cienciasaude.uniceub.br/rdi/article/view/8502.

[62] T Markus, *Rechtsvergleichung im Völkerrecht* (Tübingen: Mohr Siebeck, 2021) 3.

shortcomings. First, beyond specific examples, it is often unclear what exactly can be compared. Thus, in section C these units of comparison will be used as a starting point in order to map the field of comparative international law. Second, much of the literature outlined in this section contains few, if any, references to key works of comparative law.[63] To address this blind spot, section D will therefore attempt to show precisely what contributions comparative law can make to this field.

C. Mapping the Substance of Comparative International Law

A convenient way of dividing comparative international law is between vertical and horizontal variants.[64] This division can then lead to further sub-divisions. In the field of vertical comparative international law, some studies give equal weight to the domestic and international levels, for example, comparisons between international adjudicatory bodies and their domestic counterparts. In other studies of the vertical variant, the main interest is a comparative understanding of international law, for example, where the interpretation of international law suggests (or even requires) a comparison with domestic legal systems. With regard to horizontal comparative international law, there are also two sub-categories: it can be about research that compares units of the international level, or it can concern a comparison between countries or groups of countries as related to international law.

Figure 1.3 Types of comparative international law

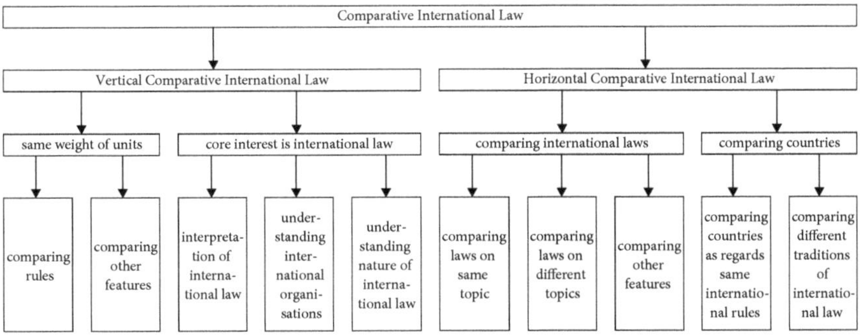

[63] For example, while a Google Scholar search (conducted on 16 December 2024) for 'comparative international law' leads to 2,440 hits, adding the names Zweigert Kötz as the authors of the main textbook on comparative law (K Zweigert and H Kötz, *An Introduction to Comparative Law*, 3rd edn (Oxford: Clarendon, 1998) reduces the number of hits to 88, ie, less than 4 per cent of the former publications.

[64] Roberts et al, 'Conceptualizing' (n 31) 10; M Siems, *Comparative Law*, 3rd edn (Cambridge: Cambridge University Press, 2022) 335–40. See also A Momirov and A Naudé Fourie, 'Vertical Comparative Law Methods: Tools for Conceptualising the International Rule of Law' (2009) 2 *Erasmus Law Review* 291; R Scarciglia, *Methods and Legal Comparison: Challenges for Methodological Pluralism* (Cheltenham: Edward Elgar, 2023) 172–74.

Figure 1.3 presents the general divide and the further subcategories. This section explains the 10 sub-categories as those will subsequently be used to identify the possible contribution of comparative law (section D). For this purpose, the following makes use of some of the literature cited in the previous section but also draws on further research.

First, studies of vertical comparative international law in which domestic and international levels have equal weight can compare specific legal rules. In a simple case, these are entirely different rules: for example, in environmental law, research has compared domestic rules with international ones, not yet implemented by the country in question.[65] But it is also possible to compare the rules as they exist in international law with the way they are implemented at the domestic and local levels.[66] Thus, as we have seen in some of the definitions in the previous section,[67] the aspiration of comparative international law in such studies is often to provide a concrete understanding of the way international law is re-made within a certain domestic context.

Second, vertical studies can also compare other features of international and domestic legal systems. For example, this can concern adjudicatory bodies, be they arbitral bodies or courts or tribunals. Such bodies exist at the domestic level, but they are also increasingly used at the international level, as we observe a growing constitutionalisation of international structures.[68] Many 'other features', broadly understood, could also fall under this sub-category: for example, comparing the personnel of international organisations and state administration, comparing professors of international law with other professors, comparing public attitudes about international and domestic law etc.

Third, vertical research can concern the interpretation of international law while then also considering domestic law. In the past, it was sometimes claimed that international law's *sui generis* character precluded an analysis of its norms from the perspective of domestic laws.[69] Yet today's scholarship is more open to comparative insights, while also asking us to consider the different contexts between both levels.[70] For example, research and practice have managed to identify some common general principles which can then be adapted to more specific rules of international law.[71] When international laws are based on legal concepts that already appear in a particular country, the law of this country can be helpful for the interpretation of the international rule.[72] Moreover, there are the prominent cases

[65] S Vermeylen, 'Comparative Environmental Law and Orientalism: Reading beyond the "Text" of Traditional Knowledge Protection' (2015) 24 *Review of European Community and International Environmental Law* 304.

[66] See, eg, Bùi (n 56) and Riegner (n 57).

[67] See nn 31, 44 and 45.

[68] See, eg, CPR Romano et al, 'Mapping International Adjudicative Bodies, the Issues, and Players' in CPR Romano et al (eds), *The Oxford Handbook of International Adjudication* (Oxford: Oxford University Press, 2014) 3.

[69] See CB Picker, 'International Law's Mixed Heritage: A Common/Civil Law Jurisdiction' (2008) 41 *Vanderbilt Journal of Transnational Law* 1083, 1090.

[70] Peat (n 35) 221; E Ellis, 'General Principles and Comparative Law' (2011) 22 *European Journal of International Law* 949, 959, 968.

[71] H Waldock, 'General Course of Public International Law' (1962-II) 106 *Recueil des Cours* 1, 56.

[72] Momirov and Naudé Fourie (n 64) 295 (for domestic and international tort law).

of the statutes of the International Court of Justice (ICJ) and the International Criminal Court (ICC) that explicitly require a comparative approach.[73]

Fourth, the vertical variant can also be about understanding international organisations, making use of information from domestic legal systems. For example, the design and internal organisation of the ICJ are said to be based on the French legal culture,[74] despite its procedural rules indicating that appointments to the ICJ should represent 'the principal legal systems of the world'.[75] Such research can then also examine whether the background of judges of international courts matters: for example, whether judges show biases in the application of international law depending on the parties in question.[76]

Fifth, the final topic of vertical comparative law is the understanding of the very nature of international law. A prominent example of research that combines a critical and comparative perspective are the Third World Approaches to International Law (TWAIL).[77] This view argues that today's international law is not universal and neutral, but is shaped by the interests of Western countries. Thus, this line of research may also be seen as an example of critical legal studies, as it shows the inevitably political nature of legal rules and institutions.[78]

Sixth, and turning to horizontal comparative international law, it is possible to compare sets of international rules that address the same topic but for different countries. This type of comparison may be particularly relevant due to the increased fragmentation of international law,[79] and comparing such international norms has even been called comparative international law '*stricto sensu*'.[80] A typical example in this field is the research on the many investment treaties that exist today.[81] An atypical one may be a comparison between international humanitarian

[73] ICJ Statute, art 38(1)(c) (referring to 'the general principles of law recognized by civilized nations'); ICC Statute, art 21(1)(c) (referring to the 'general principles of law derived by the Court from national laws of legal systems of the world').

[74] M Cohen, 'The Continuing Impact of French Legal Culture on the International Court of Justice' in Roberts et al, *Comparative International Law* (n 30) 181.

[75] ICJ Statute, art 9. Likewise, ICC Statute, art 36(8)(a).

[76] For example, this has been researched for the judges of the Court of Justice of the European Union; see AH Zhang, J Liu and N Garoupa, 'Judging in Europe: Do Legal Traditions Matter?' (2018) 14 *Journal of Competition Law & Economics* 144.

[77] See, eg, JT Gathii, 'The Agenda of Third World Approaches to International Law' in J Dunoff and M Pollack (eds), *International Legal Theory: Foundations and Frontiers* (Cambridge: Cambridge University Press, 2019) 153; L Eslava, 'Twail Coordinates', *Critical Legal Thinking*, 2 April 2019, http://criticallegalthinking.com/2019/04/02/twail-coordinates.

[78] See, eg, AC Hutchinson and PJ Monahan, 'Law, Politics, and the Critical Legal Scholars: The Unfolding Drama of American Legal Thought' (1984) 36 *Stanford Law Review* 199; M Tushnet, 'Critical Legal Studies: A Political History' (1991) 100 *Yale Law Journal* 1515.

[79] Butler, 'Comparative International Law' (n 33) 250.

[80] S Besson, 'International Courts and the Jurisprudence of Statehood' (2019) 10 *Transnational Legal Theory* 30, 60.

[81] See, eg, T Broude, YZ Haftel and A Thompson, 'Who Cares about Regulatory Space in BITs? A Comparative International Approach' in Roberts et al, *Comparative International Law* (n 30) 527; L Cotula, 'Expropriation Clauses and Environmental Regulation: Diffusion of Law in the Era of Investment Treaties' (2015) 24 *Review of European Community and International Environmental Law* 278.

law and Islamic laws (specifically as regards armed conflict) if one assumes that Islamic law also has an international (or perhaps transnational) dimension.[82]

Seventh, a variant of the previous type is a horizontal comparison that compares rules that do not deal with exactly the same subject matter, but where – in the terminology of comparative law – there is another *tertium comparationis*. For example, such a study may compare how different international treaties deal with different types of environmental damage,[83] or whether and how World Trade Organization (WTO) and international investment law should follow common principles.[84] Though some suggest that a comparison of branches of international law should not belong to comparative international law,[85] there are better reasons to include such types of studies as, here too, some of the key methods and tools of comparative law can be applied.[86] In other words, as comparative law is open to new units of analysis,[87] the same should apply to comparative international law.

Eighth, a horizontal comparison can also be concerned with other features of international law. For example, research has been conducted on general features of international treaties: their legal form and scope,[88] and how far they include a multilingual dimension.[89] It is also possible to focus on the structure and rule-making practices of international organisations.[90] In relation to international courts and tribunals, it is possible to compare, for example, whether they allow dissenting and separate opinions,[91] whether they borrow ideas from other international courts,[92] and whether it is possible to measure the processes and outcomes of international courts and the compliance of states with their decisions in order to compare their performance.[93]

Ninth, horizontal comparative international law can compare countries (or groups of countries) as they relate to international law. Thus, this is similar to

[82] N Badawi, 'Regulation of Armed Conflict: Critical Comparativism' (2016) 37 *Third World Quarterly* 1990.

[83] *cf* E Morgera, 'Global Environmental Law and Comparative Legal Methods' (2015) 24 *Review of European Community and International Environmental Law* 254, 257.

[84] J Kurtz, *The WTO and International Investment Law: Converging Systems* (Cambridge: Cambridge University Press, 2016).

[85] MA Damirli, 'Comparative International Law in the Quest for Academic Identity' (2016) 11 *Journal of Comparative Law* 59, 75.

[86] See section D, as well as the research by Vordermayer-Riemer discussed in section B.

[87] M Siems, 'The Power of Comparative Law: What Type of Units Can Comparative Law Compare?' (2019) 67 *American Journal of Comparative Law* 861.

[88] A Guzman, *How International Law Works: A Rational Choice Theory* (Oxford: Oxford University Press, 2008) 119–81 (identifying a trade-off between form and substance).

[89] F Prieto-Ramos, 'Global Law as Translated Text: Mapping Institutional Legal Translation' (2017) 22 *Tilburg Law Review* 185 (comparing the United Nations (UN), the WTO and the EU).

[90] See, eg, Organisation for Economic Co-operation and Development (OECD), *International Regulatory Co-operation: The Role of International Organisations in Fostering Better Rules of Globalisation* (Paris: OECD Publishing, 2016).

[91] N Garoupa and T Ginsburg, *Judicial Reputation: A Comparative Theory* (Chicago: University of Chicago Press, 2015) 182.

[92] E Voeten, 'Borrowing and Nonborrowing among International Courts' (2010) 39 *Journal of Legal Studies* 547.

[93] T Squatrito et al, *The Performance of International Courts and Tribunals* (Cambridge: Cambridge University Press, 2018).

non-international comparative law, but the relevance of international law also justifies its inclusion in the field of comparative international law. For example, such research can be about the different ways in which international law is incorporated into domestic law,[94] the commitment of states to international law,[95] their participation in international organisations or the decision to remain neutral.[96] With respect to courts (or other actors), it can for instance be concerned with differences in domestic compliance with decisions of international courts,[97] or the way in which domestic courts interpret rules of international law, including the question of whether they also consider case law from other jurisdictions for this purpose.[98]

Tenth, a final prominent line of horizontal research examines different traditions of international law. Such research has, for example, compared how international law is researched and taught across countries.[99] It can also be about the question of whether there are distinct approaches among countries towards international law, for which it has even been said that '[t]he comparative method is a sine qua non for coming to terms with subsystems of international law'.[100] Indeed, as already mentioned, in the Cold War period, such research often compared the role of ideology as regards Western and Soviet approaches to international law.[101] Other works compare historical traditions and contemporary perspectives of countries and regions on international law.[102] As we have seen in the previous section, this also includes literature that discusses, for example, whether the relevance of such traditions is a problem for the universal claim of international law or whether it fosters a realistic understanding of what international law can and cannot achieve.[103]

[94] See, eg, P-H Verdier and M Versteeg, 'International Law in National Legal Systems: An Empirical Investigation' in Roberts et al, *Comparative International Law* (n 30); D Shelton (ed), *International Law and Domestic Legal Systems: Incorporation, Transformation, and Persuasion* (Oxford: Oxford University Press, 2011).

[95] For research in the fields of human rights law, see, eg, KL Cope, CD Creamer and M Versteeg, 'Empirical Studies of Human Rights Law' (2019) 15 *Annual Review of Law and Social Science* 155; Z Elkins, T Ginsburg and B Simmons, 'Getting to Rights: Treaty Ratification, Constitutional Convergence, and Human Rights Practice' (2013) 54 *Harvard International Law Journal* 61.

[96] As in the first study by Descamps (n 16). See also the research on the relationship between foreign relations law and international law in nn 47 and 48.

[97] Roberts et al, 'Conceptualizing' (n 31) 14–16; SM Mitchell and EJ Powell, *Domestic Law Goes Global: Legal Traditions and International Courts* (Cambridge: Cambridge University Press, 2011).

[98] See references in nn 21, 35, and 38.

[99] See references in nn 22 and 36 and previously; see also F Baetens and WL Cheah, 'Being an International Law Lecturer in the 21st Century: Where Tradition Meets Innovation' (2013) 2 *Cambridge Journal of International and Comparative Law* 974.

[100] WE Butler, 'Comparative Approaches to International Law' (1985) 190 *Collected Courses of the Hague Academy of International Law* 9, 45.

[101] See, eg, Butler (n 9); Mamlyuk and Mattei (n 24).

[102] See, eg, A Becker-Lorca, *Mestizo International Law: A Global Intellectual History 1842–1933* (Cambridge: Cambridge University Press, 2015); R Derrig, *The New Haven School: American International Law* (Oxford: Oxford University Press, 2025); JM Beneyto and D Kennedy (eds), *New Approaches to International Law: The European and the American Experiences* (The Hague: TMC Asser, 2012); C Giorgetti and G Verdirame, *Whither the West? International Law in Europe and the United States* (Cambridge: Cambridge University Press, 2021); A Kjeldgaard-Pedersen (ed), *Nordic Approaches to International Law* (Leiden: Brill, 2017); as well as the references in nn 19, 27, 29, and 54–57. See also chs 3 to 7 in this volume.

[103] See, eg, the statements by Butler (n 33); Carcano (n 46); and Stephan (n 50).

To conclude, these 10 categories capture in a condensed manner the main types of research that are pursued in the field of comparative international law. Of course, in practice, research may often combine multiple categories, for example, including both a vertical and a horizontal dimension. Still, these categories remain helpful for the purpose of the next section, showing the contributions that comparative law can make to this field.

D. Contributions of Comparative Law to Comparative International Law

It is not easy to quickly grasp the core of comparative law as it covers a great variety of substantive and methodological topics that reflect the disagreement of whether it should be seen as a more theoretical or practical field of research.[104] Drawing on previous work,[105] the following uses the existing body of knowledge of comparative law as a starting point in order to identify seven representative methods and concepts that are frequently discussed in the comparative law literature.

Figure 1.4 Comparative international law (CIL) and methods/concepts of comparative law

yes | partly | no

		Key concepts and methods of comparative law:						
Categories of comparative international law:		*legal families*	*legal diffusion*	*foreign legal culture*	*functional method*	*socio-legal relations*	*law reforms by transplant*	*possibility of unified rules*
vertical CIL	same weight of units and rules	partly	partly	partly	yes	partly	yes	partly
	same weight of units and other features	partly	partly	yes	partly	partly	yes	partly
	interpretation of international law	yes	partly	partly	partly	no	no	yes
	understanding int'l organisations	yes	yes	partly	partly	no	no	partly
	understanding nature of international law	partly	yes	partly	no	partly	no	yes
horizontal CIL	international laws on same legal topic	partly	partly	partly	yes	yes	yes	yes
	international laws on different topics	partly	partly	partly	partly	partly	yes	yes
	other features of international laws	partly	partly	partly	partly	yes	yes	yes
	how countries relate to specific int'l law	yes	yes	yes	partly	yes	yes	yes
	different traditions of international law	yes	yes	yes	no	partly	partly	partly

[104] See, eg, U Kischel, *Comparative Law* (Oxford: Oxford University Press, 2019) 45–85.
[105] Siems (n 87).

Figure 1.4 displays a matrix of seven methods and concepts of comparative law and the 10 types of comparative international law identified in the previous section. The black, grey and white shading of the cells refers to the likely relevance of those methods and concepts for the new units. In other words, responding to the question whether these methods and concepts are relevant to these categories of comparative international law, black means 'yes', white means 'no' and grey designates ambiguous cases. The following will mainly explain the 'yes' cases in order to illustrate how insights from comparative law can be valuable for comparative international law.

The topic of *legal families* is often at the centre of debates in comparative law. Some of the main comparative law books are structured according to legal families, for example, with chapters on the common law, the civil law, religious legal systems etc,[106] while critics challenge the relevance of such broad country groupings today.[107] Applied to comparative international law, there are at least four categories in which legal families play a key role (while, in the other categories, it may also matter in some instances).[108] First, in the aforementioned cases where the ICJ and the ICC need to apply a comparative approach,[109] a common approach is to consider representative legal systems, for instance, countries of different legal families.[110] Second, as regards the understanding of international organisations through a vertical comparison, there is some debate on whether international law is closer to the common law or civil law model,[111] while other research has examined whether judges show biases in the application of international law based on their common/civil law origins.[112] Third, horizontal comparisons between countries in their application of international law can incorporate insights from legal families: for example, it has been explored whether commitment to international courts reflects differences between legal families.[113] Fourth, different traditions of international law may be correlated to legal families, at least in some circumstances, for example, where legal families refer to different political regimes (eg, historically, the socialist legal family).

[106] See, eg, R David, M Goré and C Jauffret-Spinosi, *Les grands systèmes de droit contemporains*, 13th edn (Paris: Dalloz, 2025); HP Glenn, *Legal Traditions of the World*, 5th edn (Oxford: Oxford University Press, 2014).

[107] For critical positions, see, eg, Siems (n 64) 92–108; M Pargendler, 'The Rise and Decline of Legal Families' (2012) 60 *American Journal of Comparative Law* 1043.

[108] For an example of a horizontal comparison of different international laws, see F Duina, 'Making Sense of the Legal and Judicial Architectures of Regional Trade Agreements Worldwide' (2016) 10 *Regulation & Governance* 368 (interventionalist or minimalist regional trade agreements (RTAs) depending on whether mainly civil and common law member countries).

[109] See n 73.

[110] See A Pellet and D Müller in A Zimmermann and C Tomuschat, *The Statute of the International Court of Justice: A Commentary*, 3rd edn (Oxford: Oxford University Press, 2019), art 38, para 264; K Ambos, *Treatise on International Criminal Law, Vol 1: Foundations and General Part* (Oxford: Oxford University Press, 2013) 77.

[111] See, eg, CB Picker, 'International Law's Mixed Heritage: A Common/Civil Law Jurisdiction' (2008) 41 *Vanderbilt Journal of Transnational Law* 1083.

[112] See Zhang et al (n 76).

[113] See references in n 97.

The concept of *legal diffusion*[114] also aims to make sense of the complexity of the legal world. It may be associated with the belonging of countries to the same legal family, but this is not always the case. For example, it is often debated whether we are witnessing an Americanisation of legal systems in both common and civil law countries.[115] In the vertical variant of comparative international law, it can again be a means of understanding international organisations, for example, where they follow models of specific countries (and not legal families as a whole). It is also helpful for an understanding of the nature of international law, notably the narrative that classical international law has a European or Western bias.[116] For horizontal comparative international law, we can again refer to the categories of comparing countries as they apply international law or follow different traditions of international law. More generally, it is worth adding that all other categories may also apply the notion of legal diffusion when it comes to the identification of similarities and differences,[117] while also noting that diffusion would not mean that the rule or institution is exactly the same in all units of analysis.[118]

A further element of comparative law is that it is typically concerned with the understanding of a *foreign legal culture*. This is seen as a distinct challenge as comparatists 'have to be able to reconstruct the meaning of legal rules that are foreign to them'.[119] Some authors then discuss how cross-cultural understanding can be achieved, for example, the need for an immersion into a foreign legal culture (as opposed to a mere superficial understanding of the black-letter rules),[120] while others emphasise the inevitable limitations of one's own understanding of foreign law.[121] In comparative international law, such considerations again play a natural role when examining different countries, that is, in the horizontal categories of how different countries relate to the same international rules and how we can compare different traditions of international law. In the vertical variant, it can be used to show how the court structures of domestic courts differ from international adjudicatory bodies, as the former closely reflects a particular domestic culture,

[114] See, eg, W Twining, 'Diffusion of Law: A Global Perspective' (2004) 49 *Journal of Legal Pluralism* 1.

[115] See, eg, M Langer, 'From Legal Transplants to Legal Translations: The Globalization of Plea Bargaining and the Americanization Thesis in Criminal Procedure' (2004) 45 *Harvard International Law Journal* 1; RD Kelemen and EC Sibbitt, 'The Americanization of Japanese Law' (2002) 23 *University of Pennsylvania Journal of International Economic Law* 269.

[116] McWhinney (n 18).

[117] For an example, see KJ Alter 'The Global Spread of European Style International Courts' (2012) 35 *West European Politics* 135.

[118] This argument has been raised in particular in the debate about legal transplants, notably by P Legrand, 'The Impossibility of Legal Transplants' (1997) 4 *Maastricht Journal of European and Comparative Law* 111 in critiquing A Watson, *Legal Transplants: An Approach to Comparative Law*, 2nd edn (Athens, GA: University of Georgia Press, 1993).

[119] Adams (n 3) 239.

[120] V Grosswald Curran, 'Cultural Immersion, Difference and Categories in US Comparative Law' (1998) 46 *American Journal of Comparative Law* 43.

[121] P Legrand, 'Negative Comparative Law' (2015) 10 *Journal of Comparative Law* 405, 40: '[T]o interpret foreign law is immediately and necessarily to disfigure it.'

while the latter can be designed more freely.[122] In all the other categories, the 'partly' classification means that the idea of scrutinising law from a legal culture perspective can be relevant if one extends the notion of a foreign legal culture to the 'many different legal cultures involved in the international legal order'.[123]

An alternative to a legal cultural approach is the *functional approach* of comparative law.[124] At the most basic level, it recommends that the starting point of a comparative analysis should be a scenario of facts followed by the question of which legal rules different countries use to address those facts. It is also possible, though disputed, to infer further elements from functionalism, for example, that, across the world, laws usually have a functional agenda in pursuing particular goals. It follows that, in the present case, this approach is most useful for the categories of comparative international law that compare rules on the same topic, be it at the vertical or the horizontal level.[125] In other cases, it can be relevant if one uses a broadly phrased functional question. For example, for questions such as 'How are disputes resolved?' or 'How can law contribute to economic development?', it is clear that studies of other categories of comparative international law may also be seen as functional types of comparison.

The interest of comparative law in understanding *socio-legal relations* can be thought of as an extension to a functional approach. It is based on the idea that the multiplicity of laws under investigation can foster our understanding of the relationship between law and society. For example, a frequent debate is whether law is primarily a reflection of society or whether it is primarily a means to shape society in a particular way.[126] Such research can also be extended to empirical methods: for example, there is now a growing field of quantitative research that aims to test hypotheses about socio-legal relations with comparative data.[127] With respect to comparative international law, a socio-legal approach is relevant for any research that includes an understanding of rules at the ground level.[128] But using comparative information as a test case is likely to work best if the laws are at the same level, ie, horizontal comparative international law. For example, international laws on the same topic may be used as a test case for empirical research.[129] As mentioned above, one study on international courts aimed to develop criteria to measure and

[122] For the importance of differences in context, see also V Vadi, 'The Migration of Constitutional Ideas to Regional and International Economic Law: The Case of Proportionality' (2015) 35 *Northwestern Journal of International Law and Business* 557, 586–89.

[123] CB Picker, 'Comparative Legal Cultural Analyses of International Economic Law: A New Methodological Approach' (2013) 1 *Chinese Journal of Comparative Law* 21, 21.

[124] For a general discussion of its various elements, see R Michaels, 'The Functional Method of Comparative Law' in Reimann and Zimmermann (eds) (n 13) 34.

[125] Such as in comparative studies of investment treaties; see n 81.

[126] For this 'causality problem in socio-legal research' see Siems (n 64) 177–84.

[127] For an overview see M Siems, 'Empirical Methods' in Siems and Yap (eds) (n 7) 157.

[128] In this sense, see also EJ Powell, 'Comparative International Law and the Social Science Approach' (2021) 22 *Chicago Journal of International Law* 147.

[129] For an example, see Broude et al (n 81).

compare their performance.[130] A comparison of domestic legal systems as they relate to the same international law can also be of a socio-legal nature: it may aim to show whether international rules have led to actual similarities. Or, to provide a more specific example, if international laws have been drafted as multilingual laws, studies may examine how far this makes a difference for the application of these laws in different countries.[131]

Policy-related comparative law often recommends *law reforms by transplant*. This view also acknowledges that simply copying foreign legal models does not work well if the foreign model leads to a mismatch with the existing legal and extra-legal context of the transplant country. However, if transplants are well chosen and designed,[132] it is held that foreign experience can provide helpful information for law making.[133] For comparative international law, it is – with the exception of categories that mainly aim for the understanding of certain phenomena – also intuitive that some comparative learning is possible. For example, in the vertical variant that compares international and domestic law, research may include the recommendation that a domestic rule or institution should diffuse 'upwards' as a 'vertical legal transplant'. This has been discussed, for example, regarding the migration of the principles of reasonableness and proportionality to international investment law and the procedure of amicus curiae participation to the European Court of Human Rights.[134] In the horizontal variant, the learning may be between international laws or between countries as they implement international law. In both cases, this is clear as far as rules concern the same topic. However, it can also be suggested that learning between international laws may sometimes be feasible if they deal with different topics; as already mentioned, it has, for example, been proposed that some concepts from international human rights law may be applied to environmental agreements.[135]

Finally, comparative law has a long tradition of being interested in the *possibility of unified rules*.[136] Here too, this position is not naïve. A frequent view is that comparative law can help us to answer two questions: first, whether there should be unified rules at all; and, second, if this is affirmed, what the substance

[130] Squatrito et al (n 93).

[131] See, eg, FM Mucciarelli, '*E Pluribus Unum?* Language Diversity and the Harmonization of Company law in the European Union' (2019) 26 *Maastricht Journal of European and Comparative Law* 669.

[132] See, eg, H Xanthaki, 'Legal Transplants in Legislation: Defusing the Trap' (2008) 57 *International and Comparative Law Quarterly* 659.

[133] In the words of Zweigert and Kötz (n 63) 47: '[T]he comparatist is in the best position to follow his comparative researches with a critical evaluation … If he does not, no one else will do it.'

[134] V Vadi, *Proportionality, Reasonableness and Standards of Review in International Investment Law and Arbitration* (Cheltenham: Edward Elgar, 2018); A Dolidze, 'Bridging Comparative and International Law: Amicus Curiae Participation as a Vertical Legal Transplant' (2015) 26 *European Journal of International Law* 851 (also suggesting the terms downward and upward diffusion).

[135] Vordermayer-Riemer (n 42).

[136] See, eg, C Jamin, 'Saleilles' and Lambert's Old Dream Revisited' (2002) 50 *American Journal of Comparative Law* 701.

of these unified rules should be.[137] In the present case, the use of comparative law in the interpretation of international law is an example where the former can help the latter to determine the substance of unified rules. In the vertical variant, the understanding of the nature of international law can also benefit from the debate about the possibility of unified rules as the latter may show where the unification of the law is not appropriate (eg, because it disregards the interests of less powerful states).[138] As regards horizontal international law, it is suggested that the categories are the same here as for legal transplants, namely that instead of transplanting rules, unified rules may, for example, combine ideas from different legal systems.[139]

Overall, the foregoing analysis, as summarised in Figure 1.4, shows that insights from comparative law can contribute to all of the 10 categories of comparative international law. It should not be seen as a surprise that the horizontal variants have more (clear) 'yes' cases than the vertical ones as the methods and concepts of comparative law have mainly been developed for horizontal comparisons. Yet it is also worth noting that, across all categories, the majority of fields are at least 'grey'; thus, this confirms that it is indeed possible to say that comparative international law is a distinct field of research.

E. Conclusion

The state of the art in comparative international law, as presented in this chapter, has shown that we can be optimistic about the development of this field. First, we have seen that its use has increased in recent years as researchers have applied this notion to a variety of topics. Second, this chapter has shown that it is possible to taxonomise this field into two broad categories – vertical and horizontal comparative international law – and then into 10 more specific categories. Third, as we saw in the previous section, comparative law can indeed contribute to all of these 10 categories.

Comparative international law thus has the potential to become an established field of research. Of course, this does not exclude other approaches to international law. Drawing a parallel to other fields, we can see that there is, for example, comparative contract law (or comparative constitutional, criminal law etc), but

[137] Together with the previous category, such research can also be seen as advocating for an applied comparative law; see, eg, DL Finnegan, 'Applied Comparative Law and Judicial Reform' (2006) 8 *The Thomas M Cooley Journal of Practical and Clinical Law* 97; R Pardolesi and M Granieri, 'The Future of Law Professors and Comparative Law' (2013) 21 *The Digest* 1.

[138] For a similar point, see D Kennedy 'New Approaches to Comparative Law: Comparativism and International Governance' (1997) *Utah Law Review* 545, 614–22 (comparatists bring in cultural differences).

[139] For a similar point, see K Pistor, 'The Standardization of Law and its Effect on Developing Economies' (2002) 50 *American Journal of Comparative Law* 97, 108–11 (standardised rules may be based on the national model, lowest cost denominator or synthetic concept).

also transnational contract law, critical contract law, empirical contract law etc. Thus, for comparative international law, it may also be valuable (but beyond the scope of this chapter) to explore how far it may benefit from close interaction with, say, critical or empirical international law.

Future developments may well change some of the orientations and topics outlined in this chapter. Change may come from comparative law, as we have seen the rise and fall of certain methods and themes of comparative law in recent decades.[140] Moreover, change may come from the international sphere: for example, it has been said that the cooperation of independent sovereign states has been today often replaced by an interdependence of states,[141] that there is a growing weight of non-state players and emergence of non-state regulators,[142] and that dynamic and non-hierarchical forms of networked and experimental governance have complemented traditional forms of international law.[143] Thus, comparative international law needs to remain attentive to developments in both of its parent fields.

[140] For some trends, see data in Siems (n 13); for a more speculative account, see M Siems, 'Comparative Law in the 22nd Century' (2016) 23 *Maastricht Journal of European and Comparative Law* 359.

[141] S Hobe, 'Globalisation: A Challenge to the Nation State and International Law' in M Likosky (ed), *Transnational Legal Processes: Globalisation and Power Disparities* (London: Butterworths, 2002) 378, 386.

[142] J-B Auby, *Globalisation, Law and the State* (Oxford: Hart Publishing, 2017) 66–68. See also ch 12 by Infantino in this volume.

[143] See, for instance, G de Búrca, RO Keohane and CF Sabel, 'New Modes of Pluralist Global Governance' (2013) 45 *New York University Journal of International Law and Politics* 723; M Fenwick, S Wrbka and S van Uytsel (eds), *Networked Governance, Transnational Business and the Law* (Berlin: Springer, 2014). See also ch 13 by Husa in this volume.

2

Comparative International Law

A Historical Reconstruction

ROBERT SCHÜTZE

A. Introduction: Butler and the International-Systems Approach

When was 'comparative international law' born and what is the best definition of this field in light of its disciplinary history? Profoundly diverse 'orders' or 'systems' of international law have existed in modern history.[1] These various systems began to be studied comparatively at the end of the eighteenth century – not just from an historical perspective but also from a geographical perspective. An early example of this comparative analysis of international law can be found in the work of Robert Ward.[2] Faced with a plurality of regional international systems, Ward came to believe that there was no universal international law: 'that what is commonly called the Law of Nations, falls far short of universality; and that, therefore, the Law is not the Law of all nations, but only of particular classes of them; and thus there may be a *different Law of Nations for different parts of the globe*'.[3]

However, this relativist conception of international law was increasingly challenged – and supplanted – by the expansion of 'European' international law in the nineteenth century. The story of this legal 'transfer' and diffusion has been told in the past, especially as regards Asia and Latin America.[4] By the early twentieth

[1] O Yasuaki, 'When was the Law of International Society Born?' (2000) 2 *Journal of the History of International Law* 1. See also, more generally, O Yasuaki, *A Transcivilizational Perspective on International Law* (Leiden: Martinus Nijhoff, 2010).

[2] R Ward, *An Enquiry into the Foundation and History of the Law of Nations in Europe*, vol I (Dublin: Butterworth, 1795).

[3] ibid xiv (emphasis added).

[4] For excellent discussions here, see especially S Kroll, *Normgenese durch Re-Interpretation: China und das europäische Völkerrecht im 19. und 20. Jahrhundert* (Baden-Baden: Nomos, 2012); A Becker Lorca, *Mestizo International Law: A Global Intellectual History, 1842–1933* (Cambridge: Cambridge University Press, 2016).

century, it therefore seemed that only one single universal system of international law governed the world. Yet three developments soon qualified this picture. With the rise of the Soviet Union, a new socialist system of international law gradually emerged in the 'Second World', which was soon itself complemented by a 'Third World' conception of international law. And, the arrival of regional international organisations like the EU led to a discussion whether 'new legal order[s] of international law' were being created.[5] By the 1960s, it thus appeared that the universal system of general international law had been 're-particularised' into distinct normative sub-systems for different 'classes' of states.

It is at this point that the modern discipline of (public) comparative international law is born. One of its founding fathers is William E Butler, who tirelessly re-introduced comparative approaches back to international law.[6] Butler's pioneering work has largely been ignored by the post-2011 scholarship.[7] However, his Hague Lectures on 'Comparative Approaches to International Law' in particular remain a landmark in the development of the field. Noting that 'international law' and 'comparative law' have traditionally been treated as 'two discrete realms'

[5] Case 26/62 *Van Gend en Loos v Netherlands Inland Revenue Administration* [1963] ECR (English Special Edition) 1, 12.

[6] Butler's most important contributions to comparative international law are: WE Butler, 'International Law and the Comparative Method' (1977) 30 *Current Legal Problems* 105; WE Butler (ed), *International Law in Comparative Perspective* (Alphen aan den Rijn: Sijthoff & Noordhoff, 1980); WE Butler, 'Comparative Approaches to International Law' (1985) 190 *Collected Courses of the Hague Academy* 9. A second person who made important contributions to the post-1945 English-language discipline of comparative international law was Butler's contemporary, Edward McWhinney. See here especially E McWhinney, 'Comparative International Law: Regional or Sectoral, Inter-systemic Approaches to Contemporary International Law' in Hague Academy (ed), *The Future of International Law in a Multicultural World* (Leiden: Brill, 1984) 211. While both authors often use the label 'comparative approaches to international law' instead of 'comparative international law', the overlap between both labels cannot be doubted. See, eg, WE Butler, 'American Research on Soviet Approaches to Public International Law' (1970) 70 *Columbia Law Review* 218, 224: 'a course in comparative international law is now being offered at the Harvard Law School'; and the earlier E McWhinney, 'Operational Methodology and Philosophy for Accommodation of the Contending Systems of International Law' (1964) 50 *Virginia Law Review* 36, 54: 'The operational problem for the present-day international lawyer who is genuinely concerned with the attempt to accommodate the contending legal systems may in some sense seem to reduce to an exercise in comparative law-comparative international law, if one wishes to be precise.'

[7] The main exception to the rule is B Mamlyuk and U Mattei, 'Comparative International Law' (2011) 36 *Brooklyn Journal of International Law* 385. By contrast, in a striking act of omission, the introductory chapter of A Roberts et al (eds), *Comparative International Law* (Oxford: Oxford University Press, 2018) entitled 'Conceptualizing Comparative International Law' does not discuss Butler's (or McWhinney's) methodological work, and when listing 'antecedents in earlier scholarship', Butler is not mentioned (ibid fn 7). This omission seems to only serve the authors' foundationalist claim to be discovering 'this emerging field' (ibid 6) and 'to establish comparative international law as a field of research'. This misleading view stems from Roberts' earlier article – A Roberts, 'Comparative International Law' (2011) 60 *International and Comparative Law Quarterly* 81 – according to which '[c]omparative international law is a unique phenomenon that has not received distinct treatment in the literature'. It is hardly surprising that Butler was not amused and rightly chastised this disappointing lack of intellectual generosity in his critical review of Roberts et al's book in WE Butler, 'Comparative International Law: A Review' (2018) 13 *Journal of Comparative Law* 242.

rather than the latter constituting a method for the analysis of international law,[8] a number of disciplinary intersections are identified:

> Without in any way attempting to restrict the concept of comparative law, it will be suggested there are at least six different but inter-related domains of comparative legal studies, four of which appertain to public international law. It is the latter with which these lectures shall be primarily concerned: (1) the comparative analysis of the international legal system per se, including postulated subsystems and doctrinal writings; (2) the comparative analysis of the relationship(s) between international law and municipal or community legal systems and cultures; (3) the comparative analysis of the internal or 'administrative' law of international organizations and institutions; (4) the application of the learning and lore of 'traditional' comparative legal concerns to the domain of public international law.[9]

With acute sensitivity towards the comparative dimension of international legal history,[10] the special focus of Butler's own work has thereby been on the first dimension, even if his clairvoyance as regards the third dimension should also be noted.[11] In the course of his Hague Lectures, he thus finds:

> Although we speak quite properly of the universality of contemporary international law, the international system has entertained for the past three centuries divergent understandings of 'universal' and the co-terminus existence of regional, theological and ideological subsystems (in some cases, alternative systems). These may only be studied comparatively, with a view to better comprehending the international legal order and, on occasion, resolving conflicts of rules that may emerge between them ... The fountainhead of modern international law not so long ago was known as 'European international law' ... There are at least four postulated subsystems of contemporary international law: the Islamic law of nations, the Latin American (or simply American) international law, African international law and the so-called socialist international law.[12]

This 'systems' or 'sub-system' approach to comparative international law contrasts with what Butler calls 'national approaches to international law' or 'comparative foreign relations law', which primarily focus on single countries' interpretations of international law.[13] An analysis of the modern Chinese approach to international law would, according to him, fall into this category, as 'China is a single system, rather than a legal "family"'.[14] Comparative foreign relations law is, of course, comparative law, yet it is – strictly speaking – not an integral part of the discipline of comparative *international* law, which Butler in a later publication defines

[8] Butler, 'Comparative Approaches to International Law' (n 6) 30.
[9] ibid 17.
[10] ibid 33–35. See also Butler, *International Law in Comparative Perspective* (n 6) pt IV, 'International Legal History in Comparative Perspective'.
[11] Butler, *International Law in Comparative Perspective* (n 6) pt V, 'The Role of Comparison in International Organizations'.
[12] Butler, 'Comparative Approaches to International Law' (n 6) 42.
[13] ibid 44 and 83.
[14] ibid 76.

as relating to 'the identification and analysis of similarities and differences within *systems of international law*, historical and contemporary, and between *international legal systems* and all other legal systems'.[15]

This international systems focus of the discipline of comparative international law does not, unlike the methodology recently championed by Roberts et al, concentrate on diverse national actors and the way they understand, interpret and apply international law.[16] For if comparative international law is primarily understood in terms of how international law is *received* at the national level (especially by its courts or academics),[17] it squarely falls within the discipline of *international* law because the existence of one universal system of international law behind these national receptions is always assumed.[18] Conversely, if a critical-constructivist perspective is chosen, this approach collapses into comparative foreign relations law, which is, ultimately, comparative *national* law.[19] Butler's international systems conception, by contrast, focuses not on individual states, but on 'families' of states that *share* a distinct conception of international law.[20] That perspective allows him to simultaneously acknowledge the normativity of international law above each state, while equally being able to recognise different normative systems in which a particular 'style' of thinking prevails.

This chapter wishes to revisit Butler's core domain of the discipline of comparative international law. It offers a broad outline of the diverse systems or legal

[15] Butler, 'Comparative International Law: A Review' (n 7) 246 (emphasis added).

[16] A Roberts et al, 'Conceptualizing Comparative International Law' in Roberts et al (eds), *Comparative International Law* (n 7) 6. The 'national' perspective is particularly prevalent in A Roberts, *Is International Law International?* (Oxford: Oxford University Press, 2017), which 'explores how different *national* communities of international lawyers construct their understandings of international law in ways that belie the field's claim to universality' (ibid 1, emphasis added). But see also (ibid 2 and 3 – emphasis added): '[T]his study represents one strand in a broader re-emerging subfield or set of approaches that I term "comparative international law," which examine cross-*national* similarities and differences in the way that international law is understood, interpreted, applied, and approached by actors in and from different *states*.'

[17] A Roberts, 'Comparative International Law? The Role of National Courts in Creating and Enforcing International Law' (2011) 60 *International and Comparative Law Quarterly* 57, as well as Roberts, *Is International Law International?* (n 16). See also D Sloss, *The Role of Domestic Courts in Treaty Enforcement: A Comparative Study* (Cambridge: Cambridge University Press, 2009); P-H Verdier and M Versteeg, 'International Law in National Legal Systems: An Empirical Investigation' (2015) 109 *American Journal of International Law* 514.

[18] See especially Roberts et al, 'Conceptualizing Comparative International Law' (n 7) 4 (emphasis added): 'On issues from Treaty interpretation to the content of customary international law, different states and international bodies may set forth different interpretations *of the same rules* …'.

[19] That a critical-constructivist perspective ultimately questions the very normativity of international law as 'law' is admitted by Roberts, *Is International Law International?* (n 16) 321. Roberts' project here converges with the critical-legal-studies approach championed by M Koskenniemi (who wrote the preface to Roberts' book).

[20] On the ambivalent and controversial notion of legal 'family' and the problems of comparative taxonomies in general, see M Pargendler, 'The Rise and Decline of Legal Families' (2012) 60 *American Journal of Comparative Law* 1043. See also M. Siems, *Comparative Law* (Cambridge: Cambridge University Press, 2022) ch 4.

families of international law that have existed in the 200 years between Ward's and Butler's versions of comparative international law.[21] Section B begins with the discovery, in the eighteenth century, of a geographical plurality of international systems, and especially the emergence of a distinctive 'European' international law that would, in the course of the nineteenth century, become the dominant 'system' of international law. Section C then explores three major counter-currents to the supposed universality of this European international law in the twentieth century: the 'socialist' conception of international law, the 'Third World' conception of international law and the 'new' EU conception of international law. A conclusion will return to the methodological question, posed at the beginning of this chapter, namely, how best to conceptualise and define the discipline of comparative international law today.

B. Out of One, Many – Part I: International Systems in the Nineteenth Century

Unlike the naturalist-rationalist conception of international law that insisted on the universality of its law of nations,[22] eighteenth-century Europe rediscovered that different civilisations had developed their own normative thinking about the relations between different peoples. An early comparative view here notoriously held that: 'All nations have a right of nations; and even the Iroquois, who eat their prisoners, have one.'[23] Yet Montesquieu's extreme national approach would not prevail in the nineteenth century; instead, it is a regional or civilisational approach to international law that gains the upper hand. Let us analyse this regional approach in a first step (section B.1), before exploring the rise of European international law in a second step (section B.2).

[21] My chapter aims to primarily present the geographical (synchronic) co-existence of parallel systems of international law over time. It is not concerned with the historical (diachronic) distinctions between 'rationalist', 'historicist' or 'positivist' systems or periods in the history of (Western European) international law. For this 'historical' variant of comparative international law, see especially P Vinogradoff, *Historical Types of International Law* (Leiden: Brill, 1923), as well as, more recently, W Grewe, *The Epochs of International Law* (Berlin: De Gruyter, 2000). The synchronic and diachronic dimensions of comparative international law may overlap. All 'socialist' authors, for example, expressly endorse different 'historical types' of international law, because international law is seen as a product or 'super-structure' of the social and economic relations of an epoch. See, eg, DB Lewin et al (eds), *Völkerrecht – Lehrbuch* (Berlin: DDR Staatsverlag, 1967) 21: 'Jedem historischen Typ der Klassengesellschaft entspricht ihr eigenes Völkerrecht.'

[22] E de Vattel, *The Law of Nations*, trans J Chitty (Johnson & Co, 1883). The book was originally published in 1758. The subtitle of Vattel's book importantly is *Or, Principles of the Law of Nature, Applied to the Conduct and Affairs of Nations and Sovereigns.*

[23] C de Montesquieu, *The Spirit of the Laws*, trans A Cohler et al (Cambridge: Cambridge University Press, 1989) 8.

1. After 'Naturalism': The Recognition of Diverse Positive International Legal Systems

In the last quarter of the eighteenth century, a number of German 'positivist' legal scholars began to closely analyse existing state practices in order to discover the 'real' international law between states. It was soon found that this positive international law could be different, according to the states or regions involved. A good illustration of this discovery is Moser's *First Principles of Today's European Law of Nations* (1778).[24] Moser here admits that there exist '*many positive* or particular' international legal orders and that 'Europe' only constitutes one such regional system with its own international customs.[25]

This positivist conception is subsequently taken up by von Martens, whose textbook *The Law of Nations* (1785) was to become an international bestseller in the nineteenth century.[26] Like Moser, Martens also believed that the existence of various positive international orders cannot be doubted. The latter were rooted in 'the resemblance of manners and religion, the intercourse of commerce, the frequency of treaties of all sorts, and the ties of blood between sovereigns'.[27] And these social ties had, within Europe, created a 'society of nations and states' that, while falling short of a 'state' or 'republic',[28] nonetheless formed a normative system in which a positive law could be found.

The most reflective and comparative version of this regional international systems theory can be found in the work of Robert Ward.[29] Ward accepts, along with his predecessors, that different positive international laws exist, and like Moser and Martens, he also thinks that for this positive law to be binding, it needs a 'binding principle' behind it. That binding principle is found in 'religion, and the moral system engrafted upon it'.[30] The world thus 'falls into different divisions or sets of nations, connected together under particular religions, moral systems, and local institutions, to the exclusion of other divisions or sets of nations'.[31] Unlike Montesquieu's national relativism, Ward here comes to embrace an *international*

[24] JJ Moser, *Erste Grundlehren des jetzigen Europäischen Völker-Rechts, in Friedens- und Kriegs-Zeiten* (Raspe, 1778). Moser considers himself to be the first to have created the idea of a 'European' international law. On Moser's empirical programme generally, see A Verdross, 'J.J. Mosers Programm einer Völkerrechtswissenschaft der Erfahrung' (1922) 3 *Zeitschrift des öffentlichen Rechts* 96.

[25] Moser (n 24) § 15.

[26] After a first Latin edition in 1785, a French edition (1789) and a German edition (1796) were followed by an English edition in 1802. The following section is based on the first English edition.

[27] GF von Martens, *A Compendium of the Law of Nations Founded on the Treaties and Customs of the Modern Nations of Europe*, trans W Cobbett (Cobbett, 1802) 27.

[28] ibid 27, fn: 'We may compare this society of European powers to a people before they form themselves into a state; that is to say, before they acknowledge any sovereign power over them. The states of Europe need then make but one step, to advance from the natural to the civil state, and to form themselves into an universal monarchy or republic; but this step they will never make.'

[29] Ward (n 2).

[30] ibid xxxv.

[31] ibid xiii.

relativism: each 'system of morality' generates one particular system of international law. Next to a Christian Law of Nations – that applies to the European nations – there co-exists an Islamic Law of Nations, as well as a Chinese Law of nations and so on.[32]

By the time that Ward was writing, the central normative principles of the 'Islamic' and the 'Chinese' international law systems had become well known. There had, of course, been extensive cultural and diplomatic contacts between Europe and the Ottoman Empire, and just two years prior to the publication of Ward's book, a notorious encounter between the European and the Chinese conception of international law had taken place, when the English ambassador to China had refused the acknowledge the universal supremacy of the Chinese emperor over the rest of the world.[33]

What, then, were the main differences and similarities between these international systems? The classic Islamic international system divided the world into two spheres: the realm of Islam (*dār al-islām*), in which a single law was to govern all Muslims, and the realm of war (*dār al-harb*), in which no law was to apply.[34] Unlike the European idea of a sovereign equality between states, under this normative conception, there cannot be 'a family of nations composed of states enjoying sovereign rights and equality of status' because 'the law of Islam recognizes no other nation than its own'.[35] And while there may appear to be international 'treaties' with non-Islamic states, these were not seen as implying equality or permanency; instead, they were regarded as unilateral concessions that temporarily suspended the holy war (*jihad*) against non-Muslims.[36] Classic Islamic international law is thus, in essence, a 'law of war', which is regarded 'as an instrument for universalising' Islam to the entire world.[37]

The classic Chinese system, by contrast, assumed the universal superiority of China. While according to Fairbank, it distinguished three different cultural zones,[38] these three zones nonetheless formed part of a 'unified and centralised'

[32] Ward lists seven 'classes of nations' expressly (ibid 139), but appears to be open to more: 'Thus then, distinct Classes of Nations have distinguishing Sets of customs. The North American Indians have one; The Indians of the South Sea another; The Negroes a third; the Gentoos a fourth; The Tartar Nations a fifth; The Mahometans a sixth; The Christians a sevenths, and so on.' Ward also accepts that some nations may exist 'in a kind of twilight' between two international systems, and here mentions the Ottoman Empire as an example (ibid 163).

[33] For this famous encounter, see D Mungello, *The Great Encounter of China and the West, 1500–1800* (Lanham, MD: Rowman & Littlefield, 2005), esp 126 et seq.

[34] For overviews here, see M Khadduri, *War and Peace in the Law of Islam* (Baltimore, MD: Johns Hopkins Press, 1955); IK Salem, *Islam und Völkerrecht: Das Völkerrecht in der islamischen Weltanschauung* (Thatcham: Express, 1984); and, more recently, S Laghmani, *Islam et droit international* (Leiden: Brill, 2023).

[35] M Khadduri, 'Islam and the Modern Law of Nations' (1956) 50 *American Journal of International Law* 358.

[36] ibid 360.

[37] Khadduri (n 34) 51. For the same point, see Laghmani (n 34) 60 and esp 150: 'Ce que l'on appelle *siyar*, est, de ce point de vu, le droit d'un empire et plus précisément un droit impérial.'

[38] JK Fairbank, 'A Preliminary Framework' in JK Fairbank, *The Chinese World Order: Traditional China's Foreign Relations* (Cambridge, MA: Harvard University Press, 1968) 1, 2.

Chinese world order. The latter was, once more, 'not organised by a division of territories among sovereigns of equal status'; rather, its 'organising principle' was that of 'superordination-subordination' under a universal Chinese 'empire'.[39] International agreements between China and a 'barbarian' nation were considered impossible;[40] they were but unilateral concessions granted by the Chinese emperor.[41] And, again, unlike the classic European conception of sovereign equality, 'all other non-Chinese nations had to be submissive and obedient',[42] because the Chinese 'state' was charged with 'the administration of civilised society *in toto*'.[43]

2. 'European' International Law: From Particular to Universal Order

How would the nineteenth century deal with these three international systems? The European law of nations was quickly adopted by the United States. It can, for example, be found in Kent's *Commentaries on American Law* (1826).[44] Following Ward, 'Europe' is here identified with 'Christianity',[45] as this normative conception of European international law allowed the United States – geographically remote from Europe – to explain why it could adopt (and benefit from) the customs and laws of the old continent.[46] Ward equally influenced Henry Wheaton, whose 1836

[39] ibid 9. See also Li Zhaojie, 'Traditional Chinese World Order' (2002) 1 *Chinese Journal of International Law* 20, 29 and 34: '[T]he concept of Chinese universal empire was that of an all-embracing domain, which included the whole world known to it … Such a hierarchically-structured world order was therefore characterized by the absence of state-to-state relations on the basis of principles of sovereign equality and territorial independence like the European world order.'

[40] On the Chinese notion of 'barbarians', see ICY Hsü, *China's Entrance into the Family of Nations: The Diplomatic Phase, 1858–1880* (Cambridge, MA: Harvard University Press, 1960) 7: 'Not only the Chinese language, but the Chinese people in their attitude toward the barbarians, often compared them to animals … Barbarians, in a strict sense, were not foreigners, for they were not outside the domain of the universal Chinese empire. They were but "uncivilized and outlandish" peoples awaiting assimilation into the Chinese orbit through cultural transformation.' It is only with the 1858 Treaty of Tientsin that China was prohibited from using the word 'barbarian' with regard to certain Western states. See, eg, art LI of the Peace Treaty between the Queen of Great Britain and the Emperor of China, in FL Israel (ed), *Major Peace Treaties of Modern History, 1648–1967*, vol II (Maidenhead: McGraw-Hill, 1967) 1065.

[41] According to Yasuaki, 'When was the Law of International Society Born?' (n 1), this conception even applied to the 1842 Treaty of Nanjing that, from the traditional Sinocentric worldview, saw the Chinese Emperor unilaterally allowing the 'barbarians' to settle their own disputes in China (ibid 31).

[42] Zhaojie (n 39) 34.

[43] ibid 48 (with reference to Mancall).

[44] J Kent, *Commentaries on American Law* (Halsted, 1826).

[45] Robert Ward is quoted already in Lecture 1 (ibid 4), and when Kent went on to assert that of all causes 'the most weight is to be attributed to the intimate alliance of the great powers as one Christian community', he relied heavily on Ward.

[46] However, in one important way, the 'New World' quickly opposed the old one, for with the emergence of the European Concert and the Holy Alliance in post-Napoleonic Europe, the young American Republic could not accept the monarchic principle and the 'Monroe Doctrine' would become a cornerstone of an 'American' international doctrine – especially the later (Latin) American conception of international law.

Elements of International Law were to shape Anglo-Saxon thinking for almost a century.[47] Here we read:

> There is … no universal immutable law of nations, binding upon the whole human race – which all mankind in all ages and countries, ancient and modern, savage and civilized, Christian and pagan have recognised in theory or in practice … The ordinary jus gentium is only a particular law, applicable to a distinct set or family of nations, varying at different times with the change in religion, manners, government, and other institutions, among every class of nations. Hence the international law of the civilized, Christian nations of Europe and America, is one thing; and that which governs the intercourse of the Mohammedan nations of the East with each other, and with Christians, is another and a very different thing.[48]

The passage was undoubtedly influenced by Montesquieu and Ward;[49] yet, unlike the latter's normative relativism, Wheaton's identification of European international law with 'civilisation' as such was to increasingly establish a hierarchy between the various regional systems of international law. How did this happen? European states came to assume that, despite their belief in sovereign equality, there was a hierarchical chain of being in which other societies reflected lower evolutionary stages when measured against the 'most advanced' European standard of civilisation.[50] In the nineteenth century, the key representative of this kind of hierarchical thinking was John Stuart Mill.

Mill had worked on the idea of 'civilisation' since 1836,[51] and in his *A Few Words on Non-intervention* (1859),[52] he famously made a categorical distinction between those international law principles governing civilised nations and those principles that would govern situations in which one party was at a 'high' and the other at a 'low' stage of civilisation.[53] In the former situation, 'civilised peoples' were seen to be 'members of an equal community', whose independence and sovereignty would need to be respected; yet, the same principles could not apply to the relationship between civilised and uncivilised states.[54]

[47] H Wheaton, *Elements of International Law* (Caray, Lea & Blanchard, 1836). The influence of Wheaton's *Elements of International Law* can hardly be exaggerated. In addition to the editions Wheaton published himself, posthumous American editions by WB Lawrence and RH Dana ran alongside separate English and French editions. Italian, Chinese and Japanese editions started to be published after 1860.

[48] ibid 44–45.

[49] ibid 44: 'Montesquieu deduces the peculiar law of nations prevailing among different races from their peculiar moral and psychological circumstances, in the same philosophical spirit with which he traces the origin and history of the civil laws of different nations.' However, Wheaton also heavily borrowed from Ward, whose work on the *History of the Law of Nations in Europe* was cited.

[50] G Gong, *The Standard of 'Civilization' in International Society* (Oxford: Clarendon Press, 1984).

[51] JS Mill, *Civilisation* (1836) in *The Collected Works of John Stuart Mill*, vol XVIII, ed J Robson (Toronto: University of Toronto Press, 1977) 117.

[52] JS Mill, *A Few Words on Non-intervention* (1859) in *The Collected Works of John Stuart Mill*, vol XXI, ed J Robson (Toronto: University of Toronto Press, 1984) 109.

[53] ibid 118.

[54] ibid: 'To suppose that the same international customs, and the same rules of international morality, can obtain between one civilized nation and another, and between civilized nations and barbarians, is

Part and parcel of Mill's dual conception of international law is, thereby, his 'civilisational' imperialism. For in seeing Europe – and especially the United Kingdom and the British Empire – as the highest civilisation on earth, and considering humankind as 'one not because it [is] everywhere the same, but because the differences [represent] different stages in the same process',[55] a hierarchy of states comes to be established, and that hierarchy ultimately justifies advanced states to lead and teach non-civilised states in the general interest of humanity as a whole. This hierarchical view will soon come to mean the following:

> Strictly speaking, there is not one International Law, but several. Wherever a group of peoples are compelled by local contiguity or other circumstances to enter into relations with each other, a set of rules and customs is sure to grow up among them, and their intercourse will be regulated thereby. The rules will differ at different times and among different groups. Their nature will be determined by the ideas current upon the subject of international intercourse and the practices permissible in warfare ... But though there are several systems of International Law, there is but one important system, and to it the name has been by common consent appropriated. It grew up in Christian Europe, though some of its roots may be traced back to ancient Greece and ancient Rome. It has been adopted in modern times by all the civilized states of the earth.[56]

The European society of states and 'its' international law is here portrayed as a universalistic society-in-becoming. For if the European standard is the most advanced standard, each society that wishes to interact with the Western world would have to conform to this standard. Ward's earlier relativist conception of different 'classes' of states having *each* developed their own (regional) international system is here rejected. There exists only *one* proper system of international law, membership of which is, however, still 'incomplete' because it depends on whether the 'European' standard of civilisation has been reached.[57]

This European conception of international law would conquer the world, by force and by assimilation, in the long nineteenth century. After the United States, it was 'appropriated', albeit with caveats, by Latin America;[58] and by the middle of the nineteenth century, the Ottoman Empire – the leading Islamic power – was

a grave error, and one which no statesman can fall into, however it may be with those who, from a safe and irresponsible position, criticize statesmen.'

[55] JW Burrow, *Evolution and Society: A Study in Victorian Social Theory* (Cambridge: Cambridge University Press, 1968) 98.

[56] TJ Lawrence, *The Principles of International Law* (Heath, 1898) 4.

[57] L Oppenheim, *International Law: A Treatise*, vol I (London: Longmans, 1912) § 103: 'Doubtful is the position of all non-Christian States except Turkey and Japan, such as China, Morocco, Siam, Persia, and further Abyssinia, although the latter is a Christian State, and although China, Persia, and Siam took part in the Hague Peace Conferences of 1899 and 1907. Their civilisation is essentially so different from that of the Christian States that international intercourse with them of the same kind as between Christian States has been hitherto impossible.'

[58] For a detailed story of this development, see A Becker Lorca, 'Universal International Law: Nineteenth-Century Histories of Imposition and Appropriation' (2010) 51 *Harvard International Law Journal* 475. However, by the beginning of the twentieth century, some Latin American authors started to insist on a specifically (Latin) American conception of international law. See A Alvarez, 'Latin America and International Law,'(1909) 3 *American Journal of International Law* 269, esp 273; and, more

admitted into the European family of nations.[59] The integration of the Chinese international system took place in the second half of the nineteenth century. The Treaty of Nanjing (1842) here represents an infamous starting point.[60] In the course of the next decades, the Chinese Empire reluctantly began to absorb the 'European' counter-conception,[61] and by the end of the nineteenth century, this European conception had imposed itself on much of Asia, with Japan and China in particular having entered into the (European) family of nations.[62]

After the First World War, it appeared to many (European) contemporaries that the European international order had become 'universal'. With the creation of the League of Nations in 1919, a first universal international organisation had been created that, while still dominated by European states, was open to any fully self-governing state of the world.[63] And yet, in one of history's many ironies, it is at the very moment when the universal 'League of Nations' is conceived that a 'New World' is born. For with the success of the Bolshevik Revolution and the creation of the first socialist state in 1922, a new – Marxist – way of thinking about international relations and international law appeared on the world stage.

C. Out of One, Many – Part II: International Systems in the Twentieth Century

The twentieth century gradually saw the re-emergence of new 'families' of nations. A socialist conception of international law would gain prominence after the Second World War, when the Union of Soviet Socialist Republics (USSR) extended its

recently, JP Scarfi, *The Hidden History of International Law in the Americas: Empire and Legal Networks* (Oxford: Oxford University Press, 2017).

[59] For an excellent summary of this story, see Yasuaki, 'When was the Law of International Society Born?' (n 1) 33–39.

[60] Y Zewei, 'Western International Law and China's Confucianism in the 19th Century: Collision and Integration' (2011) 13 *Journal of the History of International Law* 285; and now also S Hong-Lam, 'The Gentle Civilizer of the Far East: A Re-examination of the Encounter between "China" and "International Law"' (2024) 26 *Journal of the History of International Law* 1.

[61] Part and parcel of this legal 'transplantation' was the translation of classic 'European' authors like Wheaton. For a wonderful discussion of this aspect, with regard to China in particular, see Hsü (n 40), esp ch 8.

[62] The exact dates of this collapse of the Sinocentric system and its replacement by the Eurocentric system of international law are disputed. For excellent accounts here, see ibid, as well as R Svarverud, *International Law as World Order in Late Imperial China: Translation, Reception and Discourse, 1847–1911* (Leiden: Brill, 2007). For a brief discussion of the Japanese case, see M Zachmann, 'The Reception and Use of International Law in Modern Japan, 1853–1945' (2014) 19 *Zeitschrift für Japanisches Recht* 109.

[63] Article 1 of the 1919 Covenant of the League of Nations provided that: 'Any fully self-governing State, Dominion or Colony … may become a Member of the League if its admission is agreed to by two-thirds of the Assembly.' On China's position here especially, see Y Zhang, *China in the International System, 1918–1920: The Middle Kingdom at the Periphery* (London: Palgrave, 1991).

ideology to the 'Second World' (section C.1). Simultaneously, the decolonisation of the 'First World' created a 'Third World' of newly independent and developing states, with their own conception of international law (section C.2). And, once more with a degree of historical irony, even within Europe, a 'new legal order of international law' was beginning to emerge among the Member States of the European Union (section C.3). Let us look at this refragmentation of international law in more detail.

1. The 'Second World': The Socialist Family of Nations

What was the international law conception of the socialist family of nations? With the birth of the USSR, an explicitly Marxist-materialist conception of law entered the international arena. From its perspective, modern international law was 'the legal form of the struggle of the capitalist states among themselves for domination over the rest of the world', and, as such, it was nothing but 'the continuation of one armed conflict and the prelude to the next'.[64]

But if international law was merely the result of the capitalist 'mode of production' and the legal expression of bourgeois 'class domination', how can a socialist state engage with it? The first tentative answer that Soviet international law scholarship here gives is the idea of a temporary compromise:

> With the emergence of Soviet States in the historical arena, international law assumes a different significance. It becomes the form of a temporary compromise between two antagonistic class systems. This compromise is effected for that period when one system (the bourgeois) is already unable to ensure its exclusive domination, and the other (proletarian and socialist) has not yet won it. It is in this sense that it seems possible, to us, to speak of international law in the transitional period … International law becomes inter-class law.[65]

This first socialist approach had originally been proposed by Yevgeny Korovin, according to whom this inter-class law was not only a 'temporary' but also a 'non-universal' international law.[66] There simply could not be a universal international law because the economic base structures of capitalism and socialism were radically different. However, this view would soon fall out of favour with the Stalinist state, yet rather than offering its own positive conception of international law, the attitude of Soviet scholars during this second stage remained purely negativistic: 'The USSR does not accept all institutions and models of bourgeois international

[64] E Pashukanis, 'International Law' (1925) in E Pashukanis, *Selected Writings* (Cambridge, MA: Academic Press, 1980) 168, 169.

[65] ibid 172–73.

[66] EA Korovin, 'Das Völkerrecht der Übergangszeit' (1925), as discussed in AN Makarov, 'Die Völkerrechtswissenschaft in Sowjetrussland' (1936) 6 *Zeitschrift für ausländisches öffentliches Recht und Völkerrecht* 479, 481.

law – it openly rejects those which emerged as institutions for the enslavement of small and weak peoples by the groups of imperialist government.'[67]

Finally, in a third stage, Soviet scholarship returned to a more positive conception of socialist international law. It came to accept the existence of a historically conditioned capitalist *general* international law in addition to a more *specific* and 'higher' socialist international law.[68] Rejecting the 'constitutionalist' reading of the United Nations, because it undermined its pluralist conception of international law,[69] capitalist and socialist international law were here seen as 'law', yet the normative principles that animated both systems of international law were different. General international law was governed by the principle of 'peaceful coexistence'; socialist international law was, by contrast, informed by the idea of 'proletarian internationalism'.[70]

What are the main characteristics of this proletarian internationalism? The latter was given legal shape through three socialist legal principles – namely, the principles of fraternal friendship, close cooperation and mutual assistance.[71] The last principle in particular plays a distinct role for socialist international law and means the following:

> Proletarian internationalism has signified and does signify above all the unity of the proletariat of various countries in the class struggle against capital for a socialist reconstruction of society … An important part of this struggle is the joint defence of the socialist system from any attempt of forces of the old world to destroy or subvert any socialist state of this system … A vivid manifestation of this policy is the assistance of the Soviet Union to the Hungarian people of 1956 and the assistance, together with other socialist countries, to the people of Czechoslovakia in 1968 in protecting socialist gains and, ultimately, in defending their sovereignty and independence from sudden swoops of imperialism.[72]

Proletarian or socialist internationalism was thus based on the concept of 'limited' or 'socialist' sovereignty, which subjected the independence of each socialist state to the higher values of Marxist-Leninism.[73] This was to preserve the unity and

[67] A Vyshinsky, as quoted in E Green, 'Socialist Internationalism: *Theoria* and *Praxis* in Soviet International Law' (1988) 13 *Yale Journal of International Law* 306, 309.

[68] This idea of a specific socialist law had originally been rejected; yet post-Stalinist scholarship comes to emphatically accept this point, see, eg, DB Lewin et al (eds), *Völkerrecht: Lehrbuch* (Berlin: Staatsverlag der DDR, 1967) 20; and GI Tunkin, *Theory of International Law* (Cambridge, MA: Harvard University Press, 1974) 427.

[69] On this anti-mondialism, see E McWinney, 'Ideological Conflict and the Special Soviet Approach to International Law' (1971) 3 *University of Toledo Law Review* 215, 217.

[70] Tunkin (n 68) 432: 'The principles of proletarian internationalism have become international legal principles of relations between countries of the socialist system by way of custom and, partially, by treaty. These principles, which have been applied in the practice of relations between socialist countries, have been recognized by all states of the world system of socialism as international legal principles.'

[71] ibid 434–35. See also T Schweisfurth, *Sozialistisches Völkerrecht?* (Berlin: Springer, 1979) 273.

[72] Tunkin (n 68) 434–36. Similarly, see Lewin et al (eds) (n 68) 85.

[73] For an excellent discussion of the relationship between 'sovereignty' and 'socialism', and the idea of 'socialist sovereignty', see RA Jones, *The Soviet Concept of 'Limited Sovereignty' from Lenin to Gorbachev: The Brezhnev Doctrine* (London: Macmillan, 1990) esp 257–58.

integrity of the Socialist Commonwealth – the Second World, where individual national interests ought to always be subordinated to the fraternal common will of all other socialist states, and especially that of its oldest and most powerful member: the Soviet Union. It is this Soviet-centredness against which Chinese socialism would, after a while,[74] rebel through the development of its own 'Third World conception' of international law. And in denouncing the idea of socialist sovereignty as a form of 'imperialism', Chinese communism came to adopt its own specifically socialist conception of international law.[75]

2. 'Third World' Approaches to International Law (TWAIL)

The 'Third World' conception of international law originally grew out of the desire for a 'non-aligned' anti-imperialist alternative to the Western-capitalist (First World) and Eastern-socialist (Second World) conceptions of international law.[76] Formally starting with the 1955 Bandung Conference that brought together a number of African and Asian states – especially China[77] – it came to be embraced by most of the decolonised states that had, after 1960, become independent.

These 'new states' originally shared the Soviet-socialist scepticism towards the 'liberal' nineteenth-century international law, because of its Eurocentric and imperialist nature.[78] And reclaiming their own histories,[79] they began questioning the binding nature of those 'European' customs and international treaties that seemed to contradict the interests of decolonised states:

> [I]t is incumbent upon the Third World countries to re-examine the principles, rules and regulations of traditional international law and to decide which of them ought

[74] Originally, communist China had closely followed the Soviet-socialist conception of international law: see H Chiu, Communist China's Attitude towards International Law, (1966) 60 *American Journal of International Law* 245; and more generally JA Cohen and H Chiu, *People's China and International Law: A Documentary Study*, vol 1 (Princeton: Princeton University Press, 1974).

[75] On this point, see S Jaschek, 'Die Chinesische Völkerrechtsdoktrin im Lichte der Drei-Welten-Theorie' (1978) 21 *German Yearbook of International Law* 363; and W Butler, 'Anglo-American Research on Soviet Approaches to Public International Law' in Butler (ed), *International Law in Comparative Perspective* (n 6) 169, 181–82. For a more recent analysis, see T Ruskola, *Legal Orientalism: China, the United States, and Modern Law* (Cambridge, MA: Harvard University Press, 2013).

[76] W Tieya, 'The Third World and International Law' in Chinese Society of International Law, *Selected Articles from the Chinese Yearbook of International Law* (Beijing: China Translation & Publishing Corporation, 1983), 6.

[77] C Yifeng, 'Bandung, China, and the Making of World Order in East Asia' in L Eslava et al (eds), *Bandung, Global History, and International Law: Critical Pasts and Pending Futures* (Cambridge: Cambridge University Press, 2017) 177.

[78] RP Anand, *New States and International Law* (Noida: Vikas, 1972) 45: '[E]ven a cursory look at the history of international law leaves no doubt about the Eurocentric nature of this law developed by and for the benefit of the rich, industrial, and powerful states of Western Europe and the United States.'

[79] See, eg, TO Elias, *Africa and the Development of International Law* (Leiden: Sijthoff, 1972), esp ch 1; RP Anand, *Studies in International Law and History: An Asian Perspective* (Leiden: Brill, 2004).

> to be rejected and which ought to be retained or even reaffirmed and given renewed emphasis.[80]

According to the 'clean slate' theory, therefore, only those norms to which these new states could have expressly or implicitly consented to were to be binding on them.[81]

Yet unlike the Soviet view in favour of a special socialist international system, the early Third World conception of international law rejects the idea of distinct subsystems of international law.[82] On the contrary, to many Third World scholars, only through decolonisation had international society become truly universal and the future task of legal scholarship was to make international law reflect this new universality. In the words of Anand:

> Today, with the reappearance of the new African-Asian states, the international society has become universal. The traditional international law, the parochial law of the European Powers, is bound to be affected by the new sociological structure of the society. While a large part of this law is fairly reasonable, useful and adjustable to the new international social structure, and cannot and should not be discarded, it requires complete overhaul and adaption to new circumstances. Like the present society and the classical international law, it must become universal to serve the interests of all the states, and help in the establishment of peace and security. In order to command respect to all the states it must extend from a European national law to a common law of mankind.[83]

What should this 'common law of mankind' look like? It would need to reflect the interests of all states, and in a demand that parallels nineteenth-century socialism, only a degree of *material* equality was ultimately seen to guarantee the sovereignty of all states. It followed that post-colonial international law would need to contain a global-solidaristic project that pursued economic development,[84] and it is in that context that a 'New International Economic Order' (NIEO) was envisaged.[85] The NIEO was the first attempt to institutionalise the 'welfare state' at the international level and it represents, to date, the 'biggest departure' from the Western liberal conception of (European) international law.[86]

[80] Tieya (n 76) 20.

[81] A Krueger, *Die Bindung der Dritten Welt an das postkoloniale Völkerrecht* (Berlin: Springer, 2018) 54–64.

[82] GM Abi-Saab, 'The Newly Independent States and the Rules of International Law: An Outline' (1962) 8 *Howard Law Journal* 95, 105.

[83] Anand (n 78) 114.

[84] Krueger (n 81) 101.

[85] Most famously here, see M Bedjaoui, *Towards a New International Economic Order* (Teaneck, NJ: Holmer & Meier, 1979). For a subsequent account, see PN Agarwala, *The New International Economic Order: An Overview* (Oxford: Pergamon, 1983).

[86] A Gotachew, *Worldmaking after Empire: The Rise and Fall of Self-Determination* (Princeton: Princeton University Press, 2019) 12.

The vehicle to adopt and implement the NIEO was quickly identified – universal international organisations: '[I]nternational organizations, and especially the United Nations, provide an ideal context for the drafting of a legal new deal with a view to the transformation of the international economic order and the development of all peoples.'[87] The special role of the United Nations, and its 'political' organs in particular,[88] here also led to another significant feature of the Third World international law project – the demand to transform the UN General Assembly into a formal international legislature. In the words of Bedjaoui:

> Through its egalitarian character, its majority basis and hence its democratic origins, the [General Assembly] resolution seems to [Third World States] to present sufficient guarantees as a method for the elaboration of international norms responding to today's needs. The preference of Third World States for resolutions as instruments for the progressive development of international law can thus be explained: first, by the conception these States have of the role of international organizations and especially the General Assembly of the United Nations; next by the speed of adoption of a resolution; and last, by the resolution's flexibility, since it can quite easily be changed to take account of developments in the world.[89]

Yet in the absence of a convincing concept of international democracy or demoicracy,[90] and in the face of powerful 'Western' resistance, the democratic and redistributive Third World conception of international law eventually fails. Worse, from the early 1980s onwards, an alternative neoliberal philosophy swept over international law and has today almost completely eradicated the conditions of possibility behind this democratic-redistributive common-law-of-mankind conception. Reacting to this dramatic failure, a new generation of Third World scholars began, henceforth, to reconceptualise TWAIL in the 1990s.[91] However, this 'TWAIL II' scholarship differs significantly from its precursor. For in its most extreme version, it altogether rejects international law,[92] while even its more

[87] Bedjaoui (n 85) 140. See also G Abi-Saab, 'Introduction: The Concept of International Organization: A Synthesis' in G Abi-Saab (ed), *The Concept of International Organization* (Paris: UNESCO, 1981) 9, esp 23.

[88] R Higgins, *The Development of International Law through the Political Organs of the United Nations* (Oxford: Oxford University Press, 1963).

[89] Badjaoui (n 85) 140.

[90] I Claude, *Swords into Plowshares: The Problems and Progress of International Organisation* (Maidenhead: McGraw-Hill, 1984) 126: 'Majority decisions in the equalitarian General Assembly are likely to be undemocratic in the sense that they do not represent the majority of the world's population, unrealistic in the sense that they do not reflect the greater portion of the world's real power, morally unimpressive in the sense that they cannot be identified as expressions of the dominant will of a genuine community, and for all these reasons ineffectual and perhaps even dangerous.' For a discussion of the concept of demoicracy in the international arena, see R Schütze *We, the Peoples: Models of Demoicracy* (Oxford: Oxford University Press, in preparation).

[91] On the distinction between TWAIL I and TWAIL II, see A Anghie and BS Chimni, 'Third World Approaches to International Law and Individual Responsibility in Internal Conflicts' (2003) 2 *Chinese Journal of International Law* 77.

[92] The most radical TWAIL II critique has thus contended that the entire 'regime of international law is illegitimate' as a 'predatory system that legitimizes, reproduces and sustains the plunder and

moderate expressions have replaced the constructive and affirmative TWAIL I with a negative 'critical legal studies' approach.[93]

3. Supranational 'International' Law: The New 'European' Legal Order

With the disappearance of the real-existing 'Socialist Commonwealth' after 1989, and the gradual fading of the original Third World conception of international law, did the Western-liberal conception of international law again become universal? By the early twenty-first century, it indeed seemed to some that a 'new world order', based on Western liberal-capitalist principles, had arrived.[94] General international law, while open to internal critiques and distinct methodological approaches,[95] appeared to have become truly 'international'.[96] And yet what this 'end of history' view neglects is an important 're-particularising' development that had already started early in the twentieth century: the rise of regional international organisations (RIOs).[97] Important post-1945 milestones here are the founding of the Organization of American States (1948),[98] the European Community (1957, since 1993 the European Union), the Association of Southeast Asia (1961, since 1967 Association of Southeast Asian Nations (ASEAN)) and the Organization of African Unity (1963, since 2002 the African Union).

What stands behind this 'new regionalism' in the second half of the twentieth century? It is, along with Alvarez, the realisation that '[t]o pretend that all states

subordination of the Third World by the West'. See MW Mutua, 'What is TWAIL?' (2000) 94 *Proceedings of the Annual Meeting (American Society of International Law)* 31.

[93] For this excellent point, see J Haskell, 'TRAIL-ing TWAIL: Arguments and Blind Spots in Third World Approaches to International Law' (2014) 27 *Canadian Journal of Law and Jurisprudence* 383. Similarly, see G Abi-Saab, 'The Third World Intellectual in Praxis: Confrontation, Participation, or Operation behind Enemy Lines?' (2016) 37 *Third World Quarterly* 1957, esp 1958: 'I am with two minds about the label TWAIL. If it is taken literally – Third World Approaches to International Law – then, of course, I am a TWAILer or TWIALian. But if it is taken, as presented or perceived by some, as an off-shot of the Critical Legal Studies school, I am not.'

[94] Nothing signals this self-celebratory arrival more than AM Slaughter, *New World Order* (Princeton: Princeton University Press, 2005).

[95] SR Ratner and AM Slaughter (eds), 'Symposium on Method in International Law' (1999) 93 *American Journal of International Law* 291.

[96] It is against this post-1989 'universalistic' background that Roberts et al 'discover' comparative international law at a moment in time when earlier alternative regional conceptualisations of international law had largely disappeared from the textbooks of international law; and it is for this reason, it seems to me, that the 'national' diversity route appears to them as the only way forward for reconceptualising the discipline of comparative international law. Yet are major disagreements between Russia or China (or the United States) and other states really something new and distinctive? Has the invisible college not always been divisible along 'ideological' lines during much of the twentieth century? Historical amnesia is, of course, an infallible ingredient to 'discovering' new fields.

[97] JR de Orúe Y Arregui, 'Le Regionalism dans l'Organisation International' (1935) 53 *Collected Courses of the Hague Academy* 1.

[98] For an overview here, see OC Stoetzer, *The Organization of American States* (Westport, CT: Praeger, 1993).

that form the community of nations should be always governed by the same identical rules, would be equivalent to a denial of the right of groups of nations of special origin and geographical situation to develop in conformity to their nature when they are able to so develop.'[99] And by the twenty-first century, it had also become clearer that modern international law simply lacked the normative and decisional structures for collective international government. Not only does it still adhere to the 'sovereign equality' of all states;[100] its adherence to state voluntarism and the unanimity rule has blocked all major government initiatives on all important global goods (peace, welfare and the environment).

A regional approach, by contrast, promised better collective solutions by inviting states to share their sovereignty within a supranational 'union' of states.[101] The best analysed example in this context is the European Union.[102] From the very start, European integration contrasted with international 'coordination' in two essential ways. Normatively, the status of European law within the domestic legal orders would not depend on national law and, decisionally, the creation of many supranational norms would not require unanimous consent. In both respects, the EU had created '*a new legal order of international law*',[103] and the most iconic new legal principles here were the doctrines of direct effect and primacy:

> By contrast with ordinary international treaties, the [EU] Treaty has created its own legal system which, on the entry into force of the Treaty, became an integral part of the legal systems of the Member States and which their courts are bound to apply … The integration into the laws of each Member State of provisions which derive from the [Union], and more generally the terms and the spirit of the Treaty, make it impossible for the States, as a corollary, to accord precedence to a unilateral and subsequent measure over a legal system accepted by them on a basis of reciprocity.[104]

Ever since its creation, the EU legal system has thus insisted on its 'autonomy', and it has defended this autonomy against the normative demands of international law.[105] The UN Charter, for example, while having 'special importance' within the European legal order, could thus – at best – have primacy over European legislation, but '[t]hat primacy at the level of [European] law would not, however, extend to primary law' as the constitutional basis of the European legal order.[106] The EU

[99] A Alvarez, 'Latin America and International Law' (1909) 3 *American Journal of International Law* 269, 346.

[100] Article 2(1) of the UN Charter: 'The Organization is based on the principle of the sovereign equality of all its Members.'

[101] R Schütze (ed), *Globalisation and Governance: International Problems, European Solutions* (Cambridge: Cambridge University Press, 2018).

[102] See, eg, R Schütze, *European Union Law*, 4th edn (Oxford: Oxford University Press, 2025).

[103] *Van Gend en Loos* (n 5) 12 (emphasis added).

[104] Case 6/64 *Costa v ENEL* [1964] ECR 585, 593–94.

[105] Case C-402/05 P *Kadi and Al Barakaat International Foundation v Council and Commission*, EU:C:2008:461.

[106] ibid para 308.

legal system therefore constituted a special 'international' regime that no longer derived its authority and normativity from general international law.

How should one think of the European Union and its 'new' legal system? In light of its historical evolution, the European Union today occupies a place somewhere in between an international organisation and a super-state.[107] This 'middle ground' is hard to conceptualise, and from the very beginning, the European Union was said to have been 'established on the most advanced frontiers of the [international] law of peaceful cooperation', with its principles of solidarity and integration having taken it 'to the boundaries of federalism'.[108] But was the European Union inside those boundaries or outside them? Comparative international law can here assist in finding answers to these conceptual questions, as much as it can help in analysing the ways in which the European Union has itself become a supranational 'model', whose ideas and structures are increasingly diffused and transplanted elsewhere.[109]

D. Conclusion: Re-aligning Comparative International Law with its History

What should the domain of comparative international law be? As sections B and C have shown, a wide range of different international normative systems have existed over the last 250 years, and from Ward to Butler, several academic writers have engaged in 'comparative' work contrasting these different systems. Furthermore, related work has focused on the legal 'diffusion' or 'transplantation' processes, especially of European international law, as well as the resulting hybridity that this process has brought about.[110] But, importantly, the main historical focus has thereby always been on comparing 'systems', 'orders' and 'regimes' of *international* law.

This system-centric approach is very different from the more recent approach taken by Roberts et al in which the field of comparative international law is defined by how different actors, especially *national* ones, understand and interpret international law. However, the conceptual tensions within this actor-centric definition are serious. For while its national-reception version, ironically, preserves the idea of one underlying universal international law that is only refracted into a plurality

[107] R Schütze, 'On "Federal" Ground: The European Union as an (Inter)National Phenomenon' (2009) 46 *Common Market Law Review* 1069.

[108] P Pescatore, 'International Law and Community Law: A Comparative Analysis' (1970) 7 *Common Market Law Review* 167, 182.

[109] For interesting comparisons between the African Union and the EU, see O Amao et al (eds), *The Emergent African Union Law: Conceptualization, Delimitation, and Application* (Oxford: Oxford University Press, 2021); and from a political science perspective, see L Fioramonti and F Mattheis, 'Is Africa Really Following Europe? An Integrated Framework for Comparative Regionalism' (2016) 54 *Journal of Common Market Studies* 674.

[110] See n 4.

of subjective author-perspectives,[111] its national-constructivist version ultimately leads to a denial of international law as law. In essence, and as section A has already argued, the Roberts et al approach to comparative international law either leads to a version of international law proper or it becomes comparative foreign relations law. However, any good conception of comparative international law, should take all three elements of 'comparative', 'international' and 'law' seriously. With Butler, *national* approaches to international law, à la Montesquieu or Roberts, should categorically be excluded from its domain.[112]

This refocusing of the discipline in light of its history does not empty its twenty-first century subject matter. For while the socialist-materialist conception of international law no longer seriously rivals the Western-liberal conception (and TWAIL has transformed itself from a universal-welfarist into a critical-negative project), there continue to be different variations of inter-state law today. Indeed, with the rise of regional international organisations, like the European Union, an important new branch of comparative international law has emerged.[113] The African Union, for example, here offers brilliant possibilities for the international comparativist. For not only has it tried to learn from the legal experiences of the European Union (and the Council of Europe), the 'innovative principles' within its own Constitutive Act will also themselves inspire others in turn;[114] and its integrated 'regionalism within regionalism' approach might especially be a future guide for other continents, including Europe.

But apart from the horizontal comparisons between 'regional' international orders – whether at the systemic level or in respect to specific issues, such as human rights[115] – what ought to be included and what excluded from the field of comparative international law?

From the perspective of one regional 'inter-state' system, vertical comparisons can of course go upwards and downwards. The European Union may, for example, be compared to universal organisations, like the United Nations or the World Trade Organization,[116] but it can equally be compared to national phenomena, like

[111] See again n 17.

[112] For the same reason, one might be equally sceptical towards the more recent plea to 'renationalise' the history of international law. For this Roberts-like attempt to create a 'new' discipline of 'comparative international legal history', see now I de la Rasilla, 'Towards Comparative International Legal History?' (2025) 27 *Journal of the History of International Law* 1.

[113] For good recent overviews of the new 'field' of comparative regionalism, see T Börzel and T Risse (eds), *Oxford Handbook of Comparative Regionalism* (Oxford: Oxford University Press, 2016); and C Closa and L Casini, *Comparative Regional Integration* (Cambridge: Cambridge University Press, 2016). See now also S Besson and E Kassoti, 'The International Law of Regional Organizations: Mapping the Issues' (2024) 21 *International Organizations Law Review* 1, which locates this branch specifically within 'comparative international law' (at 3).

[114] AA Yusuf, *Pan-Africanism and International Law* (Leiden: Brill, 2014), esp 186 et seq.

[115] See, eg, H Gros Espiell, 'La Convention américaine et la Convention européenne des droits de l'homme : Analyse comparative' (1989) 218 *Collected Courses of the Hague Academy* 167.

[116] Schütze (n 101).

the United States or the German Federal Republic.[117] Legal diffusion or transfers may also happen in both directions: US American and German federalism has thus inspired the European Union in the past, while the latter's hybrid federalism has more recently informed British constitutional law with regard to devolution.[118] Yet it should be noted that in every comparison mentioned so far, one unit of analysis has always been an inter-state system, like the European Union. For as soon as two states are compared – even as regards their approaches to international law, we are in the realm of comparative constitutional law, not comparative international law.[119]

What about comparisons between different branches of international law? In the last 100 years, the scope of international law has expanded enormously. In addition to dealing with 'war and peace', 'trade' and diplomatic relations, modern international law now covers, inter alia, international human rights, international crimes and international environmental issues. This ever-increasing specialisation has led to the 'fragmentation' of general international law into distinct parts or specialised 'legal regimes'.[120] To some, a comparison of these special 'systems' or 'regimes' should also fall within the discipline of comparative international law, whereas others have been more critical.[121] Yet there are good reasons to include these horizontal inter-branch comparisons, as long as their functional or cultural 'comparability' is given.[122] And the discipline of comparative international law can here be especially useful in its vertical dimension: for each special international system can not only be compared upwards to general international law;[123] equally, the more international law specialises, the more useful downwards comparison to national law will become.

[117] R Schütze, *From Dual to Cooperative Federalism: The Changing Structure of European Law* (Oxford: Oxford University Press, 2009); and R Schütze, 'Classifying EU Competences: German Constitutional Lessons?' in S Garben and I Govaere (eds), *The Division of Competences between the EU and the Member States* (Oxford: Hart Publishing, 2017) 33.

[118] The most recent example here is the United Kingdom Internal Market Act 2020. For a comparative analysis, see M Dougan et al, 'Sleeping with an Elephant: Devolution and the United Kingdom Internal Market Act 2020' (2022) 138 *Law Quarterly Review* 650.

[119] In a similar way, the analysis of various *national* approaches to private international law would not be comparative international law, but rather comparative 'conflicts' law. By contrast, *inter-state* approaches to private international law would fall within comparative international law: see E Abdallah, 'La Convention de la Ligue arabe sur l'exécution des jugements. Étude comparative du droit conventionnel comparé avec le droit interne' (1973) 138 *Collected Courses of the Hague Academy* 503. With the engagement of the EU in this area, there is also (arguably) again a 'European' conception of private international law; see G van Calster, *European Private International Law* (Oxford: Hart Publishing, 2024.

[120] B Simma, 'Self-Contained Regimes' (1985) 16 *Netherlands Yearbook of International Law* 111; and, more recently, B Simma and D Pulkowski, 'Of Planets and the Universe: Self-Contained Regimes in International Law' (2006) 17 *European Journal of International Law* 483.

[121] Roberts et al, 'Conceptualizing Comparative International Law' (n 7) 9: 'Unlike the fragmentation debate, comparative international law focuses primarily, though not exclusively, on interpretations of international law put forward by states and substate actors, such as national courts.'

[122] M Siems, 'The Power of Comparative Law: What Type of Units Can Comparative Law Compare?' (2019) 67 *American Journal of Comparative Law* 861.

[123] J Kurtz, *The WTO and International Investment Law: Converging Systems* (Cambridge: Cambridge University Press, 2016).

Figure 2.1 Overview of units of comparative international law

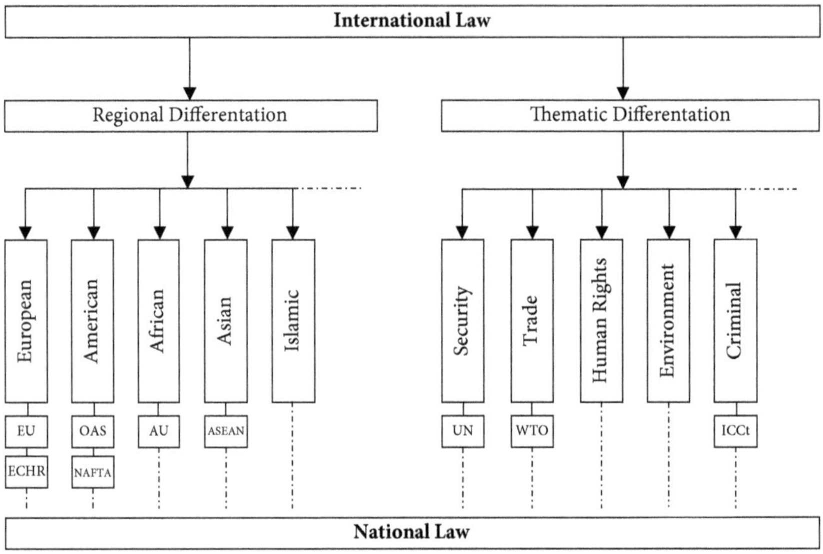

In conclusion, then, and building on Butler's definition, quoted in the Introduction above, the field of comparative international law can be historically and conceptually redefined as follows. *Comparative international law is concerned with the identification and analysis of similarities and differences among regional or specialised systems of international law (horizontal comparison) or between them and general international or national law (vertical comparison), whereby at least one unit of comparison is international or supranational in nature.* Figure 2.1 gives an overview of the various international 'units', whether regional or thematic, that fall within the discipline of comparative international law. This new definition is primarily focused on synchronous comparisons, yet – with Butler – a broadened temporal frame might here also accommodate inter-period comparisons of different historical systems of international law.[124]

[124] See n 21.

PART II

Historical and Comparative Perspectives

3

'African' International Law

KEHINDE FOLAKE OLAOYE

A. Introduction

More than a century after the phrase 'African international law' appeared for the first time in academic literature, we might still ask if it is misplaced or inappropriate to ask what AIL is.[1] In 1929, during an American Society of International Law Conference, Dr Scott Brown rejected the notion of 'African international law', arguing that continents had nothing to do with international law.[2] When these arguments were being made, some comparativists argued that Africa had no legal existence in the law of nations. While a few scholars recognised the existence of international law in pre-colonial Africa,[3] it was acceptable to refer to parts of colonised Africa as backward territory,[4] uncivilised, exotic and primitive.[5] At the final session of the 1932 General Section of the International Congress of Comparative Law, a resolution was passed recommending:

> [T]he study of written and customary laws of the people of Africa, Asia and Oceania in order to bring the study of *exotic* law into the field of consideration in comparative law, and give opportunity for the ethnology of law and the archaeology of law to be of greater mutual aid.[6]

[1] A Koagne Zouapet, 'Is There an African Approach to International Law? Is it Even Needed?' in A Koagne Zouapet (ed), *Sixty Years after Independence, Africa and International Law* (Pretoria: Pretoria University Press, 2023) 3.

[2] 'Proceedings of the American Society of International Law at its Annual Meeting April 24–27 1929' (1929) 23 *ASIL Proceedings* 25.

[3] Baron SA Korff, 'Introduction to the History of International Law' (1924) 18 *American Journal of International Law* 246, 250.

[4] M Lindley and M Frank, *The Acquisition and Government of Backward Territory in International Law: Being a Treatise on the Law and Practice Relating to Colonial Expansion* (London: Longmans, 1926).

[5] JC Gardner, 'The Study of Comparative Law in Great Britain' (1932) 14 *Journal of Comparative Legislation and International Law* 201, 205.

[6] MH Colvin, 'International Congress of Comparative Law' (1932) 7 *Tulane Law Review* 53, 58.

Since 1908, when Judge Alejandro Alvarez first made his famous thesis on regional international law,[7] the African continent has undergone significant change, development and progress.[8] The existence of a separate field of international law called 'African international law' has been a subject of scholarship since the late 1950s when the first African colonies began to prepare for self-governance.[9] However, this term has fallen into disuse, in favour of a broader notion of 'African approaches to international law'.[10] Over the last seven decades, Africa has achieved several international milestones, including decolonisation and the establishment of regional international organisations.[11] It has also been confronted with challenges and problems. Collective historical experiences, common challenges and the proliferation of sub-regional organisations have also created opportunities for developing distinct scholarship and jurisprudence in specific sub-fields, including international investment law, international trade law, the law of international development, the international law of the sea, international refugee law, international environmental law, international human rights law and international environmental law.[12] African approaches to international law, which encompass how Africa as a continent collectively interacts with principles of international law, are recognised in academic literature, in international reports, in international treaties and in the decision making of international courts and tribunals.[13]

[7] A Alvarez, 'Latin America and International Law' (1909) 3 *American Journal of International Law* 269.

[8] T Maluwa, 'Reassessing Aspects of the Contribution of African States to the Development of International Law through African Regional Multilateral Treaties' (2020) 41 *Michigan Journal of International Law* 327.

[9] PF Gonidec, 'Note sur le droit des conventions internationales en Afrique' (1965) 11 *Annuaire français de droit international* 866; R Yakemtchouck, *L'Afrique en Droit international* (1969) 7 *Cahiers économiques et sociaux* 383; J-M Bipoun-Woum, *Le droit international africain: problèmes généraux, règlement des conflits* (Paris: LJDJ, 1970); FC Okoye, *International Law and the New African States* (London: Sweet & Maxwell, 1972); TO Elias, *Africa and the Development of International Law* (Leiden: AW Sijthoff, 1972).

[10] F Viljoen, H Sipalla and F Adegalu (eds), *Exploring African Approaches to International Law: Essays in Honour of Kéba Mbaye* (Pretoria: Pretoria University Law Press, 2022).

[11] Maluwa (n 8) 327.

[12] JT Gathii, *African Regional Trade Agreements as Legal Regimes* (Cambridge: Cambridge University Press 2011); M Geboye Desta and M Hirsch, 'African Countries in the World Trading System: International Trade, Domestic Institutions and the Role of International Law' (2012) 61 *International and Comparative Law Quarterly* 127; F Ouguergouz, *La Charte africaine des droits de l'homme et des peuples: Une approche juridique des droits de l'homme entre tradition et modernité* (Geneva: Graduate Institute Publications, 2015); CC Jalloh, KM Clarke and VO Nmehielle (eds), *The African Court of Justice and Human and Peoples' Rights in Context: Development and Challenges* (Cambridge: Cambridge University Press, 2019); YN Hodu and MM Mbengue (eds), *African Perspectives in International Investment Law* (Manchester: Manchester University Press, 2020); J Sarkin-Hughes and ETM Siang'andu (eds), *Africa's Role and Contribution to International Criminal Justice* (Cambridge: Intersentia, 2020); N Negm, *An Introduction to the African Union Environmental Treaties* (Leiden: Brill, 2023); WL Kidane, *Africa's International Investment Law Regimes* (Oxford: Oxford University Press, 2023); M Blakeney and GM Alemu, *African Free Trade Agreements and Intellectual Property* (Cheltenham: Edward Elgar, 2024).

[13] B Fagbayibo, *African Approaches to International Law* (Oxford Bibliographies), available at www.doi.org/10.1093/obo/9780199796953-0225.

Although the contributions of Africa to international law have been examined in detail in previous scholarship, including from a comparative perspective, few recent studies examine this strictly from a comparative international law perspective. Comparative international law has been defined as using comparative law insights and methods to order to identify, analyse and explain similarities and differences in how international law is understood, interpreted, applied and approached by different national and international actors.[14] From an African perspective, comparative study of international law can be defined as using comparative law methods to study the convergence and divergence of African treaties, the decisions of African regional courts and the practice of African states to understand how Africa is using international law to solve Africa's international law problems.

As this chapter shows, while we all are inherently comparative international lawyers, we must yet again confront centuries-old arguments on culture, universalism, regionalism and newer arguments on the fragmentation of international law. For the African international legal scholar, the choice of comparativism as a legal methodology comes with the legal baggage of 'African law' and its colonial ethnography.[15] In a similar vein, we must ask again: what is Africa and what is Africanness? Is Africa a geographical legal fiction, or is there a true pan-AIL[16] that has survived inordinate geographical mappings carved out by the coloniser? Unlike the first generation of international law scholars who grappled with these questions with much difficulty, we have more experience and practice, which allows us to focus on important issues like African peoples-centred international law.

This chapter is a response to attempts to reinvigorate comparative international law, and thus comes with an imperative to revisit the notion of 'African international law'. It builds on decades of AIL intellectual traditions and examines future directions for African approaches to comparative international law. The basic question it asks is: what role has comparative methodology played and what role can it play in the further identification of Africa approaches to Africa's international law problems? This chapter shows that while we may disagree on the practical relevance of identifying African approaches to international law, African attitudes to international law, African contributions to international law or African solutions to Africa's international law problems, we can all agree that Africa provides a rich canvas for comparative international legal studies. This chapter uses three main illustrations – namely treaty ratification, dispute

[14] A Roberts et al, 'Conceptualizing Comparative International Law in Comparative International Law' in A Roberts et al (eds), *Comparative International Law* (Oxford: Oxford University Press, 2018) 3, 4; DH Rached and CHubner Mendes, 'Comparative International Law' in M Siems and PJ Yap (eds), *The Cambridge Handbook of Comparative Law* (Cambridge: Cambridge University Press 2024) 561; see also chs 1 and 2 by Siems and Schütze in this volume.

[15] L Rosen, 'Comparative Law and Anthropology' in M Bussani and U Mattei (eds), *The Cambridge Companion to Comparative Law* (Cambridge: Cambridge University Press, 2012) 73, 75.

[16] AA Yusuf, *Pan-Africanism and International Law* (Leiden: Martinus Nijhoff Publishers, 2015).

resolution and the sources of international law – to show the practical relevance of comparative international law.

This chapter is divided into four main sections. Section B examines why the quest for AIL was a main project until the 1990s, linking this quest to the preoccupation with African law. Sections C and D focus on the role that comparative law has played in the identification of AIL, showing that the imperative for comparative approaches intensified with the birth of new era of African regionalism in the 1990s. Section E examines in detail the practical relevance of an African regional approach to international law. The conclusion in section F shows that even though the notion of African regional law may be antithetical to true economic integration within the continent, it provides future directions for theoretical and practical studies. The conclusion also makes a case for a peoples-centred African approach to international law.

B. Approaches to 'African International Law'

Although it is now commonplace to consider African approaches to international law, it is also possible to identify national approaches and sub-regional approaches. These include pre-decolonisation notions of 'West African international law'[17] and 'Southern African international law'. Notable contemporary national approaches include South African perspectives,[18] Egyptian perspectives, Nigerian approaches[19] and Abyssinian approaches.[20] Clear evidence of national approaches is found in the different national societies of international law and newly formed regional branches of the International Law Association in Cameroon, Senegal, Nigeria, South Africa, Mauritius and East Africa. Other examples are the African Society of International Law and the Africa International Economic Law Network. Sub-regional yearbooks of international law, like the recently published *Congolese Yearbook of International Law*, and conferences held annually are also an indication of this trend.[21] Societies are not a new trend. The Egyptian Society of International Law was established in 1944 by Mr Jasper Y Brinton, a British national in the mixed courts of Egypt, 'to encourage the study of public and private international

[17] L Solanke, *United West Africa (or Africa) at the Bar of the Family of Nations* (London: West African Students' Union, 1927); RS Smith, *Warfare & Diplomacy in Pre-colonial West Africa* (Madison: University of Wisconsin Press, 1989) 144; MM Mbengue and N Odili, 'West African Approaches to International Water Law and Treaty Practice' in SC McCaffrey, C Leb and RT Denoon (eds), *Research Handbook on International Water Law* (Cheltenham: Edward Elgar, 2019) 361.

[18] J Dugard et al, *Dugard's International Law: A South African Perspective*, 5th edn (Claremont: Juta, 2018).

[19] See C Eboe-Osuji, E Emeseh and OD Akinkugbe (eds), *Nigerian Yearbook of International Law 2018/2019* (Cham: Springer, 2021).

[20] R Parfitt, 'Empire des Nègres Blancs: The Hybridity of International Personality and the Abyssinia Crisis of 1935–36' (2011) 24 *Leiden Journal of International Law* 849. See also *The Ethiopian Yearbook of International Law* (published by Springer since 2016).

[21] *Annuaire congolais de droit international 2023* (Brussels: Bruylant, 2024).

law in Egypt'.[22] More than two decades later, the Nigerian Society of International Law was founded in 1968.[23] These associations are not to be confused with the International African Law Association, which was established in the mid-1950s, with several national branches for the study of African law.

The much older notion of 'African law'[24] laid the foundation for disciplines of international law in Africa, especially Africa's peoples-centred human rights framework. It was these notions of 'African law', established by the 'greatest' comparativists, that the first generation of African trained international lawyers sought to counter through organisations like the Organization of African Unity (OAU) Commission of Jurists.[25] The notion of African law originated from anthropological societies established by colonial exploration societies popularised by colonial officers like Federick Lugard, who sought to understand 'uncivilized' systems.[26] These perceptions of 'Africa' flourished until the 1960s. For example, in his 1957 Foreword, which launched the *Journal of Africa Law*, Sir Alfred Denning (better known as Lord Denning) described African law as a jumble of pieces, a jigsaw that had to be sorted and put into one whole if the peoples of Africa were to emerge into a great civilisation.[27] In 1962, Hans Wolfgang Baade wrote that there was at least at the present no typical African school of thought in public international law, as contrasted with the Latin American doctrine.[28] He argued that little danger to traditional 'Western' values and concepts lurked in a specific 'African' conception of law, whether national or international, and that:

> [F]inally the really singular telescoping of articulate societal and legal development into an unprecedentedly short time-span affords the comparative scholar a splendid opportunity not only to see other societies in actual development, but also to comprehend his own legal frame of reference more thoroughly and more modestly.[29]

Baade's arguments are compounded, as he also noted that if the uniqueness of African legal problems did not result primarily in its 'unusual and frequently archaic character of major legal institutions', but in the stage of its economic

[22] 'Current Notes: Meeting of the Inter-American Bar Association' (1944) 38 *American Journal of International Law* 473, 474; JI Kunz, 'Revue Égyptienne de Droit International' (1949) 43 *American Journal of International Law* 792.

[23] Proceedings of the First Annual Conference of the Nigerian Society of International Law, 1969 (Lagos: Faculty of Law, University of Lagos, 1970).

[24] JH Driberg, 'The African Conception of Law' (1934) 16 *Journal of Comparative Legislation and International Law* 230.

[25] K M'Baye, 'The African Conception of Law' in *International Encyclopedia of Comparative Law* (Leiden: Brill, 1974) 138.

[26] F Lugard, 'Colonial Administration' (1933) 41 *Economica* 248; R Akande, *Entangled Domains: Empire, Law and Religion in Northern Nigeria* (Cambridge: Cambridge University Press, 2023) 18. See also H Dedek, 'The Tradition of Comparative Law: Comparison and its Colonial Legacies' in Siems and Yap (eds) (n 14) 387.

[27] A Denning, 'Foreword' (1957) 1 *Journal of African Law* 1.

[28] HW Baade, 'African Law: Foreword' (1962) 27 *Law & Contemporary Problems* 537, 541.

[29] ibid 544.

development, much of what had been written about African law by comparative and international lawyers would require a careful re-examination.[30]

Keba Mbaye portrayed African law as sufficiently unique and distinct to support nationalist exceptionalism and pan-African solidarity. He viewed an African family of law in the immemorial rules of customary African law, expressed by religion and morality and populated by kinship groups, elders, spirits and living ancestors. This would form the foundation for Mbaye's future international law projects on development and human rights.[31] For the straitjacket comparativist, African law had nothing to do with the law of nations. Noting this oversight, in 1996, Anthony Allott, a jurist of African and comparative law, noted that a major gap in the first 40 years of the *Journal of African Law* was the absence of international law.[32] The *Journal* had focused on publishing 'comparative material on the non-common-law jurisdictions of Africa' and papers that showed that Islamic law prevailed not only in the north of Africa but also other Muslim majority countries.[33]

In 1962, Alejandro Alvarez extended his famous 1910 thesis to Africa as a result of the emergence of new states in Africa.[34] African scholars approached AIL from different perspectives with Latin American being the archetype for comparison. While some African scholars sought to highlight the contributions of Africa, other scholars focused on 'African International Law.'[35] Scholars like Fatouros and Gonidec expressed optimism that although embryonic, AIL would emerge in the future.[36] Scholars like Elias sought to show that international existed in pre-colonial Africa. Scholars like Felix Okoye argued that as African states had not yet developed doctrines like the Latin American Calvo Doctrine and the Drago Doctrine, there was no AIL.[37] However, Okoye provided a good definition of AIL, defining it as '"a body of conventional and customary law, complementary to general international law, and governing inter-States relations" in the Pan-African world'.[38] Ginther's definition of AIL as *jus publicum africanum* consisting of international legal principles of an African state was also an important definition.[39] In contemporary times, these early definitions of AIL show why there has been a shift away from AIL towards African contributions to international law.

[30] ibid 537.

[31] M'Baye (n 25).

[32] AN Allott, 'The Journal of African Law 1957–96: Then and Now' (1996) 40 *Journal of African Law* 143, 150. See P-H Verdier, 'Comparative International Law and the Rise of Regional Journals' (2024) 49 *Yale Journal of International Law* 154.

[33] ibid 147. See also RS Elsaman, 'Middle East and North Africa' in Siems and Yap (eds) (n 14) 331.

[34] A Alvarez, *El nuevo derecho internacional en sus relaciones con la vida actual de los pueblos* (Santiago: Editorial Jurídica de Chile, 1962).

[35] R Yakemtchouk, 'Le Regime International des Voies d'Eau Africaines' (1969) 5 *Revue belge de droit international* 480.

[36] AA Fatouros, 'International Law and the Third World' (1964) 50(5) *Virginia Law Review* 783, 820.

[37] Okoye (n 9) 209.

[38] ibid. The first part of this statement quotes the dissenting opinion by Judge Read in the ICJ's Asylum Case (Colombia v Peru) of 20 November 1950, *ICJ Reports* 1950, 316.

[39] K Ginther, 'Re-defining International Law from the Point of View of Decolonisation and Development and African Regionalism' (1982) 26 *Journal of African Law* 49, 51.

In the 1960s, international society underwent rapid change.[40] The first leaders of Africa's independent states recognised that 'a United States of Africa' was a legal fiction created from maps drawn by the coloniser. Yet compromises were made from the lines of division in the Brazzaville, Pan-African Freedom Movement for East and Central Africa (PAFMESCA), Monrovia and Casablanca groups to form the OAU in 1963. At the inaugural meeting of the OAU, President Abdel Nasser of the United Arab Republic (Egypt) stated:

> [A]ll the traditional divisions which imperialism tried to impose on the continent to rend it apart to North of the Sahara and South of the Sahara, to white, black and coloured Africa, to East and West, to French-speaking Africa and English-speaking Africa have all collapsed and were swept away by the genuine African reality. There remains but one language on African land … the language of the one destiny no matter what the method of expression.[41]

Unity in Africa and Asia raised concerns for international law in a divided world.[42] However, fears for the disunity of international law as a result of newly independent states were greatly exaggerated. While some Western publicists expressed scepticism, others embraced and welcomed new approaches from the newly independent states of Africa. Wolfgang Friedmann described new approaches to international law as 'an artificial inflation of cultural distinctiveness', asking if law was not 'more than just a harmless exercise in hypocrisy and narcissism'.[43] While some non-African scholars welcomed the idea of African international law, many leading international lawyers viewed African attitudes with disdain and scepticism. For most scholars, there were fears that the emergence of regional international law was a 'menace to the survival of a universal system of international law'.[44]

The period between the 1950s and the 1990 can be described as a period when the existence of a unique AIL was considered extremely important. The 1955 Bandung Conference, the establishment of the OAU and the Asian Legal Consultative Committee (ALCC) were not exactly welcomed in the family of nations. Notable events in no particular order, between 1960 and 1989, include the oil embargo against Portugal, South Africa and Rhodesia,[45] wars of national liberation and the declaration of a New International Economic Order in 1974.[46] UN General Assemblies, the United Nations Conference on Trade and Development

[40] *International Law and African Problems*, African Conference, Lagos, 14–18 March 1967 (Carnegie Endowment for International Peace, 1968).

[41] Information Department, *President Gamal Abdel-Nasser's Speeches and Press Interviews* (1963) 95.

[42] OJ Lissitzyn, 'International Law in a Divided World' (1961) 34 *International Conciliation* 3.

[43] W Friedmann, 'The Position of Underdeveloped Countries and the Universality of International Law' (1961–63) 1 *Columbia Journal of Transnational Law* 78, 86.

[44] YZ Blum, 'Review of *New Nations and the Law of Nations. International Law – Indian Courts and Legislature*' (1969) *American Journal of Comparative Law* 485, 486.

[45] IFI Shihata, 'Destination Embargo of Arab Oil: Its Legality under International Law' (1974) 68 *American Journal of International Law* 591, 596.

[46] TO Elias, 'New Perspectives and Conceptions in Contemporary Public International Law' (1980–81) 10 *Denver Journal of International Law and Policy* 409.

(UNCTAD) conferences, Resolutions of the ALCC and African regional organisations reflected these changes. Ethiopia and Liberia instituted proceedings against South Africa before the International Court of Justice concerning the continued existence of the League of Nations Mandate for South West Africa.[47] Other areas of concern were the settlement of boundary disputes[48] and the nationalisation of foreign-owned property.[49] As these developments in international law continued,[50] scepticism towards AIL remained in the 1970s and 1980s, although this scepticism was already at its vanishing point. In his introduction to an African legal history project published under the aegis of the UN Institute for Training and Research in 1975, Kodwo Mensah-Brown noted:

> In the early 1960s, the concept of an African International law might legitimately have been dismissed as premature; for international order was then being confronted more with defiant attitudes than with the development of new doctrines identifiable as African. Today, this view seems untenable as the defiant attitudes of the last decade have been and still are being collated and crystallized into principles of jurisprudential concepts. The spate of literature in recent years on the multifarious aspect of the impact of Africa in international law is progressively brining the concept into focus of an emergent field of study. Although in an embryonic phase of development, African international law is currently being investigated by means of different approaches.[51]

Yet in his 1980 Hague Academy lecture on comparative international, William Elliott Butler recognised the possibility of the future emergence of AIL as a regional approach to international law as against its full existence.[52] In the same year, the South African jurist John Duggard recognised the emergence of AIL. Even though he acknowledged that AIL was not as distinct as communist and Latin American approaches, he recognised that a distinct regional African law could be seen in the use of force against colonial and racist powers, the binding force of UN General Assembly resolutions, the status of liberation movements in Africa, the right to self-determination, state succession and international adjudication.[53] By the end of the 1990s, a new form of economic regionalism emerged in Africa. The end of apartheid in South Africa, the end of the Cold War, and new forms of African regionalism like the 1991 Treaty establishing

[47] UO Umozurike, 'International Law and Self-Determination in Namibia' (1970) 8 *Journal of Modern African Studies* 585.

[48] OA Cukwurah, *The Settlement of Boundary Disputes in International Law* (Manchester: Manchester University Press, 1967).

[49] SKB Asante, 'Restructuring Transnational Mineral Agreements' (1979) 73 *American Journal of International Law* 335.

[50] TO Elias, *New Horizons in International Law* (Leiden: Brill, 1979).

[51] AK Mensah-Brown, 'Introduction' in AK Mensah-Brown (ed), *African International Legal History* (New York: UN Institute for Training and Research, 1975) 1, 3.

[52] WE Butler, 'International Law and the Comparative Method' in WE Butler (ed), *International Law in Comparative Perspective* (Leiden: Brill, 1980) 25, 37.

[53] J Duggard, 'Book Review of AJGM Sanders, *International Jurisprudence in African Context*' (1980) 13 *Comparative and International Law Journal of Southern Africa* 128, 129.

the African Economic Community heralded a new era of African international regional law. This new form of regionalism was sealed with the transformation of OAU into the African Union in 2000.

Post-2000, AIL was finally permitted to flourish. However, scholarship has continued in the AIL contributionist tradition, focusing on the African origins of the right to development[54] and the African origins of international law.[55] There have also been more studies of private international law in Africa, including studies on the 'transplanted' Organisation for the Harmonisation of Business Law in Africa.[56] Older terms like 'Africanisation' and new terminology like 'an African Union law' have also emerged.[57] International scholars like Tiyanjana Maluwa have emphasised less focus on the theoretical paradigms and contributions of individual African scholars in favour of more focus on the actual practice of African states. He defines Africa's contributions as international law norms arising within Africa that have created new legal concepts or elaborated on existing ones, and which have subsequently exerted influence beyond the continent.[58] This 'Addis Ababa Effect', which can be likened to the 'Brussels Effect', is replacing the original focus on AIL. However, Mohammed Bedjaoui has described African contributions to international law as half-hearted. He has noted that due to the continued domination by ex-colonisers, African states have failed to change international law.[59] Political and economic problems like the imposition of sanctions on undemocratically elected governments, challenge the peace and security and show that there is some practical value in examining more closely what Bedjaoui has described as *demi-teinte*.

C. The Practical Value of 'African International Law'

Express references to 'African international law' or 'African approaches to international law' are sparse in international treaties and international reports, and in the decisions of international tribunals and courts. Nevertheless, the recognition of African practices is evident in different sources of international law. These include reports of the International Law Commission (ILC) and international

[54] JT Gathii, 'Africa and the Radical Origins of the Right to Development' (2020) 1 *Third World Approaches to International Law Review* 28.

[55] JI Levitt, 'The African Origins of International Law: Myth or Reality' (2015) 19 *UCLA Journal of International Law & Foreign Affairs* 113; MJC Moco, 'Contribuição para uma apreciação Jus-Internacional da integração Regional Africana' (PhD dissertation, University of Lisbon, 2016).

[56] R Oppong, 'Private International Law in Africa: The Past, Present, and Future' (2007) 55 *American Journal of Comparative Law* 677. See J Neels, *African Principles on the Law Applicable to International Commercial Contracts* (Johannesburg: UJ Press, 2023).

[57] O Amao, M Olivier and KD Magliveras (eds), *The Emergent African Union Law: Conceptualization, Delimitation, and Application* (Oxford: Oxford University Press, 2021).

[58] Maluwa (n 8) 330.

[59] M Bedjaoui, 'La contribution en demi-teinte de l'Afrique au developpement du droit international' (2004) 47 *German Yearbook of International Law* 63, 68.

decisions. Recent commentaries of the ILC include those on the Draft Articles on the Protection of Persons in the Event of Disaster, the Draft Articles on Prevention and Punishment of Crimes against Humanity, the Draft Guidelines and Draft Annex Constituting the Guide to Provisional Application of Treaties, the Draft Guidelines on the Protection of the Atmosphere, and the Draft Principles on Protection of the Environment in Relation to Armed Conflicts. In the Commentary to the Draft Conclusions on Identification of Customary International law, the ILC notes that the case law of the International Court of Justice (ICJ) shows that some rules of customary law are limited in terms of their impact to the African continent.[60]

While to a large extent African practice has contributed to universal international law, controversial practices have also emerged. For example, it has been shown that the practice of intervention by invitation is an intra-African phenomenon, which has emerged from successive coups within the continent.[61] International criminal law and prosecution of Africa leaders has attracted criticism. For example, based on a database of 16,192 citations of the ICC, a recent article shows that the ICC rarely cites African national laws or cases.[62] This is notable considering that Africa states are frequently named in ICC investigations. All the same, African treaties are frequently referred to in the judgments of the European Court of Human Rights and other courts.[63] In their reasonings, international courts inevitably adopt a comparative approach in decision making. A good example is the *Diallo* decision. In its reasoning, the ICJ compared Article 12(1) of the African Charter with interpretations of the European Court of Human Rights and the Inter-American Court of Human Rights, the Convention for the Protection of Human Rights and Fundamental Freedoms, and the American Convention on Human Rights, noting the consistency of these treaties.[64] To a certain extent, it can be argued that efforts made over the last few decades in terms of promoting the study of international law by Africans and promoting the study of Africa's international law, including the preoccupation with 'African law', have made this possible. These include broadening peoples' rights as a distinct category of human rights law, recognition of the right to development, the right of humanitarian intervention and expansion of the rights of children, women and the internally displaced.[65]

[60] ILC Draft Conclusions on Identification of Customary International Law, with Commentaries (2018) 33.

[61] E de Wet, 'The Modern Practice of Intervention by Invitation in Africa and its Implications for the Prohibition of the Use of Force' (2015) 26 *European Journal of International Law* 979.

[62] S Manley, PM Tehrani and R Rasiah, 'The (Non-)Use of African Law by the International Criminal Court' (2023) 34 *European Journal of International Law* 555.

[63] *Ramadan v Malta* App No 76136/12 (ECtHR, 21 June 2016).

[64] *Republic of Guinea v Democratic Republic of the Congo* (Merits, Judgment) [2010] ICJ Rep 639, 663.

[65] Maluwa (n 8).

D. The Role of Comparative Methods

In the 1960s, comparative international lawyers recognised the emergence of the international law of the Afro-Asian or newly merging states. It was argued that in the absence of a comparative approach, it would be possible to identify as many international laws as there are states.[66] Wilfred Jenks, while noting the value of comparative law to international law, recognised that the law of the Asian members of the Commonwealth, Chinese law and at a later stage African law must be added to the training of international lawyers.[67]

In 1986, the African Society of International and Comparative Law (ASICL) was established to promote education in African law and to promote Africa's contribution to international law. Notably, in his editorial to the first issue of the *African Journal of International and Comparative Law*, Emile Yakpo stated that it was important to 'establish co-operation between African lawyers of the various legal systems in Northern, Eastern, Anglophone and Francophone Africa, in order to benefit from Comparative Law'. It can be argued that the Society was trying to fill the gaps now left by the OAU jurists, the disunity of African and Asian approaches to international law and the initial focus on Africa law. Emile Yakpo's editorial also admonished African publicists to abandon 'dubious' expressions like 'African law' or 'Tribal law', describing them as colonial-era concepts that were unhelpful for identifying the richness of African legal systems. The goals of the ASIC can be contrasted with those of the African Association of International Law, also established in 1986, to 'foster the development and dissemination of African perspectives and practices of international law'.[68]

Comparative law has been developed and used in African international law studies, although overshadowed by critical approaches and schools of thought like Third World Approaches to International Law (TWAIL).[69] In his infamous paper on Asian and African attitudes, which is considered foundation reading for TWAIL, Ram Prakash Anand argued that in the absence of a comparative approach, arguments made by international law scholars that non-Christian African states objected to international law because of their different cultural, religious, ethical, social and legal backgrounds had no value.[70] The main methods used and developed by African scholars include historical, critical and functional approaches

[66] LC Green, 'Comparative Law as a Source of International Law' (1967) 42 *Tulane Law Review* 52, 55.

[67] WC Jenks, 'Craftsmanship in International Law' (1956) 50 *American Journal of International Law* 32, 41.

[68] 'African Association of International Law: Statutes' [1994] 1 *African Yearbook of International Law* 327.

[69] S Mancuso and CM Fombad (eds), *Comparative Law in Africa: Methodologies and Concepts* (Claremont: Juta, 2015).

[70] RP Anand, 'Attitude of the Asian-African States toward Certain Problems of International Law' (1966) 15 *International and Comparative Law Quarterly* 55, 71.

to the study of Africa's mixed legal systems.[71] Critical theorists notably scholars who represent TWAIL have highlighted the invisibility of Africa in international law[72] and have criticised the contributionist tradition. Malalu Costa argued that the teaching of international law in anglophone Africa must include subjects like African regional integration, which have to be very comparative. Malalu defined comparative study as examining achievements or failures, while stressing the development of an AIL. Although he considered this AIL as non-existent in 1986, he favoured at least identifying Africa's contribution to international law.[73] Kamba noted that comparative law was useful for the ascertainment, creation, formulation and application of principles of international law in Africa.[74] It is now well recognised that comparative legal research is key to any research aimed at drafting harmonised laws or drawing up international conventions and agreements.[75]

Pierre-François Gonidec, who was a prominent believer in AIL, highlighted the importance of comparative law methodology for realising AIL. Under his direction, Joseph-Marie Bipoun-Woum published *Le droit international africain* in 1970. In addition to directing the African and Malagasy series publications, Pierre-François Gonidec was a frequent contributor to the *African Journal of International and Comparative Law*.[76] In 1997, he published a defining journal article, for good reason in both French and English, in which he made a case for a treatise on 'African International Law'. In the article, Gonidec acknowledged the complexities of Africa's diversity, asking:

> Would not a project aiming to establish the unity of African international law be doomed by this institutional and normative diversity? We do not think so. Such diversity only entails the need to make use of the comparative method, which has its value not only in the study of municipal law, but also of international law. Thus, it is out of the question to review all the African international organisations, nor even all the pan African NGOs. On the other hand, it is possible, by use of the comparative method to show their common philosophy which is a drive towards unity even though this unity may be conceived differently by the various States or peoples. It is also possible to compare the structures of these organisations, their means of action, their respective competences, their results … Overall, a Treatise of African international law should make it possible through the use of the comparative method, to move from the

[71] CN Okeke, 'Comparative Law in Africa: Methodologies and Concepts' in Mancuso and Fombad (eds) (n 69) 34.

[72] JT Gathii, 'Mapping African International Law' (2011) 2 *Transnational Legal Theory* 429, 439.

[73] CR Mahalu, 'The Teaching of International Law in Anglophonic Africa' (1986) 24 *Archiv des Völkerrechts* 196, 214.

[74] WJ Kamba, 'Comparative Law: A Theoretical Framework' (1974) 23 *International and Comparative Law Quarterly* 485, 504.

[75] CM Fombad, 'Comparative Research in Contemporary African Legal Studies' (2018) 67 *Journal of Legal Education* 984, 991.

[76] P-F Gonidec, *Les organisations internationales africaines: étude comparative* (Paris: Harmattan, 1987); P-F Gonidec, 'Existe-t-il un droit international africain?' (1993) 5 *African Journal of International and Comparative Law* 243; P-F Gonidec, 'Droit international de droit interne en afrique' (1996) 8 *African Journal of International and Comparative Law* 789.

national to the regional level, without prejudice of comparisons between the latter and the universal level[77]

A lot has changed since Gonidec's profound proposals for a textbook on 'African International Law'. Several books on AIL have been published, and comparative international law is taught in leading African law schools. In February 2009, the Statute on the African Union Commission on International Law (AUCL) was adopted, following the proposal by the AU Executive Council held in Addis Ababa, Ethiopia, in July 2004. The AUCL emphasises the contemporary relevance of African approaches to international law. As the next section will show, despite this growth and progress, comparative international law still holds lots of promise.

E. Method and the Future of Approaches to African Comparative International Law

Within Africa, different legal traditions and legal families have been identified in legal scholarship.[78] These include civil law, common law and Sharia law. Most African countries adopt a mix of legal systems, combining pre-colonial traditions with colonial-era laws and post-colonial laws. These include countries like Cameroon, in which both common law and civil law apply differently in Southern and Northern Cameroon.[79] On both sides of the Sahara, legal transplants from the colonial era remain the main source of law. However, legal transplants have historically not fallen into straightforward compartments. Some jurisdictions have modernised their laws through legal transplants from other common law countries or other civil law countries. Translating the legal families used by comparative scholars into international law studies is not very straightforward either. And as Gonidec noted in 1997, to a large extent, comparative methodology could even be fatal to AIL. This section examines future directions for legal scholarship by focusing on the sources of international law, the law of treaties and dispute resolution. It provides some practical directions for the following looming questions: what do we compare, why should we compare and how should we compare?[80] A full analysis is beyond the scope of this chapter.[81] This section can form a basis for expanding legal education, informing the decision making of tribunals and work of the AUCL.

[77] P-F Gonidec, 'Towards a Treatise of African International Law' (1997) 9 *African Journal of International and Comparative Law* 807, 820.

[78] WF Menski, *Comparative Law in a Global Context: The Legal Systems of Asia and Africa*, 2nd edn (Cambridge: Cambridge University Press, 2006); C Ntampaka, *Introduction aux systèmes juridiques africains* (Namur: Presses universitaires de Namur, 2005).

[79] EN Ngwafor, 'Cameroon: The Law across the Bridge: Twenty Years (1972–1992) of Confusion' (1995) 26 *Revue générale de droit* 69.

[80] EG Bello, 'How Advantageous is the Use of Comparative Law in Public International Law?' (1988) 66 *Revue de Droit International, de Sciences Diplomatiques et Politiques* 77.

[81] See A Cuyvers, 'Comparing Regional Law' in Siems and Yap (eds) (n 14) 649.

1. The Law of Treaties and Patterns of Treaty Ratification

The law of treaties is a great foundation for deploring comparative methods in the study of African approaches to international law. Existing studies have identified poor ratification of regional treaties which is compounded by overlapping regionalism.[82] The law on treaties raises several issues, including the interpretation of treaties, treaty reservation and withdrawal from treaties. In the 1960s, a key concern was whether newly independent African states could be bound by treaties created before their creation.[83] Traditionally, comparative approaches have focused on the distinction between dualism and monism. Patterns of treaty practice that are traceable to different legal traditions can be explored further. This may include studies, for example, on why only a few African common law countries are signatories to the UN Convention on Contracts for the International Sale of Goods (CISG). Analogies can be made with the OHADA (Organization for the Harmonization of Business Law in Africa) Uniform Acts and their application in francophone states and Equatorial Guinea, which is a former Spanish colony. While some of these studies can aid the role of Africa in the development of international law, they may not be helpful in identifying AIL. For example, it is widely known that the early entry into force of the International Centre for Settlement of Investment Disputes (ICSID) occurred due to the ratification of African states. At the same time, even though Ethiopia was one of the first states to sign the ICSID Convention in 1965, to date it has not ratified the Convention. While this is an indication of an Ethiopian approach, it does little to promote the identification of one single African approach. Reservations of states to international treaties is also an area for comparative studies. For example, in its general reservation to the 1979 UN Convention on the Elimination of All Forms of Discrimination against Women, Egypt states that it is willing to comply with Article 2 so long as this does not run counter to Islamic law. Reservations to Article 2 have also been made by Niger concerning the taking of all appropriate measures to abolish all customs and practices that constitute discrimination against women, particularly in respect of succession. Another key area of research is treaty withdrawal and departure from international organisations. In January 2024, Niger, Mali and Burkina Faso announced their withdrawal from the Economic Community of West African States. These three states, which share a common currency as members of the Communauté financière d'Afrique, have not announced their withdrawal from the West African Economic and Monetary Union or from the African Union. Future regional projects like the ECO currency, the realisation of the African Economic Community and full operationalisation of the African Continental Free Trade Area can only be fully realised and understood through comparative legal studies.

[82] Gathii (n 12) 73.
[83] GM Abi-Saab, 'The Newly Independent States and the Rules of International Law: An Outline' (1962) 8 *Howard Law Journal* 95, 107.

2. Sources of International Law

The Protocol of the Court of Justice of the African Union provides that in carrying out its functions, the Court shall have regard to: (a) the Constitutive Act; (b) international treaties, whether general or particular, ratified by the contesting states; (c) international custom, as evidence of a general practice accepted as law; (d) the general principles of law recognised universally or by African states; (e) subject to the provisions of paragraph 1 of Article 46 of the present Statute, judicial decisions and writings of the most highly qualified publicists of various nations well as the regulations, directives and decisions of the Union, as subsidiary means for the determination of the rules of law; and (f) any other law relevant to the determination of the case.[84] This provision, which is the African equivalent to Article 38 of the ICJ Statute, presupposes that there are general principles of law recognised only by African states. Identification of customary law has been a core function of the ILC. Dire Tladi notes that in its adoption of *jus cogens*, the ILC has adopted an approached favoured by the African group, which encompasses legal texts, state practices, precedents and doctrine.[85] Comparisons between Article 31 of the Court of Justice Statute and other African treaties show the importance of articulating African principles on international law. However, the applicable law provisions of African regional courts and international organisations do not necessarily articulate an African approach. A good starting point is the 2018 African Continental Free Trade Area Agreement (AfCFTA). The preamble to the AfCFTA refers to respective rights and obligations under the Constitutive Act of the African Union of 2000, the Abuja Treaty and, where applicable, the Marrakesh Agreement Establishing the World Trade Organization (WTO) of 1994. While the WTO was established in 1994, its goals were really developed in the General Agreement on Tariffs and Trade (GATT) era with the participation of very few African states. As a group, African states have not been very active in the WTO. In 2019, the 44 Member States of the WTO who are part of the African Group requested that the African Union be granted observer status at the WTO.[86] The letter noted that Africa remains committed to the rules-based multilateral trading system in which the WTO serves as the principal global organ of governance, and that the African Union has been given the mandate to coordinate and harmonise the position of African countries and regions within international trade negotiations.[87]

[84] Protocol of the Court of Justice of the African Union (adopted 1 July 2003), art 31.

[85] D Tladi, *The International Law Commission's Draft Conclusions on Peremptory Norms* (Oxford: Oxford University Press, 2024) 14.

[86] Statement by Ambassador Albert M Muchanga, African Union Commissioner for Trade and Industry Delivered at the Third Regional Dialogue on WTO Accessions for Africa: Deepening Economic Integration in Africa through WTO Membership and AfCFTA Implementation (12 February 2020), available at www.wto.org/english/thewto_e/acc_e/commissioner_muchanga_speech_at_wto_accession_workshop_003.pdf.

[87] ibid.

The key principles of the AfCFTA are driven by: (a) Member States of the African Union; (b) Regional Economic Communities (RECs)' Free Trade Areas (FTAs) as building blocks for the AfCFTA; (c) variable geometry; (d) flexibility and special and differential treatment; (e) transparency and disclosure of information; (f) preservation of the *acquis*; (g) most-favoured-nation (MFN) treatment; (h) national treatment; and (i) reciprocity. With the exception of 'variable geometry', which has been elaborated on by the East African Court of Justice, these principles are universal law principles.

A recent case that illustrates the practical implications of comparative approaches for regional international law is *Southern African Customs Union Poultry Safeguards*.[88] In this dispute, the South African Customs Union (SACU) argued that WTO obligations invoked by the EU were not applicable to the dispute, meaning that it was not mandatory for them to be taken into consideration. The SACU further pointed out that Article 34(10) of the Economic Partnership Agreement (EPA) explicitly barred the parties from bringing a dispute about safeguards under the aegis of the WTO. In its 2022 ruling, the arbitral tribunal noted that trade agreements like the EU–SACU EPA do not emerge in a vacuum; they do not seek to isolate their parties from the multilateral trade regime, but only to deepen and qualify their common relationship in light of Article XXIV GATT.[89] This decision points to the value to comparative approach, but also to a Southern African regional approach to international economic law. Effectively, comparative approaches point towards what was first conceived by Lauterpacht as analogies that have become the foundation for developing transnational law. While some African regional treaties refer exclusively to regional treaties, most African treaties refer to general principles. For example, the SADC Tribunal, which has been the subject of several comparative studies, can be said to be a reflection of the unique history of Southern Africa and the South African approach to international law.[90] Article 35 of the SADC Treaty refers exclusively to its own applicable law.[91] Recent protocols of the AfCFTA, namely the Digital Protocol and the Gender Protocol, are examples of the divergent approaches to applicable law. For example, the Preamble to the Protocol to the Agreement Establishing the African Continental Free Trade Area on Digital Trade (2024) refers to the Digital Transformation Strategy for Africa and digital trade matters incorporated into the instrument of the African Union, regional economic communities, as well as international instruments and agreements.

[88] *Southern African Customs Union Poultry Safeguards*, Panel Ruling – Final Report of the Arbitration Panel (3 August 2022).

[89] ibid para 233.

[90] KJ Alter, JT Gathii, and LR Helfer, 'Backlash against International Courts in West, East and Southern Africa: Causes and Consequences' (2016) 27 *European Journal of International Law* 328.

[91] Treaty of the Southern African Development Community (1992), art 35.

3. Dispute Resolution

In the 1960s, the attitude of newly developing countries to international dispute resolution was a major concern. Some issues that have emerged include exclusive jurisdiction over disputes, exhaustion of local remedies, direct access to dispute settlement for individuals and availability of remedies. In the 1990s, proliferation of African regional courts and dispute resolution institutions laid the groundwork for Africa's trade courts, which have become global laboratories.[92] Nevertheless, African states have turned to the ICJ to settle territorial disputes.[93] Yet within the settlement of disputes, an African approach can be distilled from the practices of states. While this approach is not very different from the universal approach, core tensions that were raised in the 1960s remain. The African Court has noted that, unlike its European and Inter-American counterparts, the African Charter does not specify the territorial scope of its application. However, the Court has always examined its territorial jurisdiction as part of other aspects of its competence.[94] African regional courts frequently refer to decisions of Latin American and European courts.[95]

It has always been argued that African culture promotes non-adversarial dispute methods like mediation, yet the AfCFTA adopts WTO-style dispute resolution. In international investment law, an African approach similar to the Latin American approach should promote the settlement of disputes using domestic courts and institutions. While previous drafts of the AfCFTA's investment protocol recognised international arbitration, the most recent draft postpones the negotiation of the dispute resolution clause. This is indicative of a failed consensus between the different regional groups within the African Union. There may also be indications that the South African regional approach will influence the eventual compromise provisions on dispute settlement. This is evident in the 2011 disbanding of the SADC Tribunal after the regional court held that the Zimbabwean government unlawfully seized the land of white farmers, and South Africa's move away from international arbitration after the Piero Foresti arbitration.[96] In 2018, the South African Constitutional Court ruled that participation of the South African President in the 2011 abolishment of the SADC Tribunal was unconstitutional,

[92] TO Elias, 'The Role of the International Court of Justice in Africa' (1989) 1 *African Journal of International and Comparative Law* 1.

[93] D Akande, 'The Role of the International Court of Justice in the Maintenance of International Peace' (1996) 8 *African Journal of International and Comparative Law* 592.

[94] African Court on Human and Peoples Rights, *Bernard Anbatayela Monrah v Republic of Benin, Burkina Faso, Republic of Côte d'Ivoire, Republic of Ghana, Republic of Malawi, United Republic of Tanzania and Republic of Tunisia* (Application No 028/2018) (22 September 2022) 146.

[95] San Jose Declaration: The African Court on Human and Peoples' Rights, the European Court of Human Rights and the Inter-American Court of Human Rights at Dialogue among Regional Human Rights Courts (26 May 2023).

[96] L Nathan, 'The Disbanding of the SADC Tribunal: A Cautionary Tale' (2013) 35 *Human Rights Quarterly* 870.

unlawful and irrational. Notably, in its ruling the Court stated that South Africa's ratification of the SADC Treaty was not merely a consequence or misfortune of the imperatives of *geopolitical location*, but a thoughtful and appropriate decision to take for the good of our people, our democracy, the image of the SADC region and, by extension, of Africa.[97] It also noted that 'disagreement with other SADC family members is healthy, and typical of the richness that diversity at a regional level ought to bring into the fold'.[98] The Court also stated that the correct South African perspective to international law should protect the rights of citizens, and that this was 'especially so in a region that has a long and painful history of struggling for the attainment of these good governance, economic development, growth and stability-enhancing goals of universal application'.[99] This decision is significant, as it shows the challenges of African community law and the political interference with the powers of regional courts. In Kenya, the Attorney General has recently approached the Supreme Court for an opinion on the legal consequences and effects of decisions of the East African Court of Justice.

Amendments to the ICSID rules in 2022 now permit regional economic communities to be parties in investment treaty arbitration disputes. The possibility of African regional economic communities as respondents or claimants may not yet be as pronounced as within the European Union. However, this points to the important and complexities of continental approaches to dispute resolution. At the WTO, the African Group has supported accessibility and finding a solution to ensure the effective functioning of the WTO's Appellate Body as a legitimate forum where all members have equal opportunities in terms of enforcing their rights.[100]

F. Conclusion

This chapter has shown that comparative international law is an appropriate methodology for understanding and developing African approaches to international law. To a large extent, classical comparative studies still continue in the tradition of 'African law', which held sway in the 1960s.[101] While we are all inevitably comparative scholars, more can be done to develop comparative international law. Difficulties exist in terms of doing proper and effective comparative research of Africa's complex and overlapping regional regimes. For example, the decisions of African regional courts are published only in French or English and not in Arabic, Portuguese, Spanish or Kiswahili.

[97] *Law Society of South Africa and Others v President of the Republic of South Africa and Others* [2018] ZACC 51 (11 December 2018) para 50.
[98] ibid para 90.
[99] ibid para 91.
[100] WTO Communication from the African Group on Dispute Settlement Reform (12 July 2023).
[101] S Mancuso, *African Law(s): Comparative Insights on the African Lawscape* (Leiden: Brill, 2023).

It is perhaps time to move beyond 'African international law' and continue in the tradition of studying African approaches to Africa's international law problems. In practice, solutions to successive coups, terrorism, piracy, refugee crises and economic inequalities require stronger political will and stronger international law institutions. African approaches should not be an opportunity for exceptionalism, which worsens these problems. While African regional international law has provided some remedies for the individual, contrary to the fundamental principles of African law, it has failed the African peoples. As newer sub-fields of international law develop in cross-border digital trade, space exploration, artificial intelligence, climate change, economic security law and international taxation, a peoples' approach must take centre stage.[102]

[102] A Titus, 'The Perspective of the EAC on International Tax Law' in F Haase and G Kofler (eds), *The Oxford Handbook of International Tax Law* (Oxford: Oxford University Press, 2023) 899.

4

'American' International Law

RÍÁN DERRIG

A. Introduction

The 53rd annual meeting of the American Society of International Law (ASIL) convened in The Mayflower Hotel in Washington DC on the afternoon of 30 April 1959. The meeting's theme was 'Diverse Systems of World Public Order Today'. The goal was a comparative exploration of legal systems thought to represent different world cultures. Panels discussed the Soviet system, the Islamic system, the Shi'ite system and the Latin American system. Speakers attempted to identify characterising principles of the systems they examined, and they moved on to discuss the implications of this condition of systemic diversity for substantive legal sub-fields like the use of force, jurisdiction, the distribution of natural resources, trade, the law of treaties, and human rights. The panels were populated by figures now viewed as among the most prominent of twentieth-century Anglo-American international law, who discussed what were then considered the most pressing issues of American foreign policy and world politics.

This chapter uses the 1959 ASIL meeting as a fulcrum about which to turn its analysis for four main reasons. First, this meeting shows significant continuities with characteristics of the earlier twentieth-century field of international law. The account developed here emphasises continuities and commonalities, between the meeting's participants in debate over what American international law should be at mid-century and between fundamental, animating themes of that meeting and of the earlier twentieth-century field of American international law. Continuity is emphasised over the perception of any moment of significant rupture. As a question of method, focusing on the ideas that were recurrent over this three-day meeting in Washington DC, and by extension in scholarship in the field in the late 1950s and early 1960s, illustrates most about what it was like to participate in, and think about, American international law at that time. As a question of history, the material presented below will demonstrate the extent to which the methodological anti-formalism, and the anthropological, psychologised tradition of ideas about a national American character examined in this chapter as animating themes of the 1959 meeting, date from at least the late nineteenth century.

Rather than taking at face value the recurrent claims to novelty and unprecedented change made by many of the meeting participants, it is more fruitful to read those claims as a constitutive part of this tradition ideas, whereby thinkers assumed the role of explaining Americanness in response to recurring but perpetually unprecedented crises.

Second, the 1959 meeting exemplifies a strong comparative impulse in international law scholarship in the United States at that moment. As Mathias Siems' findings show, this was a moment when the possibility of distinctly Western and Soviet approaches to international law was a point of focus for comparative international law scholarship, although the term 'comparative international law' itself was infrequently used before the early 2000s.[1] The 1959 ASIL meeting included participants whose legal training had not been in the United States, and more than might have been typical of such meetings because of its comparative theme. Nevertheless, most had significant familiarity with the ideas that were influential in American international law scholarship and practice, often working largely in that context.

Third, the perceived confrontation between the 'free world' and Soviet communism, as well as the position of non-aligned states, animated many of the meeting's attendees, who saw a reality not of one world legal order, but of blocs of political power advancing apparently differing visions of international law.[2] In this way, the 1959 ASIL meeting took place in a moment not unlike our own. After the Cold War, hubristic expectation of a universal liberal international order, we again find ourselves in a moment when several geopolitical power centres advance contesting and plausible models of what an international legal order should look like and do. It again seems pressing to examine how law structures world power in a plural way.

Fourth, the 1959 ASIL meeting is a useful entry point because it opens a window on to mid-century American international law and practice through one of the most prominent and, I have argued elsewhere, quintessential of schools of American legal theory – the New Haven School.[3] The meeting was convened during Myres McDougal's tenure as President of the ASIL. McDougal was a professor of law at Yale Law School and, with Harold Lasswell, a prominent political scientist, he developed an approach to legal theory and pedagogy that became known as the New Haven School. This school was made up of McDougal and former students who rose to prominent positions in academia, government and the judiciary in the United States and around the world. In 1959 it was perhaps near the height of its influence, though it would be another decade before it would be named as a 'school' of thought, first by McDougal's former students. The 1959

[1] See Siems, ch 1 in this volume.

[2] Wilfred Jenks, among others, makes this point: *Proceedings of the American Society of International Law at Its Fifty-Third Annual Meeting, Held at Washington, DC* (Washington DC: American Society of International Law, 1959) 85.

[3] R Derrig, *The New Haven School: American International Law* (Oxford: Oxford University Press, 2025).

meeting highlights one moment in a slow process, of which the New Haven School is emblematic, of the field of international law becoming increasingly theoretically concerned. Although in 1959 it remained the case that in the United States, international law was typically a specialism developed as an appendage to another core area of expertise in domestic law, rather than a field that would sustain a scholarly career by itself, the beginnings of the dense Anglo-American field of international legal theory that exists today can be seen at this meeting.

Panels at the 1959 annual meeting included many self-described New Haven School associates. The panels show flashes of the way of viewing and using law so characteristic of the New Haven School, which I have argued also typify trends ascending in the field more broadly at mid-century and still characteristic of American international law practice and scholarship today. This chapter describes and examines implications of those ways of viewing and using law, and of international law in particular. It identifies ideas drawing formative influences from intellectual and social movements of the early twentieth-century and inter-war period, being especially prominent at mid-century, and with resonances still today.

The first such body of ideas is a methodological anti-formalism that has shaped legal argument in the field, but a particular tradition of anti-formalism. The argument made in this chapter is that this anti-formalism has often supported, and has at least been an accommodating companion to the projection of American power in international politics. The second set of ideas examined supports the argument that what animated this methodological anti-formalism has been less a moralism, or a transcendental claim of some kind, but instead an anthropology of what it is, or should be, to be American. This constitutes an ontologically particular understanding of what is of value in social life, and one more psychologised than is usually acknowledged. It can be seen especially clearly in the writings of people who have called themselves liberal internationalists, from the 1990s to today.

The chapter aims to both outline characteristics of how American international law was practised at mid-century and to reflect on how those characteristics connect to politics of what law was used to do.[4] This amounts to two claims. One claim concerns the place of a specific methodological tradition in scholarship. Another claim is that across several sub-fields of international law, the ideas and methods of that tradition have tended to accompany, albeit without necessarily being causative of, how the US government approaches international law and politics at moments when its interests appear prima facie to conflict with the law. In other words, when American interests have been at stake and the most obvious interpretation of the law appears to run against the American position, ideas and methods from the anti-formalist tradition described here have been heavily relied upon in arguments of scholars supportive of that position and in arguments made by official representatives of the United States. This pattern has simultaneously

[4] An aim like this is placed within one of a number of categories of 'horizontal' comparative international law research by Siems (n 1).

been compatible with the deployment of a 'ferocious and uncompromising' formal legalism to the actions of other states contrary to American interests, in scholarly and official legal arguments.[5]

One aim of the chapter is to carry analysis of theoretical ideas about international law through to consequences those ideas had when deployed in legal arguments attached to concrete consequences in social life – whether those consequences might be, for example, the deployment of violence; the recognition or not of acts of another state; or using economic tools to harm another state's economy and population. The chapter concludes by reflecting on what the story told here allows us to conclude about how politics connects to specific methodological traditions in American legal thought and in international legal thought.

B. A Tradition of Methodological Anti-formalism

The methodological anti-formalism identified in this chapter refers to a way of viewing and using law that descended from the classical pragmatists' turn-of-the-century critique of metaphysical absolutes and transcendental value orders. This is the critique developed by William James, Charles Sanders Peirce and John Dewey, and, within law, of Nicholas St John Green and Oliver Wendell Holmes. Much has been written about the arguments between, and the different identities of, prominent American international lawyers, but if a stranger from another culture had stumbled into the ASIL meeting of lawyers and diplomats in the East Room of The Mayflower Hotel in 1959, most of whom were white, Protestant men of an ascendant East Coast policy elite, what would have been most striking would have been how similarly they all spoke about and imagined uses for law in international affairs.

With differing levels of disparagement, most referred to the international law of a past era as inadequate to the complexity, movement and danger of their own moment. Reflecting on the world to which Elihu Root referred when he addressed ASIL's first annual meeting in 1907, in 1959, then Assistant Director General of the International Labor Office Wilfred Jenks concluded that:

> Political, economic and social changes and scientific and technological developments have so transformed contemporary international relations that a fundamental re-thinking of international law has become necessary … [N]uclear experiment and space research have given an importance and immediacy to the mutual relations of international law with science and advanced technology which are together new.[6]

[5] N Bhuta, 'A Global State of Exception? The United States and World Order' (2003) 10 *Constellations* 371, 380; D Kennedy, 'The Twentieth-Century Discipline of International Law in the United States' in A Sarat, B Garth and RA Kagan (eds), *Looking Back at Law's Century* (Ithaca, NY: Cornell University Press, 2002) 412.

[6] *Proceedings of the American Society of International Law at Its Fifty-Third Annual Meeting* (n 2) 85. On Jenks, see G Fiti Sinclair, 'C Wilfred Jenks and the Futures of International Organizations Law' (2020) 31 *European Journal of International Law* 525.

Speaking to the topic of 'The Politics of Survival and the Bases of World Public Order', the international relations and law scholar William TR Fox announced that: 'An increased diversity in the public order systems of the leading states and a drastically changed military technology distinguish the world of the 1950's [*sic*] from that of the turn of the century.'[7] The political science and international law scholar Ruth C Lawson identified a theme of a panel on international security as the forced 're-examination of traditional legal concepts concerning what we have been accustomed to refer to as "international security"'.[8] The Canadian international law scholar Maxell Cohen mused: 'What is there that has driven so many scholars in recent years to seek a reappraisal of the foundations, the substance, and the method of international law?'[9]

If the meeting's attendees spoke of what they cast as classical problems of international law, it was to complain of their outdated persistence, or to marvel at the extent to which these problems were being resolved, or at least reformulated through modern methods of planning and management, especially by the expanding administrative world of UN agencies. Jenks reminded the meeting that in the 15 years since the end of the Second World War, the United Nations and 'some sixteen specialized agencies and analogous bodies have been vigorously developed; half of these have already attained virtual universality'.[10] He made the potentially significant suggestion that the rapidly growing role played by international 'judicial, legislative and administrative agencies and procedures' could herald the advent of the concept of 'international public policy', something that could shift the traditional presumption against the restriction of state sovereignty towards a presumption that what he thought was the factually obvious interdependence of states must imply the effectiveness of international law.[11] Jenks thought that taken together, changes in contemporary world politics alongside modern scientific knowledge placed on the meeting's attendees a 'responsibility unparalleled since the age of Grotius' to fundamentally rethink the nature and role of law in world affairs.[12]

As against what the meeting's attendees saw as the formalist, logical reasoning and detached concepts of what they called 'traditional' or 'classical' international law, hopelessly abstracted from real social life, they contrasted their own attention to law moulded by, and self-consciously deployed to control, powerful social forces always in flux. Kenneth S Carlston, a professor at the University of Illinois College of Law, derided the definition of 'jurisdiction' offered by Joseph Henry Beale, a long-time favourite foil of legal realists representative of an outdated legal formalism, and by the American Law Institute's *Restatement of the Conflict of Laws*, another fond target of realists, saying: '"Jurisdiction" thus viewed is an abstract

[7] *Proceedings of the American Society of International Law at Its Fifty-Third Annual Meeting* (n 2) 137.
[8] ibid 162.
[9] ibid 99.
[10] ibid 86.
[11] ibid 88.
[12] ibid 89.

notion. It is its own little domain. It is postulated as something which can be dealt with separately and apart from the world of fact from which it is taken.'[13]

Also speaking to the topic of jurisdiction, Louis Henkin bemoaned a tendency to speak of jurisdiction 'exclusively in conceptual terms', when he thought the operation of jurisdiction in relations between states was better explained by whether the states in question shared conceptions of 'public policy' in specific legal fields.[14] Quincy Wright opened his address on a panel on the use of force by affirming his agreement with Myres McDougal and Harold Lasswell's premise that 'changes in the law of a community grow out of its public policy', and took an anthropically and sociologically informed view of the goals of the United Nations Charter, placing it firmly in a social context of states, nations and a legal system intended to universalise in world society.[15]

All of these premises, of law socially situated and instrumentalised, the meeting's participants owed to the tradition of ideas descending from the classical pragmatists, which by mid-century permeated American intellectual life. Carlston, who was enthusiastic about reheating the most tried and tested classics of legal realism, even quoted one of Holmes' aphorisms.[16] The meeting's records highlight a common adherence to a set of premises about how law could be used, about its interpretive limits, about what was plausible to argue about it, and to do with it. Here, this is called a methodological tradition. As well as indicating transmission over time, denoting it as a tradition is a way of saying that it amounted to more than a set of rationally conceived premises. It was a set of ideas and practices closer to a mood operative, to varying extents in different contexts and moments, in many areas of twentieth-century American intellectual and cultural life.[17]

A deeply pragmatist tradition, Cornell West's definition of American pragmatism captures the mood-like character of this body of ideas when he calls it 'a particular set of social practices that articulate certain American desires, values, and responses that are elaborated in institutional apparatuses controlled by a significant slice of the American middle class'.[18] West's reading of American pragmatism centres what he calls its 'evasion of epistemology-centred philosophy', its sidestepping of a European rationalist tradition of philosophy preoccupied with identifying rationally sound grounds for knowledge in preference for:

> [A] conception of philosophy as a form of cultural criticism in which the meaning of America is put forward by intellectuals in response to distinct social and cultural crises. In this sense, American pragmatism is less a philosophical tradition putting forward solutions to perennial problems in the Western philosophical tradition initiated by

[13] ibid 171.
[14] ibid 182.
[15] ibid 145–46.
[16] ibid 171.
[17] Legal realism is described as an intellectual mood by MJ Horwitz, *The Transformation of American Law 1870–1960: The Crisis of Legal Orthodoxy* (Oxford: Oxford University Press, 1992).
[18] C West, *The American Evasion of Philosophy: A Genealogy of Pragmatism* (Madison: University of Wisconsin Press, 2009) 3–5.

Plato and more a continuous cultural commentary or set of interpretations that attempt to explain America to itself at a particular historical moment.[19]

This tendency of philosophical pragmatism to find animation in a perceived need to explain what it is to be an American to Americans, to be an anthropology of Americanness, will be examined in section C below. Here, for the purposes of characterising the anti-formalist tradition exhibited at the 1959 meeting, it is useful to emphasise West's description of this tradition as an ongoing 'cultural commentary'.

In his classic examination of the same tradition, which he views as a 'Revolt Against Formalism' that swept through the disciplines and American intellectual life at the turn of the twentieth century, Morton White draws together the movements of this tradition within respective fields:

> Pragmatism, instrumentalism, institutionalism, economic determinism, and legal realism … are all suspicious of approaches that are excessively formal; they all protest their anxiety to come to grips with reality, their attachment to the moving and the vital in social life.[20]

Concerned with fitting the tools of their fields not to the demands of logical deduction, but to 'experience in some streaming sense', White's anti-formalists (Holmes, Dewey, the economist Thorstein Veblen, and the historians James Harvey Robinson and Charles A Beard) were preoccupied by 'life, experience, process, growth, context, function'.[21] White framed his narration of the influence of these ideas on American intellectual life as one of decline from the 1930s onwards, but within legal scholarship they remained highly influential in the late 1950s, and, as this chapter argues, left a lasting legacy in international legal thought in the United States that is still evident today.

One way in which these ideas would have influenced some of this largely male group in The Mayflower Hotel was through the community planning of the New Deal of the 1930s, a political manifestation of pragmatist impulses.[22] Myres McDougal, who had been a New Deal property lawyer during the 1930s, thought the role of democratic elites undertaking world planning was to formulate universal claims that would de facto apply at first to the portion of the globe over which the United States was dominant. He said that in his writings, at meeting after meeting of the ASIL, including in The Mayflower in 1959. Five years before, intervening in discussions at a previous ASIL annual meeting, he had said:

> The whole function of international law is to permit such intervention in affairs which would otherwise be regarded as internal … The whole purpose of the United Nations

[19] ibid 5.

[20] M White, *Social Thought in America: The Revolt against Formalism* (Oxford: Oxford University Press, 1976) 6.

[21] ibid 13.

[22] Afroditi Giovanopoulou has also traced the influence of former New Dealers in the United States State Department after the Second World War; see A Giovanopoulou, 'Pragmatic Legalism: Revisiting America's Order after World War II' (2021) 62 *Harvard International Law Journal* 325.

> and its host of subsidiary international organizations is, again, to permit external elites to intervene in the affairs of nation-states which would otherwise be regarded as internal – to intervene for the purposes of promoting international peace and security, of promoting co-operation with respect to economic well-being and human rights, and of promoting all the other values specified in the organizational charters. It must be recognized that we created these institutions for the very purpose of intervention.[23]

Generally, the predominant substantive legacy of these ideas within American international law scholarship and practice is that they have been used as McDougal said they should be used: to constitute freedom of movement for American foreign policy. They have become a constitutive part of a project of projecting power around the world. This can be illustrated by identifying some particularly significant debates that took place during the 1959 meeting over issues that were then topical, and drawing lines from those debates to contemporary American international law practice.

To put the argument most bluntly, what is telling is that in these examples, a person advancing a legal argument that seeks to achieve freedom of movement for American power typically leans into the anti-formalist mood described above, whereas a challenger to that position will typically emphasise relatively more impermeable legal forms. However, the examples will also show that while this politics of legal method can be observed in a patterned way over time, it is by no means immutable over time, being sub-field-specific and potentially shifting as the content of legal forms in a specific sub-field changes. The examples examined here and drawn from the 1959 meeting concern debate about the legality of the expropriation of assets of American investors in socialist and communist states, and those over the use of force.

1. Expropriation

Alarm over expropriation of investor assets outside the United States was a centrepiece of the meeting. Loftus E Becker, then Legal Advisor to the Department of State, dedicated the entirety of his address at the annual dinner to the topic. Becker wanted to criticise states and international lawyers that were building a growing body of practice and scholarship around the view that expropriation of foreign, privately owned assets without compensation or with partial compensation was lawful where those expropriations took place in the context of 'wholesale' change to the expropriating state's economic structure.[24] He cited a series of what he thought were comparable examples of states nationalising property, from the Soviet government of 1917, through socialist states in Eastern Europe undertaking agrarian reforms, in Nazi Germany, Mexico, of the Anglo-Iranian Oil Company,

[23] *Proceedings of the American Society of International Law at its Forty-Eighth Annual Meeting* (Washington DC: American Society of International Law, 1954) 120.

[24] *Proceedings of the American Society of International Law at Its Fifty-Third Annual Meeting* (n 2) 342.

the Suez Canal and Dutch-owned property in Indonesia.[25] Becker argued that legal arguments by then being increasingly widely made in support of expropriation contravened what he presented as the fundamental, classical principle that just compensation must be paid to foreign citizens for property taken by a host state.

For Becker, before the First World War, the basis of what he argued was a principle of customary international law 'in considerations of reason, equity, and justice was so obvious that general acceptance of the principle was virtually tacit in character … [it] went without saying'.[26] By 1959, however, Becker said it was being widely contravened in practice and scholarship, and he called on 'the American international lawyer and his foreign colleagues' to help the State Department to shore up this beleaguered principle by counterattacking its critics.[27] Despite its appeal to a classically respected lineage, the line of counter-attack suggested by Becker was substantively functionalist. He said that this principle was necessary because if it was not respected, international business could not be undertaken with the necessary certainty, 'and without it the economic development so ardently desired in every quarter of the world will be slow to come'.[28] Becker was correct that had he been making the same argument in the 1920s or 1930s, a more strictly formalist position might have been plausible. The prominent international arbitrations of that period, often over oil concessions granted to Western companies in the Middle East, shaped a body of international economic law populated by formal principles (like the doctrine of acquired rights) skewed in favour of Western interests.[29]

However, by 1959, decolonising states were increasingly in a position to advance claims based on formal legal principles (like territorial sovereignty) against private Western companies that were trying to retain extractive rights gained in colonial situations, or in contexts approximating colonialism. To respond to this growing body of legal claims against Western economic power being made by newly independent states on sovereigntist grounds, Becker was forced to lean on more and more functionalism as his argument proceeded. He criticised state practice as though it were a mistake when viewed in the light of his functionalism. This is not to say that a doctrine like acquired rights could not be invoked. It could and was, but Becker was forced to add more functionalist anti-formalism to his reasoning to make it convince.

The same debate had seized the panellists on a panel that discussed jurisdiction the day before. The growing number of situations in which American courts were being called on to determine the legality of expropriations of assets of American investors in communist and socialist states called into question the jurisdiction

[25] ibid 337.
[26] ibid 337.
[27] ibid 343.
[28] ibid 337.
[29] See Derrig (n 3), where McDougal's advocacy on behalf of Saudi Arabia in the Aramco arbitration is examined. For a wider study of this topic, see A Leiter, *Making the World Safe for Investment: The Protection of Foreign Property 1922–1959* (Cambridge: Cambridge University Press, 2023).

of those courts – could they hold that these expropriations were unlawful or should the act of state doctrine prompt them to defer to the acts of the other state? Carlston launched precisely the kind of counterattack for which Becker would call the following evening:

> A state's exclusive sovereignty or jurisdiction over its natural resources becomes virtually meaningless when it is the international use of these resources which gives them meaning and value as property. The grasp of jurisdiction may try to encompass what a United Nations General Assembly resolution termed 'natural wealth and resources', but the interests of the international society which gives value to those resources through their international use cannot become the captive of a single state … the supplanting of the impersonal forces of the international market by the personal dictate of the sovereign, the withholding of access by all countries to mineral resources essential to the mineral-based economies of industrialized states, except on political terms agreeable to the sovereign of the source state, would create unendurable strains on the international legal system.[30]

Carlston leaned heavily on the anti-formalist tradition to deconstruct legal claims to jurisdiction based on territorial sovereignty or sovereignty over natural resources. Carlston concluded that 'answers to the formal question of legitimacy or the practical question of physical power will never provide an answer to the ultimate question of the wisdom of action'.[31] The wisdom of an action was, for Carlston, determined by the 'interest of all peoples in the international economy as a means for national integration and individual welfare'.[32] Formal legal principles or, indeed, military force must not obstruct the practical imperatives of international markets.

This pattern of anti-formalist arguments against the legitimacy of expropriation can be juxtaposed against the argument made by Richard Falk on the same panel, which landed on a position of favouring general deference on the part of domestic courts towards such acts of state. Falk was trained by Myres McDougal and identified as a member of the New Haven School, but in political terms he occupied a pole at the opposite end of the field to McDougal's vigorously asserted and much-discussed legal arguments in support of anti-communist policies of the United States. Falk consistently argued for an American foreign policy characterised by restraint. This was true of his arguments across many fields of international law, but his address immediately following Carlston offers a particularly clear example.

Falk also spoke about jurisdiction to expropriate. His remarks departed from anti-formalist premises, developing a sociological and contextual explanation of the kinds of actions and actors to which the legal concept of jurisdiction typically refers. From this anti-formalist point of departure, he built to the preliminary

[30] *Proceedings of the American Society of International Law at Its Fifty-Third Annual Meeting* (n 2) 172.
[31] ibid 173.
[32] ibid.

conclusion that deference and restraint was usually a prudent approach when taken by states. A line of case law of the US Supreme Court, Falk suggested, demonstrated this approach. He cited the *Pink* and *Bernstein* cases, which had held in favour of domestic courts deferring to foreign acts of state unless the executive branch of the US government had explicitly articulated a policy indicating otherwise.[33]

Having departed from a thoroughly anti-formalist, sociologically thick view of how law operated in such situations, Falk used those premises to build a growing emphasis on the importance of legal form by effectively arguing that it had a sociologically real function.[34] His conclusion both endorsed the possibility, in principle, of instrumentalising law to defend one's 'preferred system of public order' (ie, liberal democracy, socialism or communism), but also settled on the strong view that in most conceivable cases, including the expropriation examples under discussion, domestic courts should defer to what he saw as the restraining function of legal form. Domestic American courts should respect expropriations undertaken by foreign states.

Falk's legal arguments are typically read as examples of the anti-formalist tradition examined here, directly descending from the New Haven School stream of that tradition. What tends to be neglected is the extent to which Falk consistently boiled off the potent conclusions to which that anti-formalism might have been expected to lead, and which would have favoured freeing American power from the restraint of deference to legal form. By the time Falk reached substantive legal positions, he had typically deployed his anti-formalism to support the taking seriously of legal doctrine and form on the part of the United States. The end points of these arguments can then be better read as a self-aware, instrumentally deployed formalism. From within the American traditional of legal anti-formalism, Falk consistently endeavoured to walk back the legal conclusions that tradition was being used to reach within international law.

2. Use of Force

A similar pattern could be observed on the panel focused on the law of war and of laws in war. Quincy Wright, one of the most prominent of the inter-war generation of American international law scholars and by 1959 close to retirement as a professor of international law at the University of Virginia, played the role of the restraining formalist. Like Falk, he departed from a socially situated view of law, agreeing, like most of the American field at the time, that 'changes in the law of a community grow out of its public policy'.[35] More quickly than Falk, Wright rounded back to an argument that centred legal form as a medium that should

[33] ibid 179.
[34] This emphasis is apparent in Falk's remarks (ibid 180).
[35] ibid 145.

facilitate the peaceful co-existence 'of diverse nations and ideologies'.[36] Although it was true that changes in law grew out of a community's public policy, Wright said that that was beside the point for the international lawyer:

> If statesmen wholeheartedly pursue the task, not of winning the 'cold war' but of ending it, not of seeking to universalize any ideology by force but of stabilising conditions of peaceful coexistence among diverse nations and ideologies, and not of asserting an international law favourable to any doctrine, but of discovering and maintaining an international law which reflects the values shared by all nations, the world may acquire such stability that arts, sciences and ethics may progress through peaceful communication and discussion among the peoples of the world.[37]

Wright thought that the jurist's role should be to identify principles ascribed to by all peoples of the world, analyse those committed to in the United Nations Charter and other international instruments, and deductively apply those principles to specific situations.

If this view rang with the naiveté of a pre-realist artificiality, which it likely did for many of Wright's mid-century audience in The Mayflower Hotel's East Room, it nonetheless had real consequences when he attached it to concrete legal arguments. Wright took as his target the tendency of the United States to intervene in other state's civil wars. He quoted disapprovingly John Foster Dulles, who had resigned as Secretary of State days before the ASIL meeting, when he had said that the United States recognised parties to conflict with other states as legitimate governments of those states as 'an instrument of national policy, to serve enlightened self-interest'.[38] Wright specifically targeted cases like the 1958 American intervention in Lebanon, relying on an extensively argued *American Journal of International Law* editorial he had published in January 1959 to briskly conclude at the meeting that this had been a primarily internal revolt and the United States' intervention was difficult to justify under international law.[39]

His arguments about such concrete situations were conventional, clear and effective in their conclusions. Intervention by a state in conflict internal to another state was rarely permitted under international law, and justifications for intervention based on human rights abuses, or to promote the self-determination of peoples could only properly attach to acts of the United Nations itself, not of individual states. Threats to international peace and security might require United Nations intervention, and the General Assembly, not the Security Council, was the most appropriate organ to decide whether such contravention of state sovereignty was required.[40]

[36] ibid.

[37] ibid 153.

[38] ibid 150.

[39] ibid; Q Wright, 'Editorial Comment: United States Intervention in the Lebanon' (1959) 53 *American Journal of International Law* 112.

[40] *Proceedings of the American Society of International Law at Its Fifty-Third Annual Meeting* (n 2) 152.

Florentino Feliciano, a former student of McDougal's then working for the Department of Justice of the Philippines and later to become a Justice of the Supreme Court of the Philippines, stepped into the role of the panel's anti-formalist. His presentation reproduced arguments he had published in a triptych of pieces co-authored with McDougal, and which they were then developing into a monograph to be published in 1961. The theme of Feliciano's presentation, as of his writings with McDougal generally, was to use an unremitting anti-formalism to make as porous as possible boundaries between legal concepts and admittedly often binary thresholds classically used to translate situations of armed conflict into legal idiom.

For example, in his presentation, Feliciano argued that the determination of whether a particular deployment of violence by a state constituted an illegitimate act of aggression or a legitimate, defensive use of force must be made by reference to an extensive set of criteria, including '[t]he character of the structures and processes of authority and control maintained within the participant charged' and 'what kind of public order a state envisions in the international arena'.[41] In the characteristic New Haven School vocabulary, what Feliciano was basically saying was that in an open-ended, highly fluid way, characterisations of a state's domestic order – democratic, communist, socialist and totalitarian – could legitimately be part of determining the legality of their use of force, as could their ideological aims in international affairs. All of Feliciano and McDougal's arguments of this sort worked assiduously to open up and look behind legal forms – above all, that of sovereignty – which scholars like Wright would argue were kept in a state of artificial separation from social life specifically to allow them to be used to limit the grounds on which states could claim that their use of violence was legal.

After the floor was opened for questions, McDougal quickly launched an attack against Wright's faith in law as a universal medium between different ideologies and value orders. McDougal drew on the address he had made to the meeting on the evening before, in which he had argued that the Soviet Union and societies in its orbit were cannibalistic because their ideology was premised on totalising expansion rather than co-existence: 'There can be no law, he [McDougal] insisted, transcending the systems of "cannibals" and "non-cannibals".'[42]

3. Expropriation and Use of Force in Contemporary American International Law

More often than not, it has been arguments like those of Carlston, Feliciano and McDougal, rather than of Falk and Wright, that have proved their worth as a justificatory substructure to the projection of American power in the later twentieth

[41] ibid 159.
[42] ibid 167.

century. Following the two fields chosen as examples in the discussions at the 1959 ASIL meeting forward to today, it can be said that this observation holds most clearly in the case of the use of force.

Critiquing how the presidential administration of George Bush was using legal argument in support of American policy aims in 2003, Nehal Bhuta traces anti-formalist arguments about the use of force similar to those of Feliciano and McDougal through American interventions widely viewed as legally dubious in the Dominican Republic (1965), in Panama (1989) and in Iraq (2003):

> The statements and posture of the Bush administration imply a vision of international order where 'law' is merely one policy consideration among others, not a binding obligation – except when applied to the enemy, with respect to whose illegal acts the notion of 'legality' adopts a ferocious and uncompromising polemical content. The restraints of legality to which an enemy is subject have no application to the United States, whose power permits – and *can be shown to permit* – it to arrogate to itself the entitlement to determine the boundary between law as principle and law as coercion.[43]

Martti Koskenniemi built the argument that he made for a 'culture of formalism' in his book *The Gentle Civilizer of Nations* around similar observations about the use to which de-formalised legal reasoning has been put in the history of American military interventions in other states. Koskenniemi recounts an argument between Adolf A Berle and Wolfgang Friedmann over the United States' 1965 military intervention in the Dominican Republic in response to the election of a leftist government. Berle, a professor at Columbia Law School and former Assistant Secretary of State, played the anti-formalist in support of the intervention, while Friedmann, also a professor at Columbia Law School, countered his caustic anti-formalism. Berle's argumentation was quintessentially of the tradition of American anti-formalism described in this chapter: 'We here deal seriously with inter-national affairs, where life and death are at stake and not with interminable Byzantine legalistics without point or outcome.'[44] Playing an almost tragic role, Friedmann countered, '[w]e all know that many legal situations are open and subject to different interpretations, but law is ultimately a matter of black and white, or we should have no business to sit here and profess to be lawyers'.[45]

The literature on the extent to which legal arguments that are best read as anti-formalist supported American-led 'humanitarian' interventions in the 1990s, legal arguments presaged in Feliciano and McDougal's writing as early as the mid-1950s, is extensive.[46] The much-discussed 'Bethlehem Principles' on when self-defence

[43] Bhuta (n 5) 380. A good example of the United States employing such polemical, uncompromising legality to claims of other states is the annual 'Freedom of Navigation Report' released by the US Department of Defense, which details the 'excessive maritime claims' challenged by the United States in the preceding year.

[44] M Koskenniemi, *The Gentle Civilizer of Nations: The Rise and Fall of International Law 1870–1960* (Cambridge: Cambridge University Press, 2001) 498; Bhuta (n 5) 384–85.

[45] Koskenniemi (n 44) 498.

[46] See, eg, A Orford, *International Law and the Politics of History* (Cambridge: Cambridge University Press, 2021), discussed, for example, at 25–26, although Orford takes what she argues is a contemporary formalism of historical methodology as the target of her critique more generally.

might be claimed in response to an actual or imminent armed attack by non-state actors offer a yet more recent example of the centrality of this tradition of anti-formalism to legal reasoning in support of arguments that have broadened the scope of the United States and allied states to legally use force. Publishing these principles and the reasoning behind them as a note in the *American Journal of International Law* in 2012, Bethlehem, a prominent barrister and former legal advisor to the United Kingdom's Foreign and Commonwealth Office, claimed reliance on previously non-public discussions between government officials animated by perceived new necessities to use force after the attack on the World Trade Center in 2001. Seeking to expand the scope for relying on a very broad understanding of what might be viewed as legitimate self-defence in response to imminent or actual armed attacks by non-state actors, Bethlehem writes in terms that would have been at home in the anti-formalist role on a panel of the 1959 ASIL meeting. He laments a divide in the scholarly literature on self-defence:

> [B]etween those who favor a restrictive approach to the law on self-defense and those who take the view that the credibility of the law depends ultimately upon its ability to address effectively the realities of contemporary threats … The reality of the threats, the consequences of inaction, and the challenges of both strategic appreciation and operational decision making in the face of such threats frequently trump a doctrinal debate … it is important that principle is sensitive to the practical realities of the circumstances that it addresses.[47]

This reasoning deployed, by the end of the short note, Bethlehem articulates principles in a legalistic style. This note is a useful example of how this style of legal reasoning frequently operates. At key moments, it turns on an exasperated, purportedly clear-eyed, contextual realism that caustically and often sarcastically dismisses 'Byzantine', 'doctrinal' or legalistic inaction in favour of a posture of adept movement in concert with a rush of social change.[48] Thereafter, a more classically legalistic tone and style can be re-adopted, the key turn having been made. The distinctive anti-formalist tradition examined here having been leaned upon, with concepts having been made more porous and thresholds more contextually situated and blurred, the argument can rest back upon a more easy emphasis on the forms of those concepts with their new content.

If snapshots of this anti-formalism at work are plentiful and easily found in contemporary debates over how the United States uses force, the story is different in the case of the other example drawn from discussions at the 1959 meeting, that of expropriation. In that debate, legal acts implementing economic policies of ideologically distinct domestic legal orders were being forced into a condition

[47] D Bethlehem, 'Notes and Comments: Principles Relevant to the Scope of a State's Right of Self-Defense Against an Imminent or Actual Armed Attack by Nonstate Actors' (2012) 106 *American Journal of International Law* 4.

[48] P Schlag, 'Formalism and Realism in Ruins (Mapping the Logics of Collapse)' (2009) 95 *Iowa Law Review* 195, noting the parasitic character of realism (ibid 208), and the extent to which legal realists of the 1920s and 1930s employed ridicule and sarcasm as rhetorical tools, coupled with a tone of incredulity and outrage (ibid 204).

of reluctant conversation with each other. Established principles of deference to acts of state were available as material for formalist conclusions like Falk's. As in the use of force examples, politics mapped on to legal methods in a patterned way. However, if that pattern has remained largely unchanged in debates over the use of force, it has changed in fields of law concerning economic interests.

The pattern instantiated by Falk and Carlston at the 1959 meeting remained through the 1970s, with former colonies making sovereigntist arguments concerning economic policies and control over resources engineered to force a more fair international economic order. However, through the 1980s and 1990s, what is today narrated as the ascendance of neo-liberal economic principles alongside the collapse of the Soviet Union forced a concomitant reconstruction of international economic law, and the institutions implementing it, to the advantage of industrialised, capitalist states. Generally, this has meant that the politics that tended to pattern on to formalist or anti-formalist legal arguments within that field shifted. As the predominating content of the legal forms leaned towards the ideological premises of the United States and states like it, formalism became once more a frequently useful posture for those states, as Becker had observed had been the case earlier in the twentieth century.

Put bluntly, the window, from perhaps the mid-1950s to the end of the 1970s, when formalism had been possible for those contesting international economic inequality through international economic law, has largely closed. To take some examples from practice, when discussing how and to what extent the lawyer's role and legality itself can be instrumentalised by Third World lawyers and intellectuals pursuing political change, Georges Abi-Saab has noted that his experience of sitting on the Appellate Body of the World Trade Organization led him to the view that although 'the agreements are rather tilted against the Third World', there proved to be some possibility of influencing the body to interpret them in a more balanced way. However, of his experience as an arbitrator in arbitrations of the International Center for the Settle of Disputes, he said that both the procedure and many of the actors in the system were 'tilted in favour of foreign investors … the enemy is clearly there'.[49]

C. An Anthropology of the American Experience

The examples examined above have shown a posture of supporting maximising freedom of movement for American power in international affairs tending to map on to anti-formalist legal arguments in a patterned way. They have shown that this relationship between politics and legal method has not necessarily remained static over time or across sub-fields of international law, while suggesting that it has the

[49] G Abi-Saab, 'The Third World Intellectual in Praxis: Confrontation, Participation, or Operation behind Enemy Lines?' (2016) 37 *Third World Quarterly* 1957, 1969.

potential to do so. They also show that anti-formalism is an oppositional posture. In the tradition identified in this chapter, it was defined by what it derided – a formalism associated by the classical pragmatists at the turn of the twentieth century with European rationalist philosophy, and in law especially with the conservativism and anti-modernism of the English common law. As an oppositional posture, it operates to create space for decisions to be made on the basis of some new criteria. As Ruth C Lawson observed at the 1959 meeting, the realist contextualism deployed in The Mayflower Hotel prompted the question: 'What do we do now?'[50]

When the pattern between politics and anti-formalist method examined here has been observed, what then was the substance introduced in the wake of the oppositional work done by anti-formalism – what criteria for decision filled the space it hollowed out? The argument made here is that what was introduced is not best understood as a moralism, or a natural law throwback, although it is frequently portrayed as such.[51] If its anti-metaphysical, anti-transcendental premises are taken seriously, and because their lineage to classical pragmatism holds fast it is most accurate to do so, it cannot be those things.[52]

[50] *Proceedings of the American Society of International Law at Its Fifty-Third Annual Meeting* (n 2) 162.

[51] An example from the 1959 meeting, Richard Baxter, later and briefly a judge of the International Court of Justice, criticises the 'Thomistic' quality of McDougal's remarks (ibid 161). McDougal is also called a natural law proponent by other attendees in discussion.

[52] Debate exists over the extent to which the body of post-1990s international law scholarship associated with American liberal internationalism is best read as de-formalised/anti-formalist, or as a version of 'neo-formalism'. Some of this debate, as can be seen in Samuel Moyn's engagement with Martti Koskenniemi's influential casting of the American field as de-formalised, hangs on how de-formalisation and formalism are defined. Koskenniemi attributes de-formalisation to the influence of Carl Schmitt, which prompts Moyn to argue that contemporary liberal internationalists are too moralist to be Schmittian, and hence best read as formalists or at least only relatively de-formalised in non-operative ways. See S Moyn, 'The International Law That is America: Reflections on the Last Chapter of the Gentle Civilizer of Nations' (2013) 27 *Temple International & Comparative Law Journal* 399, 404–05 and generally. In a study of hermeneutic techniques in American law generally, Duncan Kennedy describes American human rights lawyers, and briefly by extension international human rights lawyers, as neo-formalist because of what he sees as their abuse of inductive or deductive reasoning (for Kennedy this abuse makes them formalist) to realise what they believe is 'an immanent rationality corresponding to a particular vision of society'; see D Kennedy, 'The Hermeneutic of Suspicion in Contemporary American Legal Thought' (2014) 25 *Law & Critique* 91, 117, 123. Regardless of the influence of Schmitt (I have argued elsewhere that this is not significant – see Derrig (n 3)), and setting to one side how formalism is defined (this chapter defines it negatively in keeping with the anti-formalism of classical pragmatism, differently from Kennedy and compatibly with the moralism Moyn rightly identifies in American liberal internationalism and which is also examined in this chapter), it can in any case be said that the conclusion that prominent contemporary American liberal internationalist lawyers, like Anne Marie Slaughter and Harold Koh, are formalists, which is where this argument leads, is implausible based on a plain reading of their work. These scholars typically identify themselves with the tradition of anti-formalism described here, and their work does find animation at key moments from the caustic scepticism towards abstract legal forms with which that tradition is associated. As David Kennedy has said of this generation of American liberal internationalists, 'the leading "new" scholars of my generation-people like Koh, Slaughter, Alvarez, Kingsbury, Teson … urge movement toward a new understanding of international community and a new appreciation for an antiformalist international law. In the process, they reaffirm some of the field's most familiar and dogmatic propositions: that sovereignty has eroded, that international law should be understood

Rather, it is best read as relying on an anthropology of what it was, or should be, to be a twentieth-century American. This was a tendency, still widely observable, of Americans using anthropological premises to explain themselves to themselves. As Cornell West has argued and as quoted above, the pragmatist tradition has amounted to a conception of philosophy as 'a continuous cultural commentary or set of interpretations that attempt to explain America to itself at a particular historical moment'.[53] Having considered examples of this tradition at work in legal argument in this chapter, it is also possible to see manifestations of what West has cast as American pragmatism's:

> [P]rofound insights and myopic blindnesses, enabling strengths and debilitating weaknesses, all resulting from distinctive features of American civilization: its revolutionary beginnings combined with a slave-based economy; its elastic liberal rule of law combined with an entrenched business-dominated status quo; its hybrid culture in combination with a collective self-definition as homogenously Anglo-American; its obsession with mobility, contingency, and pecuniary liquidity combined with a deep moralistic impulse.[54]

The arguments made at the 1959 meeting show both the persuasive power of the legal anti-formalism that is a descendent of the tradition that West describes, and what it can obscure, the way it can serve power while dismissing the vulnerable with a shrug of brusque modernism.

This tradition has very close connections to Anglo-American disciplinary anthropology of the early twentieth century. Anthropological works of that period, many of which were widely read as popular literature, can be interpreted as a manifestation of a trend of cultural introspection in societies that were industrialising, which were anxious about perceived change in social structures, and which were at the same time projecting violence and extractive practices onto colonies and people geographically removed from them. In his study of the work of Holmes, Dewey and Veblen, Morton White emphasises the 'epoch-making' character of anthropological research that strongly influenced their works. He quotes Veblen's conviction that: 'Anthropology is destined to revolutionize the political and the social sciences as radically as bacteriology has revolutionized the science of medicine.'[55] By mid-century, it was common to think in terms of the rise and fall of cultures, explaining what a new elite class of American world planners should do with the power they had claimed by reference to a story of cultural development that had purportedly led them to the cusp of this great task.

politically, that the boundary between international and municipal law is porous, that international law may not be as universal as it pretends, that the international regime is better understood as a process or multilevel game than as government by legal norms. They have taken ideas that have been part of disciplinary common sense for a century – pragmatism, antiformalism, interdisciplinarity and turned them into a fighting faith.' D Kennedy, 'My Talk at the ASIL: What is New Thinking in International Law' (2000) 94 *American Society of International Law Proceedings* 104, 119.

[53] West (n 18) 5.

[54] ibid.

[55] White (n 20) 19 and 22.

Myres McDougal closed his address to the 1959 ASIL on a note of such quivering grandeur, quoting the fourth volume of the British historian Arnold Toynbee's much-read *A Study of History*:

> The dead civilizations are not 'dead by fate'; and therefore a living civilization is not doomed inexorably in advance *migrare ad plures*: to join the majority of its kind that have suffered shipwreck … [W]e need fear no evil from the encompassing shadow of Death; for we are not compelled to submit our fate to the blind arbitrament of statistics.[56]

Before turning to the bane of expropriation, Becker opened his remarks at the meeting's dinner on a more prosaic but similar note, musing that: 'By nature and tradition we [Americans] tend to be an optimistic people. To us the idea of progress, of strong steadfast advance towards a known goal, is almost second nature … [R]etrogression is repugnant to us.'[57] Of manifestations of this temper of thought in legal method, and in the New Haven School specifically, Richard Falk said that some of the essence of that method was 'to work out explicitly and fully the implications for a given subject-matter of common-sense rationality as understood in mid-twentieth century America.'[58]

It is also important to recognise the strongly psychologised character of this tendency to anthropologise the experience of American-ness. In a disciplinary sense, this is unsurprising. The overlap between anthropology and psychology in the first half of the twentieth century was very significant. Peter Mandler's reconstruction of the career of Margaret Mead lays out the story of the deep interaction between anthropology, psychoanalytic theory and mid-century theories of American foreign policy clearly.[59] Many presentations in The Mayflower reflected these interactions. The entire meeting had a comparative, anthropological framing. But it was anthropology and comparison instrumentalised for the sake of introspection. The presentations and discussions make it clear that the point is less to better connect to the premises of Islamic, or Soviet or Latin American legal thought than to harvest material to fuel introspection. Morton White also connects these themes of anthropology and psychology when he observes that historicism in the anti-formalist tradition is not necessarily veneration of the past, but is 'instrumental to the solution of present problems – to the elimination of contemporary irrationality'.[60]

Many of the presentations to the 1959 meeting exhibit a preoccupation with relations between identities, values, personalities of people on the one hand, and political and legal orders on the other. This relationship is felt to be shifting and would ideally be controlled. One of the best formulations of this kind of

[56] *Proceedings of the American Society of International Law at Its Fifty-Third Annual Meeting* (n 2) 132.
[57] ibid 336.
[58] R Falk, 'On Treaty Interpretation and the New Haven Approach: Achievements and Prospects' (1968) 8 *Virginia Journal of International Law* 323, 332.
[59] P Mandler, *Return from the Natives: How Margaret Mead Won the Second World War and Lost the Cold War* (New Haven, CT: Yale University Press, 2013).
[60] White (n 20) 18.

preoccupation was made by Ruth C Lawson, a political scientist who worked almost exclusively on international law. Summarising the basic point of the meeting's discussions, she concluded that 'different conceptions or systems of world order are in conflict with references to the nature of man, his values and his goals'.[61] This explained the presence of divergent concepts of political and legal order. Lawson understood what was required to overcome this condition anthropologically:

> There remains the substantial task of clarifying within those communities dedicated to human freedom the principles to which men attach fundamental importance ... In the long run, nevertheless, the empirical experience of the European and Atlantic communities ... may prove to be of greater significance for the ultimate achievement of world peace and world law than the withstanding of the threat to the security, freedom and economic well-being of their peoples.[62]

Lawson's point brings together the two main currents running through the meeting – a psychologically attuned sense that legal orders are manifestations of types of human natures, personalities, sets of values, and an anthropological assumption that we might find ways to control this relationship (between personalities and legal order), by scientifically studying the collective lived experience of American and European societies. At the same time, a barely concealed note of dissent from the paranoia of 1950s anti-communism is discernible when Lawson draws emphasis away from a discourse of fighting for survival in the face of what McDougal called a cannibalistic totalitarianism, and towards an anthropological, historicising focus on the 'empirical experience of the European and Atlantic societies'.

1. Anthropologising Americanness in Contemporary American Liberal Internationalism

This psychologised, anthropology of American-ness today continues to do a lot of the same conceptual work within the tradition that has called itself American liberal internationalism. The most recent United States National Security Strategy, prepared by the former administration, of President Joe Biden, was published in 2022 and uses heavily psychologised language to express concern about autocracies. The document presents these political systems as having inherent 'pathologies' because of their personalised character.[63] As against the maladjusted personality of autocracies is juxtaposed the messier but healthier figure of American democracy. In the few places where some explanation is offered for why the United States seeks to project itself around the world as it does, to 'shape the international order' as the document describes it, a story of cultural development is flagged. This is a story of having found certain values in the lived experience of the nation, of having

[61] *Proceedings of the American Society of International Law at Its Fifty-Third Annual Meeting* (n 2) 164.
[62] ibid 166.
[63] *National Security Strategy* (The White House, Washington DC, 2022) 8.

identified a reality of human dignity by living it collectively. It is an anthropological account of the American experience of living, rather than logically deriving, democratic values and human dignity.

As Ruth Lawson put it in The Mayflower, it is an 'empirical experience' of democratic values and human dignity, asserted at both the individual psychological and collective levels. Some of the New Haven School were among the first to place this account of values and human dignity so centrally within a theory of international law, but this was a successful formulation of a broader view. It quickly connected comfortably to the vocabulary of international human rights law, as the panels on human rights at the 1959 meeting showed. As others have argued, this too has been a comfortable companion to the projection of American power.[64]

Although this anthropologised, psychologically inflected tradition of introspection about a uniquely American moral mission of world leadership has animated key foreign policies of both Democratic and Republican presidents, especially of the later twentieth century, it has tended to be a tradition most ardently invoked by liberals. It was, after all, liberals who for the most part prosecuted the Vietnam War, laid the intellectual foundations of neo-conservatism and pursued violent intervention in other states under the guise of 'humanitarian' interventions in the 1990s, always in furtherance of such a moral mission.

Whether this tradition will feature in the foreign policy of President Donald Trump is unclear, and possibly unlikely. In fact, the extent to which his statements and those of his administration appear tone deaf to this kind of view of what the United States should do with its power might be what distinguishes him most clearly from past twentieth century presidents, both Democratic and Republican. His inauguration speech was one of many examples of that. He spoke of greatness and power, but not of assuming responsibility for the prosecution of any moral mission, or for much at all, outside the borders of the United States.[65]

D. Conclusion: Patterns in the Politics of Form in Anglo-American International Law and Theory

This chapter has argued that in the second half of the twentieth century, American international law has frequently been characterised by a specific tradition of anti-formalist legal methods. It has also been argued that an animating, to an extent justifying theoretical core of that anti-formalism can be identified in an anthropological and psychologised account of how American society has lived, rather than derived, democratic values and human dignity. This story about ideas has

[64] There is a wide body of scholarship on this topic. The most influential work is S Moyn, *The Last Utopia* (Cambridge, MA: Harvard University Press, 2012).

[65] Donald J Trump, The Inaugural Address (20 January 2025, The Capitol, Washington DC), available at www.whitehouse.gov/remarks/2025/01/the-inaugural-address.

moved from bodies of thought associated in the early twentieth century with broadly progressive politics – philosophical pragmatism, psychoanalytic critiques of conservative social norms, and the New Deal – to the later twentieth century, when those same ideas supported defensive, paranoid and often violent politics of the Cold War United States. This is not an unusual story. One observation it prompts is that New Deal politics and law making may have had broadly progressive aims when pursued within the domestic United States, but as made explicit in McDougal's intervention at the 1954 ASIL meeting, quoted in section B above, projecting it unilaterally onto other states was an oppressive act. This trajectory is also explained by the fact that both anthropology and psychoanalysis became more disciplining sciences in the later twentieth-century United States, tools to remake and even control, rather than emancipate the human self.

The story told above about political patterns in how legal methods have been used has had consequences, although not the ones that might have been expected. It might have been reasonable to think that after Carlston used his legal realism to deconstruct claims of permanent sovereignty over natural resources; after Feliciano and McDougal called for an approach to the use of force that was as blurry and open ended as possible; after Becker asked international law scholars to defend American capital by using functionalist arguments to shore up the State Department's vociferous attacks on expropriation; and after other arguments in the same anti-formalist style were consistently found to neatly align with American interests, arguing for conclusions relying on more adherence to legal form like those of Falk and Wright might have seemed the progressive thing to do. A critic of American power attending the 1959 ASIL meeting might have concluded that what was required was for a generation of international lawyers to revive some version of a clear eyed, contextual and strategically crafted formalism. They might have taken up the project of opposing legal forms to power pursued by developing states in the form of the movement for a New International Economic Order in the 1970s, for example. But at least in Anglo-American international law scholarship and practice, this did not happen.

Instead, anti-formalist methods became associated with approaches to law identified as 'critical'. Formalism has been largely unavailable as a position on the political left in Anglo-American international law scholarship. As Koskenniemi noted of Friedmann's arguments against Berle's de-formalised legitimation of the American invasion of the Dominican Republic, many contemporary lawyers likely feel sympathy for Friedmann's position, but 'are perhaps uncertain about how to articulate that sympathy into a professionally respectable position'.[66] The revolt against formalism has apparently been so thorough as to have foreclosed any possibility of returning to what now appears a naive faith in formalist abstraction.

However, notwithstanding the persuasiveness of the ideas that constituted that revolt in the early twentieth-century United States, or of the frequently distinct

[66] Koskenniemi (n 44) 499.

anti-formalist premises descending from continental European philosophical traditions that shaped what is now denoted as the critical legal studies movement, the specific association of anti-formalism with the often violent projection of American power through international law is empirically observable. The extent to which the critical observation that anti-formalism has been a comfortable companion of American power requires extensive justificatory reasoning when made in a theoretical register is almost inversely proportionate to the near-banality of this observation when made by reference to untheorised legal practice of the United States.

The story told in this chapter suggests some possible reasons for this situation. First, the anti-formalist tradition highlighted here had different political consequences when it was deployed in support of projects of domestic reform in the United States – the New Deal – as compared to American-backed projects of intervention in the affairs of other states. It is, of course, a different thing for the Federal Government of the United States to insist that the State of Tennessee cede authority to a new agency that will re-plan the organisation of social services and industry in its jurisdiction (a flagship example of New Deal social planning), to the US government insisting that the Government of the Dominican Republic cede authority to another government preferred by the United States. However, for some New Dealers turned world planners, these acts were not so different, existing on a spectrum that was not bisected by any strict conception of what they might have dismissed as the artificial abstraction of sovereign equality.

Second and relatedly, in the contemporary United States the idea that anti-formalism is appropriately the method of the legal left can be attributed largely to the influence of the critical legal studies movement. This rich school of thought was primarily, and through its successor movements today remains, focused above all and often to the exclusion of much else, on the domestic law of the United States, and especially on constitutional law. In turn, anti-formalist and formalist legal methods have acquired distinct political valences in legal fields of domestic American law. These valences can shift and are consistently subject to debate, as contemporary contestation within conservative legal thought over the political utility of 'originalist' interpretations of the US Constitution shows.[67]

It is this mutability that should be emphasised. There is no reason to think that politics of method present in debates over domestic law of the United States would map on to international legal arguments across different sub-fields. It is also the case that although the anti-formalist methods within critical legal studies scholarship sit on strong theoretical premises, drawn variously from both the tradition examined in this chapter and from post-war French sociological theory, those premises need to be adapted if they are applied to laws concerning relations between states. It is not always analytically useful to assume that the condition of an individual within a social structure shaped by law is co-extensive with the

[67] Initiating this ongoing debate, see A Vermeule, 'Beyond Originalism' *The Atlantic* (31 March 2020).

condition of a state that, in principle, can claim sovereign equality as both a maker and subject of the law by which it may be oppressed. The oppressions to which each is subject and the opportunities of which each can avail are different.

Catharine MacKinnon has noted that critical legal studies' anti-formalism can render it 'less useful for those for whom law is all too determinate'.[68] A similar observation might be made about weak states. For such states, anti-formalism is unlikely to be as useful as it is for the United States, which is in a position to plausibly backstop its legal interpretations with violence. In some cases, weaker states may make more persuasive arguments by abandoning law altogether and adopting ethical or emotional registers. In other cases, although law might inevitably instantiate a status quo, there may be instances in which an actor with the power of a state will find resources within that status quo that are useful in prosecuting a change they seek. A distinct theory of the social context within which international law operates is required.

Third, the fact, as illustrated by the examples given in this chapter, that patterns in the politics of legal method are mutable over time and across sub-fields of law have made it possible to proceed with the idea that anti-formalism is the most appropriate style of left legal critique, because in some cases that may be so. However, although it is easy to find systematic, explicit explanations of why formalist methods of reasoning and interpretation have necessarily had reactionary consequences within, for example, private law doctrines in the United States, it is harder to find any such systematic explanations of why this has been so within international law. It is more common to find this idea implied.

However, within the detail of studies on specific legal fields, the mutability of the politics associated with legal method is often noted. As David Kennedy, responsible for much of the project of applying insights of critical legal studies to international law, has observed:

> It is important to remember … that what we think of as the classical system, of both legal philosophy and doctrine, has never been as thoroughly rejected as this conventional picture suggests. It survives in the most progressive of contemporary polemics for a new international law. Sovereignty, formalism, positivism, and a rule of coexistence rather than cooperation, all remain with us, not only as echoes and remnants to be excised root and branch, but as dreams, projects, and goals for our work. This continuity in twentieth century disciplinary argument leaves me skeptical of the claim that a shift away from formalism or sovereignty can ensure, or even mark an argument as progressive, or internationalist, or modern.[69]

[68] Quoted in S Moyn, 'Reconstructing Critical Legal Studies' (2024) 134 *Yale Law Journal* 77, 114 with fn 144.

[69] D Kennedy, 'International Law and the Nineteenth Century: History of an Illusion' (1997) 17 *Quinnipiac Law Review* 99, 102–03. Also convincingly making a related argument, see BR Roth, 'The Trajectory of the Democratic Entitlement Thesis in International Legal Scholarship: A Reply to Akbar Rasulov' (2021) 32 *European Journal of International Law* 49. Developing a contextual analysis of the political possibilities of formalism and anti-formalism, and concluding that anti-formalism and

In a similar vein and offering examples from practice, when reflecting on his seminal mid-1970s work on the legality of wars of national liberation, Georges Abi-Saab notes that while at first 'the West did, as they do with many Third World issues, try to shrug it off, saying this is political and it should be treated in the General Assembly rather than at a legal conference where we should discuss exclusively legal matters', this strategy failed: 'When I formulated the case for wars of national liberation as international armed conflicts from a legal perspective, they understood they had to answer; they could not simply push it aside.'[70] Similarly, of his work as an advocate in delimitation cases, Abi-Saab notes that 'the public interest was to make legality prevail over effectivity, which in general serves the stronger party who usually imposes a status quo of her or his own doing, or rather often her or his misdoings'.[71]

As Abi-Saab's reflections on when emphasis on legal forms (the term 'formalism' is not used by Abi-Saab) has or has not been useful in his legal practice show, this utility might be present in a patterned but not immutable way across time or fields of legal doctrine. This is also the pressing conclusion to be drawn from later twentieth-century American international law practice and scholarship. It is pressing because this practice and scholarship has been shaped by a unique American tradition of anti-formalism, and has had so much scope to prosecute its ideological commitments through law.

indeterminacy critique cannot be viewed as having some 'critical essence', see M Craven et al, '"We are Teachers of International Law"' (2004) 17 *Leiden Journal of International Law* 363, 374.

[70] Abi-Saab (n 49) 1965.

[71] ibid 1966.

5

China's Contemporary Approach to International Law

GE CHEN AND MING DU

A. Introduction

Widely regarded as 'the most significant geopolitical challenge of our times',[1] the rise of China has arguably had a greater impact on contemporary world politics than any other developments in recent decades. Currently, China is the world's second-largest economy, the largest manufacturer and trader in goods, the second-largest trader in services, a leading recipient of foreign direct investment flows, and the top trading partner of over 120 countries and regions.[2] At the same time, China's increasing investments in military modernisation have significantly enhanced its military capabilities.[3] On its current trajectory, many analysts predict that China will surpass the US as the world's largest economy well before the middle of the century.[4]

China's rapid ascent to superpower status – economically, politically, militarily and, to some extent, culturally – has sparked considerable speculation about whether it will seek to revise the current rules-based international order to better reflect its power and status. Some observers argue that China has already emerged as a revisionist power, intent on reshaping international relations and the rules governing them, particularly within East Asia. Others view China's efforts as part of a broader ambition to replace or fundamentally alter international law and governance on a global scale.[5]

[1] M Wu, 'The "China Inc.": Challenges to Global Trade Governance' (2016) 57 *Harvard International Law Journal* 261.

[2] Hong Kong Trade Development Council, 'Economic and Trade Information on China' (15 July 2022), https://research.hktdc.com/en/article/MzIwNjcyMDYx.

[3] US Department of Defense, *Military and Security Developments Involving the People's Republic of China 2022*, Annual Report to Congress (26 October 2022).

[4] JD Moyer et al, 'Measuring and Forecasting the Rise of China: Reality over Image' (2023) 32 *Journal of Contemporary China* 191, 205–06.

[5] N Rolland, *China's Vision for a New World Order*, National Bureau of Asian Research Special Report no 83 (January 2020); R Mitter, 'The World China Wants: How Power Will – and Won't – Reshape Chinese Ambitions' (2021)(1) 100 *Foreign Affairs* 161.

Such speculation is not surprising, given that there is little precedent for a great power rising within a normative framework not of its own creation without substantially altering or revolutionising that framework to reflect its values and interests.[6] Like other rising powers throughout history, China is likely to challenge the status quo, which, in practical terms, often involves contesting existing international norms and advancing alternative ones.[7] Based on these assumptions, some have predicted that a new Cold War is inevitable, driven by the inadequacies of international institutions to manage China's rise and prevent superpower conflict.[8]

This chapter examines China's evolving approach to international law, with a particular focus on its complex views and practices during Xi Jinping's 'new era'. Our narrative adopts a national 'approach to international law' rather than explicitly using 'comparative international law', as the recent comparative international law movement has not widely extended to China. While this does not mean China has never been influenced by comparative international law, the trend towards the nationalisation of international law seems prevalent, making a 'scholarly withdrawal into national approaches to international law' a more realistic choice when studying China.[9] Nonetheless, the topics explored in this chapter cover two fundamental areas of comparative international law: China's reception and adaptation of international law. The key questions addressed are: how unique or particularistic is China's approach compared to that of other major powers? What is the gap between China's policy pronouncements and its actual behaviour? What domestic and external factors have shaped China's approach to international law? Finally, how is the international legal order itself being affected by China's rise?

B. A Traditional Rule Taker: Unpacking China's Approach to International Law

1. The Historical Evolution of China's Perspective on International Law

As a nation without a modern legal tradition, China's initial encounter with international law in the mid-nineteenth century was marked by deep distrust.[10] Despite its millennia-old history as a state and civilisation, Western powers and legal

[6] S Chesterman, 'Asia's Ambivalence about International Law and Institutions: Past, Present and Futures' (2016) 27 *European Journal of International Law* 945, 950.

[7] EA Posner and JC Yoo, 'International Law and the Rise of China' (2006) 7 *Chicago Journal of International Law* 1, 10.

[8] P Heer, 'There Will Be a US–China Cold War' *The National Interest* (3 October 2021).

[9] See El Boudouhi, ch 8 in this volume, 206.

[10] S Ogden, 'Sovereignty and International Law: The Perspective of the People's Republic of China' (1974) 7 *NYU Journal of International Law and Politics* 1, 8–9.

theorists deemed China insufficiently 'civilised' to join the 'family of nations'.[11] In contrast, China perceived international law as a tool used to justify foreign invasions and impose unequal treaties following its military defeats during the nineteenth and early twentieth centuries.[12]

During this period, China began formally studying and adapting international legal theories and systems, with translated foreign treatises playing a crucial role.[13] Notably, the works of Emmerich de Vattel and Henry Wheaton were translated into Chinese during the late Qing dynasty, marking a significant turning point in China's understanding of public international law.[14] These translations facilitated China's transition from the 'Law of Nations' to the modern framework of international law.[15] From the perspective of 'comparative international law' advocated by this volume, this shift is significant: the earlier approach can be viewed as China's initial comparative engagement – using a foreign-law perspective – to transplant international law, whereas the latter marks China's initial acceptance of public international law as a conceptual framework.[16]

However, within China, this transition is often viewed as part of a Eurocentric process of globalising international legal norms, profoundly shaping China's value judgements and applications of international law.[17] This Eurocentric influence persisted into the twentieth century, further evident in the translation of *Oppenheim's International Law* into Chinese in 1955, which significantly influenced Chinese legal scholarship.[18] Thus, China's initial approach could be characterised as one of 'European international law'.[19]

A different ideological perspective emerged following the Second World War, shaped largely by Soviet influence.[20] After the founding of the People's Republic of China (PRC) in 1949, the Chinese Communist Party (CCP) adopted a dogmatically Marxist-Leninist view of international law, viewing 'bourgeois international law' as an instrument of Western capitalist states used to defend imperialist policies.[21] Additionally, although China was a founding member of the United Nations (UN) Security Council, the PRC was denied its legitimate seat at the UN from the late 1940s until the early 1970s. During this period, China was excluded from most intergovernmental organisations and major international law-making

[11] A Sheikh, 'The Peoples' Republic of China and International Law' (1973) 7 *The International Lawyer* 770, 775–76.
[12] ibid 777.
[13] A Roberts, *Is International Law International?* (Oxford: Oxford University Press, 2017) 139.
[14] W Li, 'From Law of Nations to International Law: Historicism and Translation in the Late Qing Dynasty' (2024) 39(1) *Journal of Tsinghua University (Philosophy and Social Sciences)* 45, 45–46.
[15] ibid 50.
[16] For a similar discussion of 'monistic' and 'dualistic' systems, see Boudouhi (n 9) 190.
[17] Li (n 14) 46.
[18] Roberts (n 13) 140.
[19] See Schütze, ch 2 in this volume, 34–37.
[20] ibid 139–40.
[21] H Chiu, 'Communist China's Attitude toward International Law' (1966) 60 *American Journal of International Law* 245, 261–63.

processes, fostering the country's hostility towards the UN and the broader international legal order in the context of the Cold War.[22] In this era, China adopted an entirely Soviet-influenced 'socialist international law'.[23]

China's revolutionary stance on international law began to shift in 1971, following its entry to the UN. This shift became more pronounced after the adoption of economic reforms and the opening-up policy in 1978,[24] marking a departure from Soviet ideological influence. Over the past half-century, China has sought deeper engagement with international regimes, integrated into the global economy, and intensified its participation in international institutions.[25] During this period, Chinese scholars began producing domestic works on international law. However, these publications often lacked independent scholarly perspectives due to censorship and self-censorship.[26] Instead, they reflected official government positions, omitting or minimising content that might challenge the state narrative.[27] Nevertheless, China's international legal strategy during this period was no longer purely Soviet-influenced socialist international law; rather, it incorporated various strategies, including elements of 'Third World international law',[28] laying the groundwork for a more significant shift.

Today, China holds membership in nearly all universal intergovernmental institutions and benefits significantly from open global economic rules and institutions. Unlike its earlier hostility, China no longer openly disdains the institutions and norms of the international community. Furthermore, China has not advocated for fundamental changes to the core principles or values of international law in most areas. According to mainstream Chinese scholars, international law now serves as a normative framework for managing China's international relations.[29] From this perspective, China's 'comparative approach' to international law can be perceived as 'comparative foreign relations law'.[30]

Nevertheless, in areas of critical national interest, China continues to assert its own interpretations of international norms and often disregards the positions of other states or international entities. This tendency is particularly evident in Chinese scholarship of international law on issues of paramount importance to

[22] A Kent, *Beyond Compliance: China, International Organizations, and Global Security* (Stanford: Stanford University Press, 2007) 38–39.

[23] Schütze (n 19) 38–40.

[24] SS Kim, 'The Development of International Law in Post-Mao China: Change and Continuity' (1987) 1 *Journal of Chinese Law* 117, 158–59.

[25] Z Pang, 'China and the Struggle over the Future of International Order' in HW Maull (ed), *The Rise and Decline of the Post-Cold War International Order* (Oxford: Oxford University Press, 2018) 235, 237.

[26] A Roberts, 'Crimea and the South China Sea: Connections and Disconnects among Chinese, Russian, and Western International Lawyers' in A Roberts et al (eds), *Comparative International Law* (Oxford: Oxford University Press, 2018) 111, 113, 127–28.

[27] Roberts (n 13) 156.

[28] Schütze (n 19) 40–43.

[29] H Xue, *Chinese Contemporary Perspectives on International Law: History, Culture and International Law* (Leiden: Brill, 2012) 23–26.

[30] Schütze (n 19) 29–30.

the nation.[31] It is in this context that some scholars categorise China's current international law strategy as part of 'authoritarian international law'.[32] While this characterisation is insightful, China's approach warrants a more precise and nuanced definition from a comparative law perspective, reflecting its uniquely distinctive style of legal thinking.

2. Theoretical Foundations of China's Current Approach to International Law

a. An Overview

Since the legal reforms of the late Qing Dynasty, China has adopted a civil law system heavily influenced by German law.[33] This foundational framework rooted in comparative law continues to shape China's theoretical approach to international law. Unlike the British and American traditions, which emphasise case law and the practical application of legal principles to specific issues, Chinese international law scholarship traditionally prioritises theoretical and conceptual analysis.[34] This preference underscores a systematic approach to legal frameworks over pragmatic jurisprudence.[35]

After China's economic reforms and opening-up, international law scholars began exploring how domestic courts should interpret and apply international law. One of the most notable contributions in this field comes from Zhou Gengsheng, a leading Chinese international jurist, who introduced the concept of 'automatic coordination' to address the relationship between international and national law.[36] Zhou's approach advocates incorporating binding international legal rules into the domestic legal system and implementing them as national law to minimise conflicts.[37] This perspective, widely recognised in Chinese international law scholarship, avoids prioritising the supremacy of international law over national law, thereby granting the Chinese government considerable flexibility in interpreting and implementing international legal obligations.[38]

Generally, Chinese scholars play a less prominent role in judicial interpretation compared to their counterparts in classic civil law systems, where academics often have significant influence on judicial reasoning.[39] Moreover, Chinese courts have

[31] Roberts (n 13) 161. See also Roberts (n 26) 130.

[32] T Ginsburg, 'Authoritarian International Law' (2020) 114 *American Journal of International Law* 221.

[33] PR Luney, 'Traditions and Foreign Influences: Systems of Law in China and Japan' (1989) 52 *Current Legal Problems* 129, 130–32.

[34] Roberts (n 13) 136.

[35] ibid.

[36] G Zhou, *International Law* (Beijing: The Commercial Press, 1983) 16.

[37] ibid.

[38] B Ahl, 'Chinese Law and International Treaties' (2009) 39 *Hong Kong Law Journal* 737, 740.

[39] Roberts (n 13) 137.

traditionally had a limited role in interpreting and applying public international law, often described as marginal or even non-existent.[40] This disconnect between theoretical scholarship and judicial application has long been a defining feature of China's legal system.

However, in recent years, this approach has evolved significantly. Chinese international law authorities increasingly examine China's distinctive strategies towards international law, adopting a comparative legal approach with greater boldness and clarity. For example, the Chinese legislature frequently incorporates international law rules into areas involving private law disputes, such as intellectual property.[41] Conversely, this practice is often excluded in public law contexts, such as administrative law.[42] On the judicial front, the Supreme People's Court of China has issued 'guiding cases' encouraging courts to apply international treaties in areas like international economic law and international environmental law through the principle of 'consistent interpretation'.[43] In contrast, such guidance is notably absent in the realm of international human rights law, where courts are often reluctant to apply international legal norms directly.[44] In these cases, Chinese courts exercise significant 'ideological discretionary power',[45] reflecting a selective approach shaped by broader state policies.

The following sections explore two theoretical elements that form the cornerstones of China's current approach to international law, illustrating their impact on both academic discourse and practical application.

b. *China's Sovereignty-Based Approach to International Law*

The concept of sovereignty lies at the heart of Chinese international legal discourse.[46] In the late nineteenth and early twentieth centuries, many nations adhered to the 'Westphalian' principle of absolute immunity, which granted states complete exemption from the jurisdiction of foreign courts. China has embraced this tradition, with its Five Principles of Peaceful Co-existence – first articulated in the 1950s and enshrined in its Constitution – manifesting a strong commitment to absolutist sovereignty.[47] Furthermore, China underscores that the fundamental

[40] ibid 136.

[41] B Ahl, 'China's Perspectives on Public International Law: Selective Adaptation of International Treaties and the Community of Common Destiny Concept' (2022) 64 *German Yearbook of International Law* 97, 101–14.

[42] ibid 102.

[43] ibid 103–04.

[44] ibid 107; C Cai, 'International Law in Chinese Courts during the Rise of China' (2016) 110 *American Journal of International Law* 269, 283–84.

[45] MYK Woo, 'Law and Discretion in the Contemporary Chinese Courts' (1999) 8 *Pacific Rim Law & Policy Journal* 581, 592–93.

[46] T Wang, 'International Law in China: Historical and Contemporary Perspectives' (1990) 221 *Recueil des Cours de l'Académie de Droit International* 228.

[47] H Xue, 'Chinese Observations on International Law' (2007) 6 *Chinese Journal of International Law* 83, 86.

principles of sovereignty and non-intervention in the internal affairs of states are enshrined in the UN Charter, bolstering its position on the primacy of sovereignty in international law.[48]

Despite the abundance of examples that illustrate China's practices concerning sovereign immunity, there is a noticeable lack of detailed discussion on this topic in Chinese international law scholarship. Chiefly, China invokes the principle of sovereignty to prioritise national sovereignty over universalist values.[49] For instance, China relies on sovereign immunity as a shield against foreign criticism or interference in its domestic policies and practices and as a justification for its reluctance to intervene in what it considers the internal affairs of other states.[50] China remains hostile to international adjudication and prefers political or diplomatic approaches when issues related to its 'core sovereign interests', such as sovereignty and territorial integrity, are at stake.[51] Similarly, China has levied sovereignty-focused critiques of other countries' foreign policies, such as democracy promotion and humanitarian intervention.[52]

China's emphasis on sovereignty is often attributed to its traumatic historical encounters with international law, spanning from the Opium War in the 1840s to its prolonged isolation from the UN and other international organisations during the early years of the PRC.[53] These experiences, marked by military defeats and the imposition of unequal treaties, fostered a lasting sense of victimhood and scepticism towards the international order. This historical context has instilled in China a mentality that international law and the prevailing global order were instruments of foreign domination, against which China must protect itself both externally and internally.[54] Sovereignty therefore functions as a legal tool to safeguard China's independence and shield it from foreign interference and aggression. However, as Benjamin Schwartz has argued, while China's historical experiences may have shaped its earlier worldview, their causal weight in explaining present or future Chinese policies should not be overstated: Schwartz cautions against attributing China's contemporary stance on sovereignty solely to its historical grievances, emphasising the need for a more nuanced interpretation.[55]

[48] ibid 84–85.

[49] J Men, 'Between Human Rights and Sovereignty: An Examination of EU–China Political Relations' (2011) 17 *European Law Journal* 534, 540–44.

[50] W Muller, 'China's Sovereignty in International Law: From Historical Grievance to Pragmatic Tool' (2013) 1 *China–EU Law Journal* 35, 56–57.

[51] Y Hao and I de la Rasill, 'China and International Adjudication: Picking up Steam? (2021) 12 *Journal of International Dispute Settlement* 637, 639–58.

[52] J Shi, 'China Blames Aggressive US Wars for Humanitarian Disasters around the World as it Hits back at Criticism of Human Rights Record' *South China Morning Post* (9 April 2021).

[53] J deLisle, 'China and Sovereignty in International Law: Across Time and Issue Areas' (2024) 6(1) *UC Irvine Journal of International, Transnational, and Comparative Law* 4, 28–29.

[54] PCW Chan, *China, State Sovereignty and International Legal Order* (Leiden: Brill, 2015) 16.

[55] BI Schwartz, 'The Chinese Perception of World Order: Past and Present' in J King Fairbank (ed), *The Chinese World Order: Traditional China's Foreign Relations* (Cambridge, MA: Harvard University Press, 1986) 276, 284.

An alternative explanation suggests that China's emphasis on sovereignty serves as a convenient legal mechanism to protect the legitimacy and stability of the communist regime and the leadership of the CCP.[56] For China, maintaining the CCP's power and ensuring national stability are paramount, with a strong focus on political unity and social harmony as prerequisites for the country's advancement.[57] By invoking the principle of sovereignty, the party-state seeks to deflect international scrutiny and criticism of its internal policies while promoting the peaceful co-existence of different political systems.

c. *China's Instrumentalist Approach to International Law*

China's emphasis on sovereignty, territorial integrity and non-interference is not absolute but instrumental, reflecting a fundamentally realist rather than normative approach to international law.[58] Above all, China cooperates with and implements those international rules that the party-state deems consistent with its political objectives or supportive of its strategic needs. For instance, while China has traditionally exhibited extreme caution towards binding third-party international dispute settlement mechanisms due to sovereignty concerns, it has embraced international adjudication in the context of trade and investment disputes.[59] Similarly, although 'non-interference' remains a cornerstone of Chinese foreign policy, the imperative to protect its rapidly expanding overseas interests has led to domestic recalibration of the relevance and applicability of this principle.[60] China has also selectively endorsed the Responsibility to Protect doctrine, applying it narrowly while advocating for constrained, multilateral use of force.[61]

Conversely, China distances itself from, ignores or entirely abandons international rules that conflict with the political goals of the party-state or predominantly aim to restrict state power.[62] For example, in the South China Sea arbitration, China dismissed the rulings of the Permanent Court of Arbitration as mere 'waste paper' and denounced the arbitration as a 'farce', despite its prior agreement to binding

[56] J Stokes, 'Does China Really Respect Sovereignty?' *The Diplomat* (23 May 2019).

[57] D Kennedy and JE Stiglitz, *Law and Economics with Chinese Characteristics: Institutions for Promoting Development in the Twenty-First Century* (Oxford: Oxford University Press, 2013) 25.

[58] BA Duben and Hangwei Li, 'The Sovereignty Paradox in China's Response to the Russia–Ukraine War' (2024) 45(4) *Contemporary Security Policy* 1, 11–12; J Wang and H Cheng, 'China's Approach to International Law: From Traditional Westphalianism to Aggressive Instrumentalism in the Xi Jinping Era' (2022) 10 *Chinese Journal of Comparative Law* 140, 144–46.

[59] M Du, 'Explaining China's Approach to Investor-State Dispute Settlement: A Contextual Approach' (2022) 28 *European Law Journal* 281, 294.

[60] TJ Baum, 'The Responsibility of Power: Shifts in Chinese Conceptualization of the Legitimacy of Overseas Intervention to Protect Nationals Abroad' (2020) 32 *Global Change, Peace & Security* 259, 272–73.

[61] Z Chen, 'China and the Responsibility to Protect' (2016) 25(101) *Journal of Contemporary China* 686, 700.

[62] C Wang and X Xiang, 'The Constitution of China and International Law: From Selective Adaptation to Normative Consensus' in I de la Rasilla and C Cai (eds), *The Cambridge Handbook of China and International Law* (Cambridge: Cambridge University Press, 2024) 73, 78–79.

arbitration under the UN Convention on the Law of the Sea.[63] Similarly, China has occasionally engaged in transnational oppression through covert overseas security operations, actions that arguably violate the sovereign rights of other states.[64] Most recently, China's non-response to Russia's violation of Ukraine's sovereignty and territorial integrity underscores its selective application of international norms.[65]

The most fundamental divergence between China and Western nations lies in the conception and protection of human rights. China emphasises that national and regional particularities – along with political, economic, social, cultural, historical and religious contexts – can justify the prioritisation of collective over individual rights.[66] For example, framing itself as a developing country, China has consistently argued that the 'rights to subsistence and development' constitute the most fundamental human rights.[67] It contends that civil and political rights are secondary to socioeconomic development, asserting that their fulfilment depends on local conditions and the prioritisation of economic growth.[68] China often cites significant poverty reduction and extensive investments in infrastructure and education as evidence of its commitment to economic and social rights.[69]

China's relativist approach to human rights has drawn considerable criticism. Scholars argue that prioritising economic and social rights over political and civil rights is artificial, as the latter are instrumental in holding governments accountable for delivering on the former.[70] Critics also contend that China's focus on economic and social rights often comes at the expense of civil and political freedoms, citing restrictions on free speech, assembly and the press as clear divergences from international human rights norms.[71] Moreover, there is broad concern that China is expanding its approach to curtailing civil and political rights beyond its borders. Examples include China's global advocacy during the COVID-19 pandemic and the implementation of the Hong Kong National Security Law, which many view as emblematic of its broader effort to erode freedoms.[72]

[63] S Denyer and E Rauhala, 'Beijing Claims to South China Sea Rejected by International Tribunal' *Washington Post* (12 July 2016).

[64] G Chen, 'The "Constitutional" Rise of Chinese Speech Imperialism' (2023) 2 *Journal of Free Speech Law* 483, 552–58.

[65] Duben and Li (n 58) 1.

[66] Chan (n 54) 121–22.

[67] 'A People-Centered Approach for Global Human Rights Progress', remarks by HE Wang Yi (22 February 2021), www.fmprc.gov.cn/eng/wjb_663304/wjbz_663308/2461_663310/202102/t20210222_9889339.html.

[68] D Chen, 'Explaining China's Changing Discourse on Human Rights, 1978–2004' (2005) 29 *Asian Perspective* 155, 169–72.

[69] The State Council Information Office White Paper, 'Poverty Alleviation: China's Experience and Contribution' (6 April 2021).

[70] JA Cohen, 'Law and Power in China's International Relations' (2019) 52 *NYU Journal of International Law and Politics* 123, 156.

[71] Y-J Chen, 'China's Challenge to the International Human Rights Regime' (2019) 51 *NYU Journal of International Law and Politics* 1179, 1203–04.

[72] S Richardson, 'China's Influence on the Global Human Rights System: Assessing China's Growing Role in the World' (*Brookings Institution*, September 2020), www.brookings.edu/wp-content/uploads/2020/09/FP_20200914_china_human_rights_richardson.pdf.

China's stance on human rights enables it to advocate for norms that prioritise state sovereignty and collective rights over individual freedoms, challenging the Western-dominated human rights discourse. By promoting alternative values and principles internationally, China seeks to shield its domestic governance model from external criticism under the pretence of non-interference and state sovereignty. Simultaneously, it positions itself as a global leader offering an alternative path for international relations and human rights, reflecting its vision of a multipolar world order.[73] This strategy underscores China's broader ambition to re-interpret and reshape international human rights law in ways that serve its governance model and strategic interests.[74]

In summary, China's approach to international law – marked by its emphasis on sovereignty, a nominal commitment to human rights protection, and a substantial reliance on an efficient international system for trade, finance and investment law – resonates strongly with, and indeed exemplifies, the broader concept of 'authoritarian international law'.[75] This pragmatic and flexible approach allows China to act as a 'rule taker', benefiting from and exploiting the existing international legal order without advocating for fundamental changes to the letter of the law in most areas.[76]

3. From Theory to Practice: China's 'Turn against' International Law

a. Underlying Factors in China's Challenge to the International Legal Order

China has long expressed dissatisfaction with certain aspects of the Western-led international order, seeking to reshape it to better reflect its own values and strategic interests. Official pronouncements repeatedly criticise an 'unfair and unreasonable' global order that, in Beijing's view, is ill-suited to addressing contemporary global challenges.[77] Several key factors explain China's increasing assertiveness and its recent 'turn against' some aspects of international law, particularly given its historical role as a largely passive 'rule taker' until the early twenty-first century.

First, China's objections stem from its belief that the existing international order is rooted in norms that privilege Western liberal democratic values such as universal rights, free markets and the rule of law. These principles are

[73] Chen (n 71) 1197–1208.
[74] ibid 1193–95.
[75] Ginsburg (n 32) 230–31.
[76] R William, 'International Law with Chinese Characteristics: Beijing and the "Rules-Based" Global Order' (*Brookings*, 2020) 1, www.brookings.edu/wp-content/uploads/2020/10/FP_20201012_international_law_china_williams.pdf.
[77] S Zhao, 'A Revisionist Stakeholder: China and the Post-World War II World Order' (2018) 27 *Journal of Contemporary China* 643, 646.

fundamentally at odds with the core tenets of the CCP system, which emphasises absolute party leadership, state-driven governance, and centralised control over economic and societal development.[78] Beijing perceives these ideological differences as a direct challenge to the legitimacy of its governance model.[79] For example, China views the US-led security architecture in Asia as a structural impediment to its development and national security objectives, particularly its ambitions concerning the 'unification' of Taiwan.[80] Similarly, while Western liberal democracies advocate for universal values to promote global peace and prosperity, China emphasises the importance of 'civilisational diversity' and attributes global conflicts to the imposition of universal values.[81] In this context, China prefers an interpretation of international norms that accommodates different governance models, ensuring that its authoritarian approach is regarded as equally legitimate as liberal democracy within the international community.[82]

Second, China's dissatisfaction with the current international order reflects a perceived gap between its material power and its international status.[83] Many observers argue that the world is witnessing the rapid and profound redistribution of power in the international system.[84] The post-Cold War condition of unipolarity marked by America's position as a peerless superpower has been shaken by the relative downturn of the US economy and the relative decline of US power. Global power is shifting from the unipolarity to greater multipolarity, and from an era of a Western-led international order to one marked by greater competition.[85] In particular, China is rapidly emerging as a serious contender for the US dominance, and future decades will see even greater increases in China's power and influence.[86] Unsurprisingly, its rise as a world power is a source of confidence and pride in China. Ebullient rhetoric such as 'the east is rising while the west is declining', 'China has stood up, grown rich, become strong, and is moving towards centre stage', 'time and momentum are on our side' and 'China can finally look at the world as an equal' have become

[78] J deLisle, 'China's Approach to International Law: A Historical Perspective', *Proceedings of the Annual Meeting of American Society of International Law* (April 2000) 267, 273–74.

[79] N Rolland, 'A World Order Modelled by China', testimony before the US–China Economic and Security Review Commission Hearing on the 'China Model' (13 March 2020).

[80] D Sevastopulo and K Hille, 'China Accuses US of Seeking "Asia-Pacific Nato"' *Financial Times* (1 June 2024).

[81] Remarks by Ambassador Zhang Jun at the UN Security Council High-level Briefing on the Maintenance of International Peace and Security (14 June 2023).

[82] See Mattei and Singh, ch 9 in this volume, 224.

[83] Rolland (n 79).

[84] See SE Goddard, 'The Rise and Fall of Great-Power Competition' (2025) 104(3) *Foreign Affairs* 8.

[85] F Zakaria, 'The Self-Destruction of American Power: Washington Squandered the Unipolar Moment' (2019) 98(4) *Foreign Affairs* 10.

[86] C Layne, 'The US-Chinese Power Shift and the End of the Pax Americana' (2018) 94(1) *International Affairs* 89, 94–103; A Goldstein, 'US-China Rivalry in the Twenty-First Century: Déjà Vu and Cold War II' (2020) 2 *China International Strategy Review* 48, 53–54.

a common refrain in Chinese official discourse.[87] China believes that its growing power entitles it to have greater influence in global affairs, and that China no longer has to accept a subordinate role as a 'rule taker' rather than a 'rule maker'.[88]

However, Beijing believes that the current international order perpetuates the dominance of a US-led West even if its power has declined, enabling Washington to dictate the rules and norms that are accepted and respected by others. In contrast, as China's power grows, it advocates for a 'fairer' international order that would grant it greater 'discourse power' and enable it to set terms for institutions and norms that reflect its own preferences, commensurate with the reality of its material power.[89] To achieve this, China seeks to re-interpret and repurpose existing international laws and institutions, advancing new norms that align with its interests.[90] This reflects a fundamentally selective engagement with international law.

b. China's Selective Adaptation of International Law

Whilst China officially demonstrates a considerable commitment to upholding international law, its reception of international norms is often characterised by the paradigm of 'selective adaptation', where interpretative communities selectively adapt non-local standards for local application in light of their own normative perspectives.[91] For example, recognising that the World Trade Organization (WTO) membership comports with China's domestic policy priority of growing economic power, China repealed, revised, amended and adopted more than 3,000 national laws, regulations and decrees to establish a comprehensive legal framework consistent with the requirements of the WTO rules.[92] In contrast, China has adopted a sovereigntist approach to international human rights law. While Western states assert that international human rights law possesses a universal character derived from treaties, customary international law and moral values, China emphasises sovereignty over human rights, asserting that 'the issue of human rights falls by and large within the sovereignty of each country'.[93] Such an approach stands in stark contrast to the Western focus on individual freedoms and democracy, highlighting a deep-rooted

[87] L Yuan, 'Why China's Confidence Could Turn to be a Weakness' *New York Times* (9 August 2022); F Zhang, 'The Xi Jinping Doctrine of China's International Relations' (2019) 14(3) *Asia Policy* 9, 12–15.

[88] Z Wang, 'The Economic Rise of China: Rule-Taker, Rule-Maker, or Rule-Breaker?' (2017) 57 *Asian Survey* 595, 597–98.

[89] Y Zhang, 'China and Liberal Hierarchies in Global International Society: Power and Negotiation for Normative Change' (2016) 92 *International Affairs* 795, 797.

[90] Ginsburg (n 32) 230–31.

[91] PB Potter, 'China and the International Legal System: Challenges of Participation' (2007) 191 *China Quarterly* 699, 700–01.

[92] J Y Qin, 'Trade, Investment and beyond: The Impact of WTO Accession on China's Legal System' (2007) 119 *China Quarterly* 720.

[93] Men (n 49) 540–44.

conflict of values and frequent tensions between relativist and universalist practices of human rights.[94]

More recently, China's approach to international law has shifted from selectively adapting its domestic laws with its international law obligations, thereby minimising conflicts between its national legal framework and international standards (a 'norm taker') to one of consciously promoting alternative global norms and standards across various domains of international relations to make them more in line with China's authoritarian governance model, interests and values (a 'rule shaper' or 'norm maker').[95] For example, in opposition to a free and open approach to govern cyberspace, China has championed a guiding principle of 'cyber sovereignty', which emphasises the right of each state to establish its own rules governing content, data storage and the flows of information that are permitted to cross borders.[96] Similarly, by providing sources of finance to authoritarian regimes with 'no strings attached', China's practice is contrary to other countries and international organisations that require democratic reform, good governance and social responsibility in recipient countries as conditions of receiving development finance.[97] In addition, China is poised to set the standards for rapidly developing technologies such as artificial intelligence and robotics, and Chinese companies' technological infrastructure – built to Chinese standards – has spread to numerous countries, further amplifying China's global influence.[98]

China's advocacy for alternative global norms, standards and conventions, combined with its growing influence in spreading them across regions, represents a transformative shift for the future of the international order.[99] The emergence of China as a rule maker is viewed by countries such as the US and the UK – two powers that historically dominated global norms – as one of the greatest geopolitical challenges of the coming decades.[100] The critical question remains: are there fundamental differences between China's approach to shaping international norms and the approaches historically employed by Britain and the US?

[94] J Neagli, 'Bend, Don't Break: China's Approach to the International Human Rights Order' (2023) 64 *Harvard International Law Journal* 489, 499–500.

[95] Rolland (n 5) 6; EC Economy, *The World According to China* (Cambridge: Polity Press, 2021) 29–60.

[96] C-H Wu, 'Sovereignty Fever: The Territorial Turn of Global Cyber Order' (2021) 81 *Zeitschrift für ausländisches öffentliches Recht und Völkerrecht* 651, 656–57.

[97] J Yuan et al, 'China's Evolving Approach to Foreign Aid', Stockholm International Peace Research Institute Policy Paper 62 (May 2022) 24.

[98] MS Erie and T Streinz, 'The Beijing Effect: China's Digital Silk Road as Transnational Data Governance' (2021) 54 *NYU Journal of International Law and Politics* 1, 11–42.

[99] M Leonard, 'The Rule-Maker Race' *Project Syndicate* (31 December 2021).

[100] US–China Economic and Security Review Commission, *2023 Annual Report to Congress* (November 2023) 187–204; K Golubkova, 'UK's Sunak Says China Poses World's Biggest Security Challenge' *Reuters* (21 May 2023), www.reuters.com/world/uks-sunak-says-china-poses-worlds-biggest-security-challenge-2023-05-21/.

c. A Historical Comparison: Rising Powers' Approaches to International Law

The ascent of great powers has historically been accompanied by shifts in their engagement with international law, offering valuable precedents for understanding contemporary challenges.[101] A comparison of Britain and the US during their respective rises to global prominence reveals patterns of adaptation, re-interpretation and norm setting that resonate with China's current approach but also highlight key differences.[102]

During the nineteenth century, as Britain established itself as the pre-eminent global power, it shaped international law to reflect and reinforce its imperial dominance.[103] The principles of free trade and maritime law, championed under the Pax Britannica, served dual purposes: they protected Britain's economic interests while also embedding its values and norms within the global order.[104] Britain's approach to international law was deeply pragmatic, ensuring that the rules it promoted correlated with its geopolitical objectives, often at the expense of emerging rivals and weaker states.[105] For instance, the abolition of the transatlantic slave trade was framed as a moral and humanitarian achievement, but also functioned as a means to undermine competing colonial powers reliant on slave labour.[106]

The US, during its rise in the early twentieth century, similarly engaged in reshaping international law, albeit under the banner of liberal internationalism.[107] Initiatives like the creation of the League of Nations and, later, the Bretton Woods institutions exemplify America's efforts to institutionalise its values – democracy, free markets and individual freedoms – within the global order.[108] However, the US has also employed a selective approach, endorsing international norms that support its interests while resisting those perceived to constrain its sovereignty,[109] such as the delayed ratification of the UN Convention on the Law of the Sea. This strategic ambiguity allowed the US to act as both a promoter and a critic of international law, depending on the context.[110]

[101] SC Neff, *Justice among Nations: A History of International Law* (Cambridge, MA: Harvard University Press, 2014) 247–49.

[102] SC Neff, 'A Short History of International Law' in MD Evans (ed), *International Law*, 6th edn (Oxford: Oxford University Press, 2024) 3, 14–15.

[103] M Koskenniemi, *The Gentle Civilizer of Nations: The Rise and Fall of International Law 1870–1960* (Cambridge: Cambridge University Press, 2001) 110–12.

[104] JH Elliott, *Empires of the Atlantic World: Britain and Spain in America 1492–1830* (New Haven: Yale University Press, 2006) 221–24.

[105] A Anghie, *Imperialism, Sovereignty and the Making of International Law* (Cambridge: Cambridge University Press, 2004) 91–97.

[106] JS Martinez, 'Antislavery Courts and the Dawn of International Human Rights Law' (2008) 117 *Yale Law Journal* 550, 554–55.

[107] Neff (n 101) 427–32.

[108] ibid 396, 400–01.

[109] MJ Glennon, *The Fog of Law: Pragmatism, Security, and the International Rule of Law* (Stanford: Stanford University Press, 2010) 13–21.

[110] A-M Slaughter, *A New World Order* (Princeton: Princeton University Press, 2004) 15–18.

Unlike Britain and the US, which framed their engagement with international law as a universalising project tied to their respective visions of governance, China's approach remains more overtly instrumentalist.[111] China's recent advocacy for concepts reflects a similar ambition to shape global norms, but does so through the lens of its governance model, emphasising state sovereignty, collective development and non-interference.[112] However, while Britain and the US sought to export their values and consolidate leadership through rule setting, China seeks to re-interpret existing norms to legitimise its governance model and challenge liberal democratic dominance without explicitly dismantling the current international legal framework.[113]

This historical perspective illuminates the nuances of China's selective strategy: while it shares the ambition of earlier rising powers to reshape international law in its image, it diverges in its cautious navigation of existing structures, leveraging them to advance its influence without fundamentally rewriting the rules. This duality – challenging liberal norms while benefiting from the system's stability – represents a distinct feature of China's 'new model' of engagement with international law. In the following section, we will examine these 'new' theories and practices underpinning China's contemporary approach to international law in Xi Jinping's new era.

C. A Twenty-First-Century Rule Maker? China's 'New Model' of International Law in Xi Jinping's New Era

While China's dissatisfaction with aspects of international law is not new, its foreign policy was long guided by the cardinal doctrine articulated by former paramount leader Deng Xiaoping: 'hiding its capabilities and biding its time'.[114] Deng advised that China should 'keep moderate and prudent, not serve as others' leader or a standard bearer, and not seek expansion or hegemony'.[115] The rationale behind this strategy was that, as a relatively weak power, China needed a peaceful international political environment to facilitate its economic development. During this phase, China refrained from challenging US global leadership, aiming to avoid provoking fear about its growing power among other nations.[116]

[111] A Peters, 'Constitutional Theories of International Organisations: Beyond the West' (2021) 20 *Chinese Journal of International Law* 649, 690–91.

[112] C Cai, 'New Great Powers and International Law in the 21st Century' (2013) 24 *European Journal of International Law* 755, 788–90.

[113] E Pils, 'Autocratic Challenges to International Human Rights Law: A Chinese Case Study' (2022) 75 *Current Legal Problems* 189, 230–31.

[114] State Councillor Dai Bingguo, 'Adhere to the Path of Peaceful Development' (6 December 2010), www.china.org.cn/opinion/2010-12/13/content_21529346.htm.

[115] ibid.

[116] X Yan, 'From Keeping a Low Profile to Striving for Achievement' (2014) 7 *Chinese Journal of International Politics* 153, 155–57.

However, as China has grown wealthier and more powerful over the past decade, its foreign policy has moved beyond the restrained posture of this doctrine, aspiring to be respected as a global leader.[117] In particular, China has leveraged its increasing capabilities to safeguard more resolutely what the CCP defines as its 'core interests', which include national sovereignty, national security, territorial integrity, national reunification, the stability of China's political system, and overall social order.[118] This shift is evident in actions such as the declaration of an Air Defence Identification Zone in the East China Sea and the undertaking of more regularised patrols challenging Japanese sovereignty over the Diaoyu Islands.[119] In the South China Sea, China has advanced its contested sovereignty claims over land features and associated maritime rights by constructing artificial islands on reefs and low-tide elevations it controls in the Spratly Islands. When faced with an adverse ruling by the Permanent Court of Arbitration, China adhered to its position of 'Four Nos': no acceptance, no participation, no recognition and no implementation, dismissing the arbitral award as 'nothing more than a piece of waste paper'.[120]

In short, what has notably changed in Xi's new era is the Chinese leadership's increased self-confidence that conditions are now ripe for China not only to criticise and dissent within the existing international order, but also to proactively promote its own alternative vision of a global order, aiming to have its interpretations of international law recognised as legitimate and acceptable alongside liberal democratic interpretations.[121] President Xi has explicitly called for China to 'lead the reform of the global governance system', with the goal of transforming institutions and norms to better reflect Beijing's values and priorities.[122] Guided by this fundamental shift in foreign relations, China is advancing its vision of 'a new model of great power relations' and, arguably, a new model of international law.[123] This section delves into the core elements of this approach, analysing Xi's key policy instruments aimed at redefining and repurposing certain concepts of international law, scrutinising their normative effects and institutional influence on key international law principles such as human rights, development, security and democracy.

[117] J Chen Weiss, 'The China Trap: US Foreign Policy and the Perilous Logic of Zero-Sum Competition' (2022) 101(5) *Foreign Affairs* 40, 43; N-C Chang Liao, 'The Sources of China's Assertiveness: The System, Domestic Politics or Leadership Preferences?' (2016) 92 *International Affairs* 817, 817–18.

[118] A Goldstein, 'China's Grand Strategy under Xi Jinping: Reassurance, Reform, and Resistance' (2020) 45(1) *International Security* 164, 187–91; K Rudd, 'How Xi Jinping Views the World: The Core Interests that Shape China's Behaviour' *Foreign Affairs* (10 May 2018).

[119] R Denny, 'Assertive China: Irredentism or Expansionism' (2019) 61 *Survival* 51, 52–53.

[120] Y Fu, 'Why China Says No to the Arbitration on the South China Sea' *Foreign Policy* (10 July 2016).

[121] Pang (n 25) 238–40.

[122] Y Huang and J Kurlantzick, 'China's Approach to Global Governance' *The Diplomat* (25 June 2020).

[123] R Xiao, 'Modeling a "New Type of Great Power Relations": A Chinese Viewpoint' (*Open Forum*, 4 October 2013), https://theasanforum.org/modeling-a-new-type-of-great-power-relations-a-chinese-viewpoint/.

1. Normative Repurposing under a New Model of International Law

The Community of Shared Future for Mankind (CSFM) is a pivotal concept articulated by Xi, encapsulating Beijing's long-term ambition to transform the international environment to conform to China's governance model and its emergence as a global leader.[124] This concept plays a dual role in international law and global governance. On the one hand, it seeks to consolidate and affirm existing principles of international law by advocating for peace, development and cooperation based on mutual respect and equality among states.[125] By championing the CSFM, China positions itself as a proponent of a new type of international law that ostensibly values collective prosperity over hegemonic dominance.[126] On the other hand, the CSFM advances China's strategic interests by facilitating its rise as a global power and promoting a governance model consistent with its own system.[127] Thus, the CSFM subtly advocates for adjustments to the international legal framework that could legitimise and reinforce governance systems that are more authoritarian, diverging from liberal democratic models.[128]

For instance, under the CSFM discourse, China re-interprets and repurposes the 'right to development' as a prerequisite for other rights, often emphasising collective over individual rights.[129] The Chinese leadership highlights its contributions to international dialogues and legal instruments supporting the right to development, advocates in international forums for recognising development as a fundamental human right, and underscores the implications of prioritising state-led development for individual freedoms and rights.[130] This approach supports China's domestic policies and international aspirations, portraying 'peaceful development' as a means to enhance state sovereignty and national rejuvenation, while potentially conflicting with Western emphasis on individual rights.[131]

As a central pillar of Xi's norm entrepreneurship, the CSFM has been incorporated into some UN resolutions, demonstrating its capacity to influence

[124] L Tobin, 'Xi's Vision for Transforming Global Governance: A Strategic Challenge or Washington and its Allies' (2018) 2(1) *Texas National Security Review* 154, 165.

[125] Ahl (n 41) 113–14.

[126] HE Xi Jinping, President of the PRC, 'Working Together to Forge a New Partnership of Win-win Cooperation and Create a Community of Shared Future of Mankind', General Debate of the 70th Session of the UN General Assembly, 28 September 2015.

[127] Research Group on the Community of Shared Future for Mankind and International Law, 'Building a Community of Shared Future for Mankind via International Law' (2019) 3 *Wuhan University International Law Review* 1, 13.

[128] Ahl (n 41) 114.

[129] R Mitchell, 'The Emerging Chinese Model of Statist Human Rights' (2022) 37 *American University Law Review* 617, 648–49.

[130] X Wang, 'China's Theoretical Innovation and Practical Contribution to the Right to Development: In Commemoration of the 30th Anniversary of the United Nations' Declaration on the Right to Development' (2017) 16 *Journal of Human Rights* 5.

[131] R Dai, 'China and International Human Rights Law' in de la Rasilla and Cai (n 62) 261, 262–65.

international legal norms and standards.[132] By embedding this concept into UN resolutions, China aims to legitimise its vision on the global stage, thereby enhancing its soft power and international standing.[133] On top of outlining the concept of the CSFM, Xi has recently introduced a series of specific proposals aimed at reinforcing the normative influence of the CSFM and presenting an alternative model of global governance.[134] By proposing these initiatives, Xi claims to provide global public goods that emphasise multilateralism, security, cultural exchange and sustainable development.[135] Each initiative reflects a different aspect of Xi's vision for a new world order matching its broader ambition of fostering a CSFM, advocating for a multipolar world that contrasts with perceived Western hegemony.[136]

Through these global initiatives, China challenges the legitimacy of the traditional security alliances and the liberal conception of human rights. In particular, China redefines and reconfigures the UN human rights system as a source of legitimacy for its human rights proposals rather than merely an impediment to be circumvented.[137] For instance, the Chinese government prioritises the concept of 'universal acceptance' for human rights, which emphasises diplomatic consensus, over the principle that human rights are universal and inherent to all individuals.[138] It is well documented that China uses the Universal Periodic Review process at the UN Human Rights Council to present its human rights achievements and counter criticisms. These efforts often involve extensive reports highlighting progress in economic and social rights while downplaying or rejecting concerns related to civil and political rights.[139] China's strategic use of its diplomatic influence to garner support or neutrality from other countries during these reviews exemplifies its efforts to shape international human rights discourse and avoid censure.[140] Thus, China's active participation in – and sometimes manipulation of – international bodies, including the UN Human Rights

[132] UN Human Rights Council, Promoting Mutually Beneficial Cooperation in the Field of Human Rights, resolution adopted by the Human Rights Council on 23 March 2018, UN Doc A/HRC/RES/37/23, 6 April 2018; A Skordas, 'Authoritarian Global Governance? The Russian-Chinese Joint Statement of March 2022' (2021) 81 *Zeitschrift für ausländisches öffentliches Recht und Völkerrecht* 293, 299.

[133] R Mitchell, 'Was the UN Human Rights Council Wrong to Back China's "Shared Future" Resolution?' (10 April 2018), www.ejiltalk.org/was-the-un-human-rights-council-wrong-to-back-chinas-shared-future-resolution.

[134] Editorial, 'Global Civilization Initiative Outlines the Way to Transcend Estrangement, Clashes and Superiority' *China Daily* (16 March 2023).

[135] J Shi, 'The Belt and Road Initiative and International Law: An Analysis from the Perspective of the Supply of International Public Goods' (2021) 42 *Social Sciences in China* 156, 160–63.

[136] F Liao, 'Multilateralism and the International Rule of Law' (2023) 8 *Social Science China* 60, 70–71.

[137] Neagli (n 94) 503, 507.

[138] R Foot, 'Institutional Design and Rhetorical Spaces: China's Human Rights Strategies in a Changing World Order' (2024) 33 *Journal of Contemporary China* 1, 5.

[139] B Ahl, 'The Rise of China and International Human Rights Law' (2015) 37 *Human Rights Quarterly* 637, 648–55.

[140] DL Sloss, *Tyrants on Twitter: Protecting Democracies from Information Warfare* (Stanford: Stanford University Press 2022) 76–81.

Council, to prevent criticism of its human rights record is widely perceived as an attempt to solidify its role as a rule maker.[141]

2. Institution Building of a New Model of International Law

To realise this new model of international law, China has embarked on building its own set of regional and international institutions, such as the Asian Infrastructure Investment Bank (AIIB), the New Development Bank (NDB) and, most notably, the Belt and Road Initiative (BRI). While these new institutions and programs have granted China significant agenda-setting and convening power, they often diverge from the standards and values upheld by existing international institutions.[142]

Take the BRI as an example. Xi's signature initiative, the BRI, is the most visible means by which Beijing is executing his vision. Launched in 2013, the BRI, which encompasses a wide range of transnational projects, including railways, highways, oil and gas pipelines, and ports, seeks to connect Asia with Africa and Europe via land and maritime networks with the goal of improving regional integration, increasing trade and stimulating economic growth.[143] At the 19th CCP Congress in October 2017, the CCP amended its Constitution by adding mandates to pursue the BRI and build a CSFM, thereby elevating both the initiative and its underlying vision within the party's long-term strategy. This move not only cements these strategies but also signals China's normative commitment to reshaping the international order according to its vision.[144]

One frequent criticism of the BRI is that it provides alternative sources of finance to authoritarian regimes without the conditions often imposed by Western countries and international organisations, such as requirements for democratic reform, good governance and social responsibility. This 'no strings attached' approach has raised concerns about undermining global efforts to promote these values.[145] Moreover, the terms of China's BRI deals frequently lack transparency. Some infrastructure investments under the BRI are suspected of constituting 'debt-trap diplomacy', a strategy where recipient countries incur unsustainable debts for ambitious projects, allowing China to extract concessions that may compromise their sovereignty.[146] A particularly contentious aspect of the BRI is the 'Digital Silk

[141] Foot (n 138) 7–10.

[142] S Kondapalli, 'Regional Multilateralism with Chinese Characteristics' in D Shambaugh (ed), *China and the World* (Oxford: Oxford University Press, 2020) 313.

[143] Xinhua, 'The Belt and Road Initiative: A Key Pillar of the Global Community of Shared Future' (10 October 2023), www.scio.gov.cn/zfbps/zfbps_2279/202310/t20231010_773734.html.

[144] J Kynge, 'China's Blueprint for an Alternative World Order' *Financial Times* (22 August 2023).

[145] Yuan et al (n 97) 24.

[146] M Bennon and F Fukuyama, 'The Obsolescing Bargain Crosses the Belt and Road Initiative: Renegotiations on BRI Projects' (2022) 38 *Oxford Review of Economic Policy* 278, 283. But this allegation has been widely dismissed as a 'myth'. See L Jones and S Hameiri, *Debunking the Myth of 'Debt Trap Diplomacy': How Recipient Countries Shape China's Belt and Road Initiative* (London: Chatham House, 2020) 28.

Road' initiative, which extends beyond traditional infrastructure development to include the export of surveillance and censorship technologies.[147] This practice has resulted in a significant backlash, with critics arguing that it risks spreading China's authoritarian governance model under the guise of development aid.[148]

3. Constitutional Amendment by a New Model of International Law?

Although there is no explicit international constitutional law, certain principles such as the protection of human rights, democracy and the rule of law are widely regarded as fundamental cornerstones of international law. For instance, democratic principles like transparency, accountability and public participation in decision-making processes are endorsed in various international treaties and declarations supporting human rights and fundamental freedoms.[149] As a result, even within its one-party autocracy framework, the Chinese party-state cannot entirely silence global discussions about the merits of democracy.[150]

Nevertheless, China's official narrative on democracy has evolved under Xi Jinping, drawing from his assertion that 'consultation is an important form of democracy, and it should also become an important means of exercising international governance'.[151] In this top-down narrative, China defines its 'democratic system' around three Cs – consultation, cooperation and consensus – which contrasts sharply with what it characterises as the 'three different Cs' of Western-style democracy: competition, confrontation and conflict.[152]

Under Xi's new model of international law, the CCP has advanced the concept of 'Whole-Process People's Democracy', further developing its Marxist-Leninist discourse on governance.[153] This model emphasises citizen involvement in political processes beyond 'empty electoral' participation, encouraging engagement in policy discussions, feedback mechanisms and social governance.[154] It underscores the importance of 'feedback' mechanisms, where public opinion can influence

[147] A Bradford, *Digital Empires: The Global Battle to Regulate Technology* (Oxford: Oxford University Press, 2023) 294–313.

[148] ibid 313–23.

[149] TM Franck, 'The Emerging Right to Democratic Governance' (1992) 86 *American Journal of International Law* 46. For a most recent account, see T Ginsburg, *Abusive Internationalism? On Democracies and International Law* (Cambridge: Cambridge University Press, 2021) 20–26.

[150] H Holbig and G Schucher, '"He Who Says C Must Say D": China's Attempt to Become the World's Largest Democracy' (2016) 2 *GIGA Focus Asia* 5, www.giga-hamburg.de/en/publications/giga-focus/he-d-china-s-attempt-world-s-largest-democracy.

[151] Tobin (n 124) 157.

[152] 'China's Two Sessions Clear Reflection of System Designed to Achieve Consultation, Cooperation and Consensus' *Global Times* (9 March 2024), www.globaltimes.cn/page/202403/1308510.shtml.

[153] The Ministry of Foreign Affairs of the PRC, 'China's Whole-Process People's Democracy Revolutionizes Understandings on Democracy' (17 May 2022), www.mfa.gov.cn/eng/topics_665678/ddzggcd/qgcrmmz/202208/t20220801_10731231.html.

[154] ibid.

policy adjustments and reforms, ostensibly ensuring that governance reflects the 'interests of all Chinese citizens'.[155] It allegedly merges the leadership of the CCP with mechanisms for public consultation and input, suggesting that the Party's leadership and the people's democratic participation are not mutually exclusive but complementary.[156]

In essence, the differences between China's perspective on democracy and Western views within the context of international law are rooted in the conceptual foundations and practical implications of their respective constitutional systems. Liberal democracies prioritise competitive elections, the protection of individual rights, and systems of checks and balances to prevent the concentration of power and ensure government accountability as their 'minimum core' principles.[157] In contrast, China's socialist narrative emphasises collective 'harmony' and state-guided 'consensus', arguing that these elements lead to stable governance and societal progress.[158] This contrast illuminates the fundamental divergence in their constitutions prescribing legitimacy, good governance and the role of the individual vis-a-vis the collective in political life.[159] Consequently, the 'Whole-Process People's Democracy' can have nuanced impacts on democracy, one of the existing 'constitutional' principles in international law, reflecting China's growing influence and its alternative governance model.

D. The Prospects of China's 'New Model' of International Law

China's assertive foreign policy has prompted extensive speculation about its ultimate objectives. One view suggests that China's actions are primarily defensive, aimed at creating a global environment that secures the CCP's rule and facilitates co-existence between authoritarian states and democracies.[160] An opposing view contends that China is pursuing a grand strategy to reshape the international order in its authoritarian image and displace the US as the dominant power at both the

[155] RL Kuhn, 'Human Rights and Whole-Process People's Democracy' *Xinhua* (20 June 2023), https://english.news.cn/2023062<0/c9b0d7dec7d94b19bb2634790ea9948a/c.html.

[156] The State Council of the PRC, 'A Deep Dive into Xi Jinping's Stewardship of Whole-Process People's Democracy' (3 March 2024), https://english.www.gov.cn/news/202403/03/content_WS65e47e91c6d0868f4e8e494c.html.

[157] R Dixon and D Landau, 'Competitive Democracy and the Constitutional Minimum Core' in T Ginsburg and A Huq (eds), *Assessing Constitutional Performance* (Cambridge: Cambridge University Press, 2016) 268.

[158] Xinhua, 'China: Democracy That Works' (4 December 2021), www.news.cn/english/2021-12/04/c_1310351231.htm.

[159] Holbig and Schucher (n 150) 5–8.

[160] J Chen Weiss, 'A World Safer for Autocracy?' (2019) 98(4) *Foreign Affairs* 92, 93–94; TJ Christensen, *No New Cold War: Why US–China Strategic Competition Will Not Be Like the US–Soviet Cold War* (Seoul: Asian Institute for Policy Studies, 2020) 11–16.

regional and global levels.[161] Other observers, disillusioned with American and European international law, even look to China's international law strategy as a dreamland on the opposite shore.[162]

We argue that China's ambition is best encapsulated by the term 'China Dream', as proposed by Xi Jinping. This discourse is built upon three foundational goals. First, it seeks to ensure national security and consolidate the leadership of the CCP. Second, it aims to achieve 'great national rejuvenation', encompassing economic growth, technological progress, military modernisation and cultural influence to restore China's historical prominence as a major global power.[163] Anchored in Marxist materialism and economic determinism, Chinese leadership believes that the international order will naturally evolve in China's favour as its economic power grows, obviating the need for direct confrontation.[164] Third, it seeks to enhance China's global influence, advocating for a multipolar world in which China plays a pivotal role in global governance, norms and values.[165] The message underpinning the 'China Dream' positions it as an alternative governance model, no less legitimate – if not superior – to the 'American Dream'. This narrative has the potential to erode conventional faith in liberal democracy and empower illiberal actors seeking economic success without adhering to the constraints of democratic societies.

Despite China's autocratic domestic rule, there is limited evidence to suggest that it is instituting new authoritarian norms within international law or significantly altering its foundational principles.[166] Instead, China selectively utilises international law to justify its actions, particularly in response to criticism over its repressive measures. This calculated approach fosters what has been described as a 'synergic corrosive effect' on the development of international law.[167] Operating within a dualistic scenario where legal norms and lawlessness co-exist, China avoids overhauling the international legal framework, opting instead to employ systematic lawlessness to reinforce state power where it deems fit.[168] Clearly, the notion that 'globalisation of law leads not to legal unity but fragmentation'

[161] R Doshi, *The Long Game: China's Grand Strategy to Displace American Order* (Oxford: Oxford University Press, 2021) 5–6; M Pillsbury, *The Hundred-Year Marathon: China's Secret Strategy to Replace America as the Global Superpower* (New York: Henry Holt and Company, 2015); D Tobin, 'How Xi Jinping's "New Era" Should Have Ended US Debate on Beijing's Ambitions' (CSIS Report, 2020) 3–7.

[162] See Mattei and Singh (n 82) 225–32.

[163] 'Full Text of Xi Jinping's Report at 19th CPC National Congress' *China Daily* (4 November 2017), www.chinadaily.com.cn/china/19thcpcnationalcongress/2017-11/04/content_34115212.htm.

[164] J Li, 'The Evolving Rule of Law with Chinese Characteristics and its Impacts on the International Legal Order' (2023) 8 *UC Irvine Journal of International, Transnational, and Comparative Law* 151, 170.

[165] J deLisle, 'The Chinese Model of Law, China's Agenda in International Law, and Implications for Democracy in Asia and beyond' *The Asian Forum* (24 October 2018), https://theasanforum.org/the-chinese-model-of-law-chinas-agenda-in-international-law-and-implications-for-democracy-in-asia-and-beyond/.

[166] Pils (n 113) 228–29.

[167] ibid 220–24.

[168] ibid 230–31.

is prominent in China's strategic development of international law, sometimes paradoxically viewed as strengthening the efficacy and legitimacy of international law.[169]

For instance, China's evolving approach to international governance demonstrates its ambition to establish a 'new model' that appeals to those prioritising innovation and sustainable development. This model seeks to address global challenges such as resource depletion and environmental degradation by transitioning from a manufacturing-based economy to one driven by human capital, technological advancement and green initiatives.[170] Unlike the US-dominated framework, which often prioritises intellectual property monopolies, China's approach emphasises inclusive innovation diffusion, particularly in life-saving and adaptive technologies. This is evident in its strategies for scaling renewable energy and addressing climate change.[171]

China's global governance initiatives, particularly within the climate change domain, demonstrate its increasing influence over international regulatory frameworks. As highlighted in the 'Green Investment Principles for the Belt and Road', endorsed by major global financial institutions, China is leveraging its BRI to create a vast market of three billion people for low-carbon technologies, offering unparalleled opportunities for scaling and innovation in clean energy solutions.[172] Additionally, partnerships with entities such as the EU on emissions trading schemes demonstrate China's efforts to align its initiatives with global climate governance strategies, solidifying its role as a pivotal player in the transition to a sustainable energy future.[173] By challenging dominant economic paradigms, China positions itself as both a global competitor and a potential leader in addressing systemic ecological and economic crises.[174]

Regardless of the perspective, China perceives the US as an adversary and the greatest external threat to its national security, sovereignty and internal stability.[175] Chinese leaders are convinced that the US is determined to isolate, Westernise and fragment China, weaken the CCP's grip on power and prevent China from attaining great power status, much as it once sought to contain and ultimately dismantle the Soviet Union.[176] With its new model of international law, China seeks global legitimacy for its authoritarian governance model, asserting that its model of development is 'blazing a new trail for other developing countries to achieve

[169] See Husa, ch 13 in this volume, 313–14, 323.

[170] P Drahos, *Survival Governance: Energy and Climate in the Chinese Century* (Oxford: Oxford University Press, 2021) 117.

[171] ibid 119.

[172] ibid 46.

[173] ibid 42.

[174] ibid 120.

[175] C Xia, 'China-US Relations in the Eyes of the Chinese Communist Party: An Insider's Perspective', Hoover Institution CGSP Occasional Paper Series No 1, 2021, 20–22.

[176] J Wang, 'The Plot against China? How Beijing Sees the New Washington Consensus' (2021) 100(4) *Foreign Affairs* 48, 54–55.

modernisation' and offering 'a new option for other countries and nations who want to speed up their development while preserving their independence'.[177] Even if Beijing does not seek global hegemony, the eradication of liberal democracy or the destruction of capitalism as the Soviet Union did, it aims to maximise its wealth, power, influence and legitimacy, and to establish a global order that is more coercive, illiberal, more hostile to liberal democratic values and less US-centric.[178]

We conceptualise China's approach to international law as its assertions about the globalisation of legal principles it views as correct or just. In other words, since any 'global' legal approach implicitly excludes competing claims, such assertions constitute part of 'global law' – albeit a hegemonic, fluid extension and reaction to traditional international law, which effectively creates an 'international law+' formula.[179] Consequently, we argue that China's international law claims transcend the 'authoritarian international law' concept, extending beyond previous comparative law perspectives on international law. Ultimately, it may not matter what China's precise endgame is: the strategic competition between the US and China presents a more complex and challenging struggle than the Cold War of the late twentieth century.[180]

E. Conclusion

China's approach to international law has often been described as 'a return to Westphalia', emphasising principles of mutual non-interference, sovereignty and the formal equality of states.[181] Sovereignty, in particular, remains central to many of China's practices on the global stage. Additionally, China exhibits a flexible and functional approach to international law, treating it as an instrument to advance national interests. This fundamentally realist approach allows China to benefit from and exploit the international legal order without necessitating fundamental changes to the letter of the law in most areas.

China's perception of the current international order as unreasonable and unfair has driven its growing efforts to shape legal norms across various domains of international relations. These efforts have intensified in Xi Jinping's new era,

[177] J Xi, 'Secure a Decisive Victory in Building a Moderately Prosperous Society in All Respects and Strive for the Great Success of Socialism with Chinese Characteristics for a New Era' (delivered at the 19th National Congress of the Communist Party of China, 18 October 2017), www.xinhuanet.com/english/download/Xi_Jinping's_report_at_19th_CPC_National_Congress.pdf.

[178] Tobin (n 161) 316–18.

[179] Husa (n 169) 10–12.

[180] T Harshaw, 'China's Challenge to the US is So Much More Than Cold War II' *Bloomberg* (19 February 2022), www.bloomberg.com/opinion/articles/2022-02-19/china-challenge-to-u-s-is-more-than-cold-war-2; C Edel and DO Shullman, 'How China Exports Authoritarianism: Beijing's Money and Technology is Fueling Repression Worldwide' *Foreign Affairs* (16 September 2021), www.foreignaffairs.com/articles/china/2021-09-16/how-china-exports-authoritarianism.

[181] T Ginsburg, 'Eastphalia as a Perfection of Westphalia' (2010) 27 *Indiana Journal of Global Legal Studies* 27, 45.

reflecting China's aspiration to correct or reform perceived inequities within the existing system. In this chapter, we have critically examined how China's foreign policies under Xi Jinping have influenced its interactions with international legal norms and practices, particularly in relation to principles such as state sovereignty and human rights. By analysing China's recent initiatives that contribute to its 'new model' of international law, we have evaluated their potential normative, institutional and constitutional impacts on the foundational principles of international law.

While China demonstrates considerable ambition in shaping international law, caution is warranted regarding the potential for undermining these foundational principles. Despite China's apparent disregard for the erosion of certain essential components, it has stopped short of pursuing a wholesale transformation of international law. Understanding this dynamic is essential for comprehending China's evolving role as a significant yet controversial actor on the international stage. As China continues to challenge conventional perceptions, its approach has the potential to reshape the legal and diplomatic landscape, posing both opportunities and significant challenges for the existing international order.

6

'European' International Law

Nineteenth-Century Exceptionalism and Universalism

MAX H MAYER*

A. Introduction

For a long time, the European tradition of international law used to see itself as *the tradition* of international law.[1] It was conscious of the fact that what later expanded

* I would like to thank Jochen von Bernstorff for the extensive discussions while developing this chapter, and both Jochen and the editors for their valuable comments on earlier version of it. Any mistakes remain my own.

[1] *cf* A Becker Lorca, 'Eurocentrism in the History of International Law' in B Fassbender and A Peters (eds) *The Oxford Handbook of the History of International Law* (Oxford: Oxford University Press, 2012) 1034, 1040–42. From the voluminous literature on international legal history and Eurocentrism, see especially N Tzouvala, 'The Specter of Eurocentrism in International Legal History' (2020) 31 *Yale Journal of Law & the Humanities* 413, but also J T Gathii, 'International Law and Eurocentricity' (1998) 9 *European Journal of International Law* 184; Y Onuma, 'When was the Law of International Society Born? An Inquiry of the History of International Law from an Intercivilizational Perspective' (2000) 2 *Journal of the History of International Law* 1; M Koskenniemi, 'International Law in Europe: Between Tradition and Renewal' (2005) 16 *European Journal of International Law* 113; M Koskenniemi, 'Histories of International law: Dealing with Eurocentrism' (2011) 2011 *Rechtsgeschichte – Legal History* 152; B Fassbender and A Peters, 'Introduction: Towards a Global History of International Law' in B Fassbender and A Peters (eds) *The Oxford Handbook of the History of International Law* (Oxford: Oxford University Press, 2012) 1; A-C Martineau, 'Overcoming Eurocentrism? Global History and the Oxford Handbook of the History of International Law' (2014) 25 *European Journal of International Law* 329; M Craven, 'Theorizing the Turn to History in International Law' in A Orford, F Hoffmann and M Clark (eds), *The Oxford Handbook of the Theory of International Law* (Oxford: Oxford University Press, 2016) 21; A Anghie, 'Europe and International Law: Colonial Legacies' in A van Aaken et al (eds), *The Oxford Handbook of International Law in Europe* (Oxford: Oxford University Press, 2023) 34; MM Mbengue and OD Akinkugbe, 'The Criticism of Eurocentrism and International Law: Countering and Pluralizing the Research, Teaching, and Practice of Eurocentric International Law' in A van Aaken et al (eds), *The Oxford Handbook of International Law in Europe* (Oxford: Oxford University Press, 2023) 225; J von Bernstorff and M Mayer, 'The Historical School and German International Legal Thought in the 19th Century' (2023) 25 *Journal of the History of International Law* 311. On contemporary approaches to international law from Europe, see the contributions in P Hilpold (ed), *European International Law Traditions* (Cham: Springer, 2021) and in A van Aaken et al (eds), *The Oxford Handbook of International Law in Europe* (Oxford: Oxford University Press, 2023, contributions published online on a rolling basis).

into a universal international legal order, through the independence of almost all former colonies in Africa and Asia, had taken its historical origins in an international legal order that had developed in Europe after the Peace of Westphalia of 1648. With this perspective, it saw its intellectual origins as tracing back to European antiquity, especially to ancient Rome.[2] International law, it knew, was a European invention, crafted in the course of European history until the end of the nineteenth century by a series of European, mostly Protestant authors, from its shared intellectual heritage.[3] In the eighth edition of his treatise on international law, published posthumously in 1955 by Hersch Lauterpacht, the German-British international lawyer Lassa Oppenheim expressed this perspective as follows:

> The modern Law of Nations is a product of Christian civilisation. It originally arose between the States of Christendom only, and for hundreds of years was confined to these States. Between Christian and Mohammedan nations a condition of perpetual enmity prevailed in former centuries. And no constant intercourse existed in former times between Christian and Buddhistic States. From about the beginning of the nineteenth century matters gradually changed. Many interests which knit Christian States together, knit likewise some non-Christian and Christian States. Positive International Law no longer recognises any distinctions in the membership of the community of nations based on religious or cultural differences.[4]

This European legacy of international law has, since the decolonisation after the Second World War, become a contested field. The influence of colonialism on its concepts are weighed, the contributions of non-European societies to its thought pointed out, and its relationship to the emergence and globalisation of capitalism discussed by scholars worldwide.[5] As many have pointed out, non-European

[2] See, eg, RP Ward, *An Enquiry into the Foundation and History of the Law of Nations in Europe, From the Time of the Greeks and Romans, to the Age of Grotius*, vol 1 (London: J Butterworth, 1795); H Wheaton, *History of the Law of Nations: From the Earlyest Times to the Treaty of Washington, 1842* (Leatherhead: Gould Banks, 1845); R Lesaffer, 'Roman Law and the Intellectual History of International Law' in Orford, Hoffmann and Clark (n 1) 38. For English-language discourses, see J Pitts, *Boundaries of the International: Law and Empire* (Cambridge, MA: Harvard University Press, 2018) 158–59.

[3] Paradigmatically, see HS Maine, *International Law: A Series of Lectures Delivered before the University of Cambridge, 1887* (London: John Murray 1888) 16; L Oppenheim, *International Law: A Treatise*, vol 1: *Peace*, ed H Lauterpacht, 8th edn (London: Longmans, Green 1955) §§ 43–50; more recently, see also MN Shaw, *International Law*, 6th edn (Cambridge: Cambridge University Press, 2008) 22–42.

[4] Oppenheim (n 3) 48.

[5] From the vast literature, see, eg, GM Abi-Saab, 'The Newly Independent States and the Rules of International Law' (1962) 8 *Howard Law Journal* 95; RP Anand, *New States and International Law* (Delhi: Vikas Publishing House, 1972); M Bedjaoui, *Towards a New International Economic Order* (Paris: UNESCO; New York: Holmes & Meier, 1979); J Fisch, *Die europäische Expansion und das Völkerrecht: Die Auseinandersetzungen um den Status der überseeischen Gebiete vom 15. Jahrhundert bis zur Gegenwart* (Stuttgart: Steiner, 1984); A Anghie, *Imperialism, Sovereignty and the Making of International Law* (Cambridge: Cambridge University Press, 2005); M Koskenniemi, *The Gentle Civilizer of Nations: The Rise and Fall of Modern International Law 1870–1960* (Cambridge: Cambridge University Press, 2002); M Koskenniemi, *To the Uttermost Parts of the Earth: Legal Imagination and International Power, 1300–1870* (Cambridge: Cambridge University Press, 2021); N Tzouvala, *Capitalism as Civilisation: A History of International Law* (Cambridge: Cambridge University Press, 2020).

societies have been living under the impact and rule of European international law for a much longer time than has been suggested by the narrative of an 'accession' of non-Europeans from the peace treaty with the Ottoman Empire in 1856 until the decolonisation of Africa, Asia and Oceania after the Second World War.[6] And, accordingly, the domination of non-European peoples has itself had a profound impact on the development of the foundational concepts of European international law, including sovereignty, territory and the protection of foreign property, having made colonialism and the 'dynamic of difference' a central characteristic of the European tradition of international law.[7]

The present chapter will discuss how European lawyers during the nineteenth century reflected on the tension between the European identity of their field and the universalist aspirations they held for it within the frameworks of their legal theories of natural law and legal positivism.

This question has been the subject of some debate before. During the 1960s, Charles H Alexandrowicz had argued that it had been the methodological transition from natural law theory to legal positivism that had prompted European international lawyers to reduce the law of nations to a regional legal order in the course of the nineteenth century.[8] While the law of nations had under natural law theory formed a global and universal legal order that regulated a vibrant exchange between European and non-European nations, the law of nations became regionalised into a European legal order in which non-Europeans had lost legal personality. Against Alexandrowicz, Wilhelm Grewe then argued in 1984 that Europeans had always understood the law of nations as applicable only to European nations, especially since the colonial conquest of the American

[6] See, eg, Anghie (n 5) 34.

[7] ibid 4–8, 243–44. On the interrelationship of colonialism and idealist philosophy, see, eg, S Buck-Morss, *Hegel, Haiti and Universal History* (Pittsburgh, PA: University of Pittsburgh Press, 2009) 21–76.

[8] CH Alexandrowicz, 'Doctrinal Aspects of the Universality of the Law of Nations' in D Armitage and J Pitts (eds), *The Law of Nations in Global History* (Oxford: Oxford University Press, 2017) 168; CH Alexandrowicz, *An Introduction to the History of the Law of Nations in the East Indies* (Oxford: Clarendon Press, 1967); CH Alexandrowicz, 'The Afro-Asian World and the Law of Nations (Historical Aspects)' (1968/I) 123 *Recueil des Cours* 117; CH Alexandrowicz, *The European-African Confrontation: A Study in Treaty Making* (Amsterdam: Sijthoff, 1973) 117–25. A similar argument has been made by A Orakhelashvili, 'The Idea of European International Law' (2006) 17 *European Journal of International Law* 315, 325 et seq, who, however, draws the inverse conclusion that positivism played no role in the construction of racist concepts of international law in the nineteenth century and that these categories were all created with reference to extra-positive factors and to what the authors of the time considered as the nature of things. For more extensive critical discussions of Alexandrowicz's positions, see W Grewe, 'Vom europäischen zum universellen Völkerrecht: Zur Frage der Revision des "europazentrischen" Bildes der Völkerrechtsgeschichte' (1982) 42 *Zeitschrift für ausländisches öffentliches Recht und Völkerrecht* 449; D Armitage and J Pitts, '"This Modern Grotius"' in D Armitage and J Pitts (eds), *The Law of Nations in Global History* (Oxford: Oxford University Press, 2017) 1, 17–30; Pitts (n 2) 16–17; M Craven, 'The Time of Revolution: Decolonisation, Heterodox International Legal Historiography and the Problem of the Contemporary' in S Chalmers and S Pahuja (eds), *Routledge Handbook of International Law and the Humanities* (Abingdon: Routledge, 2021) 242–45. Alexandrowicz's thesis was then adopted by Anand (n 5) 71 and passim; Bedjaoui (n 5) 11–16; Anghie (n 5) 40–64, with a brief explicit reference to Alexandrowicz's thesis at 43.

continent since the fifteenth and sixteenth centuries, and that this European law of nations became universalised, not restricted, during the second imperial expansion of Europe of the nineteenth century.[9] Both views then later became refuted by Yasuaki Onuma. Onuma pointed out that while the early modern law of nations of the sixteenth, seventeenth and eighteenth centuries may have been conceptualised in a universalist fashion as representing a worldwide natural legal order, it was only seen so by the Europeans themselves while in fact existing in parallel to other regional orders that also described themselves in universalist terms, namely the Sino-centric system in East Asia and the Islamic system of international relations.[10] This is an important point. What both Alexandrowicz and Grewe neglected is the difference between universalism and actual universality. While the Europeans in those period thus did use their language of natural law to describe treaty relationships with non-European societies, those societies often used their own rationales to account for those same relations in very different terms, which in some instances even implied the subordination of the respective European party. The pertinent question is therefore not whether the law of nations went from a universal to a regional legal order at the break of the nineteenth century, but rather how the European dynamic between universalism and European exceptionalism changed during the course of the shift from natural law theories to positivism.

As I would like to argue, the positivists of the nineteenth century retained a strong universalism in their theories by transforming the general concept of law from a perspective of historicism and idealism.[11] It was this transition that was crucial for maintaining both universalism as well as European exceptionalism within a European theory of international law. What legal positivism provided in the nineteenth century by adopting the legal philosophy of the German Historical School of Law and Hegel's teleological philosophy of history was not a rejection of universalism, but rather a new understanding of it, which allowed it to link European exceptionalism directly with the very concept of law. It was in this way that the historicist legal positivism that developed in the nineteenth century with the Historical School of Law conceptualised non-European societies as outside of the law of nations, which it now understood as a particular historical development

[9] Grewe (n 8); GW Gong, *The Standard of 'Civilization' in International Society* (Oxford: Clarendon Press, 1984) 4, also contradicted Alexandrowicz's thesis that the law of nations had been a universal legal order since early modernity.

[10] Onuma (n 1); see also P Starski and JA Kämmerer, 'Imperial Colonialism in the Genesis of International Law: Anomaly or Time of Transition?' (2017) 19 *Journal of the History of International Law* 50, 57–58. D Schindler, 'Universelles und regionales Völkerrecht' in *Recht als Prozeß und Gefüge: Festschrift für Hans Huber zum 80. Geburtstag* (Bern: Stämpfli, 1981) 610 also highlights that the European system of natural law was actually practised only by Europeans.

[11] On historicism and European discourses on international law of the nineteenth century, see also Craven (n 1); Pitts (n 2) 148–84; R Schütze, 'From Utopia to Apologia: International Normativity in the Long Nineteenth Century' (PhD thesis, LSE, 2019) 41–78, 151–55; L Nuzzo, *Lawyers, Space and Subjects: Historical Perspectives on the Western Legal Tradition* (Lecce: Pensa MultiMedia, 2020) 38–53.

of the European nations, but simultaneously re-integrated non-European nations into the realm of the European law of nations through the philosophy of history by projecting the historical development of the European law of nations onto the future of the non-European societies. This transition from a concept of positive law dependent on natural law to a thick historicist theory of law combined with a teleological philosophy of history was complete in the person of the Swiss Professor Johann Caspar Bluntschli, while the European legal order became factually globalised through the European imperial expansion during the course of the nineteenth century.

I will outline this transition from the universalism of natural law to the universalism of historicist positivism in European international law through a study of German international legal positivism between the middle of the eighteenth century and the middle of the nineteenth century. In a first step, I will describe the transition from natural law theory to a historicist legal positivism in the theory of international law and the ensuing restriction of the formerly universalist law of nations to Europe and North America. This transition, which formed part of the reactionary backlash against the French Revolution and its Enlightenment philosophy, is complete with the Prussian professor Karl Kaltenborn (1817–1866) (see section B). In a second step, I will illustrate the combination of this historicist positivism with Hegelian *Philosophy of History* by Bluntschli from the 1860s that turned international law into the theory of an expanding empire of liberal statehood (see section C). The conclusion (section E) will summarise the findings and give a brief outlook on the further development of legal positivism.

B. Early Positivism During the Late Eighteenth and Early Nineteenth Centuries

Until the early nineteenth century, the social philosophy that provided the essential conceptual framework for both domestic law and the law of nations was the philosophy of natural law, a tradition that had reached its first peak under the Thomist-Aristotelian Spanish Scholastic around the School of Salamanca during the colonial conquest of the American continent, but then underwent a reformulation by mostly Protestant authors following the Reformation and the Thirty Years' War.[12] With respect to the law of nations, this tradition is most eminently

[12] WG Grewe, *The Epochs of International Law* (Berlin: De Gruyter, 2013) 83–92, 187–96, 349–59; A Brett, 'Sources in the Scholastic Legacy: The (Re)Construction of the Ius Gentium in the Second Scholastic' in S Besson and J D'Aspremont (eds), *The Oxford Handbook on the Sources of International Law* (Oxford: Oxford University Press, 2017) 64–82, and in that same volume, M Koskenniemi, 'Transformations of Natural Law: Germany 1648–1815', 59–81; R Lesaffer, 'The Classical Law of Nations

represented by Hugo Grotius, Gentili, Thomas Hobbes, Samuel von Pufendorf, Christian Wolff and Emerich de Vattel. Methodologically, it sought to determine a system of general concepts of a natural law that were considered universally applicable because they were seen as deriving from a general description of human nature per se. In this line of thought, the law of nations was generally constructed as an analogy to a natural law of individual human beings. First, these works derived the essential forms of law (especially property, contracts, legal societies and self-defence) from an abstract and universalist depiction of human nature as isolated beings. They then transposed these basic categories to the relations of nations, which they understood as moral persons that had emerged from the contractual union of their citizens.[13] These nations could thus engage in legal obligations through treaties that were either entered into explicitly or tacitly through customs, and this framework was considered the appropriate description of any human political society.[14] In this framework, the legal force of international treaties rested on the natural law norm 'pacta sunt servanda'.[15]

Opposition against this deductive methodology in the field of the law of nations had already formed from the 1750s onwards, particularly in Germany.[16] Here, the pragmatically oriented scholars and officials Johann Jakob Moser (1701–85), Dietrich Heinrich Ludwig von Ompteda (1746–1803), Karl Gottlob Günther (1794–1832) and Georg Friedrich von Martens (1756–1821) were unhappy with the abstraction of the treatises on what was then called *Droit Public de l'Europe.*

(1500–1800)' in A Orakhelashvili (ed), *Research Handbook on the Theory and History of International Law* (Cheltenham: Edward Elgar, 2011) 424.

[13] T Hobbes, 'De Cive' (1642) in D Baumgold (ed), *Three-Text Edition of Thomas Hobbes's Political Theory: The Elements of Law, De Cive, and Leviathan* (Cambridge: Cambridge University Press, 2017) 2.14.4; paradigmatically, see S von Pufendorf, *De Jure Naturae et Gentium Libri Octo*, vol 2, trs CH Oldfather and WA Oldfather, ed JB Scott, first published 1660 (Oxford: Clarendon Press, 1934) 2.3; G Achenwall and JS Pütter, *Anfangsgründe des Naturrechts (Elementa iuris naturae)*, ed and trans J Schröder (first published 1750; Leipzig: Insel-Verl, 1995); C Wolff, *Jus Gentium Methodo Scientifica Pertractatum*, translation of the 1764 1st edn JH Drake (first published 1749; Oxford: Clarendon Press, 1934); E de Vattel, *Le Droit des Gens: ou principes de la loi naturelle, appliquée à la conduite et aux affaires des nations et des souverains* (Nouvelle édition augmentée, 1758); later also I Kant, *Die Metaphysik der Sitten*, ed H Ebeling (Ditzingen: Reclam, 1990); see also M Koskenniemi, 'Into Positivism: Georg Friedrich von Martens (1756–1821) and Modern International Law' (2008) 15 *Constellations* 189, 191–93. This contraposition of a positivist stream focused on the collection and assessment of historical material is also true for the field of German public law (*Reichspublizistik*) of the time; see M Stolleis, *Geschichte des öffentlichen Rechts in Deutschland*, vol 1 (Munich: CH Beck, 1988–2012) 268.

[14] There were of course many variations concerning both the substance of the general natural law and its enforceability in the temporal world – and not just in the 'court of conscience' – as well as with regard to the possibility of a positive law of nations next to the general law of nations.

[15] Von Pufendorf (n 13) 2.3.23.

[16] At the time, the German discipline of public law could already look back on a fairly long tradition of legal positivism dedicated to the reconstruction of public law from the history of the German states; see M Stolleis, *Geschichte des öffentlichen Rechts in Deutschland*, vol 1 (Munich: CH Beck, 1988–2012) 230–33; M Stolleis, 'Die Historische Schule und das öffentliche Recht' in M Stolleis (ed) *Die Bedeutung der Wörter: Studien zur europäischen Rechtsgeschichte* (Munich: Beck, 1991) 496–98.

Their criticism had two dimensions. Substantially, treatises on natural law failed to account for what they saw as European positive law of nations that had formed in Europe over the past century based on a shared cultural heritage and as a result of an increasingly refined system and practice of diplomacy within the continent.[17] These rules constituted the 'actual European law of nations' and needed to be accounted for in treatises on the law of nations, rather than the abstract rules of natural law which in their eyes had become virtually irrelevant in Europe.[18] To do so, according to their second criticism, required a different methodology: rather than following the 'theoretical' sciences in drawing conclusions from established principles and applying them to the facts, the study of the law of nations should work inductively in accordance with the 'empirical' sciences and determine the actually existing legal principles from the study of European international relations, without passing normative judgement on the material.[19] By abstracting from the principles observed in practice, Moser, Martens, Günther and Ompteda hoped to reconstruct a European positive law of nations by conceiving of European diplomatic and treaty practice as a regional system of positive law that had formed as a derogation from a universal natural law of nations.[20] Even though they insisted

[17] JJ Moser, *Versuch des neuesten Europäischen Völker-Rechts in Friedens und Kriegs-Zeiten: Vornehmlich aus denen Staatshandlungen derer Europäischen Mächten*, vol 1 (Frankfurt am Main: Varrentrapp u. Wenner, 1777–1780) §§ 1–2; GF von Martens, *Versuch über die Existenz eines positiven Europäischen Völkerrechts und den Nutzen dieser Wissenschaft* (Göttingen: Dieterich, 1787) 11–13; GF von Martens, *Précis du droit des gens moderne de l'Europe fondé sur les traités et l'usage*, vol 1 (Göttingen: Dieterich, 1789) § 8; DHL von Ompteda, *Litteratur des gesammten natürlichen und positiven Völkerrechts*, vol 1 (Regensburg: Montag,1785) § 12.

[18] JJ Moser, *Grundsätze des Völkerrechts* (first published 1777; Frankfurt am Main: Klostermann, 1959) 7 (own translation). On Moser's approach, see A Verdross, 'J. J. Mosers Programm einer Völkerrechtswissenschaft der Erfahrung' (1922) III *Niemeyer's Zeitschrift für internationales Recht* 96; R Rürup, *Johann Jacob Moser: Pietismus und Reform* (Wiesbaden: Steiner, 1965) 97–105; Koskenniemi (n 13).

[19] Moser (n 17), Vorläufige Abhandlung, § 6. In England, Ward (n 2) 57–69 argued in a similar vein that moral philosophy should take its methodological approach from Newton's experimental physics through the study of the history of humankind to confirm and overhaul the moral laws of nature inductively as they appeared from what we would today call sociological study. Such study, Ward was convinced, revealed that the moral laws of nature as Christians understood them were in fact not universal but subject to different premises about the factual world, and thus to an epistemological problematic. On Ward, see Pitts (n 2) 124–29.

[20] KG Günther, *Grundriß eines europäischen Völkerrechts nach Vernunft, Verträgen, Herkommen und Analogie* (Regensburg: Montagische Buchhandlung, 1777) §§ 4, 8; most explicitly von Ompteda (n 17) §§ 3, 12; von Martens, *Versuch* (n 17) 6–7: 'they started to no longer treat each other according to the strict external natural law'; von Martens, *Précis* I (n 17) §§ 2–3. Moser mostly just rejects natural law as unclear and disputed, without specifying its relationship to the positive law of nations, but in his treatment of occupation he references the European positive law as differing from natural law: Moser (n 17) 448; see explicitly also J Schmelzing, *Systematischer Grundriss des praktischen Europäischen Völkerrechts*, vol 1 (Rudolstadt: Verlag der Hof-Buch- und Kunsthandlung, 1818–20) 36–37. According to Grewe (n 12) 462–64, the German eighteenth-century positivists did not explicitly relate natural law and the European positive law of nations to each other doctrinally and just considered the latter to be the historically concrete state of the former, but their expressions listed here disprove him. Grewe himself (ibid 464) then apparently contradicts his own position by claiming that the natural law of nations was retained as a general legal framework used to conceptualised the relationships with non-European societies.

on the practically exclusive relevance of European practice for the actual legal relations among the European states, natural law thus still occupied an important place within their theories as the universal normative background against which a European law of nations had formed. They accepted that natural law provided the principal ideological framework for the description of international relations and understood the positive European law of nations to be built on its general conceptual apparatus.[21]

The conceptual novelty of their approaches lay more in their determination to conceptualise this array of Europe-specific norms as a coherent and uniform system of *general* rules applicable to all European states, rather than a fragmented web of bilateral and plurilateral legal relations based on treaties and customs.[22] To the positivists of the eighteenth century, this was justified by their perception of its distinct history since Greek and Roman antiquity, together with its relative cultural and religious homogeneity, had formed Europe into something qualitatively different, a distinct society without a common overarching state (Wolff's and Kant's visions of universal states were mere philosophical imaginations), not a legal but at least a political corporation.[23] It were these extra-legal factors, including also its geographical vicinity and their cultural opposition to non-Christian societies, especially the Turks, that had generated a shared sense of solidarity and a common identity among European nations.[24] For the study of law, this meant for the eighteenth-century positivists that Europe formed a distinct legal space governed by a more comprehensive system of legal rules that transcended the web of bilateral and plurilateral treaty relations and other practices, and that in some cases allowed the extrapolation of general legal rules and the extension of treaty obligations to nations not party to the respective treaty out of a common sense of forming a distinct society.[25]

The doctrinal problem with this view was that the natural law of nations was not strictly speaking equipped to support this extrapolation of general rules from a fragmented practice. As a legal framework transcending the passage of time and space, it had no conceptual apparatus to account for cultural specificity or historical patina.[26] According to natural law, positive law of nations rested

[21] Moser (n 18) 7–8.

[22] Koskenniemi (n 13) 195.

[23] Moser (n 18) 13; von Martens, *Versuch* (n 17) 6–8; GF von Martens, *Précis du droit des gens moderne de l'Europe fondé sur les traités et l'usage, vol 1*, 2nd edn (Göttingen: Dieterich, 1801) §§ 3–4; Schmelzing (n 20) § 17.

[24] Moser (n 18) 13; von Martens, *Précis 1789* I (n 17) §§ 3–4; von Martens, *Versuch* (n 17) 6–8. On the growing sense of European Identity in this period, see H Duchhardt, *Europa am Vorabend der Moderne 1650–1800* (Stuttgart: Ulmer, 2003) 27–37.

[25] Moser (n 18) 8; von Martens, *Versuch* (n 17) 1–13; von Martens, *Précis* (n 17) §§ 3–4; GF von Martens, *Précis du droit des gens modernes de l'Europe: Fondé sur les traités et l'usage; pour servir d'introduction à un cours politique et diplomatique*, 3rd edn (Göttingen: Dieterich, 1821) §§ 7–8.

[26] M Craven, 'The Time of Revolution: Decolonisation, Heterodox International Legal Historiography and the Problem of the Contemporary' in S Chalmers and S Pahuja (eds), *Routledge Handbook of International Law and the Humanities* (Abingdon: Routledge, 2021) 29.

on and required each state's consent for it to be binding vis-a-vis each state, and there was no sense of how to generate a general legal obligation without falling into philosophical fantasies like the Wolffian *civitas maxima*. This was also why the so-called 'deniers' of a positive law of nations, Hobbes and Pufendorf, had concluded that there wasn't any positive law of nations in the strict sense of the word 'law', as implying a *general* rule, which meant that such rules were only prescribed for inter-state conduct by natural law.[27] In Europe, as Moser and his successors had to concede, there was not even a universal treaty, and state practice usually only involved two or few more states.[28] The specific rules of this European law of nations could usually not be traced back to every individual state's own practice.

Moser, Ompteda and Martens insisted that these deficiencies could be overcome by abstracting rules from the nominally fragmented European practice.[29] They saw a general tendency in Europe to deal with conflicts uniformly, either because the same rules became adopted in numerous formally independent treaties (such as the conditions of visitation of trading ships by conflicting parties on the open sea) or because states (especially weaker ones) would seek inspiration from other states' practice or even invoke it to their own benefit.[30] Still, each of the positivists attempted to accommodate this problematic doctrinally in slightly different ways, either by projecting higher qualities of so-called 'policed states' into variations of the law of nature, by introducing weaker variations of tacit treaties or by simply ignoring the problem.[31] During the early nineteenth century, the most prominent German authors at the time, Schmalz, Klüber and Heffter, continued on

[27] Hobbes (n 13) 2.14.5; von Pufendorf (n 13) 2.3.23.

[28] Moser (n 18) 8.

[29] Koskenniemi (n 13) 196–97; Moser (n 18) 8; von Martens, *Précis 1789* I (n 17) § 7. Günther did not reflect on this constructive problem.

[30] Von Martens, *Précis 1801* (n 23) § 7; Moser (n 18) 8.

[31] Ompteda mobilised the idea of 'policed' or more or less 'well-mannered' states and proposed that essential rules could be imputed onto them because of their higher cultural development. He called this group of norms 'modified natural law', even though it represented positive law resting on tacit consent, to highlight their close relation to the concrete quality of the states concerned and the fact actual consent would not have to be demonstrated for each state but could be presumed on account of its 'well-mannered' nature. The other norms fell under customary law that also rested on tacit consent (eg, the hierarchy between different kinds of sovereigns), but where actual approval had to be shown of each individual state, von Ompteda (n 17) §§ 3–5. This was similar to de Vattel's distinction between *droit naturel, volontaire, conventionnel* and *coutumier*: see E de Vattel, 'Préliminaires' in *Le Droit des Gens* (n 13) vol 1, § 27. Von Martens also operated with presumed consent, but distinguished proper *Herkommen* ('conventionality', as it were), comprising norms for which actual contractual consent for the future could be presumed, from *Gewohnheitsrecht* ('customary law'), denoting only revocable consent such as to the meaning of the white flag in armed conflict. The European law of nations mostly fell under the second category of revocable consent; see von Martens (n 17) 8. Moser simply maintained that it were after all the states themselves who invoked positive legal rules from precedents, so denying their existence would simply be counterfactual, see Moser (n 17) Vorläufige Abhandlung, § 5. Günther's generally brief treatise did not raise the problematic and just distinguished treaty and customary law, the latter of which rested on tacit consent: Günther (n 20) §§ 4–8. Schmelzing just spoke of a 'congruence' (*Übereinstimmung*) of positive obligations; see Schmelzing (n 20) § 13.

the track Günther, Martens and Ompteda had outlined,[32] as did Henry Wheaton in his treatise that first appeared in 1836.[33]

Relations with non-Europeans had to be treated under natural law as the presumedly universal legal system, while any positive law was only applicable among European nations. For example, the appropriation of non-European territories was solved according to natural law, where effective occupation required that the land in question was not effectively occupied by another people. This people neither had to be Christian nor 'civilised', since under natural law, the right to property as the foundation of public authority pertained to everyone (however, nomads were excluded because occupation required sedentariness).[34]

[32] T von Schmalz, *Das europäische Völker-Recht* (Berlin, Duncker und Humblot, 1817) 8–9; J Schmelzing, *Systematischer Grundriss des praktischen Europäischen Völkerrechts*, 3 vols (Rudolstadt: Verlag der Hof-Buch- und Kunsthandlung 1818–20); JL Klüber, *Droit des gens moderne de l'Europe* (Stuttgart: Cotta, 1819) §§ 1–9; AW Heffter, *Das Europäische Völkerrecht der Gegenwart* (Berlin: CH Schroeder, 1844) § 7. Schütze (n 9) 89–91 sees Heffter, who had studied under von Savigny and Eichhorn (W Ogris, 'Heffter, August' (1969) 8 *Neue Deutsche Biographie* 202), as having already adopted the central theorem of the Historical School by founding positive law on the common consciousness (ibid vi), but he strictly speaking only understood the common consciousness, more like Hegel, to be only a remote and sociological origin of law, not the formal source of positive law. Customary law was also only one of several types of positive law and among those only the last he mentions, and not the only true type of positive law from which the others derive. With the state will in a Hegelian fashion playing a central role in the creation of law, and with his acceptance of a hypothetical natural law derived from the necessities of interchange between states with 'a certain degree of culture', his account is still partially rooted the prevailing theory and can thus be seen as standing somewhat in between these two phases of German international legal positivism. See also Carl Baron Kaltenborn, *Kritik des Völkerrechts nach dem jetzigen Standpunkte der Wissenschaft* (Leipzig: Gustav Mayer, 1847) 217–18.

[33] H Wheaton, *Elements of International Law*, vol 1 (London, B Fellowes, 1836) iii–v, § 13. On Wheaton's relationship with the Historical School, see R Schütze, 'From Utopia to Apologia: International Normativity in the Long Nineteenth Century' (PhD thesis, LSE, 2019) 41–78, 151–55 and below n 69.

[34] Von Martens, *Précis 1801* (n 23) § 36; with reference to GK Pfeffel, *Principes du droit naturel: à l'usage de l'École militaire & académique de Colmar* (Neukirch: Decker, 1781) L III, ch IV, § 21 regarding the lack of occupation by nomads. Von Martens expressly remarked that the contrary incidents where European states had occupied lands already occupied by indigenous populations ('sauvages') did not change anything about that question, as did J Schmelzing, *Systematischer Grundriss des praktischen Europäischen Völkerrechts*, vol 2 (Rudolstadt: Verlag der Hof-Buch- und Kunsthandlung, 1818–20) § 216. Moser contented himself with noting that the European positive law of nations could not say anything on the matter because it did not treat the relations to non-European nations at all (Moser, *Précis 1821* (n 25) 18; JJ Moser, *Versuch V* (n 17) 488). Whether this means that Moser excluded this question from international law altogether, as Fisch (n 5) 268–70, finds, seems doubtful, given that he expressly located the positive European law of nations within the larger framework of natural law; see CH Alexandrowicz, 'Treaty and Diplomatic Relations between European and South Asian Powers in the Seventeenth and Eighteenth Centuries' (1960) 100 *Recueil des cours de l'Académie de La Haye* 203, 285; Orakhelashvili (n 8) 318; J von Bernstorff, 'Koloniale Herrschaft durch Ambivalenz: Die deutsche Völkerrechtswissenschaft und die Kolonien' in P Dann, J von Bernstorff and I Feichtner (eds) *(Post)Koloniale Rechtswissenschaft: Geschichte und Gegenwart des Kolonialismus in der deutschen Rechtswissenschaft* (Tübingen: Mohr Siebeck, 2022) 271, 281–82.

C. The Historical School and the Parochialisation of the European Law of Nations

While the authors of the late eighteenth and early nineteenth century had thus articulated the notion of a specifically European law of nations that differed substantially from international relationships beyond Europe and America, they were only able to do so within the universalist philosophy of natural law by employing its abstract concepts in order to reconstruct their idea of a European legal order within juridical terms. Their European law of nations thus appeared as a regional specification of an otherwise universal legal system. This changed profoundly when the legal philosophy of the German Historical School of Law became received in the field of European international law. Under its theoretical aegis, natural law lost its philosophical role in the foundation of the law of nations, which, now called international law, as a whole came to be seen as a specific product of European legal history.

1. The Historical School of Law

The Historical School around Friedrich Carl von Savigny, Georg Friedrich Puchta, and many others, emerged in Germany as part of a conservative and even reactionary turn against the bourgeois revolutionary movements in Europe and the often rationalist Enlightenment philosophies they rested on.[35] The rise and fall of the French Revolution had turned into an existential experience for the entire continent.[36] Politically, it had called into question the old European feudal and monarchic orders and for the first time demonstrated the ambition of democrats and liberals to consciously organise society through an act of collective political autonomy. But its having turned into an ensuing regime of terror and having inflicted a series of pan-European wars on the continent that lasted more than 20 years, it was unclear even to liberals how claims to political freedom could be asserted both intellectually and politically.[37] At the same time, the abstract

[35] On the Historical School's sociopolitical context, see W Wilhelm, *Zur juristischen Methodenlehre im 19. Jahrhundert: Die Herkunft der Methode Paul Labands aus der Privatrechtswissenschaft* (Frankfurt am Main: Klostermann, 1958) 37–41; F Wieacker, *Privatrechtsgeschichte der Neuzeit: Unter besonderer Berücksichtigung der deutschen Entwicklung*, 3rd edn (Göttingen: Vandenhoeck & Ruprecht, 2016) 348–51 and, on the Historical School generally, at 348–457; see also H-P Haferkamp, *Die Historische Rechtsschule* (Frankfurt am Main: Vittorio Klostermann, 2018). There exists an English translation of the 2nd edition of Wieacker's *Privatrechtsgeschichte* of 1967 by T Weir (*A History of Private Law* (Oxford: Clarendon Press, 1995)), but it should be noted that Wieacker has revised some of his positions for the 3rd edition referenced here.

[36] *cf* F Jaeger and J Rüsen, *Geschichte des Historismus: Eine Einführung* (Munich: Beck, 1992) 22–24; Wieacker (n 35) 348–51; J Ritter, 'Hegel und die französische Revolution', in *Metaphysik und Politik: Studien zu Aristoteles und Hegel* (Frankfurt am Main: Suhrkamp, 1977) 192–96.

[37] Jaeger and Rüsen (n 36) 23; Ritter (n 36) 196.

rationalist philosophies of the Enlightenment had, together with the experiences with the technological progress of the rising capitalism and their dissolution of traditional social forms, caused a sense of alienation and a romantic longing for unity and particular identity.[38] The Enlightenment's understanding of human history as the essentially uniform progression of societies towards a uniform ideal of free social organisation was shattered.[39]

It was in this environment that the Historical School of Law established a philosophy of law that largely removed the creation of law from the disposition of the legislator.[40] As such, it was part of a broader movement in philosophy, literature and history that tried to grasp the nature and development of societies with notions of evolutionary self-development rather than pragmatic intentional direction.[41] Methodologically, the Historical School denied that natural law had any hermeneutic or constructive value for jurisprudence whatsoever. It agreed that law was as such a divine idea, a form of social organisation that had been created and gifted by God, but it denied the proposition that this idea had entered the temporal world in the form of natural law as a perceptible general and universal set of concepts inherent in a universal human nature. Instead, it saw it as manifesting itself only in concrete versions of itself in the legal orders of individual nations, whereas the eternal 'idea' of law itself remained inaccessible to human cognition.

This was a modality of the German philosophical idealism of the early nineteenth century which saw reality as the *form* through which its ideal and metaphysical *essence* expressed itself in a historically concrete and therefore imperfect but perceptible *manifestation*.[42] It could be tracked back to Kant's critical destruction of the metaphysical conviction that stood at the heart of any natural law theory, namely that perception of the real world could produce superhistorical certainties in moral questions.[43] It was this insight that in the eyes of the Historical School also disqualified any enterprise to determine a universally true natural law and enact it through legislation.[44] The only 'existence' the eternal idea of law had in the real world was instead in the form of manifestation in the customs and cultural

[38] Jaeger and Rüsen (n 36) 23.

[39] ibid 22.

[40] Wieacker (n 35) 348, 373; Nuzzo (n 11) 40.

[41] Jaeger and Rüsen (n 36) 22. This was a pan-European phenomenon that influenced European thought on international law during the nineteenth century in the way described in this chapter in virtually all European nations. It had an early exposition in the thinking of the early Scottish Enlightenment around Francis Hutcheson, David Hume, Adam Smith and John Millar, among others, who laid the groundwork for the evolutionary understanding of law in Europe; see P Stein, *Legal Evolution: The Story of an Idea* (Cambridge: Cambridge University Press, 1980); Koskenniemi, *Uttermost Parts* (n 5) 656–74. On historicism in British international law, see C Sylvest, 'International Law in Nineteenth-Century Britain' (2005) 75 *British Yearbook of International Law* 9, 37–64; Pitts (n 2) ch 6.

[42] J Rückert, *Idealismus, Jurisprudenz und Politik bei Friedrich Carl von Savigny*, 2nd edn (Frankfurt am Main: Vittorio Klostermann, 2022, first published 1984) 232–99; Wieacker (n 35) 355–57.

[43] Wieacker (n 35) 352; H Welzel, *Naturrecht und materiale Gerechtigkeit*, 4th edn (Göttingen: Vandenhoeck & Ruprecht, 1962) 162–82.

[44] Wieacker (n 35) 351–52.

practices of individual nations.[45] The School looked at the legal orders of the various nations as part of the latter's cultural and social heritages that had grown and developed throughout the respective nation's history. Rather than enacted by the sovereign, as natural law theory imagined it for positive law, it was always already embodied in the people's customs and social practices, 'always already there', and inextricably linked to other expressions of the nation's identity.[46] It defined the nation's identity and substance in the same way as did it's language and its literature and tales.[47] Like language, it grew and developed through history according to practical needs and cultural disposition.[48] This was the concrete factual dimension of law, its ineluctable situatedness within a concrete social setting that rationalist philosophies abstracted from in the eyes of the Historical School. As Savigny put it, 'law has no self-dependent existence; on the contrary, its essence is the life of man itself, viewed on one particular side'.[49]

What captures the difference in thinking between the Enlightenment and the Historical School well is the opposition between the ideals of 'organisation' and 'organism', an opposition that advanced to become a key conception of the nineteenth century public law philosophy. 'Organisation' served as an ideal of the Enlightenment and revolution and reflected the intentional and conscious configuration of social bodies according to rationally conceived plans and criteria.[50] On the other hand, the Historical School as well as most legal philosophies of the early to mid-nineteenth century understood social bodies as organisms, a notion they borrowed from Kant's philosophy of nature. An organism in this sense was an entity composed of several constitutive parts that follows an inherent telos and in which the many parts and the encompassing whole are correlated in the way that each part fulfils its particular role and function with a view to securing the existence of the whole, while the whole provides for the preservation of all its constituent parts.[51] An organism in this changes over time, yet not as a result of interference from the outside, but driven by the force of own inherent purpose. The typical example for this understanding of organism was for Kant the tree, which is from its origin as a seed to its ultimate formation guided by the overall working of its natural organism in which every leaf, root etc contributes to the preservation and growth of the whole, while in turn being preserved by the entire tree.[52]

[45] Kaltenborn (n 32) 241–42; FC von Savigny, *Of the Vocation of Our Age for Legislation and Jurisprudence*, trans A Hayward (London: Littlewood & Co. 1831) 30, 46.

[46] Von Savigny (n 45) 24–31.

[47] ibid 24; FC von Savigny, *System des heutigen römischen Rechts*, vol 1 (Berlin: Veit und Comp, 1840–49) § 7.

[48] Von Savigny (n 45) 27–28.

[49] ibid 46.

[50] E-W Böckenförde, 'Organ, Organismus, Organisation, politischer Körper [Sections VII–IX]' in O Brunner, W Conze and R Koselleck (eds), *Geschichtliche Grundbegriffe: Historisches Lexikon zur politisch-sozialen Sprache in Deutschland*, vol 4 (Stuttgart: Klett-Cotta, 1978) 566–70.

[51] ibid 580–82, 588–89.

[52] ibid 580–81; *cf* I Kant, *Critique of the Power of Judgment*, P Guyer ed, P Guyer and E Matthews trans (Cambridge, Cambridge University Press, 2000) §§ 64–65.

This notion of the organism perfectly encapsulated the conservative view of the Historical School's protagonists of society as well-ordered, concrete living being imbued with an inherent purpose. Here, every individual had to recognise the particular role it had fatefully been assigned and exercise it to contribute to the greater whole. The organism thus became the School's central heuristic tool for how to approach the study and development of law. Fundamentally, it was imperative to investigate the legal order's inner forces that drove its development through the study of the nation's customs and social practices through which they manifested themselves in the nation's 'life'. These forces were the national specification of the divine idea of law, what the School later called the 'people's spirit' (*Volksgeist*) as the nation's metaphysical essence determining its identity and purpose like purpose of the Kantian organism. These forces were ultimately obscure, but they were also considered to be structured by a coherent internal logic that could be described as the legal logic of the legal system.[53] To ascertain and reproduce this logical legal system was the ultimate task of the lawyer.

Juridically, this meant that all law was *positive* law and that all law was ultimately *customary* law. This was the immediate form in which it 'lived' within the social practices of a people. Legislation was strictly speaking unable to create or constitute new law; it could only give expression to the underlying customary law, and only in a technical and somewhat estranged form at that.[54] The School developed a legal methodology and conceptual framework of how to retrieve the positive law inherent in the social practices and to subsequently reconstruct the systematic logic that the legal rules were presupposed to follow as part of the coherent and evolving organic whole.[55] The intellectual understanding of those legal rules constituted the so-called 'legal consciousness'.[56] Initially, at an early stage of a people's development, it would reside in the people itself and have a primitive form, but with the increasing sophistication of the legal order, it would be taken over by professional lawyers who would act as representatives of the people's consciousness in the exploration, maintenance and appropriate development of the legal order.[57] 'The

[53] Wilhelm (n 35) 61–63; Wieacker (n 35) 396–72; A Mazzacane, 'Jurisprudenz als Wissenschaft' in FC von Savigny, *Vorlesungen über juristische Methodologie 1802–1842*, A Mazzacane (ed) (Frankfurt am Main: Klostermann, 2004) 35–36.

[54] Von Savigny (n 45) 25–29; von Savigny (n 47) § 7.

[55] Von Savigny (n 47) xxxvi–xlii; Mazzacane (n 53) 1–56; Wilhelm (n 35) 17–69.

[56] Von Savigny (n 47) §§ 12–14.

[57] Von Savigny (n 45) 28–29; Kaltenborn (n 32) 231–39. These theorems can ultimately not be properly understood without considering the School's primary concern for the preservation of German private law at the dawn of the nineteenth century. At the time, German private law consisted of a regionally diverse mix of old Germanic and local customs, local pieces of legislation, and the body of Roman law that had selectively seeped into the European legal orders during the late Middle Ages and early modernity following the rediscovery through the work of classically trained jurists. It was this appropriation of Roman law and its development and combination with prevailing Germanic customary law that von Savigny had in mind when he spoke of the production of law through the *Volksgeist*. With his classicist, not romantic worldview, the Volksgeist was for him the harmonic self-realisation of *Kultur* in the form of higher *Bildung* through the agency of the educated lawyers. His ideal were the Roman *Praetors*, the judicial magistrates that had developed large parts of Roman private law without

sum, therefore, of this theory is, that all law is originally formed in the manner in which, in ordinary but not quite correct language, customary law is said to have been formed: i.e. that it is first developed by custom and popular faith, next by jurisprudence, – everywhere, therefore, by internal silently-operating powers, not by the arbitrary will of a law-giver'.[58] It was this theory that produced the modern concept of customary law and of customary international law as the combination of a regular practice with the accompanying legal consciousness.

At the centre of the Historical School's philosophy therefore stood a reorientation of the relationship between natural law and positive law or, as its proponents now called it, between 'legal philosophy' and 'positive jurisprudence'. The School's aim was to integrate legal philosophy into positive legal methodology in order to establish the positive jurisprudence as an independent science.[59] Its relationship to the rationalist philosophies of the Enlightenment remained highly ambivalent.[60] It rejected the notion of a superhistorical and universal natural law as imperceptible and positioned itself rhetorically as its opposite, but it still saw the world as guided by God's creation and wisdom in a way that could be perceived in the organic development of individual nations. To apprehend the concrete logic that allegedly rested within the social practice, it built on the logical constructions of legal relationships of Christian Wolff.[61] In asserting that this legal logic inherent in social reality could be perceived, it betrayed the Kantian critical epistemological scepticism it had invoked to disavow the substantial natural law theories.[62] The School's protagonists ultimately sought to bridge this Kantian epistemic gap through their deep Christian faith and believed that secure cognition could ultimately be conveyed through inward religious practice, and it was regularly referred to as the 'Historical-Christian School'.[63] The goal was really to bind historical study of law and constructive legal rationalism together as two sides of a uniform legal methodology.[64] As a result, its concept of history was fundamentally unhistorical, in that legal history

legislative reason from the exigencies of practice. The Liberal's project of his own time to advance unification of the politically and legally fragmented German nation through the enactment of a codification of private law after the French Code Civil, von Savigny feared, would cut the nation off of his Roman-Germanic legal traditions through what he saw as a technically deficient code and thereby also implement a politically liberal legal order. See von Savigny (n 45) 43–60; Wieacker (n 35) 363–67, 384–86 and, on the reception of Roman law in the Germanic states, at 97–248.

[58] Von Savigny (n 45) 30.

[59] Mazzacane (n 53) 39.

[60] Wieacker (n 35) 367–77; H-P Haferkamp, 'Naturrecht und Historische Rechtsschule' in M Armgardt and T Repgen (eds), *Naturrecht in Antike und früher Neuzeit* (Tübingen: Mohr Siebeck, 2014).

[61] Wieacker (n 35) 372–74; Wilhelm (n 35) 61–63.

[62] Mazzacane (n 53) 35–36.

[63] H-P Haferkamp, 'Einflüsse der Erweckungsbewegung auf die "historisch-christliche" Rechtsschule zwischen 1815 und 1848' in P Cancik et al (eds), *Konfession im Recht: Auf der Suche nach konfessionell geprägten Denkmustern und Argumentationsstrategien in Recht und Rechtswissenschaft des 19. und 20. Jahrhunderts* (Frankfurt am Main: Klostermann, 2009); Haferkamp (n 35) 139–268.

[64] Wieacker (n 35) 367–77.

only served to reconstruct the necessary unfolding of the contemporary order according to an immanent principle.[65]

2. Kaltenborn's Transformation of International Legal Theory

During the first half of the 19th century, the Historical School's theory and methodology quickly became the predominant legal theory in German private law and public law.[66] It was only a matter of time until it would also transform the international legal thought of the time in Germany and beyond. During the first decades of the century, treatises on international law increasingly started emphasising that their object was a product of European history, culture and religion. In 1817, Schmalz already held that treaties merely codified positive legal rules that were already established in customary international law, as did Schmelzing a year later, who also highlighted that 'actual life' was 'the true source of international law' and that legal science had to outline as it 'revealed' itself through history.[67] Heffter in his influential treatise defined customary international law as general practice 'accompanied by belief of having an obligation vis-à-vis the other and on the other side of having a right', and not as a tacit treaty.[68] In the US, Henry Wheaton, who had met and engaged with Savigny during his term as US ambassador in Berlin, described international law as a specific product of European-American history, tracing back to the reception of Roman law in Europe, affirmed its limitation to the two continents and explicitly recited a brief description of Savigny's theory.[69] But it was the Prussian Professor Karl Baron Kaltenborn von Stachau who in 1847 properly translated the concepts of international law into the nomenclature of the School in a way that would – ultimately through Bluntschli – lastingly determine its central concepts to this day.[70]

[65] E-W Böckenförde, 'Die historische Rechtsschule und das Problem der Geschichtlichkeit des Rechts' in *Collegium Philosophicum: Studien/Joachim Ritter zum 60. Geburtstag* (Stuttgart: Schwabe & Co, 1960) 16.

[66] J Schröder, *Recht als Wissenschaft: Geschichte der juristischen Methode vom Humanismus bis zur historischen Schule (1500–1850)* (Munich: Beck, 2001) 191; C Kletzer, 'Custom and Positivity: An Examination of the Philosophic Ground of the Hegel-Savigny Controversy' in A Perreau-Saussine and JB Murphy (eds), *The Nature of Customary Law* (Cambridge: Cambridge University Press, 2007) 135–36.

[67] Von Schmalz (n 32) 10; Schmelzing (n 20) 21, 25–26.

[68] Heffter (n 32) § 7.

[69] H Wheaton, *Elements of International Law*, vol 1 (London: B Fellowes, 1836) 9–12, 50–51 (§ 9). On Wheaton's indebtedness to the German Historical School, see Nuzzo (n 11) 50–53; Schütze (n 11) 146–47, and Pitts (n 2) 131–33 on his limitation of international law to Europe and America.

[70] Kaltenborn (n 32); on Kaltenborn, see also Koskenniemi, *Gentle Civilizer* (n 5) 24–28; Schütze (n 11) 91. On the emergence of the Historical School of Law in Germany and its influence on German concepts of international law, see von Bernstorff and Mayer (n 1); and A Carty, *The Decay of International Law: A Reappraisal of the Limits of Legal Imagination in International Affairs* (Manchester: Manchester University Press, 2019, first published 1986) 65–71; Nuzzo (n 11) 58–70.

To give the European international law its new foundation, Kaltenborn rejected the philosophy of natural law altogether and instead saw international law as inherent in the international relations of the European nations. Kaltenborn considered Europe an organism in itself that had over the past two centuries slowly developed into a system of independent states according to its own inherent principle and which had finally found stability in the Pentarchy's governance after the upheavals of the Coalition Wars.[71] Within this organism, both small and large states had their particular role to play in the preservation of the whole.[72] Its unity was defined by the Europeans' shared cultural historical tradition, especially by their common Christian religion.[73] The European international law lived as customary law within what Kaltenborn called its 'international life'. It was a specific expression of the divine 'idea' of law on an international level and the constituted legal side of the political relationships that had formed through the development of intra-European international relations.[74] The task of international lawyers was to analyse these relationships in order to uncover legal rules that Kaltenborn presupposed as inherent in them and to determine how all of them were interrelated in the legal system of the greater organism.[75] The understanding of these rules then formed a European legal consciousness that had to be developed and refined.[76] From the time of his writing just before the 1848 revolutions, Kaltenborn looked backwards in history to see the history of European international relations as the unfolding of the European organism's inherent logic from its initial stages before Westphalia into the Pentarchy of his own time. The history of international legal scholarship and philosophy in Europe was accordingly the development of the intellectual reflection on the nature of those international relations in the form of a growing European legal consciousness.[77]

Kaltenborn then reformulated the central concepts of international law based on the Historical School's methodology. Customary international law was not a tacit treaty, but the reverse: customary law was the law inherent in practice and reflected in the legal consciousness, while treaties were unsubstantial expressions of this legal consciousness, ie, really customary law, and not themselves origins of legal rules.[78] By rejecting the idioms of natural law and its distinction of a state of nature and a state of law, Kaltenborn also integrated war into international law as both its ultimate means of procedural enforcement and inherent agent of further development, rather than seeing it as a pre- or a-legal condition. If the nature of

[71] Kaltenborn (n 32) 187, 170–71, 214–15; C von Kaltenborn, 'Rezension Heffter und Oppenheim' [1846] *Berliner Jahrbücher für wissenschaftliche Kritik* 868, 878–79.
[72] Kaltenborn (n 32) 264.
[73] ibid 215–16, 268–269; Kaltenborn (n 71), 880, 393–96.
[74] Kaltenborn (n 32) 241–42.
[75] ibid.
[76] ibid 234–39.
[77] See the references in n 73; and C Kaltenborn, 'Rezension Roßbach' [1846] *Berliner Jahrbücher für wissenschaftliche Kritik* 190, 190–92.
[78] Kaltenborn (n 32) 178, 231–39.

war was enforcement, not simply self-help, war could be understood as realising an objective social order, and as developing it further at the same time.[79]

Significantly, also with respect to the European particularism, Kaltenborn also saw the *form* and not just the substance of international law as a product of European culture. This was an essential difference to the older natural law philosophy which had considered the legal form of social relations as a universal faculty invested into a universal human nature by God upon the creation of human beings, with the consequence that European legal orders were merely sub-categories of a theoretically global mode of social organisation and dependent in their validity on the modalities of natural law.[80] And while other authors like Schmalz, Schmelzing, Heffter and Wheaton had argued that positive international law had grown out of Europe, they had still retained this basic foundation of international law in the law of nature. It was only Kaltenborn who for the first time expressed the general sentiment of the nineteenth century that modern international law *itself*, in the sense of the legal organisation of international relations per se, was an exclusive product of European culture on a philosophical level.

Kaltenborn did so through a modification of the concept of law. According to Kant and Austin, an obligation was legal if it was external to the legal subject and enforceable. Kaltenborn added another condition: what gave principles of social organisation their specifically legal character the reconciliation of individual freedom and collective organization.[81] Only a social order that had this conciliation of these formally incommensurate principles as its central principle could lay claim to being a *legal* order in the proper sense.[82] For international law, these principles were represented in the essential principles of state sovereignty and the international society.[83] Kaltenborn followed Hegel in identifying the development of this opposition and reconciliation of individuality and collectivity as the specific accomplishment of European substantial and intellectual history since antiquity: after the principle of collectivity had been formulated in Ancient Greece and Rome, it had been the achievement of the Christian religion to have introduced and asserted the principle of individuality in European culture and philosophy. The Enlightenment philosophies and the French Revolution had taken the principle of individuality to its extreme and had made it the founding principle even of

[79] ibid 310–11; see also extensively in C Kaltenborn, 'Zur Revision der Lehre von den internationalen Rechtsmitteln' (1861) 17 *Zeitschrift für die gesammte Staatswissenschaft* 69.

[80] This is why Alexandrowicz saw legal positivism as a reduction in scope of an originally allegedly global legal order; see above n 8.

[81] Kaltenborn (n 32) 256–69.

[82] ibid 215–16; Kaltenborn (n 71) 880.

[83] Note how the following determination of the essence of international law by Grewe echoes this definition: 'In sum, an international legal order can only be assumed to exist if there is a plurality of relatively independent (although not necessarily equal-ranking) bodies politic which are linked to each other in political, economic and cultural relationships and which are not subject to a superimposed authority having comprehensive law-making jurisdiction and executive competence. In their mutual relations these bodies politic must observe norms which are deemed to be binding on the basis of a legal consciousness rooted in religious, cultural and other common values.', Grewe (n 12) 7.

society, leading to terror and alienation. But the Restauration had reasserted the independent existence of the objective principle in the substantial collective and established to the organic mediation of both individual freedom and collective historical substance within the monarchic nation and established it as the leading principle of the European international law.[84] It was this organic unity of individuality and substantive collectivity, or 'subjectivity' and 'objectivity', within the organism of Europe that the history of Europe had developed towards since the emergence of the (subjective) principle of state sovereignty two centuries ago and which gave European international law its singular legal character.[85] With all law ultimately constituted in society, the objective principle was the higher of the two, ie, international law had to be understood as a legal order *above* the states and state sovereignty as a subordinate principle of that objective legal order.[86]

3. A New Perspective on Parochialism

With Europe at its centre, this theory acted as a catalyst for the ideological distinction of Europe as a distinct society of nations. The doctrine's emphasis on cultural and especially religious identity as the origin of law had an ostensible tendency to further undermine the respect towards the international relations with non-European peoples and tended to fragment global legal relations further into separate regional orders. International law had to be determined by considering practice in light of 'the general nature, the inner essence, the proper character of the Christian Germanic states'.[87] To Kaltenborn, legal reciprocity, as suggested, for example, by Heffter, was too technical a concept to bridge a difference that now affected the very foundations of law itself. A true 'international life' could only be sustained on the basis of a sufficient '*cultural-political* reciprocity' that could be measured by the degree to which the political and social organisation of other

[84] Kaltenborn (n 77) 190–222; Kaltenborn (n 71) 868–71, 878–79; Kaltenborn (n 32) 214–15; GWF Hegel, *Vorlesungen über die Philosophie der Geschichte*, eds E Moldenhauer and KM Michel (Frankfurt am Main: Suhrkamp, 1970) 520–40; on Hegel, see Ritter (n 36) 200.

[85] This distinguished Kaltenborn from Hegel, to whom international law lacked the institutional materialisation of its ethical principles in the way in which domestic law had its ethical substance that could determine the concrete realisation of freedom reflected in the institutions of the state. For Hegel, war was no sufficient substitute for this institutionalisation and even rather an expression of the fact that international law lingered in a state of a mere 'ought-to-be'; see GWF Hegel, *Outlines of the Philosophy of Right*, ed S Houlgate, trans TM Knox (Oxford: Oxford University Press, 2008) § 333.

[86] It was this conceptualisation of international law as a stateless legal order above the later moved Hans Kelsen to count it 'among the very best achievements of legal theory in the 19th century'; see H Kelsen, *Das Problem der Souveränität und die Theorie des Völkerrechts* (Tübingen: Mohr, 1920), 242–48; *cf* J von Bernstorff, *The Public International Law Theory of Hans Kelsen: Believing in Universal Law* (Cambridge: Cambridge University Press, 2010) 85–87. For a contemporary analysis of this persistent problematic of international legal theory, see M Koskenniemi, *From Apology to Utopia: The Structure of International Legal Argument* (Cambridge: Cambridge University Press, 2009).

[87] 'Die allgemeine Natur, das innerste Wesen, den eigenthümlichen Charakter der christlich germanischen Staaaten' (Kaltenborn (n 32) 180).

peoples resembled that of the 'Christian world order'.[88] With any society that didn't have the organic mediation of subjectivity and objectivity as its constitutive principle, or, in other words, that didn't assume a European state form, relationships could be maintained, but they could not be considered *legal* relationships.

What made the Historical School's parochialism and European exceptionalism so credible then as a *legal* theory was not simply its exclusive emphasis on positive law, but primarily this renovation of the concept of *positive* law itself. By making positive law directly the object of legal philosophy, without the mediation of an abstract natural law, the theory was able to pick up the cultural individuality of concrete societies that had in Moser and the positivists following him acted as mere external motivators for assembling a particular European practice and shift it to the heart of the very concept of law itself. While the adoption of the Historical School's theorem thus represented a turning point in German international legal positivism by discarding natural law, it also connected to the earlier strands of German positivism, in the theoretical development and perfection of which the Historical School saw its central task, especially within the field of international law.[89] It was this opening up of the concept of positive law to an immediate philosophical determination that then enabled Bluntschli to combine it with a universalist philosophy of history which established the European nations as the facilitators of a global legal evolution of 'civilisation'.

D. Bluntschli's Universalist Positivism

1. Natural Law, Historicism and Hegel Combined for a Legal Theory of Civilisation

From the 1860s, another exponent of the Historical School of Law in the person of the liberal Swiss Professor Johann Caspar Bluntschli developed Kaltenborn's theory further and became one of the leading European international lawyers of his time.[90] Bluntschli was as much rooted intellectually in the Historical School's

[88] ibid 215–16: 'The international exchange of Christian with non-Christian states has to be seen on a more profound level of the extent to which non-Christian states approximate in their nature to the Christian idea of the state. An international life with non-Christian states is therefore possible insofar as there exists a certain political order and moderation as the first and most incomplete aspects of a Christian state order, and they namely won't behave downright negatively or at least passively towards the other independent, especially Chistian states.' Von Savigny and Puchta had doubted even the possibility of a proper European law of nations because of a lack of regularity in the enforcement of the rules: von Savigny, *System I* (n 47) § 11; GF Puchta, *Das Gewohnheitsrecht*, vol 1 (Darmstadt: Wissenschaftliche Buchgesellschaft, 1965, first published 1828) 141–42.

[89] *cf* Kaltenborn (n 32) 228–30.

[90] On Bluntschli, see B Röben, *Johann Caspar Bluntschli, Francis Lieber und das moderne Völkerrecht 1861–1881* (Baden-Baden: Nomos, 2003); Koskenniemi, *Gentle Civilizer* (n 5) 41–47; Schütze (n 11) 97–98; Tzouvala (n 5) 44–85.

methodology as he was in Hegel's universalist philosophy of world history, and he combined the two strands from his liberal perspective into a theory of international law that was on a historical course to expand from a European into a universal, global legal order.[91] Bluntschli thus reversed the parochialist character European international legal thought had had during the preceding century and gave it a strong universalist traction, all while retaining its awareness of the particular European heritage and identity of the field. Bluntschli's account of international law thus gave expression to an expansionist and universalist sentiment that characterised the European discipline and that saw the European ideas and practices of liberty and free trade as the epitome of human 'civilization' which were bound to become globalised by all means necessary.

The positivists of the eighteenth century and the earlier, conservative and reactionary authors of the Historical School had mostly looked at Europe as a closed-off organism that was developing its own identity from within itself. Hegel's philosophy of history was very different. Hegel had a positive view of the Enlightenment tradition and while he saw the revolutionary imposition of its ideas as a failure, he admired the ambition to consciously institute society according to rational ideas (rather than mere tradition).[92] His social philosophy was dedicated to overcome the abstraction of the Enlightenment and to lay out the conditions necessary for a society to realise individual freedom as the foundational principle of its political and social organisation.[93] In line with the Enlightenments universalism, Hegel saw individual freedom as a universal principle of the ethical nature of human beings.[94] His philosophy of history interpreted world history as the gradual unfolding of the objective 'spirit' in the actual (ie, temporal) world through historical stages, each of which was associated with the characteristics of a concrete people dominating their respective age.[95] World history to Hegel was the process in which humankind became conscious of its natural individual and collective freedom and gradually actualised this freedom in concrete forms of social organisation, most importantly the state.[96] Freedom had at last become actualised through the French Revolution, and was now in the process of being universalised throughout the world.[97]

[91] Koskenniemi, *Gentle Civilizer* (n 5) 42–46; however, see Schütze (n 11) 97–99, who sees Bluntschli's theory not as continuing, but as rejecting the fundamental positions of the Historical School.

[92] Jaeger and Rüsen (n 36) 32; Ritter (n 36).

[93] Ritter (n 36) 199–200.

[94] ibid 197–98.

[95] Hegel (n 84) 86–87 et seq; a brief overview in Hegel (n 85) §§ 341–60; U Thiele, *Verfassung, Volksgeist und Religion: Hegels Überlegungen zur Weltgeschichte des Staatsrechts* (Berlin: Duncker & Humblot, 2010); Ritter (n 36) 200–01; Schütze (n 11) 56–76.

[96] Hegel (n 84) 32; Hegel (n 85) § 257.

[97] A Kojève, 'Zusammenfassender Kommentar zu den ersten sechs Kapiteln der "Phänomenologie des Geistes"' in HF Fulda and D Henrich (eds), *Materialien zu Hegels 'Phänomenologie des Geistes'* (Frankfurt am Main: Suhrkamp, 1998); Kletzer (n 66) 145; see also Buck-Morss (n 7). Because Hegel saw history as the actualisation of *reason* ('it is reason that governs the world and hence also world history': Hegel (n 84) 40), he was despised of by the 'original' historical school, which insisted on interpreting history as the actualisation of divine ideas, for being a rationalist. See Kaltenborn (n 32)

Bluntschli integrated this idea with the Historical School's theory of positive law as an emanation of history to describe the current European law of nations juridically as an episode of an ongoing universal history of humankind gradually transitioning into the political form of liberal nation-states.[98] For Bluntschli, the global order was undergoing an organic transition towards the universal establishment of economic liberalism, human rights and humanitarian principles. Positive international law was for him the form through which that transition was facilitated, and the European states were the current agents called upon to support this transition globally.[99]

Drawing on the doctrinal structure of the Historical School, and occasionally borrowing from the older natural law theories, Bluntschli translated this philosophy of history into proper juridical categories and turned the parochialist theory of the Historical School into a universalist concept with a global purview. To universalise the law of nations, he employed the notion from natural law that law was ultimately rooted in human nature and international law, and hence in principle global,[100] and he then transposed the Historical School's doctrinal concepts into this universalist setting: ideas alone did not create actual law, only the manifestation of the legal consciousness in the life of nations created the legal order.[101] This legal consciousness was that of the humankind at large as it recognised the divine ideas that were reflected in world history.[102] But at

149–50; FJ Stahl, *Die Philosophie des Rechts nach geschichtlicher Ansicht*, vol I (Heidelberg: JCB Mohr, 1830–37) 292–300; Haferkamp (n 60) 72–73.

[98] Bluntschli recalls Hegel's four main historical stages that led to the development of the European conservative-liberal state multiple times; see, eg, JC Bluntschli, 'Recht, Rechtsbegriff' in *Deutsches Staats-Wörterbuch*, vol 8 [1864] (Stuttgart: Expedition des Staats-Wörterbuchs, eds JC Bluntschli and CLT Brater (1857–70)).

[99] For a comprehensive overview the introduction in his textbook that was 'to demonstrate the progress of international law', see JC Bluntschli, *Das moderne Völkerrecht der civilisirten Staten als Rechtsbuch dargestellt* (Munich: CH Beck, 1868) 1–49; and Bluntschli (n 98); Koskenniemi, *Gentle Civilizer* (n 5) 57–70. Despite the great success of his textbook, of which multiple editions and also a French translation appeared, this sense of utopianism in his work was resented by other, more conservative German scholars; see, eg, F von Holtzendorff, 'Grundbegriffe, Wesen und Verhältnisbestimmungen des Völkerrechts' in *Handbuch des Völkerrechts: Auf Grundlage Europäischer Staatspraxis*, vol 1 [Einleitung in das Völkerrecht] (Berlin: Carl Gabel, 1885–89) 29; FH Geffcken, 'Vorwort zur siebenten Auflage' in AW Heffter, *Das europäische Völkerrecht der Gegenwart auf den bisherigen Grundlagen*, 8th ed (Berlin: HW Müller, 1888) III, who both felt that Bluntschli had overstretched the limits of legal positivism by suggesting that the law of nations was already a global order, while in their view the law of nations was still limited to Christian states and the Ottoman Empire, Egypt and Accra on account of their 'accession' to the European law of nations. The rest of the world still had to undergo the civilising education of the Christian nations before the law of nations could properly apply to them. Especially for Holtzendorff, the universality of the European law of nations could be recognised as a normative ideal within a contemporary (and hence relative) understanding of natural law, but this was only a philosophical reflection on the current state of positive law, which he saw as the only type of actual law. On the civilising mission within German scholarship of the law of nations, see von Bernstorff (n 34).

[100] Bluntschli (n 99) §§ 2, 6. Again, the Historical School shared this idea – they just disagreed with natural law theory on the relation it had to positive law. See, eg, Kaltenborn (n 60) 231, 256.

[101] Bluntschli (n 99) § 1.

[102] ibid § 4; JC Bluntschli, *Die Neueren Rechtsschulen der deutschen Juristen* (Zurich: Ch Beyel, 1862) 59–60.

the current stage of world history, the concrete scope of this formally universal legal consciousness was restricted to the European states and their former colonies: only they were the ones with the intellectual and practical sophistication required to reflect the universal law intellectually as it was emerging from world history in Europe.[103] Bluntschli thus used the Historical School's understanding of positive law as an inseparable feature of a social organism in which the development law was seen as a function of that organism's overall organic development; yet, building on the natural law's universalist cosmopolitanism, he understood this social organism to be a humanist world society and the European and American nations as the current bearers of this society's legal consciousness. For him, positive international law was thus in the process of developing in accordance with his projection for the ongoing development of that social organism. And to exclude countries outside Europe and America as a source for the global legal consciousness, he could build on the Historical School's distinction between a primitive 'Volksrecht' and scientifically developed and sophisticated 'Juristenrecht' to designate Europe and America as the representatives of the nominally global legal consciousness.

Bluntschli's combination of natural law, historicism and the idealist philosophy of history created a theory of law that was well suited to accommodate the notion that had since the beginning of the nineteenth century advanced to become the quintessence of European superiority: the notion of 'civilisation'. The concept of civilisation had emerged since the late eighteenth century against a backdrop of liberal optimism in the progress of humankind and the actual expansion of the European law of nations to the American continent through the emancipation of the former colonies there.[104] It replaced the characterisation of the law of nations as 'European' and reflected the idea of a universal history of humankind on a trajectory from a 'barbaric' into a 'civil' condition of organised statehood, free trade and the protection of individual rights, drawing on the distinction of a state of nature and a civil state of organised society that had been the hallmark of Enlightenment political philosophy from Hobbes to Kant.[105] As every society was considered to be passing through this trajectory on its own, all societies could now be classified according to how far they had progressed to the final stage of civilisation represented by the European and North American states, resulting in a co-existence of different stages of the what was imagined as essentially the same human history in different parts of the earth.[106] Like Africa, North America was

[103] Bluntschli (n 99) §§ 4–5; Röben (n 90) 100 focuses her analysis on this abstract universalism in Bluntschli's work, while its concrete limitation is not discussed.

[104] B Bowden, *The Empire of Civilization: The Evolution of an Imperial Idea* (Chicago: University of Chicago Press, 2009) 28–34.

[105] Anghie (n 5); Bowden (n 104) 40–41, 78–100; Gong (n 9).

[106] On the co-existence of different temporalities in nineteenth-century historicism and international law, see Craven (n 8). On the aforementioned classification of societies, which had early precursors during the Spanish colonisation of Central and South America, see Bowden (n 104) 53–63. On British authors, see Pitts (n 2) 130–31, 162, 167; Tzouvala (n 5) 44–87.

seen as having rested in a state of nature until the arrival of the Europeans,[107] while Turkey and Asian societies were classified as 'semi-civilised' and subjected to treaties guaranteeing the protection of property through the establishment of distinct judicial systems for Europeans ('capitulations').[108] By drawing on the Historical School's theory of law as an emanation of a concrete society, Bluntschli was able to link up the somewhat technocratic notion of 'civilisation' associated with the rationalism of the Enlightenment with the concrete historical development of Europe and thus give expression to its tension between European ownership and universal aspiration.

2. New Doctrinal Possibilities: Occupation of Non-European Territory

A case in point for this combination of natural law, idealist philosophy of history and the Historical School's doctrinal apparatus of positive law is Bluntschli's treatment of the occupation of land inhabited by so-called 'uncivilised races' in his treatise.[109] Heffter, author of the most popular German-language treatise on the law of nations before Bluntschli's *International Law*, had in line with the natural law tradition maintained that land could not be taken from indigenous populations at will.[110] But for Bluntschli, it was necessary that 'civilised nations' should install state structures in indigenous territories as soon as 'persons who have always lived in a policed state' acquired private property in land in such territories, to protect this property and 'to take over the education and guidance of the wild tribes'.[111] Referring to Vattel and Phillimore, Bluntschli started from the natural law tenet that it was the purpose of the earth's surface to serve human culture and from the philosophy of history that it was 'the destiny of the progressing humankind to disseminate the civilisation throughout the earth'. From this it followed that the expansion of 'civilised state authority' was necessary for the dissemination of civilisation, and he criticised Heffter for 'recognising the legal principle [that the earth is to become fully organised by states] but discarding its practical application'.[112] For Bluntschli, this point was decisive because in the Historical School's theorem, the probation of ideas in practice was what marked

[107] Bowden (n 104) 30. It was in this sense that Hegel considered Africa to be an 'ahistorical continent', because he held that African societies had not yet embarked on this historical trajectory of civilisation at all: Hegel (n 84) 129.

[108] Bowden (n 104) 130–31; Tzouvala (n 5) 73–84.

[109] See also von Bernstorff (n 34) 276–79.

[110] Heffter (n 32) § 70; von Bernstorff (n 34) 277.

[111] Bluntschli (n 99) § 280; for the English translation, I have borrowed partly from the French edition in JC Bluntschli, *Le droit international codifié*, 2nd edn, trans MC Lardy (Paris: Guillaumin, 1874) § 280; von Bernstorff (n 34) 277–78. This was also in line with the denigration of native populations by Hegel (n 85) § 351; *cf* Schütze (n 11) 65–66.

[112] Bluntschli (n 99) § 280; Heffter (n 32) 70; see von Bernstorff (n 34) 279. Heffter himself had relied on Grotius' assertion that a people could not be subjected to foreign authority unless by free submission,

the transition of colonial occupation from a political project to the fulfilment of positive law, for the determination of which the philosophy of history in this way acquired immediate relevance.[113]

Building on the Historical School's concept of law as an emanation of a people's culture, on Hegel's vision of world history as the coming to actuality of reason through humanity's increasing consciousness of its own freedom, as well as significant racism and misogyny in his own thought,[114] Bluntschli was thus able to integrate a hierarchical distinction between European and non-European societies into the dogmatic structure of a universal and positive international law that portrayed the European submission of the non-European world and the establishment of European economic, legal and political forms as a world-historical deed, and as the exercising of the positive international law that facilitated the universal dissemination of 'civilisation' and 'humanity'. This elevation of European states as more advanced in their self-cultivation and rationalisation continued to be the building blocks of German international legal doctrine for the decades to come,[115] and contributed to the distinction between 'civilised' and 'non-civilised' nations being integrated into Article 38 of the Statute of the Permanent Court of International Justice (hereinafter 'PCIJ Statute').[116]

3. After Bluntschli: The 'Will' of States and the Return of Formalism

Towards the end of the nineteenth century, the Historical School's theorem started to fall into disrepute and was criticised for the opacity of its concepts, as legal positivism started moving towards more tangible theories of law creation and gravitated towards the 'consent' or the 'will' of the state as the founding concept of international law (and law generally).[117] Many of its concepts nonetheless prevailed

from Hugo Grotius, *De Jure Belli ac Pacis Libri Tres*, vol 2, trans FW Kelsey (Oxford: Clarendon Press, 1925) II.9.1.

[113] On the significance of the state form in nineteenth-century colonialism and international law, see also L Eslava and S Pahuja, 'The State and International Law: A Reading from the Global South' (2020) 11 *Humanity* 118.

[114] For Bluntschli, humankind was naturally divided into agnatic 'races' with different natural characteristics, and he held that 'it was a grave mistake of the natural law theory of the state to ground the law in the individual's will. Quite the opposite, it is the race's will which is the foundation of the state's will'. See JC Bluntschli, *Lehre vom modernen Stat*, vol 3 (Stuttgart: Cotta, 1875–76) 120. On Bluntschli's racism and anti-semitism, see M Senn, 'Rassistische und antisemitische Elemente im Rechtsdenken von Johann Caspar Bluntschli' (1993) *110 Zeitschrift der Savigny-Stiftung für Rechtsgeschichte: Germanistische Abteilung* 372. On the relationship between racism and 'civilisation', see also Tzouvala (n 5) 48–49, 67–73.

[115] In German, eg, von Holtzendorff (n 99) 3–6. On the parallel development in British scholarship, see Koskenniemi, *Gentle Civilizer* (n 5) 51–54; Pitts (n 2) ch 6; Schütze (n 11) 159–69.

[116] Von Bernstorff and Mayer (n 1).

[117] Prominently from R von Jhering, *The Struggle for Law* (first published 1872, trans John J Lalor, Chicago: Callaghan, 1879); C Bergbohm, *Jurisprudenz und Rechtsphilosophie: Kritische Abhandlungen*

under legal formalism, such as the 'legal consciousness' as the origin of customary international law,[118] as did the concept of civilisation. In 1927, Joseph L Kunz, an Austrian international lawyer and part of Hans Kelsen's formalist Vienna School, published an article on the 'nation civilisée', in which he aimed to clear the concept of all references to culture or race as juridically irrelevant factors. The elimination of extra-juridical notions from the concept of law was the central project of the Vienna School.[119] 'Civilisation', as it was now also featured in Article 38 of the PCIJ Statute, was now only to signify membership in the community of positive international law.[120] The definition of the international society was now circular as consisting of those states bound by the concrete legal order of international law, which in turn only applied to the states of the international society.[121] Through the foundation of colonies and protectorates, the geographical purview of international law was now nearly universal, though only a few societies under its governance were considered sovereign states.[122] And with the material differences prevailing, the extra-legal notions of civilisation were sublimated into the factual presuppositions nominally absent from the formal structure of international law.

E. Conclusion

What becomes discernible then from this survey of German international legal positivism in the eighteenth and nineteenth centuries from the perspective of its differentiation between Western and non-Western nations is that this process involves not so much the elimination of natural in favour of positive law, but rather a redefinition of their relationship vis-a-vis each other. To set apart European from non-European legal relations was already a significant motivating factor when Moser, Günther, Martens and Ompteda looked for ways to conceive of a proper European law of nations, ostensibly to account for amendments they thought had been made to the 'original' law of nature among each other, but also for what they saw as a distinct collective history that had led to a distinct cultural identity as against especially non-Christian peoples. The Historical School's concept of international law mobilised the factors, like cultural identity, religion and history,

(Berlin: Duncker & Humblot, 1892) §§ 16–17; see also Wilhelm (n 35) 67–69. On the shifts in German legal scholarship to the 'will' of the state, Koskenniemi, *Gentle Civilizer* (n 5) ch 3; von Bernstorff and Mayer (n 1) 333–46.

[118] See, eg, L Oppenheim, 'Die Lehre vom internationalen Gewohnheitsrecht' (1915) 25 *Niemeyer's Zeitschrift für internationales Recht* 1; von Bernstorff and Mayer (n 1) 346–47.

[119] Von Bernstorff (n 86) 45.

[120] JL Kunz, 'Zum Begriff der "nation civilisee" im modernen Völkerrecht' (1927) 7 *Zeitschrift für Öffentliches Recht* 86, 89–90; A Verdross, *Die Verfassung der Völkerrechtsgemeinschaft* (Vienna: Springer, 1926) 4: 'it is precisely the unity of law that provides for the unity of the society of law' (own translation); H Kelsen, *Reine Rechtslehre*, 2nd edn (Vienna: Deuticke, 1960) 337–39.

[121] Kunz (n 120) 90.

[122] ibid 93; Fisch (n 5) 23.

which the positivists of the eighteenth century had already named as the determining factors for European distinctness, but had struggled to accommodate into their formal natural law framework, and made them the core of their theory of international law by reversing the relationship between natural and positive law. Kaltenborn, Mohl and Bluntschli made the European self-perception into the markers of law as positive law and saw the role of legal philosophy as generalising concepts from that positive law, in an effort to approach a universal and divine idea of law as such. In the 1860s, Bluntschli then gave the theory a new universalist orientation by integrating it with the Hegelian philosophy of history that saw that same European characteristics as the expression of a universal development of civilisation.[123]

In making 'civilisation' the marker for agency in international law, Bluntschli could build on an ideological landscape that permeated the theoretical boundaries of natural law and positivism, rationalism and historicism. To start with, there was already a stream of scholars who had worked on reconstructing the European law of nations on the basis of Hegel's philosophy of right as the coming into being of a universal system of law globally.[124] The Historical School's theorem itself, in its description of the internal development of the German nation as a distinct culture, had seen the essence of this development as one of cultural formation. The formation of European states and advancements in culture and sciences were interlinked, if not synonymous, and German authors could express this by drawing on the ambivalence of the German word *Bildung* as meaning both formation (in the sense of something 'taking shape') and education, and which, in German, also has a semantic allusion to the Christian idea that God had created the humans after his own image ('*Bild*': *Ebenbildlichkeit Gottes*).[125] And it had after all been the natural law tradition that had understood civilisation as the formation of a state apparatus, a transition from a state of nature into a state in which life and property of every citizen were protected.[126] It was this process of a formation of

[123] See also von Bernstorff and Mayer (n 1).

[124] KT Pütter, 'Begriff und Wesen des praktischen Europäischen Völkerrechts' in *Beiträge zur Völkerrechts-Geschichte und Wissenschaft* (Leipzig: Adolph Wienbrack, 1843); JB Fallati, 'Die Genesis der Völkergesellschaft: Ein Beitrag zur Revision der Völkerrechtswissenschaft' (1844) 1 *Zeitschrift für die gesamte Staatswissenschaft* 160–89, 260–328, 558–608; HB Oppenheim, *System des Völkerrechts* (Frankfurt: Literarische Anstalt, 1845) 1–22. Heffter (n 32) also had been significantly influenced by Hegel's philosophy. The essential difference of these theories lay in their claim that international law resulted from the states themselves and not their international 'life', as Kaltenborn and the others inspired by the Historical School would have it. This trait was both Hegelian (in its emphasis of the state's will's role) and non-Hegelian in its affirmation of an international law which Hegel himself rejected precisely for its lack of independent state policing. On the Hegel-Savigny-controversy, see in detail Kletzer (n 66).

[125] Paradigmatically, see JG Herder, *Auch eine Philosophie der Geschichte zur Bildung der Menschheit* (Nachwort von Hans-Georg Gadamer; Frankfurt am Main: Suhrkamp, 1967, first published 1774); GWF Hegel, *The Phenomenology of Spirit*, trans and ed TP Pinkard (Cambridge: Cambridge University Press, 2018) 115, § 195; see H-G Gadamer, *Wahrheit und Methode: Grundzüge einer philosophischen Hermeneutik*, 6th edn (Tübingen: Mohr, 1990) 15–24.

[126] See, eg, Hobbes (n 13) 10.1; Achenwall and Pütter (n 13) §§ 653–83; I Kant, 'The Metaphysics of Morals (1797)' trans MJ Gregor, in *Practical Philosophy*, ed MJ Gregor (Cambridge: Cambridge

states that the nineteenth-century German scholars aimed to conceive of as a long and gradual process resulting from a people's inner struggle of self-development and advancement of culture rather than as the application of an abstract tenet of a natural law that reduced this process to the juridical imagination of a contractual agreement.

What the two theories of natural law and legal positivism had in common was thus the attempt to offer a convincing description of what followed from what they each saw as the universal nature of social organisation.[127] This holds true not only for the natural law approach, which sought to describe this nature with a uniform set of basic concepts around property and contract, but also to the seemingly parochialist Historical School's theorem that not least saw its vision of law as a universally applicable concept and already from the very beginning harboured the idea that in the European world, its proponents lived in themselves represented the most refined version of that idea, indeed not too far from perfection.

University Press, 1996) §§ 43–45 ('Doctrine of Right'). In his writings on the philosophy of history, Kant posits this sense of 'civilisation' on a global, cosmopolitan level, as the central purpose of human history. See, eg, I Kant, 'Idea for a Universal History with a Cosmopolitan Aim (1784)', trans AW Wood, in G Zöller (ed), *Anthropology, History, and Education* (Cambridge: Cambridge University Press, 2011). For Kant, people living in a state of nature were considered as posing a latent threat to others and could be compelled to either organise in a state or leave: see I Kant, 'Toward Perpetual Peace: A Philosophical Sketch', trans DL Colclasure, in *Toward Perpetual Peace and Other Writings on Politics, Peace, and History*, ed P Kleingeld (New Haven: Yale University Press, 2010) 73 (Ak 8:349); *cf* Bowden (n 104) 146.

[127] See also Haferkamp (n 60) 74–77; Schütze (n 11) 76–77.

7

The Islamic Conception of International Law

AYESHA SHAHID

A. Introduction

Before the emergence of the concept of a 'nation-state' and the evolution of modern international law, rules, principles and codes of conduct were laid down to regulate the relationships between empires. The Islamic Empire, like the Greek and Roman Empires, developed *As-Siyar* (Islamic international law) as its own functioning system of international law, which has governed the international relations of Muslim states for many centuries.[1]

Oppenheim's claim that it was the 'old Christian states of Western Europe that constituted the original international community within which international law grew up gradually through custom and treaty'[2] is based on a purely Western and Eurocentric vision of international law that completely ignores that international law has been part and parcel of various religious traditions and ancient civilisations. Indeed, a vision of international law as purely 'Western' has created anxieties amongst critical legal scholars such as Martti Koskenniemi, and Third World Approaches to International Law (TWAIL) scholars such as Antony Anghie and BS Chimni, who emphasise engaging with a comparative international law scholarship while criticising the Eurocentrism of international law.[3] Koskenniemi is of the view that:

> [A] serious comparative study of international law would contribute to … thinking of the world no longer in terms of what Hegel used to call abstract universals but seeing

[1] KR Bashir, *Islamic International Law: Historical Foundations and al-Shaybani's Siyar* (Cheltenham: Edward Elgar, 2018) 1.

[2] *Oppenheim's International Law vol. I, Peace* (ed by R Jennings and A Watts), 9th edn (London: Longmans, 1997) 87–88.

[3] A Angie, *Imperialism, Sovereignty and the Making of International Law* (New York: Cambridge University Press, 2005); BS Chimni, 'Third World Approaches to International Law: A Manifesto' (2006) 8 *International Community Law Review* 3; M Koskenniemi, 'The Case for Comparative International Law' (2009) 20 *Finnish Yearbook of International Law* 1.

> all players as both universal and particular at the same time, speaking a shared language but doing that from their own, localizable standpoint.[4]

As compared to critical legal scholars, the TWAIL scholars' interventions aim to unpack and deconstruct the colonial legacies of international law and engage in efforts to decolonise the lived realities of the peoples of the Global South.[5] Anghie argues that 'the colonial and postcolonial realities of international law have been obscured and misunderstood as a consequence of a persistent and deep seated set of ideas that has structured traditional scholarship on the history and theory of international law'.[6] Anghie and Chimni consider that international law is the lived experience of the people of the Third World under colonialism, and it is not the interpretations of the court or ratifications by the states.[7]

Judge Philip Jessup of the International Court of Justice too considers that 'the effectiveness of public international law … would be seriously impaired if there were no tolerance of certain differences stemming from various legal systems'.[8] A comparative approach to international law is therefore needed to explore non-Western conceptions of international law.

It is against this background that this chapter explores the Islamic conception of international law – that is *As-Siyar* – by examining the primary and secondary sources of Islamic law, *opinio juris* of Muslim jurists from early development of *As-Siyar* to contemporary scholars, and the Muslim state practice with regard to the peaceful settlement of disputes. The central aim of this chapter is to provide a comparative perspective by assessing similarities and differences between *As-Siyar* and international law as understood, interpreted, applied and approached by various scholars and different state and non-state actors.

By using a comparative law methodology, this chapter addresses the following questions: to what extent does *As-Siyar* in general or do certain elements of *As-Siyar* have any congruence with the modern international law principles? Do principles of *As-Siyar* resonate in modern international law? Does *As-Siyar* have any relevance in achieving peaceful resolution of disputes in the present-day context? And have principles of *As-Siyar* been adopted in the state practice of present-day Muslim majority states that are members of the Organisation of Islamic Cooperation (OIC) and *Al-Jāmi'ah al-'Arabiyyah* (also known as the League of Arab States (LAS))?[9]

[4] Koskenniemi (n 2) 1–4.

[5] U Natarajan et al, 'Introduction: TWAIL – on Praxis and the Intellectual' (2016) 37 *Third World Quarterly* 1946.

[6] A Anghie 'The Evolution of International Law: Colonial and Postcolonial Realities' (2006) 27 *Third World Quarterly* 739.

[7] See A Anghie and BS Chimni, 'Third World Approaches to International Law and Individual Responsibility in Internal Conflicts' (2003) 2 *Chinese Journal of International Law* 77, 78.

[8] PC Jessup, 'Diversity and Uniformity in the Law of Nations' (1964) 58 *American Journal of International Law* 341, 343.

[9] I prefer to use the term 'Muslim majority states' and not 'Islamic states', as not all countries with Muslim majority population have a purely Islamic character, either by adopting an Islamic form of government (Iran) or by implementing Islamic laws (Saudi Arabia, Sudan and Pakistan).

This chapter is divided into five main sections. Section B provides an overview of the origin and development of *As-Siyar* to show that, like modern international law, the historical accounts reveal that *As-Siyar* was the product of a wide range of sources and juristic thought, thus reflecting a legal plurality within the Islamic legal tradition. Section C analyses *As-Siyar* as perceived by twentieth- and twenty-first-century Islamic scholars. Section D compares the commonalities and differences between *As-Siyar* and modern international law. The next two sections in this chapter focus on the issue of peaceful settlement of disputes under *As-Siyar*. Section E examines four key peace treaties as a means for peaceful settlement of disputes, entered into by Muslim rulers at various points in Islamic history with non-Muslim rulers, to demonstrate that entering into treaties has been a practice of Muslim rulers in the past for achieving peaceful settlement of disputes. To further assess the application and implementation of *As-Siyar* principles and peaceful settlement of disputes in the present-day context, section F examines the role of the OIC and the LAS to ascertain whether principles of *As-Siyar* are still practised by the Muslim majority states, and their relevance to modern international law. Section G concludes that to achieve global peace and for an effective implementation of international law, the scope of international law must be broadened by taking an inclusive approach towards non-Western legal systems.

B. The Origin and Development of *As-Siyar*: An Overview

Before examining the evolution and development of *As-Siyar*, it is pertinent to understand the concept of *Sharia* in the Islamic legal tradition(s). In classical Islamic legal tradition, there is a distinction between rules of God as laid down in the *Qur'an* (the totality of those rules is known as the *Sharia*), the rules as understood and developed by the Muslim jurists (known as the *Fiqh*) and the state law developed by the Muslim states that is consistent with the *Sharia* (known as *Siyasia Sharia*).

Sharia is considered to be a comprehensive guide that covers all aspects of human life, both legal and non-legal. Various definitions of the term, while emphasising the divine and religiously ordained nature of *Sharia*, acknowledge that it cannot be reduced to a system of law alone. An-Naim argues that the scope and subject matter of *Sharia* is much broader than legal subject matter, ranging from ritual religious practices, ethical principles and social relations to positive legal rules.[10] Abou El Fadl is of the view that '*Shar or Shari'a* in itself does not necessarily denote a set of Divine Commandments with which human beings must comply. However, it does refer to normatively transcendent and evaluative criteria for the

[10] A An-Naim, *Towards an Islamic Reformation: Civil Liberties, Human Rights and International Law* (Syracuse: Syracuse University Press, 1996).

good and for goodness'.[11] While Kusha highlights the influence of pre-Islamic customary norms, as well as other legal traditions that show *Sharia* to be a living legal system that is dynamic and evolving in its nature:

> [A]s an evolving legal doctrine had to confront pre-Islamic norms, beliefs and customs prevalent among Bedouin Arabs as well as when Islam spread to the other parts of the world other legal systems, customs and mores that existed in the Old world came into contact with Islam's evolving doctrine of law … [As a result] … this evolving doctrine neither remained a strict man-made doctrine of law … nor could it become one of strict theological doctrine such as that produced by medieval Christianity.[12]

A more nuanced definition of *Sharia* is provided by Shaheen Ali, who, in the light of epistemological meaning of the term, portrays *Sharia* 'not as a static entity but as a stream, forever flowing onward, its currents intertwining, giving rise to legally enforceable rules, principles of morality, and principles of governance and social justice'.[13] Thus, *Sharia* is not just simply a set of laws; rather, it is an umbrella term that covers both legal and non-legal aspects of human conduct.

The aspects of *Sharia* which regulate international law and the conduct of states towards each other are termed as *As-Siyar*.[14] *As-Siyar* is the plural of the noun *sīra*, which means literally a 'path, way of life, conduct, practice, attitude, or behaviour'. Bsoul explains its historical evolution as follows:

> Essentially, the concept of siyar evolved from its lexicographical meaning – in particular, from its connotation of behavior or conduct. Siyar is Sira in the singular [and] came to be used by chroniclers in their narrative accounts to mean life or biography, ie, the conduct of an individual.[15]

According to al-Zamakhshar (1144), *sīra* is from *As-Siyar* (*sara fulanan siratan hasanatan*), which means someone well behaved. Following this, it was extended and modified to mean conduct and practice. *As-Siyar al-Awaleen* and *As-Siyar al-Sharī'a* are the two other terms in which *As-Siyar* has been used in relation to the conduct of the people of the past and the issues relating to the laws of warfare.[16]

As-Siyar or Islamic international law as a branch of Islamic law derives its legal basis and general principles from the *Sharia*, *Fiqh* and *Siyasia Sharia*.[17] Muslim

[11] KA El Fadl, 'Conceptualizing Shari'a in the Modern State' (2012) 56 *Villanova Law Review* 803, 809.

[12] HR Kusha, The *Sacred Law of Islam: A Case Study of Women's Treatment in the Islamic Republic of Iran's Criminal Justice System* (London: Routledge, 2002).

[13] SS Ali, *Modern Challenges to Islamic Law* (Cambridge: Cambridge University Press, 2016).

[14] J Rehman, *Islamic State Practices, International Law and the Threat from Terrorism: A Critique of the 'Clash of Civilizations' in the New World Order* (Oxford: Hart Publishing, 2005).

[15] L Bsoul, 'Historical Evolution of Islamic Law of Nations/*As-Siyar*: Between Memory and Desire' (2008) 17 *Digest of Middle East Studies* 48, 48. See also A Shahid, 'An Exploration of the Global History of International Law: Some Perspectives from within the Islamic Legal Tradition' in I de la Rasilla and A Shahid (eds), *International Law and Islam: Historical Explorations* (Leiden, Brill-Nijhoff, 2019).

[16] A al-Zamakhshari, *Al-Kashf 'ul Haqaiq al-Tanzeel*, vol 2 (Beirut: Dar al-M'arifah, 2009) 431.

[17] CB Lombardi and NJ Brown, 'Do Constitutions Requiring Adherence to Shari'a Threaten Human Rights? How Egypt's Constitutional Court Reconciles Islamic Law with the Liberal Rule of Law' (2006) 21 *American University International Law Review* 379, 397.

jurists, while developing the rules and principles of *As-Siyar*, have relied on and drawn inspiration from the divine textual sources also known as the primary sources, that is the *Qur'an* and the *Sunnah*, as well as secondary sources *Qiyas* (analogical deduction), *Ijma* (juristic consensus) and *Urf* (customary norms and practices). To these sources, jurists have also added the practice of Islamic rulers and caliphs, their official instructions to commanders and statesmen; constitutional laws; and the internal legislation of Islamic states in both the historic and the modern era.[18]

To interpret these sources, jurists over the centuries have relied on two methodologies – *Ijtihad* and *Taqlid* (placed by many established jurists in the category of secondary sources of law) – and have used juristic techniques such as *Iikhtilaf, Takhayyur, Talfiq, Maslaha, Darura, Istishab Istihsan* and *Saddal-Dhara* to develop the corpus of Islamic law (*Fiqh*).[19] Kamali is of the view that the rules of *Fiqh*, 'being largely the result of speculative reasoning, do not have the same immutability as *Sharia* and are susceptible to new interpretations in changed circumstances'.[20] Referring to the often-blurred distinction between the two terms, Esposito comments that it is the confusion of this distinction between *Sharia* and *fiqh*, reinforced by the doctrine of *Taqlid* or adherence to established law, that has led to the overly sacrosanct attitude towards the classical *fiqh*.[21]

Ijtihad thus has remained a significant methodology for developing Islamic law over the centuries. The Islamic conception of international law *As-Siyar* was developed by Muslim jurists who exercised *Ijtihad* and used their own independent reasoning for interpreting the original divine texts. In the words of Hallaq:

> *Ijtihad* provided and still provides a legal mechanism which is indispensable to legal theory as a device for discovering judicial judgments as set out in the *Qur'an* by Allah, and by this token a means of effecting legal reforms in accordance with the times and customs of society.[22]

The origins of *As-Siyar* lay in the divine sources, and the development of *As-Siyar* as a separate branch of Islamic law is attributed to a number of Muslim jurists from the fifth century onwards, who developed the rules of *As-Siyar* using both primary and secondary sources of Islamic law. Imam Al-Sha'bi (641–723) is considered to be the first scholar to contribute to *As-Siyar*. However, Shabi's contribution was limited to the narratives of the campaigns led by the Prophet, and he did not contribute towards developing the rules of *As-Siyar*. Abdullah Ibn 'Umar had

[18] M Bassiouni, 'Protection of Diplomats under Islamic Law' (1980) 74 *American Journal of International Law* 609.

[19] For detailed discussion on sources, see A Rahim, *Muhammadan Jurisprudence* (Lahore: Mansoor Book House, 1995) 44–45; NJ Coulson, *A History of Islamic Law* (Edinburgh: Edinburgh University Press, 1994) 80–81; MH Kamali, *Shari'ah Law: An Introduction* (Oxford: Oneworld Publications, 2008).

[20] Kamali (n 19) 14.

[21] JL Esposito, 'Muslim Family Law Reform: Towards an Islamic Methodology' (1976) 15 *Islamic Studies* 19, 23.

[22] WB Hallaq, 'Was the Gate of Ijtihad Closed?' (1984) 16 *International Journal of Middle Eastern Studies* 3, 13.

heard Sha'bi talking about these campaigns and was so impressed by his knowledge and description of campaigns that he remarked 'it seems as if Al-Shabi'i has participated with us in those campaigns'. Jalaly is of the view that the earliest extant work on *Siyar* was al-Majmu fil-Fiqh, authored by Imam Zayd ibn Ali.[23]

Among Muslim jurists, Imam Abu Hanifa al-Nu'man ibn Thabit is regarded as the founder of *As-Siyar*.[24] Imam Abu Hanifa used the term *As-Siyar* for the set of rules governing relations between a Muslim state and non-Muslim states during war and peace. He introduced the notion of territoriality in the relationships between Muslims and non-Muslims. Muslims and non-Muslims were viewed as juridical personalities, both as individuals and as territorial groups.[25] He developed the rules of *As-Siyar* by using individual reasoning and *Qiyas* (analogical deduction) rather than the narratives of the Prophet and his companions.[26] It was in fact through the works of Imam Abu Hanifa's disciples that the term *As-Siyar* became so widely used in later centuries to represent this area of the law. Imam Malik ibn Anas, a disciple of Imam Abu Hanifa and founder of the Maliki School of thought, in his treatise *Al-Mudawwana al-Kubra*, included a chapter entitled 'Kitab-ul-Jihad', in which he laid down rules that prohibited the killing of women, children, elderly men and monks and hermits in their cells. He also instructed that the property of monks and hermits should not be touched, as that was their only means of sustenance. As compared to *Al- Mudawwana*, Imam Malik, in his other book *Al-Muwatta*, provides more detailed rules on granting immunity to non-combatants.

The most prolific jurist to contribute towards the development of *As-Siyar* was Mohammad ibn al-Hasan- al-Shaybani (750–805). Shaybani is often described as the Hugo Grotius of the Muslims. Joseph Freiherr von Hammer-Purgstall, an eighteenth/nineteenth-century Austrian diplomat and pioneer orientalist, was the first to compare Shaybani to Hugo Grotius. The work of Shaybani's school constitutes one of the first great contributions to the *As-Siyar* and is identified with the 'Law of Nations'; the category of *As-Siyar* includes discussions of the justification and conduct of war.[27]

Shaybani wrote many books covering different aspects of Islamic jurisprudence and *As-Siyar*. One of Shaybani's earliest works on Islamic jurisprudence was *Kitab-ul- Asl*, also known as *Kitab al Mabsut*. It was a compilation of a dialogue between Imam Abu Yusuf and Shaybani commenting upon the legal doctrines and opinions of Imam Abu Hanifa. His two exclusive books are *Kitab-Al As-Siyar Al-Saghir* (*The Shorter Book on* As-Siyar) and *Kitab Al As-Siyar Al Kabir* (*The*

[23] Z Jalaly, 'Analysis of Origin, Development and Nature of Islamic International Law' (2018) 1 *Kardan Journal of Social Sciences and Humanities* 3, 7–8.

[24] AS Bouzenita, 'The Siyar: An Islamic Law of Nations?' (2007) 35(19) *Asian Journal of Social Science* 25.

[25] LA Bsoul, 'Historical Evolution of Islamic Law of Nations/Siyar: Between Memory and Desire' (2008) 17 *Digest of Middle East Studies* 48, 58.

[26] ibid.

[27] J Kelsay, 'Al-Shaybani and the Islamic Law of War' (2003) 2(1) *Journal of Military Ethics* 64.

Longer Book on As-Siyar). *Kitab Al Kabir* is considered to be his magnum opus.[28] Judge Weeramantry considers that Hugo Grotius' writings on the *jus gentium* may have been influenced by the works of Shaybani on the subject.[29]

Shaybani contributed to the systematisation of the rules of *As-Siyar* and provided an in-depth analysis of the lawfulness of settlements of disputes over usurped property, blood-money payment, and ownership of dwellings and slaves.[30] In Shaybani's writings one also finds references to questions related to day-to-day administrative matters in war, such as the distribution of war booty, and treatment of women and children.[31] He emphasised that when women and children are captured in war, a certain code of conduct needs to be followed – for instance, transport for women and children is considered an obligation, so much so that if a means of transport is not immediately at hand and the captives are unable to walk, the commander must hire transport for them. A high degree of humane behaviour was demanded of Muslims in warfare that if not complied with would deprive the war of its meritorious character.[32]

Shaybani, in his treatise *As-Siyar Al-Kabir*, expounds in detail upon the rules granting *aman* (safe conduct or pledge of security) to non-Muslims upon entering into Muslim territory for a fixed period of time, for the purposes of safe entry and residing or carrying out trade. *Aman* was considered as a sacred promise, where the foreigner receiving it came under the full protection of the receiving state during its term and within its jurisdiction. It could be given both in times of war and peace. In times of war, if a Muslim gave *aman* to a person, then his life would be saved and security had to be provided, even if that person was fighting. Similarly, in times of peace, the objective of giving *aman* was to facilitate international trade, travel and interaction between nations through envoys.[33] Allain, while examining the translation of Shaybani's *Kitab-Al As-Siyar Al-Saghir* (*The Shorter Book on* As-Siyar) by Mahmood Ahmad Ghazi, states that 'Muhammad Shaybani is second to none in the pantheon of classic international jurists; as the first to provide a systematic account of international law, more than *eight* centuries before Hugo Grotius' *Iure Belli ac Pacis* of 1625'.[34]

[28] M Khadduri, *The Islamic Law of Nations: Shaybani's Siyar* (Baltimore: Johns Hopkins University Press, 1966) 18.

[29] CG Weeramantry, *Islamic Jurisprudence: An International Perspective* (New York: Palgrave Macmillan, 1988) 132.

[30] MA Baderin, 'Muhammad Al -Shaybani (749/50–805)' in B Fasbender and A Peters (eds), *The Oxford Handbook of the History of International Law* (Oxford, Oxford University Press, 2014) 1081, 1082.

[31] M Ibn Al-Hasan *Al-Shaybani, Kitab al-Siyar Al-Kabir* (Beirut: Dar al-Kutub al-'Ilmiyyah, 1997) 252–53.

[32] CF Amerasinghe, 'The Historical Development of International Law: Universal Aspects' (2001) 39 *Archiv des Völkerrechts* 374.

[33] For further details, see KR Bashir, 'Al-Shaybani and Aman: Treatment of Foreigners in the Classical Islamic State with Special Focus on Diplomatic Envoys' in M-L Frick and AT Muller (eds), *Islam and International Law: Engaging Self-Centrism from a Plurality of Perspectives* (Leiden: Brill, 2013) 149.

[34] J Allain, 'Khadurri as Gatekeeper of the Islamic Law of Nations?' in de la Rasilla and A Shahid (n 15) 127.

A few other jurists that need mentioning here include Abu-al- Hasan Ali-ibn-Muhammad al-Mawardi (974–1058), Muhammad-ibn-Ahmad al-Sarakshi (1009–90), Najm al-Din-ibn Hafs-al-Nasafi(1068–1142), Ala-al-Din-Abu Bakr-al-Kasani (1115–91) and Abu Ishaq Ibrahim ibn Muhammad ibn al-Harith al-Fazari (1315–1408). Mawardi's *al Hawai-al-Kabir* is the most important treatise on the topic of *jihad* from that time. It provides an analysis of the classical theories of military *jihad* and the necessity of undertaking it in specific circumstances.[35] Sarakhsi, Nasafi and Kasani used the term in a legal and technical sense to regulate several kinds of relations between Muslims and non-Muslims, including *murtaddūn* (apostates), *musta'mins* (enemy aliens) who have been given *aman* (the promise of security and safe conduct, given to an enemy by Muslims) and *ahl al-dhimma* (non-Muslim subjects of the Islamic state).[36] Fazari, an expert on *hadith* literature from Kufa, wrote a treatise on *As-Siyar*, in which he dealt with the subjects of *maghazi*, *As-Siyar*, *jihad* and other rulings.[37] In addition, he analysed the nature of the relationship between Muslims and non-Muslims, including *ahl al-dhimma* (inhabitants of territory protected by a treaty of surrender) and *muharibīn* (non-Muslims dwelling in *dār al-harb*).

These jurists transformed the concept of *As-Siyar* from a narrative to a normative character, especially with regard to rules concerning the resort to war (*jus ad bellum*), treaties and the conduct of war (*jus in bello*).[38] Rules were laid down to determine who should not be killed during the course of war, distinction between combatants and non-combatants, the protection of properties, the rights of prisoners of war and termination of their captivity, and the effects of war. A binding set of rules was laid down to deal with rebels and apostates. Similarly, it had rules regarding the immunity of envoys and territorial jurisdiction, protection of non-Muslim citizens in a Muslim state, foreigners, especially businessmen from non-Muslim nations who visited for business or requested asylum from Muslim individuals or state. Hans Kruse asserts that 'the positive international law of Europe had more than eight centuries later not yet reached the high degree of humanitarianization with which the Islamic law of war was imbued'.[39] The treatment of non-combatants during war thus suggests that the Islamic law of war formulated centuries ago respected rules that today form part of modern humanitarian law. Hamidullah argues that as the *Qur'an* and *Sunnah* provide only guiding principles, it was the Muslim jurists who, after the death of the Prophet, expanded those guiding

[35] A al-Mawardi, *Al-Hawi al-kabir fi fiqh madhhab al-imam al-shafi'i radi allahu 'anhu wa-huwa sharh mukhtasar al-muzani*, vol 14, ed 'Ali Muhammad Mu'awwad and 'Adil Ahmad 'Abd al-Mawjud (Beirut: Daral-kutub al-'arabiyya, 1994) 102.

[36] See the references in Shahid (n 15) 71.

[37] ibid.

[38] K Bennoune, 'As-Salāmu `Alaykum? Humanitarian Law in Islamic Jurisprudence' (1994) 15 *Michigan Journal of International Law* 605, 643.

[39] H Kruse, *The Foundations of Islamic International Jurisprudence* (Karachi: Pakistan Historical Society, 1956).

principles and developed 'a complete system of law which served all the purposes of the Imperial Muslims, even at the height of their widest expansion from the Atlantic to the Pacific'.[40]

The foregoing discussion demonstrates that Islamic legal scholars contributed to the development of *As-Siyar* as a unique discipline of Islamic law to regulate the relationship between Muslims and non-Muslims, and it set out the principles of war and peace. There was no scarcity of scholarly works written by Islamic scholars on various aspects of *As-Siyar* between 723 and 1400, and those works certainly precede Western scholarship on law of peoples.[41]

C. *As-Siyar* in the Eyes of Contemporary Muslim Scholars[42]

The early twentieth-century scholars Nagib Arminazi,[43] Imam Abu Zahra,[44] Majid Khadduri[45] and Hamidullah[46] have provided various definitions of the term *As-Siyar*. Nagib Arminazi defined it as:

> [T]he set of rules that are binding on Muslims in their relations with non-Muslims, whether they fight [the Muslim state] or have peaceful relations [with them], whether they are individuals or states, and whether they are inside Muslim territory or outside of it, and the set of these rules also include the situation of apostates, rebels and robbers.[47]

Whereas Imam Abu Zahra defines it as:

> The rules of jihad and war, what is allowed in it and what is not, and the rules of [permanent] peace treaties and temporary truce, and the rules of who should be granted alien status and who should not, the rules of war booty, ransom and enslavement, as well as other problems that arise during wars and its aftermath. In short, it designates the rules of international relations between Muslims and other [communities] during peace and war, although most of the discussion is about the war.[48]

[40] M Hamidullah, *The Muslim Conduct of State* (New York: Other Press, 1961).

[41] I de La Rasilla, 'The Protean Historical Mirror of International Law' in de la Rasilla and A Shahid (n 15) 15.

[42] Most parts of this section are taken from my book chapter: A Shahid, 'An Exploration of the Global History of International Law: Some Perspectives from within the Islamic Legal Tradition' in de la Rasilla and A Shahid (n 15).

[43] N Armazani, *al-Shar' al-Dawlīfi al-Islam* (Damascus: Matb'at Ibn Zaydun, Demascus, 1930) 44.

[44] M Abu Zahra in the introduction to *Sharh kitab al-Siyar al-Kabir* of Muhammad al-Shaybani with the commentary by Al–Sarakhsi (Cairo: University of Cairo Press, 1957) 33.

[45] Khadduri (n 28) 66.

[46] Hamidullah (n 40).

[47] N Arminazi 'L'Islam et le droit international' (PhD thesis, Paris, 1929).

[48] See Zahra (n 44) as translated in M Munir, 'Islamic International Law (*Siyar*): An Introduction' (2012) 35 *Hamdard Islamicus* 37.

One of the criticisms of these definitions is that they are not applicable in the present-day context, as the changes that are brought about by the obligations of Muslim states under international law are not taken into account.[49]

Majid Khadduri defines *As-Siyar* as 'an extension of Islamic law designed to govern relations of the Muslims, whether inside or outside the world of Islam', whereas Hamidullah defines it as: 'That part of the law and custom of the land and treaty obligations which a Muslim de facto or de jure State observes in its dealings with other de facto or de jure States.'[50]

The concept of a nation-state, as we understand and experience it today, did not exist in seventh-century Arabia or for a long time thereafter. Modern nation-states, including Muslim jurisdictions, have governance structures visibly different from that of the seventh-century State of Medina.[51] The use of the term *As-Siyar* as the 'Islamic Law of Nations' is a much later development that became prominent among scholars during the early twentieth century.[52]

Mohammad Fadel argues that Khadduri's understanding of the *As-Siyar* was dominated by his treatment of the *As-Siyar* as a religious dogma rather than systematic legal thought, and this reinforced pre-existing notions of Islamic law as wholly other to Western understandings of law, reducing scholarly interest in exploring the *As-Siyar*.[53] In the same vain, Allain criticizes Khadurri's writings on Shaybani's *Siyar* by stating that Khadurri:

> [D]ownplayed the importance of Shaybani and his writing, leaving a half-century's lost opportunity as to the international law scholars' knowledge of the place of the *Siyar* generally, and of Shaybani specifically, in the annals of what was to become known by the nineteenth century as international law.[54]

Hamidullah defines *As-Siyar* as: 'That part of the law and custom of the land and treaty obligations which a Muslim *de facto* or *de jure* state observes in its dealings with other *de facto* or *de jure* states.'[55]

These early twentieth-century scholars have also used various terms, such as 'Muslim Law of Nations' and 'Islamic Law of Nations', to equate *As-Siyar* with international law. In their view, just as the original *jus gentium* was a branch of municipal Roman law, the Muslim Law of Nations was a branch of the corpus of Islamic law.[56] However, recent contemporary scholars such as Khaled Ramadan Bashir, Mohammad Fadel, Anke Iman Bouzenita, Abdu Ala An-Naim and

[49] Munir (n 48).

[50] Khadduri (n 45); Hamidullah (n 40).

[51] SS Ali, *Modern Challenges to Islamic Law* (Cambridge: Cambridge University Press, 2016).

[52] Since the second half of the twentieth century, the other two terms used interchangeably with the term 'Islamic Law of Nations' are 'Muslim Law of Nations' and 'Islamic International Law'.

[53] M Fadel, 'Sovereignty, Territoriality, and Private International Law in Classical Muslim International Law' (2024) 71 *American Journal of International Law* 856.

[54] Allain (n 34).

[55] M Hamidullah, *The Muslim Conduct of State*, 5th edn (Lahore: SH Muhammad Ashraf, 1968) 3.

[56] ibid 16.

Shaheen Ali do not accept equating *As-Siyar* with the term 'Law of Nations'. Bashir defines *As-Siyar* as follows:

> *Siyar* is a branch of Islamic law that regulates relations involving a Muslim state or between Muslims and non-Muslims both domestically and internationally both in times of peace and war.[57]

Fadel is of the following view:

> Islamic rules of international law are best understood as providing legal baselines that were to regulate the conduct of the emerging Islamic State in the absence of treaty commitments with non-Muslims, while at the same time enabling that state to enter into peaceful relations with non-Muslims.[58]

Bouzenita and An-Naim also do not accept equating *As-Siyar* with the term 'Islamic Law of Nations', 'Muslim international law' or 'Islamic international law'. Bouzenita considers that as *As-Siyar* lacks the concept and definition of a territorial state, which constitutes one of the basic elements of modern international law, it cannot be equated with modern international law.[59] An-Naim argues that 'there can only be one international law, but it has to be truly international by incorporating relevant principles from different legal traditions, instead of the exclusive Euro-Centric concept, principles and institutions of international law as commonly known today'.[60]

An-Naim proposes that the relationship between Islamic law and modern international law should be seen in terms of a more inclusive approach to the latter, rather than conflict or competition between the two.[61] An-Naim also emphasises the significance of certain beliefs and values, such as equality, justice, peace and the rule of law, that are common to all legal systems. He argues that international law is based on shared belief. In his view:

> [I]t is not true that international law seeks to achieve order without belief, unless one limits the realm and scope of belief to doctrinal religious belief, which was never true of Muslims anyway. International law is indeed based on shared belief, such as belief in the rule of law, in liberal values of equality and justice, or at least in the desirability and possibility of peace.[62]

This could only be possible if the relationship between these two legal systems is founded on a clear understanding of differences in their nature and development,

[57] Bashir (n 1) 7.
[58] M Fadel, 'International Law, Regional Developments: Islam' (2009) *Max Planck Encyclopaedia of Public International Law* para 57, https://opil.ouplaw.com/display/10.1093/law:epil/9780199231690/law-9780199231690-e711.
[59] Bouzenita (n 24) 44.
[60] Workshop on Islamic Law: Islamic Law and International Law, Joint Annual Meeting of the American Society of Comparative Law and Law and Society Association (2004), https://web.archive.org/web/20121202012257/www.aals.org/am2004/islamiclaw/international.htm.
[61] ibid.
[62] ibid.

as well as appreciation of the political and sociological context in which they operate. An-Naim is not in favour of using the compatibility/incompatibility frame of reference for generating a positive debate.[63] Similarly, Gamal Bader is of the view that:

> Contemporary Islamic legal thought has no trouble subscribing to all current principles of International Law. Beyond that it aspires to enrich International Law with its own contributions. What contemporaneous legal systems can contribute to each other and to international law is a different emphasis on values, a particular pattern of juridical reasoning and a distinctive methodology in the search for solutions to common problems. In all these areas Islamic law has much to offer to the ongoing process of development of international law.[64]

Ali, while accepting the differences in remit and reach of the Islamic and Westphalian legal orders, emphasises that the overlaps between the two offer a common discursive space and engagement with a view to some mutually useful transformative processes.[65] Ali provides a more balanced and logical approach, of comparing the substantive content of *As-Siyar* with international law.

Drawing on these views, it is argued that to promote peaceful settlement of disputes and global peace, it is pertinent to take stock of commonalities and differences between *As-Siyar* and the Westphalian model of international law.

D. Commonalities and Differences between *As-Siyar* and Modern International Law

In recent years, there has been an increased interest in comparative international law as a field of research. Siems divides comparative international law methodology into two main categories: vertical and horizontal.[66] The horizontal category of comparative international law provides room for assessing the convergences and divergences between *As-Siyar* and modern international law. Using this horizontal category will be useful to explore the possibility of unifying rules that are common in Islamic and modern international law, as this could lead to legitimacy and acceptance of modern international law by Muslim states and non-state actors and in achieving peaceful settlement of disputes. To begin with, the sources of *As-Siyar* suggests that the *Qur'an* as a primary source represents divine authority; the *Sunnah*, embodying the Arabian *jus gentium*, is equivalent to custom, whereas rules expressed in treaties with non-Muslims fall into the category of agreement,

[63] ibid.

[64] GM Badr, 'A Survey of Islamic International Law' in MW Janis and C Evans (eds), *Religion and International Law* (The Hague: Martinus Nijhoff, 1999) 95, 100–01.

[65] SS Ali, 'Resurrecting Siyar through Fatwas? (Re)Constructing 'Islamic International Law' in a Post-(Iraq) Invasion World' (2009) 14 *Journal of Conflict & Security Law* 115, 124.

[66] See Siems, ch 1 in this volume.

and the juristic commentaries of Islamic scholars, as well as the utterances and opinions of the Muslim rulers in the interpretation and the application of the law, based on analogy, are said to form reason.[67] Bennoune argues that when analysed in terms of modern international law, the sources of *As-Siyar* conform to the same categories as defined by modern jurists and by the statute of the International Court of Justice – namely, authority, custom, agreement and reason.[68] Rehman, by using a comparative lens, argues that further analogies can be drawn between the sources of modern international law and Islamic law. In his view, *Ijma* or agreement of the jurists can be regarded as akin to Article 38(1)(d) of the Statute of the International Court of Justice, which allows for 'judicial decisions and the teachings of the most highly qualified publicists'.[69] However, Rehman also raises the concern that to consider *Ijma* as analogous to modern-day Western liberal democracy would be stretching the concept a bit too far.

Another commonality between *As-Siyar* and modern international law can be found in the origins of both legal traditions. *As-Siyar*'s origin in the divine sources can be compared with the sources of modern international law that lie in natural law theory. Philosophers such as St Thomas Aquinas considered that natural law formed part of the law of God. The relevance of the theory of natural law to the development of modern international law cannot be over-emphasised, for a British historical lawyer, Sir Henry Maine, stated that the birth of modern international law was the grandest function of the law of nature.[70] While the origin of modern international law is in the natural law theory, philosophers like Francisco Vitoria (1480–1546), Francisco Suarez (1548–1617), Alberico Gentili (1552–1608) and Hugo van Groot (1583–1645, also known as Hugo Grotius) have made enormous contributions to the development of modern international law from a natural law perspective. Although Grotius mentioned God in his definition of natural law, he did argue that natural law would still be valid even if there were no God. Thus, as opposed to Aquinas, Grotius secularised international law and made it supportable purely on the basis of reason.[71] Grotius, while acknowledging that there is clear evidence of the principles of natural law, believed that the existence of these principles had to be proved to others.[72] Thus, he set out to give the proof by making reference to testimonies of philosophers, historians, poets and statesmen across ages. Bluntschli, on the other hand, while drawing a distinction between civilised and non-civilised peoples, argues that international law could extend to all peoples across the world without thereby requiring any of these non-civilised peoples to forsake their culture.[73] In fact, it was Bluntschli's view that international law lay on

[67] Bennoune (n 38) 605.
[68] ibid 614.
[69] Rehman (n 14) 14.
[70] HJS Maine, *Ancient Law* (London: CreateSpace, 2017 [1861]) 56 and 64–66.
[71] ibid 64.
[72] MM Lawan, 'Al-Shaybani and Grotius: An Inquiry into Comparative International Law' (2020) 6 *Asian Yearbook of Human Rights and Humanitarian Law* 148.
[73] JC Bluntschli, *Das moderne Völkerrecht* (Nordlingen: CH Beck, 1872) 55.

a foundation of natural law, which carried universal extension and did not depend on the specificity of different cultural forms. In more recent studies, Novak and Berman have examined the influence of Christianity on secular law.[74]

Looking at the Muslim states' practice, the membership of the United Nations (UN) and acceptance of the UN Charter and its rules on the prohibition of the use of force, active participation of Muslim states in the formulation of various human rights treaties and their accession to these treaties (albeit with reservations in the name of Islam) are examples that show the congruence between modern international law and Islamic international law. The insistence on the prohibition on the use of force in international relations by Muslim states under the UN Charter and the endorsement of principles of international humanitarian law point towards compatibility between the fundamental principles of international law and *As-Siyar*.[75] Moreover, the constitutions of majority of Muslim states require states to conform both to Islamic law and international legal norms (and often specifically international human rights norms). The courts in many Muslim states have held that laws that are inconsistent with international norms are inconsistent with human welfare and justice, and thus with the general goals of the *Sharia*. Such examples offer a space for mutual dialogue and constructive engagement with Islamic international law. These common principles in the substantive content of the *As-Siyar* and modern international law show convergence of the two legal systems.

In fact, *Siyar* gives rise to and protects some of the principles of modern international law, such as reciprocity, non-aggression, the prioritisation of peaceful dispute resolutions, non-intervention in domestic affairs of other states, the unity of the human race, the fulfilment of promises in good faith and the promotion of fundamental human rights.[76]

In the *Qur'an*, saving a human life is regarded as a noble act – in particular, protecting the lives of innocent people. The *Qur'an* clearly states that 'if any one saved a life, it would be as if he saved the humanity'. Elsewhere in the *Qur'an* it says: 'If anyone slays a human being unless it be [in punishment] for murder or for spreading corruption on earth, it shall be as though he had slain all mankind; whereas if anyone saves a life, it shall be as though he had saved the lives of all mankind.' Thus, the *Qur'an* equates saving a life to the preservation of the *din* (religion) or, as the *Maqasid al-Shari'ah* (*Principles of Sharia*) contended, that protecting humanity is an integral part of the Islamic law. This is very similar to what St Augustine (354–430), in his theory of just war, emphasised – that tolerating grievances and pains to save an innocent and oppressed life follows Christian morals, and for this purpose, when needed, perpetrating war is not against Christian morals.[77]

[74] JH Berman, *Law and Revolution II: The Impact of the Protestant Reformation on the Western Legal Tradition* (Cambridge, MA: Harvard University Press, 2006); D Novak, 'Law: Religious or Secular?' (2000) *86 Virginia Law Review* 569.

[75] See section C above.

[76] Badr (n 64) 100–01.

[77] MN Hamadani, 'Protecting Human Life through Humanitarian Intervention in Islamic Law' (2024) 1(2) *Legal Transformation in Muslim Societies* 122.

Other common rules include the principles that today form the basis of *jus in bello* and *jus in bellum* in modern international law. These principles are found in the Islamic legal tradition: for instance, *As-Siyar* sets out the rules that now form part of the principle of granting immunity under modern international law by providing protection to envoys and diplomats, foreigners, especially businessmen from non-Muslim nations who visited for business or requested asylum.

Likewise, the rules about the treatment of non-combatants during war in *As-Siyar* are very similar to what today forms part of the modern humanitarian law. *As-Siyar* rules correspond to the international humanitarian law conventions, ranging from the 1856 Convention Establishing the International Committee for the Red Cross, The Hague Conventions of 1899 and 1907 and the four 1949 Geneva Conventions and their 1977 Additional Protocols. One can thus say that a common theme between the principles of international law and *As-Siyar* is the concept of humanity and extending humanitarian protection for peaceful coexistence.

However, there are certain divergences between the Westphalian model of international law and *As-Siyar*. As mentioned elsewhere, *As-Siyar* pre-dates its Western counterpart by several centuries and was developed much earlier than the present-day Western international law. The origins of *As-Siyar* can be traced back to the very early historical period of the evolution of Islamic law from the times of the Prophet Mohammad. Western international law, on the other hand, is a more recent phenomenon that developed gradually from the early sixteenth century onwards.[78] *As-Siyar*, for instance, recognised and extended protection to individuals from the very initial stages, as compared to modern international law, which granted protection to individuals at a much later stage in its development. Sexual violence in war was considered a war crime since the early days of Islam, whereas in modern international law, rape and sexual violence were not recognised as a crime until the adoption of the 1993 Statute of the International Criminal Tribunal for the Former Yugoslavia.

Another divergence between the two is that the history of Islamic international law is much larger and cannot be compartmentalised into a specific geographical region, as significant contributions to Islamic legal thought and legal practice also came from Persia, India, South East Asia (including Indonesia and Malaysia) and European localities, especially but not exclusively Spain, Italy, Greece, the Balkans and other places.[79] Modern international law, on the other hand, is Western and Eurocentric in its vision.

To further analyse the relevance of *As-Siyar* in the modern-day context, the next section examines the Islamic concept of *sulh* or peaceful settlement of disputes in order to establish that peaceful resolutions have been part and parcel of Islamic history, and that these examples from the past can provide the basis for achieving peaceful settlements of disputes in the present-day context.

[78] Al-Mawardi (n 35) 73.

[79] N Samour, 'Is There a Role for Islamic International Law in the History of International Law?' (2014) 25 *European Journal of International Law* 313.

E. Peaceful Resolution of Disputes in Islamic Law

1. Primary Sources of Islamic Law

The two primary sources of Islamic law place emphasis on moral and just relations between states, and call for a peaceful resolution of disputes and abiding by treaty obligations and agreements. The *Qur'an* places emphasis on peaceful relations between individuals.[80] In chapter 49: verse 9, it is clearly stated that Muslims should end disagreements by making peace: 'If two parties among the believers fall into a quarrel, make ye peace between them.' Similarly, in chapter 8: verse 61, the *Qur'an* states: 'But if the enemy Incline towards peace, Do thou [also] incline towards peace, and trust in God: for He is the one that heareth and knoweth [All things].'

The *Qur'an* orders Muslims to: 'Fulfil the Covenant of God when ye have entered into it, And break not your oaths after ye have confirmed them; Indeed ye have made God your surety; for God knoweth all,'[81] Similarly, the *Qur'an* commands 'but if [any] seek your aid in religion, it is your duty to help them, except against a people with whom ye have a treaty of mutual alliance'.[82] As such, all treaty obligations must be respected and be followed in good faith. These verses of the *Qur'an* show that a treaty agreement must not be coercive, unjust or oppressive towards one party, and the consent of all parties must be obtained before entering into a treaty obligation.

Similarly, the Prophet Mohammad also emphasised the observance and adherence to treaty obligations. On one occasion, he clearly stated that: 'Anyone who kills a person from among the people with whom there is a treaty [*mu'ahid*] will not smell the fragrance of Paradise, even though its fragrance extends to a walking distance of forty years.'[83] This saying of the Prophet Muhammad confirms the sanctity and observance of treaty obligations. As the founder and head of the first Islamic state, he entered into a range of international agreements and emphasised compliance with those agreements.

Alongside the *Qur'anic* verses and *Sunnah* of the Prophet Mohammad, there are a number of examples in Islamic history of treaties entered into by Muslim rulers to achieve peaceful settlement of disputes. This section analyses three other key treaties entered into by Muslim rulers at various points in history, and the *Tanzeemat* reforms during Ottoman rule, to argue that entering into treaties for peaceful co-existence and settlement of disputes is one of the core values of Islamic legal tradition and, in particular, a key principle of *As-Siyar*. In this section I focus

[80] I have used here the *Qura'nic* translations by Abdullah Yusuf Ali, available at https://quranyusufali.com.

[81] *Qur'an*, chapter 16: verse 91.

[82] ibid, chapter 8: verse 72.

[83] Sahih al-Bukhari 6914, as translated at https://fiqh.islamonline.net/en/do-the-polytheists-qualify-for-dhimmis-status.

on the Treaty of *Hudaibiya*, Caliph Harun al-Rashid's treaty with Empress Irene of Byzantium (in 802), Suleiman the Magnificent's (the tenth Sultan of the Ottoman Empire) treaty with King Francis I of France (in 1535) and the *Tanzeemat* reforms during Ottoman rule.

The Treaty of *Hudaibiya* between Muslims and infidels is a significant example that demonstrates the principle of peaceful co-existence and acceptance of reconciliation with the non-Muslims. The Treaty of *Hudaibiya* demonstrates that the fundamental rule of Western international law, *pacta sunt servanda*, formulated by Grotius in the seventeenth century, is also a fundamental rule of Islamic international law, where it is based upon *Qur'anic* injunctions and the *Sunnah* of the Prophet.[84] It is noteworthy that entering treaties was a pre-Islamic Arab customary practice that was approved and upheld by the Prophet Mohammad, and as such it became part of the *Sunnah* of the Prophet. The entering into treaties by the Prophet with his enemies and surrounding tribes demonstrates that there was already customary international law in existence, and treaties are an example of customary international law. It also confirmed the principle of freedom of religion and the prevention of religious persecution. Its negotiating history showed the sanctity of emissaries, that a violation of an ambassador's immunity is a *casus belli* and that no ambassador may be detained or harmed. One can thus argue that concluding peace treaties with the enemies is in accordance with the Islamic principles as laid down in the *Qur'an* and *Sunnah*, whether for the purposes of expediency or to eliminate conflict or a setback or defeat.

2. Treaties between Early Muslim Rulers and the Roman Byzantine Empire

When Islam spread to various parts of the world, treaties and peace agreements were entered into by the Ummayads, Abbasids and Ottomans with the Roman-Byzantine Empire. From the time of Roman rule over the Arab tribes in the first century to the rise of Islam in the seventh century, the Arabs, Roman Catholics and Byzantines were not always at war with each other; there were periods when peace prevailed between them and they were able to live together as different but not indifferent neighbours. Muslim rulers entered into treaties with the Roman-Byzantine Empires. After the consolidation of power in about 750, Islam sought to establish conditions under which relations could be conducted with non-Muslim states. There were certain kinds of legal agreements permitted with such states, which ensured safety (the basis for diplomatic missions) and were an alliance between equals – upon the defeat of Muslims by the infidels.[85]

[84] Bouzenita (n 24) 149.

[85] M Khadduri, *War and Peace in the Law of Islam* (Baltimore: Johns Hopkins University Press, 1955), as cited in Amerasinghe (n 32).

One of the significant treaties was the treaty between the Abbasid ruler, Caliph Harun al-Rashid and Empress Irene of Byzantium in 798. In this treaty, the Byzantines were the weaker party; they were forced to pay annual tribute to Baghdad, as well as to end their frequent violations of the Abbasid frontier.[86] Caliph Harun Al-Rashid also sent embassies to the Chinese Tang dynasty to establish good relations with them.[87] The emissaries and envoys were also shown due protocol.

According to Mahmassani:

> [Within] Islamic practice, diplomatic agents were generally received with gorgeous ceremony. Similar ceremonies were observed on their departure. These ceremonies were often accompanied by great hospitality and the display of extravagant pomp and lavish processions, in order to give the emissaries the impression of the grandeur and power of the State.[88]

From the fourteenth century onwards, the world saw the emergence of the Ottoman Empire, representing Islamic rule, followed by the Habsburg Empire in Europe in the fifteenth century, representing Christendom, which expanded to Eastern and South-Eastern Europe. The Ottomans became the premier Muslim empire throughout the fifteenth to nineteenth centuries. In 1517, the Ottoman Empire extended its domain to include the Arabic-speaking regions of North Africa, Egypt, Syria, Iraq and the Arabian Peninsula. With this, they now controlled the three holy sites – Makkah, Madinah and Jerusalem – and thus bore the responsibility for protection of the holy cities.

The rise of the Ottoman Empire revived Muslim power and gave fresh impetus to the development of the *As-Siyar*. The Ottoman Empire played an important role in the shaping of *As-Siyar* by entering into treaties with the Habsburg Empire. Despite the conflicting religious beliefs, the Ottomans and the Habsburgs entered into a range of contracts and economic, diplomatic and cultural treaties for territorial and regional hegemony.

One of the most significant treaties entered at that time was between the Ottoman Sultan Sulieman the Magnificent and King Francis I of France in 1535. This treaty introduced innovations in the relations between Christian powers and Islam in early modern times. The preamble treated the King of France and his representatives as equals with Sultan Sulieman and his representatives. Article 1 provided for the establishment of a 'bonne et sure paix' (valid and sure peace) between the Sultan and the King, and granted reciprocal rights to the subjects of each monarch in the territory of the other. The French were to enjoy rights of

[86] For further details on treaties, see LH Bsoul, *International Treaties (Mu'ahadat) in Islam: Theory and Practice in the Light of Siyar* (Montreal: McGill University Press, 2003).

[87] M Broomhall, *Islam in China: A Neglected Problem* (London: Morgan & Scott Ltd, 1910) 25, 26.

[88] S Mahmassani, 'The Principles of International Law in the Light of Islamic Doctrine' (1966) 117 *Recueil des Cours de l'Académie de Droit International* 201.

exemption from the poll tax, along with the right of trial in their consulates in accordance with their own laws.

According to Article 2 of the treaty, the King of France had the right to:

> [S]end to Constantinople or Pera or other places of the Empire a bailiff … The said bailiff and consul shall be received and maintained in proper authority so that each one of them may in his locality, and without being hindered by any judge, qadi, soubashi or other according to his faith and law, hear, judge and determine all causes, suits and differences both civil and criminal, which might arise between merchants and other subjects of the King [of France] … The qadi or other officers of the Grand Signior may not try any differences between the merchants and subjects of the King, even if the said merchants should request it, and if perchance the said qadis should hear a case their judgment shall be null and void.

Under the treaty, the subjects of the Habsburg dynasty were given the status of *Istiman* in the Ottoman Empire, and were allowed to visit, reside and trade in the Ottoman Empire.[89] This status provided the basis for capitulations, which allowed European merchants to reside in the Ottoman Empire and provided the framework for diplomatic relations between the Ottomans and Europeans. Moreover, this treaty received full support from Shaykh al-Islam, Abu-L-Su'ud, Grand Mufti of the Ottoman Empire.[90]

A far more radical change that took place in the Ottoman rules was about improving the position of the Christian subjects living under the Ottoman rule. France (1740), Russia (1774) and other countries were given the right to 'protect' these subjects by making representations to the Sultan (Ottoman ruler) regarding their conditions.[91] The implementation of these commitments was embodied in the *Tanzeemat* decrees, beginning with the promulgation of the *Khatti Sharif Gulkhane* of 3 November 1839.[92] It outlined anticipated changes in several substantive policies: (a) taxes, their fair assessment and collection; (b) the military, the conscription of soldiery to be equitable and proportionately spread over the provinces; (c) civil liberties, citizens to be secure in their property, criminal procedure to be public and the different religions treated equally; and (d) the new Council of Judicial Ordinances (established in 1838), designated as the consultative and legislative body, and charged to carry out this work. The *Tanzeemat* Reforms were followed by other enactments until they were finally incorporated in an elaborate constitutional document issued by the Sultan in 1876. However, neither the

[89] Khadduri (n 85).

[90] J Schacht, *An Introduction to Islamic Law* (Oxford: Clarendon Press, 1964) 90.

[91] Stanford J Shaw and Gökhan Çetinsaya, 'Ottoman Empire' in JL Esposito (ed), *The Oxford Encyclopedia of the Islamic World* (Oxford: Oxford University Press, 2009), www.oxfordreference.com/display/10.1093/acref/9780195305135.001.0001/acref-9780195305135-e-0611.

[92] WS Vucinich, *The Ottoman Empire: Its Record and Legacy* (Princeton: Van Nostrand, 1965) 89; SJ Shaw, *History of the Ottoman Empire and Modern Turkey* (Cambridge: Cambridge University Press, 1977) 59–61.

Tanzeemat decrees nor the Constitution of 1876 materialised due to the strong resistance of traditional Islam to Western concepts of law and justice.

During the *Tanzeemat* period, Britain (and France and Austria at times) emerged as the main supporter of the Ottoman Empire against Russia. However, the turning point in the history of the Empire was the introduction of capitulations and the Treaty of Paris in 1856.[93] The capitulations were unilateral concessions, granted by the sultans to foreign sovereigns, but as the Ottoman Empire went into decline, these agreements became bilateral and conferred reciprocal rights.[94]

Under the Treaty of Paris, the Ottoman Empire was formally admitted into the European state system and was allowed to participate in the public law and concert of Europe. Moinuddin is of the view that:

> [C]enturies of peaceful contacts and commercial relations between Islamic and non-Islamic States prior to the admittance of the Ottoman Empire to the European concert in 1856 had led to the emergence of a body of 'regional or Islamic' customary rules which provided the underlying basis of such relations.[95]

These legal arrangements created a protégé system guaranteeing foreign residents personal, economic and legal privileges, like the right to reside in the Ottoman territories, freedom of worship and tax-exempt status.[96] This suggests that the contact between Christian and Islamic civilisations in times of war and peace exposed the West to Islamic concepts of war and peace as well as international trade, and vice versa. In the words of Judge Al Khasawneh, there is 'a common history' of the Western and Islamic World that has contributed to the development of international law, and as a consequence international law cannot be labelled as exclusively Western.[97]

These treaties can be cited as examples of international customary law that bound both Muslim and non-Muslim rulers. However, each side interpreted these relations according to its own vision of the world and on the basis of its own legal system. The European view from the sixteenth to the eighteenth centuries was that their *jus gentium* (the law of peoples) carried universal meaning

[93] Treaty of Paris, 30 March 1856 (author translation, 'participer aux avantages du droit public et du concert Européen').

[94] G Gozzi, 'The Particularistic Universalism of International Law in the 19th Century: Responding to A Becker Lorca, 'Universal International Law: Nineteenth-Century Histories of Imposition and Appropriation' (2010) 51 *Harvard International Law Journal* 475.

[95] H Moinuddin, *The Charter of the Islamic Conference and Legal Framework of Economic Cooperation Among its Member States: A Study of the Charter, the General Agreement for Economic, Technical and Commercial Co-operation and the Agreement for Promotion, Protection and Guarantee of Investments Among Member States of the OIC* (Oxford: Clarendon Press, 1987) 39.

[96] G Gozzi, 'History of International Law and Western Civilization' (2007) 9 *International Community Law Review* 353.

[97] AS Al-Khasawneh, 'Islam and International Law' in M-L Frick and AT Muller (eds), *Islam and International Law: Engaging Self-Centrism from a Plurality of Perspectives* (Leiden: Brill, 2013) 29, 32.

and application.[98] The Ottomans' Islamic view of relations among nations, on the other hand, had nothing to do with the *jus gentium* or with natural law; instead, the Ottomans based it on *As-Siyar*.[99]

A more recent example is the India–Pakistan conflict in April 2025, which was one of the most intense military escalations between the two nuclear armed neighbours. Due to the enduring geopolitical tensions and historical grievances between the two countries, the armed conflict unfolded through a series of cross-border air strikes, drone warfare and artillery exchanges across the Line of Control in Kashmir. India also launched missile attacks and air strikes, killing innocent civilians, including children in Pakistan. However, Pakistan's response to Indian aggression was of defensive *jihad*. It clearly demonstrated that principles of *As-Siyar* were followed and women, children and places of worship in India were not attacked in retaliation. The Joint Armed Forces in Pakistan and the Pakistan government very clearly stated that Islam does not permit taking the lives of civilians and the innocent population. The ceasefire reached between the two countries later highlights the critical role of third-party mediation in de-escalating regional conflicts and also shows that peace agreements are entered by Muslim states with non-Muslim states.[100]

This shows that entering into treaties and agreements to achieve peaceful resolution of disputes has remained part and parcel of the Muslim empires. In the words of Samour, peace treaties have been an 'intra-Muslim tool of diplomacy and truces' between the Muslim and non-Muslim empires.[101] Despite conflicts, there have been periods of peaceful co-existence, mutual cooperation and cross-religious alliances between Western Catholic, Byzantine Orthodox and the Muslim Ottoman Empire. These various examples from different periods of history show that peaceful contacts and commercial relations between Islamic and non-Islamic states prior to the admittance of the Ottoman Empire to the 'European concert' in 1856 had led to the emergence of a body of Islamic customary rules that provided the underlying basis of such relations. One might thus argue that within the Islamic legal tradition, entering into treaties and the peaceful settlement of disputes is in consonance with modern international law's treaty mechanism and third-party methods such as conciliation or mediation.

To assess the relevance of *As-Siyar* principles in the present-day context, the next section examines the role of the OIC and the LAS for achieving peaceful settlement of disputes.

[98] Y Onuma, 'When was the Law of International Society Born? An Inquiry of the History of International Law from an Inter-civilizational Perspective' (2000) 2 *Journal of the History of International Law* 36.
[99] ibid.
[100] RAA Janjua, 'Four Days to the Brink: The 2025 India-Pakistan Air War' (13 May 2025), https://ssrn.com/abstract=5252595.
[101] Samour (n 79) 313–19.

F. Muslim States' Practice and International Law in the Twenty-First Century

The OIC is the second-largest organisation, with a membership of 57 states spread over four continents, and is in charge of global governance in its Member States.[102] All 57 Member States of the OIC are members of the UN. The OIC has strong relationships with the UN, the EU and major world powers such as the United States, Russia and the People's Republic of China. It collaborates with the UN and other UN agencies on numerous fronts around the globe. The OIC has played many roles and has served as an arbitrator in confrontations between Muslim states. It has interfered in the affairs of non-Muslim countries when those countries attacked Muslim minority communities, as was recently seen in the case of Rohingya Muslims in Myanmar. The OIC has also performed a humanitarian role in several places across the globe, and it serves as a vital development agent in OIC countries. For this purpose, the OIC established specialised agencies, standing committees and agencies for various objectives and specific tasks. Following the strengthening of other institutions, the OIC began focusing on topics such as financial governance, humanitarian activities, education and research.

The OIC Charter lays down the objectives and principles of the organisation, and has as its fundamental purposes to strengthen solidarity and cooperation among the Member States. The preamble to the OIC Charter pledges a commitment by the Muslim Member States to contribute to international peace and security, understanding and dialogue among civilisations, cultures and religions, and to promote and encourage friendly relations and good neighbourliness, to promote confidence and encourage friendly relations, mutual respect and cooperation between Member States and other states. Furthermore, the preamble acknowledges that Member States must uphold the objectives and principles of the present Charter, the UN Charter and international law, as well as international humanitarian law, while strictly adhering to the principle of non-interference in matters that are essentially within the domestic jurisdiction of any state. The preamble also emphasises friendly relations and good neighbourliness, mutual respect and cooperation with both Muslim and non-Muslim states.

Under Article 1(3) of the OIC Charter, Muslim Member States recognise the right to self-determination and non-interference in the domestic affairs of each Member State, and to respect the sovereignty, independence and territorial integrity of each Member State.

Article 2(3) of the OIC Charter states that all Member States must settle disputes through peaceful means and refrain from the use or threat of the use of

[102] For further details, see www.oic-oci.org/upload/journals/content/oic_journal_issue_52_en.pdf.

force in their relations. Peaceful settlement of disputes is further emphasised in Articles 27 and 28 of the OIC Charter. Article 27 provides:

> The Member States, parties to any dispute, the continuance of which may be detrimental to the interests of the Islamic Ummah or may endanger the maintenance of international peace and security, shall seek a solution by good offices, negotiation, enquiry, mediation, conciliation, arbitration, judicial settlement or other peaceful means of their own choice. In this context good offices may include consultation with the Executive Committee and the Secretary-General.

Article 28 places emphasis on cooperation with other international and regional organisations with the objective of preserving international peace and security, and settling disputes through peaceful means.

The OIC Charter clearly demonstrates that Muslim states acknowledge Islamic principles of peaceful dispute resolution and entering into peaceful treaties to achieve international peace.[103] The OIC-2025 programme is anchored in the provisions of the OIC Charter and focuses on 18 priority areas with 107 goals, which include issues of Peace and Security, Palestine and Al-Quds, Poverty Alleviation, Counter-terrorism, Investment and Finance, Food Security, Science and Technology, Climate Change and Sustainability, Moderation, Culture and Interfaith Harmony, Empowerment of Women, Joint Islamic Humanitarian Action, and Human Rights and Good Governance, among others.

The OIC endeavours to safeguard and protect the interests of the Muslim world in the spirit of promoting international peace and harmony among various people of the world. In 1975, it established the Al-Quds Committee to monitor the implementation of decisions issued by the organisation and other international organisations that care for and serve as mediators. This permanent committee's mission is to execute all decisions pertaining to the Israel-Arab problem, given the basic relationship between the Al-Quds dispute and the war. The Muslim world's collective response to the Palestine issue begins with OIC policies and actions. The issue of Palestine was the impetus for the formation of the OIC, and the Palestine issue has remained the top agenda item at all OIC conferences.

The OIC has recently adopted a resolution to underscore the need for continuous efforts to reach a total cessation of the brutal Israeli military aggression against the Palestinian people, and has condemned the horrific massacre perpetrated by Hamas and the Israeli occupation in the Gaza Strip.[104] This brutal armed conflict has resulted in the killing of thousands of innocent civilians, with many others injured. It is a war crime that contravenes all humane values and state terrorism deserving accountability and sanction. The OIC has also emphasised the need to

[103] www.refworld.org/docid/3ae6b3ab18.html.

[104] Resolution Adopted by the Extraordinary Session of the Council of Foreign Ministers of the Member States of the Organization of Islamic Cooperation to Consider the Continuing Israeli Aggression against the Palestinian People OIC General Secretariat Jeddah – Kingdom of Saudi Arabia Tuesday, 5 March 2024, https://new.oic-oci.org/Lists/ConferenceDocuments/Attachments/2614/ex_cfm_19_res_r2_en.pdf.

provide humanitarian and medical assistance, as well as basic needs, to the Gaza Strip in a sustainable manner, calling at the same time on the international community, and particularly the Security Council, to provide international protection for the Palestinian people.

However, one of the major weaknesses of the OIC is that it cannot compel its Member States to move in a particular direction. Ali and Sultan argue that the performance of both the UN and the OIC is identical, as neither the OIC nor the General Assembly of the UN can put the decisions and agreements into effect.[105] Like the UN, where, due to the veto power of its five permanent Member States, the UN Security Council can only implement decisions if all five permanent states concur on an issue, the OIC can only encourage and offer guidance, mediation and suggestions in a democratic and peaceful manner, but cannot implement its decisions. The UN Security Council's lack of power has recently been demonstrated, when the US vetoed the resolution for a ceasefire between Israel and Palestine, despite 13 out of 15 Member States voting in favour of the resolution. It was only after five unsuccessful resolutions that in March 2024 a resolution on an immediate ceasefire was adopted by a vote of 14 Member States in favour and one abstention by the US. However, in recent months we have seen that despite the resolution and all efforts for negotiating a ceasefire have been blatantly ignored by Israel. This raises serious questions about the effectiveness of the OIC as an organisation to bring peace in the region.

Another important regional organisation is the intergovernmental pan-Arab organisation of all Arab states in the Middle East and North Africa, established in Cairo on 22 March 1945. The LAS is a 22-member body that was established following the adoption of the Alexandria Protocol in 1944, which included a resolution to form a 'Council of the League of Arab States'. The member countries are Algeria, Bahrain, Comoros, Djibouti, Egypt, Iraq, Jordan, Kuwait, Lebanon, Libya, Mauritania, Morocco, Oman, Palestine, Qatar, Saudi Arabia, Somalia, Sudan, Syria, Tunisia, the United Arab Emirates and Yemen. The Charter of the Arab League was signed by delegates of Egypt, Syria, Transjordan, Iraq, Saudi Arabia and Lebanon at the General Arab Congress, with Yemen signing in May 1945.

The purpose of establishing the LAS was to form an entente of newly independent Arab states following the Second World War that would represent the Arab masses emerging from decades of subjugation by foreign powers. Article 3 of the Covenant tasked the new Council with deciding on 'the means by which the League is to cooperate with the international bodies to be created in the future in order to guarantee security and peace and regulate economic and social relations'. This article created a path for the LAS to position itself as a regional organisation in the framework of the approaching San Francisco Conference.

[105] T Ali and H Sultan, 'Emerging Role of the Organization of Islamic Cooperation in the Global Governance since 1969' (2023) 10 *Cogent Arts & Humanities* 2202052.

Article 5 of the Charter of the Arab League supports the objective of peace and the inadmissibility of the use of force. However, the mandate for peaceful resolution of disputes is limited to those disputes that do not deal with the independence, territorial integrity or sovereignty of any state. Article 9 places emphasis on entering into agreements to establish closer cooperation and stronger bonds between the Member States and other states. It emphasises that Member States of the Arab League that desire to establish closer cooperation and stronger bonds than are provided for by this Charter may conclude agreements to that end. Under this article, treaties and agreements already concluded or to be concluded in the future between a Member State and another state shall not be binding on or restrictive upon other members. Similarly, the Human Rights Charter of the Arab League also acknowledges the close inter-relationship between human rights and world peace, and rejects racism and Zionism, which constitute a violation of human rights and pose a threat to world peace.

Despite these provisions for peace and peaceful settlement of disputes in these regional documents, in recent years there has been a sharp increase in violence and armed conflicts in Muslim states like Libya, Iraq and, more recently, Syria, Palestine, Lebanon and Yemen, to name but a few. The armed conflicts in Muslim states are the outcome of several factors: for instance, the conflict between Israel and Palestine and the Iraqi invasion of Kuwait in 1990 are the result of the creation of artificial boundaries imposed by European colonial powers.[106] Other factors include the rise of religious nationalism as a counter-reaction to a secular nationalism promoted by the colonial powers and associated with corrupt and inefficient governments in the post-colonial world, and the interventionist policy of major powers, such as the Soviet Union in Afghanistan from 1979, and the US and other Western powers in several Muslim states after 9/11.[107] As a result, seemingly stable dictatorships have been replaced with unstable semi-democracies in a number of Muslim countries, such as Afghanistan, Iraq and Libya. While there were no recent outside interventions in Egypt and Syria prior to 2011, the series of events known as 'the Arab Spring' helped to spread regime change from the neighbouring countries, and Russian intervention eventually became an important factor in Syria. Some scholars argue that the increase in armed conflicts in Muslim countries is a reaction in the Muslim world to interventions by major powers.[108] This reaction has been shown in the form of terrorist attacks of 9/11 in the US, 7/7 in the UK and those in other Western countries. This clearly demonstrates that the consequences of armed conflicts are not restricted to the territories of warring states, but have an overall global impact.

Bouhamidi argues that since its establishment, the LAS has succeeded in resolving certain conflicts, has failed to resolve others and has been able to prevent others

[106] NP Gleditsch and I Rudolfsen, 'Are Muslim Countries More Prone to Violence?' (2016) 3(2) *Research and Politics* 7.
[107] ibid.
[108] ibid.

from escalating.[109] However, in the recent Palestine–Israel conflict, the LAS has declined as an organisation – from one that represents and pushes for collective, purposeful and effective Arab action to a mere façade of ineffectual institutions that reflect the prevalent disunity in the Arab world.[110] Division within the LAS, the lack of a balance of power, and individual political and economic agendas of Member States have affected the cohesiveness and ability of the LAS to achieve peace in the region. To be an effective organisation and to achieve peace in the region, the Member States of the LAS need to seriously address its weaknesses and unite so that the League can play a positive role in the region. It should revive the Arab Peace Initiative, the two-state solution and the land-for-peace principle for Palestine.

The UN, the OIC and the LAS have so far failed to arrive at a peaceful resolution of the most recent Palestine–Israel conflict that started on 7 October 2023. The persistence of armed conflicts has resulted in increased disproportionate attacks on civilian populations, including women and children, who are being targeted mercilessly. Such attacks are against the principles of both international law and Islamic law. The attack by Hamas on Israeli citizens is against the principles of *As-Siyar*, which prohibits the attacking and killing non-combatants. Similarly, the bombardment and killing of thousands of Palestinians by Israel in retaliation is against the principles of international law.

In November 2023, the Arab and Muslim leaders convened an extraordinary joint summit of the Arab League and the OIC, under the leadership of Saudi Crown Prince Mohammed bin Salman, in condemnation of Israel's war in the Gaza Strip. At this joint conference, King Abdullah II of Jordan, Palestinian Authority President Mahmoud Abbas and Egyptian President Abdel Fattah el-Sisi, as well as Iranian President Ebrahim Raissi, Turkish President Recep Tayyip Erdogan and Emir of Qatar Sheikh Tamim bin Hamad Al Thani were invited to mobilise for Gaza.

The final resolution adopted at the joint summit begins with a re-affirmation of all resolutions of the OIC and the Arab League regarding the Palestine and occupied Arab territories.[111]

This resolution also recalls all resolutions of the UN and other international organisations regarding the Palestinian cause, the crimes of the Israeli occupation, and the right of the Palestinian people to freedom and independence in all its territories, which have been occupied since 1967 and constitute a sole geographical unit.[112] Another important element of the resolution is that it called on the UN Security Council to take a decisive and binding decision that imposes a cessation of aggression and curbs the colonial occupation authority

[109] S Bouhamidi, *The Role of the League of Arab States: Mediating and Resolving Arab-Arab Conflicts* (Riga: VDM Verlag Dr Müller, 2011) 2.
[110] See https://arabcenterdc.org/resource/the-arab-leagues-many-failures.
[111] A full English translation of the Resolution is available at: www.spa.gov.sa/en/N1996072.
[112] ibid.

that violates international law, international humanitarian law and international legitimacy resolutions, the latest of which is UN General Assembly Resolution No A/ES-10/L.25 of 26 October 2023.[113] The Muslim states in this resolution also strongly condemned the Israeli aggression against the Gaza Strip, the war crimes, and the barbaric and inhuman massacres perpetrated by the government of occupation. The final resolution also rejected Israeli claims that it is acting in 'self-defence' and demanded that the UN Security Council adopt 'a decisive and binding resolution' to halt Israel's aggression.[114] Most importantly, while recognising the significance of international courts, the Muslim states also called on the Prosecutor of the International Criminal Court to complete the investigation into war crimes and crimes against humanity committed by Israel against the Palestinian people in all the occupied Palestinian territories, including East Jerusalem, as well as to seek the Advisory Opinion of the International Court of Justice.

However, the outcome of a joint summit of the LAS and the OIC has exposed regional divisions over how to respond to the war. Both the OIC and LAS Member States declined to approve punitive economic and political steps against Israel over its war against Hamas. Some states, including Algeria and Lebanon, proposed responding to the devastation in Gaza by threatening to disrupt oil supplies to Israel and its allies, as well as severing the economic and diplomatic ties that some Arab League states have with Israel, but the United Arab Emirates and Bahrain, which normalised ties with Israel in 2020, rejected the proposal.

Some mediation efforts deployed in this regard by the State of Qatar and the Arab Republic of Egypt resulted in achieving an interim ceasefire in the Gaza Strip, but Israel has continued its disproportionate action since the end of the ceasefire. The UN Office for the Coordination of Humanitarian Affairs has reported that according to the Ministry of Health (MoH) in Gaza between 30 April and 7 May, 230 Palestinians were killed and 883 were injured.[115] The MoH further reported that between 7 October 2023 and 7 May 2025, at least 52,653 Palestinians have been killed and 118,897 have been injured, including women, children and other innocent civilians, as well as the destruction of hospitals, schools and civilian-populated areas.[116] Israel's actions are in complete violation of the principles of international law and amount to war crimes.

To end the war and violence, a revamping of the UN Security Council as well as the OIC and the LAS is needed to make these international and regional organisations more effective. The mere passing of resolutions and political statements will not resolve the issue. Although the Charter of the LAS supports achieving peace, its provisions of peaceful resolution of disputes are limited in scope as they

[113] ibid.
[114] ibid.
[115] UN Office for the Coordination of Humanitarian Affairs (2025) 'Humanitarian Situation Update #286 | Gaza Strip', www.ochaopt.org/content/humanitarian-situation-update-286-gaza-strip.
[116] ibid.

do not deal with disputes relating to the territorial integrity, independence or sovereignty of any state. An engagement with Islamic international law by using comparative law methodology will help in resolving inter-state disputes and in gaining the confidence of Muslim states in international and regional adjudication mechanisms, and will lead to the attainment of world peace. It would also help in highlighting the commonalities between *As-Siyar* and international law, as well as bridging the gap between the two.

G. Conclusion

This chapter has shown that Islamic legal tradition is not a unified legal tradition; rather, it is a plural legal tradition that has developed through the use of a range of primary and secondary sources as well as diverse juristic opinions and scholarly works written over the centuries. This chapter demonstrates that within the Islamic legal tradition, a sophisticated system of *As-Siyar* was developed as an integral part of Islamic law, which regulated the relationship between the Muslim and non-Muslim states for centuries. The rules of war, peace treaties and mutual alliances, whether for peaceful co-existence or trade relations, were developed by Islamic jurists from the early days of Islam on the basis of the *Qur'an* and *Sunnah* of the Prophet.

A comparative view of both *As-Siyar* and modern international law validates that both are dynamic legal traditions that have changed and evolved over the passage of time, and, despite important differences, there are crucial similarities between the two.[117] One can thus say that *As-Siyar* and modern international law are congruent in the sense that, like modern international law, the corpus of Islamic international law, though divinely inspired, was developed over the passage of time as a result of the juridical efforts of the various authoritative jurists belonging to different schools of thought.

Within *As- Siyar*, peaceful resolution of disputes has been acknowledged and treaties were entered into to regulate relationships with non-Muslims. The interaction of Muslims with Byzantines, the Franks of Spain and the Habsburg Empires suggests that peaceful resolution of disputes was achieved by entering into treaties with non-Muslims. By using these examples of the past the OIC and the LAS need to take firm positions, and aim at achieving peaceful resolution of disputes.

Finally, the review of the role of the UN as well as the OIC and the LAS clearly suggests that these organisations have failed to bring peace in the region and stop the genocide of Palestinian Muslims. International law today has failed many of its own tests. This demonstrates the need for an alternative, or at least for an altered version of international law. In order for international law to be accepted

[117] EJ Powell, *Islamic law and International Law: Peaceful Resolution of Disputes* (Oxford: Oxford University Press, 2023) 272.

as 'international' and 'universal', there is a need to understand and appreciate the non-Western legal traditions, including the Islamic legal tradition. In the words of Judge Philip Jessup of the International Court of Justice, 'the effectiveness of public international law … would be seriously impaired if there were no tolerance of certain differences stemming from various legal systems'.[118] If the purpose of international law is to serve the interests of a wide and diverse international community of states, then it has to adopt an inclusionary and accommodative approach by accepting the commonalities and divergences amongst the Western and Islamic legal traditions.

[118] PC Jessup, 'Diversity and Uniformity in the Law of Nations' (1964) 58 *American Journal of International Law* 343.

PART III

Critical and Analytical Perspectives

8

Is Comparative International Law Really Comparative Law?

A Methodological Critique

SAÏDA EL BOUDOUHI

A. Introduction

The formula 'comparative international law' may sound inherently incongruent from a public international law perspective. How can the latter, which has always aspired to a form of universality,[1] be of interest to comparative law? How can what is *one* be *compared*? It is a truism that comparison presupposes plurality. Does speaking of comparative international law imply that there are several 'international laws'? This raises no difficulty if we refer to private international law, the subject of which are national rules on conflicts of law and jurisdiction. As these rules differ from one national legal system to another, it is only natural that they are the object of a comparative analysis. It is more puzzling in the case of public international law, which refers to the rules shared by the members of international society. Despite the reluctance, or at least the perplexity, that one may express regarding the soundness of the concept,[2] this chapter purports to examine what public international law could borrow from comparative law under the heading of 'comparative international law'. The chapter will endeavour to show that even if comparative international law were to be mostly a linguistic convenience, it nevertheless contains an added value at the methodological level.

Unlike new areas of law that have appeared over time, such as international economic law,[3] comparative international law is not a new branch of international law, despite the new scholarly attention it has attracted over the last two decades.

[1] D Kennedy, 'New Approaches to Comparative Law: Comparativism and International Governance' (1997) 1997 *Utah Law Review* 545.

[2] For a previous temptative deconstruction of the concept, see S El Boudouhi, 'Le droit international comparé: mythe ou réalité?' (2017) 121 *Revue générale de droit international public* 981.

[3] P Weil, 'Le droit international économique' in SFDI, Colloque d'Orléans, *Aspects du droit international économique* (Pedone, Paris, 1972) 31–32.

While it could expand to any comparative process taking place, horizontally and vertically,[4] in international law,[5] it is mainly understood here in a deliberately restrictive manner, as a way of approaching a subject that has long existed in international law – that is, the study of the application of international law in various domestic legal systems in a comparative manner. Indeed, if comparative international law is to have a conceptual consistency and to belong to the big family of comparative law, it may be worth restricting its scope to the comparison between different legal systems, and not between several branches of the same legal order.[6] When international judges – increasingly – refer to the practice of other international judges, they do so within the framework of the same legal order. This practice, which happens to fall within the scope of the principles of treaty interpretation,[7] is certainly part of the cognitive process of comparison, but not of comparative law as a scientific discipline. As to understanding comparative international law as encompassing, more generally, the comparison between different national or regional approaches of international law,[8] it is true that recognising the diversity of approaches amounts to laying the foundations for comparison between national approaches of the same object, international law. Nevertheless, these 'geographical' approaches often correspond to epistemological approaches, that is, a study of the way in which the science of international law is approached, and not so much of the way in which international law is applied in different legal systems. While these studies are considered as part of the 'new born discipline of comparative international law'[9] or whether they are embedded in a historic perspective of

[4] See Siems, ch 1 in this volume.

[5] For an all-encompassing approach, see the symposium on 'Exploring Comparative International Law' (2015) 109(3) *American Journal of International Law*; A Roberts et al (eds), *Comparative International Law* (Oxford: Oxford University Press, 2018). For an approach which is restrictive in a different manner, see Schütze, ch 2 in this volume.

[6] *Ahmadou Sadio Diallo (Republic of Guinea v Democratic Republic of the Congo)* (ICJ, 19 June 2012) (compensation), statement by Judge Greenwood, 394. However, for an early use of the phrase 'comparative international law', see J-F Flauss, in his reviews 'Actualité de la Convention européenne des droits de l'homme' of the journal *AJDA* in 2000, 2002 and 2009; G Cohen Jonathan and J-F Flauss, 'Cour européenne des droits de l'homme' (2008) 54 *Annuaire Français de Droit International* 529, 530; J-F Flauss, 'Du droit international comparé dans la jurisprudence de la Cour européenne des droits de l'homme' in Institut suisse de droit comparé (ed), *Le rôle du droit comparé dans l'avènement du droit européen – The Role of Comparative Law in the Emergence of European Law* (Zurich: Schulthess, 2002) 159.

[7] Article 31(3) of the Vienna Convention indeed refers to 'any applicable rule between the parties' which indirectly calls for the taking into account of what other branches of international law provide.

[8] E Jouannet, 'French and American Perspectives on International Law: Legal Cultures and International Law' (2006) 58 *Maine Law Review* 292; H Ruiz Fabri, 'Nécessité d'une approche européenne du droit international? Ni oui, ni non, ni blanc, ni noir' in SFDI/Société allemande de droit international, *Droit international et diversité des cultures juridiques* (Paris, Pedone, 2008) 223; A Becker Lorca, 'International Law in Latin America or Latin American International Law? Rise, Fall, and Retrieval of a Tradition of Legal Thinking and Political Imagination' (2006) 47 *Harvard International Law Journal* 283; F Messineo, 'Is There an Italian Conception of International Law?' (2013) 2 *Cambridge Journal of International and Comparative Law* 879; L Mälksoo, *Russian Approaches to International Law* (Oxford: Oxford University Press, 2015).

[9] BN Mamlyuk and U Mattei, 'Comparative International Law' (2011) 36 *Brooklyn Journal of International Law* 451.

international,[10] they are more akin to comparative studies more generally understood than to comparative law strictly speaking. They will thus be left out of the present analysis as they compare theories of international law rather than legal systems or legal rules which seem to be at the core of any type of comparative law, be it international or domestic law.

It is commonly agreed that comparative law is first and foremost an academic discipline rather than a branch of positive law.[11] However, the fact that comparative law does not, like administrative law or criminal law, for example, correspond to rules of positive law does not prevent it from being law.[12] It is a 'method of studying law and a stock of academic knowledge'.[13] To nevertheless distinguish comparative law from other branches of law, Picard interestingly opposes 'law as knowledge' to 'law as power'.[14] Yet, for some time now, this classical conception of comparative law seems to have been put to the test by the tendency of national and international courts to cite the decisions of their foreign or international counterparts. Some have noted that courts tend to 'give comparative law an ever more prominent place as a source of law'.[15] While comparative law cannot be understood as a source of law within the formalistic understanding of the sources doctrine, it nevertheless is an increasing source of inspiration for courts – that is, a material source of law. In this case, comparative law could be conceived not just as an academic discipline,[16] but as an aspect of positive law if only for interpretative purposes. In any case, it is undeniable that since at least the 2000s, judges have been seizing on the comparative tool,[17] especially when they take into account, expressly or tacitly, foreign case law in their deliberations or decisions.[18]

[10] For a contrary view – ie, an understanding of comparative international law as corresponding mainly to the comparison of different 'systems' or approaches of international law – see Schütze, ch 2 in this volume.

[11] E Picard, 'L'étude du droit comparé en France en 1999' (1999) 51 *Revue internationale de droit comparé* 885; M Reimann, 'Comparative Law and Neighbouring Disciplines' in M Bussani and U Mattei (eds), *Cambridge Companion to Comparative* Law (Cambridge: Cambridge University Press, 2012) 14.

[12] E Picard, 'Le droit comparé est-il du droit?' *Annuaire de l'Institut Michel Villey*, vol 1 (Paris: Dalloz, 2009) 173.

[13] Reimann (n 11).

[14] Picard (n 12) 178.

[15] M Andenas and D Fairgrieve, *Courts and Comparative Law* (Oxford: Oxford University Press, 2015) 5.

[16] Picard (n 12) 192–93.

[17] In some jurisdictions, such as the US Supreme Court, this practice is quite old, although it has long gone unnoticed. See SG Calabresi and SD Zimdahl, 'The Supreme Court and Foreign Sources of Law: Two Hundred Years of Practice and the Juvenile Death Penalty Decision' (2005) 47 *William & Mary Law Review* 743. See also R Bismuth, 'L'utilisation de sources de droit étrangères dans la jurisprudence de la Cour suprême des Etats-Unis' (2010) 62 *Revue Internationale de Droit Comparé* 105.

[18] See, among others, the series of conferences on 'comparative law, territoriality of law' organised by the Conseil d'Etat between 2015 and 2017: G Canivet, *Comparative Law before the Courts* (London: BIICL, 2004); M-C Ponthoreau and T Groppi, *The Use of Foreign Precedent by Foreign Judges* (Oxford: Hart Publishing, 2013) 422; M Andenas and D Fairgrieve (eds), *Courts and Comparative Law* (Oxford: Oxford University Press, 2015), in particular M Gelter and and M Siems, 'Networks, Dialogue or One-Way Traffic? An Empirical Analysis of Cross-citations between Ten of Europe's Highest Courts' (ch 11). The Association des Hautes Juridictions de Cassation des pays ayant en partage l'usage du

Thus, comparative international law, if it were to be recognised as a specific sub-discipline, would correspond above all to the 'old' comparative practice in international law scholarship (see section B). But we must also consider the possibility that this formula is used as a mere linguistic convenience to designate an aspect of positive law – that is, the use of comparative practice by domestic judges when applying international law (see section C). The common ground for both practices, which accounts for the added value of the label 'comparative international law', seems to be an appeal for more methodology in resorting to an increasingly complex and diverse set of rules and legal systems in applying international law (see section D).

B. Comparative International Law in International Law Scholarship: Consolidation of a Traditional Branch of International Law

There has long been a practice of comparing the various ways in which legal systems receive and apply international law in international law scholarship. In recent years, this trend has grown considerably, in line with the ever-increasing importance of international law in national legal systems. This scholarly practice, together with a certain practice of national jurisdictions,[19] is the basis for the emergence of debates around the notion of 'comparative international law'. While the tradition of comparing different ways of applying international law is of relatively long standing and has only recently been strengthened (see section B.1), it is not clear whether it should fall under the heading of 'comparative international law', since what is compared is not so much international law as foreign relations law of different legal systems (see section B.2).

1. The Consolidation of a Comparative Scholarship of the Reception of International Law within Domestic Legal Systems

Over the last few decades, we have become accustomed to comparing different ways of 'receiving' international law from a more technical and practical perspective than that of the 'major approaches to international law'.[20] The focus is on

français (AHUJCAF), which brings together around 50 French-speaking supreme jurisdictions, also illustrates the interest that national courts can have in the output of their foreign peers. See also M-C Ponthoreau and T Groppi, *The Use of Foreign Precedent by National Judges* (Oxford: Hart Publishing, 2013); F Melleray (ed), *L'argument de droit comparé en droit administratif* (Brussels: Bruylant, 2007).

[19] See section C below.

[20] See in particular the study by PM Eisemann, *L'intégration du droit international et communautaire dans l'ordre juridique national: étude de la pratique en Europe* (The Hague: Kluwer, 1996). See

the ways in which international law is integrated into domestic law, its place in the hierarchy of national norms, its direct applicability and so on. In this case, the comparison is 'macro' in the sense usually understood by comparatists: it focuses on the main principles governing the application of international law in domestic law as a whole,[21] that is, 'the global study of legal systems … with a view to characterising and classifying them'.[22] Thus, it is hard to find an international law textbook that does not refer to the classification of national legal systems according to whether they are monist or dualist in their reception of international law. In some cases, entire studies are devoted to the way in which international law is received and applied by domestic judges, with examples selected from a very wide variety of legal systems.[23] In others, the analysis focuses on one aspect of the reception of international law, studied in at least two national legal systems.[24] In the latter case, the analysis is both macro- and micro-comparative.

Today, these studies are numerous and form part of a long-standing tradition. In recent decades, the increasing importance of international law in domestic legal systems has reinforced their importance. And yet, what is striking is that the term 'comparative international law' does not appear therein, as the scholars consider that their discipline is public international law. Even studies that have appeared in publications devoted to comparative law in general do not use the term 'comparative international law'.[25] However, this is no obstacle to considering that comparative law has been practised in international law scholarship for a very long time, without necessarily claiming it as such. This is the case even when legal systems are not actually compared, but rather classified and studied in parallel in the same volume. Indeed, just as a realist approach to comparative law tends to regard all studies of foreign law[26] as falling within its scope, whether or not they

also D Shelton (ed), *International Law and Domestic Legal Systems: Incorporation, Transformation, and Persuasion* (Oxford: Oxford University Press, 2011); D Sloss (ed), *The Role of Domestic Courts in Treaty Enforcement: A Comparative Study* (Cambridge: Cambridge University Press 2009).

[21] B Jaluzot, 'Méthodologie du droit comparé: bilan et prospective' (2005) 57 *Revue internationale de droit comparé* 46.

[22] ibid.

[23] E Lagrange, 'L'efficacité des normes internationales concernant la situation des personnes privées dans les ordres juridiques internes' (2011) 356 *Recueil des cours de l'Académie de droit international de La Haye* 243; M Killander (ed), *International Law and Domestic Human Rights Litigation in Africa* (Pretoria: Pretoria University Law Press, 2010); D Shelton (ed), *International Law and Domestic Legal Systems: Incorporation, Transformation and Persuasion* (Oxford: Oxford University Press, 2011); J Nijman and A Nollkaemper, *New Perspectives on the Divide between National and International Law* (Oxford: Oxford University Press, 2007); D Sloss (ed), *The Role of Domestic Courts in Treaty Enforcement: A Comparative Study* (Cambridge: Cambridge University Press, 2009); E Benvenisti, 'Judicial Misgivings Regarding the Application of International Law: An Analysis of Attitudes of National Courts' (1993) 4 *European Journal of International Law* 159; E Benvenisti, 'Reclaiming Democracy: The Strategic Uses of Foreign and International Law by National Courts' (2008) 102 *American Journal of International Law* 241.

[24] B Taxil, 'Les critères de l'applicabilité directe des traités internationaux aux Etats-Unis et en France' (2007) 59 *Revue internationale de droit comparé* 157.

[25] These include articles on public international law published in comparative law journals such as the *Revue internationale de droit comparé*. See, for example, ibid.

[26] Reimann (n 11) 15.

are genuinely comparative, it makes no difference, a fortiori, whether studies of the various ways in which international law is applied consist of genuine comparative analyses or are simply compilations of national perspectives. Insofar as they form the very basis of a potential comparative analysis, these works belong to a possible comparative law applied to international law, even if they do not use the comparative law methods.

More recently, a scholarly trend close to, but distinct from, the previous one has consisted in collecting and analysing, sometimes in a highly technical manner, decisions handed down by the courts of other countries. There has been a marked increase in this type of study in recent years,[27] culminating perhaps with the Study Group of the International Law Association on the Engagement of Domestic Courts with International Law.[28] This comparison could be described as 'micro', insofar as the aim is no longer to analyse the major principles governing the application of international law in the domestic legal order, as is the case in most textbooks, but rather their concrete implementation in specific cases. The growth of this trend can be seen in the increasing number of sections and works devoted to foreign case law relating to international law. Sections on national case law relating to international law are a long-standing feature of all international law journals. Textbooks have equally always devoted a chapter to the application of international law in domestic law. In France, for instance, the focus has always been on the application of international law by the French courts. What may have changed in this respect is the scope of these chapters: whereas in the past, we were content with a presentation of the two main theoretical trends, monism and dualism,[29] today the precise modalities of application in the domestic legal order are increasingly developed.[30] On the other hand, it is more novel to see certain publications devoting space to the collection and analysis of foreign case law relating to international law.[31] However, comparisons are not directly included in these sections, the purpose of which is to present the case law of several national jurisdictions separately rather than to compare them as such. While this does not prevent them

[27] A Roberts, 'Comparative International Law? The Role of National Courts in Creating and Enforcing International Law' (2011) 60 *International and Comparative Law Quarterly* 57.

[28] The research group has produced a book: A Nollkaemper, Y Shany and A Tzanakopoulos, *The Engagement of Domestic Courts with International Law: Comparative Perspectives* (Oxford: Oxford University Press, 2024).

[29] In the first editions of the *Précis Dalloz*, notably the 1968 edition by C Rousseau, 'the place of international law in the legal system' was reduced to a few pages of theoretical developments, supported by examples of international case law. In an earlier work, Rousseau devoted scarcely more than a few lines in the introduction to this question: *Droit international public* (Paris: Recueil Sirey, 1953) 5.

[30] This is obvious when comparing successive versions of the same textbook. For example, in P-M Dupuy's (then P-M Dupuy and Y Kerbrat's) *Précis Dalloz*, the chapter devoted to the application of international law in the domestic legal order has been progressively expanded since 1992, until its size more than doubled in the 2016 version.

[31] See in particular the 'Foreign case law relevant to international law' section inserted in the *Revue générale de droit international public* from 2014; Oxford University Press' online *International Law in Domestic Courts* database has expanded considerably since its creation in 2006.

from falling under the heading of comparative law,[32] these headings are nonetheless an indispensable basis for truly comparative studies. They make it easy to develop a comparative approach to a wide range of international law issues. This is how studies or books devoted to an aspect of international law seen through the eyes of different national judges have multiplied, whether on the subject of universal jurisdiction,[33] humanitarian law,[34] international human rights law[35] or treaty interpretation in general before national judges.[36]

It is the intensification of this type of doctrinal practice that has given rise to an awareness among some authors of the emergence of a new disciplinary field. However, it is interesting to note that this increase in scientific production on the subject parallels, but is not the same as, the emergence of an awareness – or self-awareness – of its existence as a discipline. Thus, not all the scholars involved in this intensification seem to qualify their scientific approach as comparative international law. Perhaps this is because the notion of comparative international law appears to be particularly vague and ambiguous, especially when it refers to a certain practice of national or international jurisdictions.

2. The Inherent Ambiguity of a Potential Discipline: Comparative Studies of International Law versus Comparative Studies of National Law Relating to International Law

The difficulty in conceptually grasping comparative international law as a scientific discipline may stem from the ambiguity of the phrase: what is really being compared? Is it international law or domestic law relating to international law? Indeed, international law, insofar as it is (at least in theory) the same in all states, can hardly be compared. However, what can be compared is domestic law as it relates to international law. Assuming that it can constitute a scientific discipline, the delicate question remains as to whether it is a sub-discipline of international law or rather a sub-discipline of comparative (domestic) law.

In the first case, comparative international law could not be a branch of international law, but merely a way of studying a branch of international law – that of the application of international law in domestic law – which already existed, but the importance of which had never reached a sufficient threshold to give rise to

[32] See the second paragraph of this section.

[33] L Reydams, *Universal Jurisdiction: International and Municipal Perspectives* (Oxford: Oxford University Press, 2004) 258.

[34] B Conforti and F Francioni (eds), *Enforcing International Human Rights in Domestic Courts* (The Hague: Martinus Nijhoff Publishers, 1997).

[35] S Weill, *The Role of National Courts in Applying International Humanitarian Law* (Oxford: Oxford University Press, 2014).

[36] HP Aust and G Nolte, *The Interpretation of International Law by Domestic Courts. Uniformity, Diversity, Convergence* (Oxford: Oxford University Press, 2016).

claims of constitution as a sub-discipline. The establishment of a sub-discipline of international law would then be justified by the use of comparative law methods, which would thus be systematically integrated into the study of international law when it comes to studying its reception and application in various national legal orders. This is probably the only case where the use of the expression 'comparative international law' could refer to a certain sub-discipline of international law, understood as a scientific method of studying a given object. Nevertheless, even in this case, its status as a scientific sub-discipline would only be justified if the study of international law were to incorporate tools derived from the methodology of comparative law, which is known to provide a large space to ethics and pragmatism alongside strictly epistemological tools.[37]

In the second case, it would be comparative law (ie, a discipline of domestic law) that would find a new object (international law) or, more precisely, for dualistic systems, law of international origin. It is perhaps more accurately, or at least less ambiguously, denominated 'comparative foreign relations law'.[38] In this case, comparative international law would simply be an object of study in domestic (mainly constitutional) law. In this respect, it is perhaps revealing that many of the scholars involved in the 'comparativist project in international law'[39] are from dualist systems of incorporation of international law into domestic law, and that some have even come to doubt that international law is truly 'international'.[40] Comparative international law thus appears as an extreme manifestation of dualism in the relationship between domestic and international law. In this sense, to speak of comparative international law would be to challenge the autonomy of international law in the domestic order, since it would exist only insofar as it is transformed into domestic law. Indeed, to consider the application of international law in domestic law as an object of comparative law, in the same way as constitutional law or administrative law, is to deny to international law its specificity and its autonomy as a legal order, which consists in the fact that it is composed, at least in part, of norms that are necessarily the same in various national legal orders.

Should we then distinguish between monistic and dualist domestic legal systems? In monistic systems, comparative international law would truly be international law, whereas in entirely dualistic systems, it would merely be domestic law of external origin.[41] This latter hypothesis seems to be corroborated by some of

[37] M-C Ponthoreau, 'Le droit comparé en question(s): entre pragmatisme et outil épistémologique' (2005) 57 *Revue internationale de droit comparé* 7; on the 'methodological diversity' and 'epistemological complexity' of comparative law, see G Samuel, 'Dépasser le fonctionnalisme' in P Legrand (ed), *Comparer les droits, résolument* (Paris: PUF, 2009) 405.

[38] CR Bradley (ed), *The Oxford Handbook of Comparative Foreign Relations Law* (Oxford: Oxford University Press, 2019).

[39] The phrase is borrowed from J d'Aspremont, 'Comparativism and Colonizing Thinking in International Law' (2020) 57 *Canadian Yearbook of International Law* 89.

[40] A Roberts, *Is International Law International?* (Oxford: Oxford University Press, 2017).

[41] However, it is well known that some dualist systems contain monist loopholes – as illustrated by the famous English adage concerning customary norms, 'international law is part of the law of the land'. To this, we can add the fact, put forward by recent research, that there are other ways for domestic

the claims made by the scholars behind the concept of comparative international law: that the discipline of 'comparative international law' should concern itself not only with domestic judicial practice relating to international law, but also with the practice of all state bodies in relation to international law. Thus, it is held that comparative international law should also look at the way in which legislative or executive bodies translate their treaty obligations into domestic law,[42] following the example of the comparative studies that can be carried out on the transposition of directives in the Member States of the European Union. We could, for example, look not at the different ways in which the Aarhus Convention may be applied by national judges, but at the different national regulations that its implementation has entailed. But would this still be a study of international law? More likely, it would be a study of comparative (domestic) environmental law, with aspects borrowed from international law. In a way, it would be a study not of the application, but of the influence of international law on domestic environmental law.[43] International law would turn into a mere material source of domestic law.

This extension and de-formalisation of international law certainly has the advantage of opening up very broad research horizons for international lawyers, in a way that perhaps coincides with the wish formulated by Combacau in another context, namely, that international lawyers could have a less formalistic, more substantive and therefore more encompassing vision of their subject.[44] However, it is not clear whether this is still a matter for international law, for what is being compared here is purely domestic law, even if this domestic law has a link with the international law it claims to transpose. Indeed, while the duality of the functions of domestic judges in relation to international law justifies the comparison of their practice as a matter of comparative international law, it is not certain that this can be systematically extended to the practice of other state bodies, unless international law is completely de-formalised.[45]

These few conceptual difficulties aside, there seems to be no major obstacle to recognising that comparative international law could constitute a sub-discipline – of comparative law or of international law – consisting of the study of the application of international law in different national legal orders, the only condition being

judges to 'engage' with international than the formal application of international rules and principles (Nollkaemper, Shany and Tzanakopoulos (n 28)).

[42] A Roberts et al, 'Comparative International Law: Framing the Field' (2015) 109 *American Journal of International Law* 467, 470.

[43] For this type of international law study, see, eg, M Prieur, L'influence des conventions internationales sur le droit interne de l'environnement. Actes de la réunion constitutive du comité sur l'environnement de l'AHJUCAF' June 2008, Porto-Novo, Benin, 291, 2008, https://hal.science/hal-00499293v1.

[44] J Combacau, 'Conclusions générales' in SFDI, *Enseignement du droit international, recherche et pratique: journée d'étude du 20 janvier 1996 organisée sous les auspices de l'UNESCO* (Paris: Pedone, 1997) 268.

[45] We leave aside here the question of the functional duality – Georges Scelle's 'dédoublement fonctionnel' – of all state bodies with regard to the formation and application of customary norms, since they are both subject to these norms and can modify them through their practice (on customary norms and comparative international law).

that this study be firmly based on the methodological tools of comparative law. This is the only way in which this sub-discipline can be seen to have a specificity within the larger category of 'public international law', and thus be given scientific support. In a complementary way, the comparative practice of domestic courts in relation to international law can also fall under the label of comparative international law, notwithstanding that unlike the practice that has just been examined, this one is only a linguistic convenience.

C. Comparative International Law before Domestic Courts: Comparative Law or a Linguistic Convenience?

One of the phenomena that has led to the emergence of the debate around a new discipline of international law is the comparative practice of domestic judges when applying international law.[46] Thus, it has been said that: 'The existence of comparative international law is nowhere more evident than in national court approaches to treaty interpretation.'[47] This triggers two sets of questions. On the one hand, can it be said that this practice is truly part of comparative international law? In other words, is this phenomenon of taking foreign law into account comparable to what happens in comparative constitutional law when a domestic judge draws inspiration from foreign law to interpret their own constitutional law? On the other hand, does this mean that that comparative law is no longer just an academic discipline, but an aspect of positive law? An intermediate position would be to consider comparative law as a 'science' – that of the knowledge of law[48] – that judges and legislators, like academics, can master. It could also be argued that those practising law do not use comparative law as a scientific discipline, but only as a comparative process, without necessarily being concerned with the 'science' that lies in the comparative method. Thus, comparative law may also be merely 'the common property of contemporary legal reasoning', whether used by academics, legislators or judges.[49] In other words, it can be a linguistic convenience or shorthand for the borrowing of the comparative process by those practising law. However, the fact remains that any research into a possible concept of 'comparative international law' cannot ignore this practice by domestic courts, which is expanding rapidly in all branches of law, including public international law. Yet, it remains to be seen to

[46] On this practice, see Roberts (n 27). See also S El Boudouhi, 'Le précédent étranger relatif au droit international' in N Aloupi and C Kleiner (eds), *Colloque annuel de la SFDI 2015: Le précédent* (Paris: Pedone, 2016) 289.

[47] Roberts (n 27) 82.

[48] Picard (n 12) 193.

[49] J-M Sauvé, 'Comprendre et réguler le droit globalisé ou comment dompter la Chimère?', Opening address at the inaugural conference of the *Droit comparé et territorialité du droit* lecture series, organised by the Conseil d'Etat in association with the Société de législation comparée (SLC) and the Institut français des sciences administratives (IFSA) at the Conseil d'Etat on 20 May 2015.

what extent this practice, insofar as it concerns public international law, is merely the expression of a wider phenomenon of comparative approaches developed by national judges or is a corollary of the international sources' doctrine.

Starting from the above-mentioned definition by Picard,[50] international law sources theory shows that each of the cases in which the domestic judge has recourse to foreign law to identify or interpret an international legal norm comes under the heading of 'law as power' and not 'law as knowledge'. Indeed, the criterion used to determine whether or not a given matter falls within the scope of comparative law is whether or not the judge is required to take foreign law into account. However, it would appear that, unlike the case with the consideration of sources of domestic law, recourse to foreign law is imposed on the domestic judge by rules of recognition of international law, be they rules of identification, interpretation or implementation (see section C.1). The use of the term 'comparative law' – or comparative international law – to designate this activity of the domestic judge is therefore, if not an abuse, then at least a mere convenience of language (see section C.2).

1. The Use of Foreign Law Deriving from International Law Sources Doctrine

The difference between the comparative law argument as it may be used in domestic law and the use of foreign law by the domestic judge in their consideration of international sources is that, except in special cases, there is no legal basis for the former, whereas there are several for the latter, one being common to all sources while the others are specific to each type of source.

The common basis is to be found in Article 38(1)(d) of the Statute of the International Court of Justice: in connection with the establishment or interpretation of an international legal norm, be it customary, conventional or, a fortiori, a general principle of law, foreign case law that has already ruled on the same question of international law may be taken into account by the domestic judge. This is so according to the persuasive precedent doctrine which national judges apply when they refer to the way in which other national judges have determined or interpreted the same international standard as the one with which they are confronted.[51] While some confusion may arise from the use of comparative analysis under this provision, it is now well accepted that the 'judicial decisions' that can

[50] Picard (n 12).

[51] On the persuasive precedent, *cf* S El Boudouhi, 'Les décisions de justice comme source du droit international chez Fitzmaurice et Jennings' in *Grandes pages de la doctrine du droit international public*, vol 2, proceedings of the IHEI colloquium devoted to the sources of international law (Paris: Pedone, 2015). Amongst the many illustrations that may be found in that paper, see Tribunale di Vigevano, 12 July 2000, *Rheinland Versicherungen v Srl Atlarez and Allianz Subalpina SpA*, CLOUT case no 378, www.uncitral.org/clout/clout/data/ita/clout_case_378_leg-1602.html.

be taken into account as an 'auxiliary means of determining the rules of law' are those rendered by international courts as well as those issued by national courts.[52]

This tradition of referring to foreign case law is well established in common law jurisdictions that, historically and long before international law took on a significant role in their practice, took care to cite each other to determine common law rules, independently of any rules of international law. However, what appears to be new is the habit that some of them have recently taken on, ie, relying on non-common law jurisdictions, not to establish a principle of domestic law that they share, but to determine the applicability or interpretation of international law.[53] Yet, it should be noted that some jurisdictions continue to refer only to other common law jurisdictions, where their consideration should be broadened when examining international norms.[54]

Besides this common foundation, each of the three main sources of international law – treaties, custom and general principles of law – has its own specific legal basis for the consideration by domestic courts of foreign law relating to international law. With regard to treaty norms, two other bases can be identified. The first stems from treaty law. When a national judge charged with interpreting a treaty provision takes into account foreign case law relating to that same provision, this might appear to be a recourse to the argument of comparative law, but in reality it is no more than the – usually tacit – application of the rule relating to subsequent practice referred to in the 1969 Vienna Convention on the Law of Treaties in the section relating to the interpretation of treaties.[55] Indeed, the way in which a treaty has been applied by another national court forms an integral part of the 'subsequent practice in the application of the treaty' referred to in Article 31(3) of the Vienna Convention.[56] However, national courts seem to avoid relying on this provision when referring to foreign case law, probably because this would require that they take into

[52] ILC, Report of the International Law Commission, 74th session, 2023, A/78/10, § 117, on the first draft conclusions proposed by the Special Rapporteur on auxiliary means of determining the rules of law; see also, eg, RY Jennings, 'What is International Law and How Do We Tell When We See it?' (1981) *Annuaire suisse de droit international* 59, 76–77; S Rosenne, 'The Perplexities of Modern International Law: General Course of Public International Law' (2001) 291 *Recueils des Cours de l'Académie de Droit International de La Haye* 69.

[53] Various examples can be found in different common law systems. See, eg, the Indian Supreme Court decision *Abu Salem Abdul Qayyum Ansari v Central Bureau of Investigation and India*, 5 August 2013 (No 415-416 of 2012), available at http://supremecourtofindia.nic.in/outtoday/ar41512.pdf (discussed in R Rivier, 'Jurisprudence étrangère intéressant le droit international' (2014) 118(4) *Revue generale de droit international public* 935). For other examples, see El Boudouhi (n 46).

[54] *cf* C-E Côté's criticism of Canadian jurisdictions, which too often limit themselves to other *common law* jurisdictions in their apprehension of international sources: C-E Coté, 'Le juge canadien et la coutume internationale' in A Marie and B Tranchant (eds), *Droit international et juges internes* (Paris: Pedone, SFDI, 2024) 302.

[55] In the same vein, see Roberts (n 27) 85–86.

[56] *Johar and Others and Suri (Intervening) v India and Row Javi (Intervening)*, Decision in writ petition (Criminal), Number 76 of 2016, (2018) 10 SCC 1 (ILDC 2928 (IN 2018), 6 September 2018, India).

consideration, in accordance with a consistent interpretation of Article 31(3),[57] only the domestic case law that is genuinely concordant between the different parties to the treaty.

The second, even more specific basis is to be found only in some international conventions, notably those relating to rules of private international law, such as the United Nations Convention on the International Sale of Goods, Article 7 of which stipulates the need for uniformity of interpretation, the Warsaw Convention on International Carriage by Air, which implicitly contains such a requirement,[58] or the Athens Convention relating to the Carriage of Passengers by Sea. The effective implementation of these conventions requires, implicitly or explicitly, a uniform interpretation, which implies that national judges in charge of applying them must take into account what their foreign peers have decided in comparable situations.[59]

In the case of customary law, international law again dictates that foreign law should be taken into account, not for the purposes of interpretation, but for those of identification of international law. When domestic judges rely on foreign precedent to establish a customary norm, they are not using it as precedent, but as an element of state practice or *opinio juris*. This cannot be a case of comparative law, as the taking into account of foreign law is required by an international law rule, in this case Article 38(1)(b) of the Statute of the International Court of Justice.[60] And even if, like Merkouris, we were to accept the principle of a distinction between the existence of custom and its interpretation,[61] the latter would itself be governed, even implicitly, by international law, since nothing justifies that a norm of international law be interpreted in the light of rules of domestic law.

Finally, the association between comparative law and international law is often made in relation to the general principles of international law 'recognized by civilized nations' in Article 38(1)(c). This association is a long-standing one, since general principles of law have always been seen as the result of a comparative examination of several legal systems.[62] And yet it is not certain that this is relevant, especially when the judge at work is the national judge and not the international

[57] See, eg, I Sinclair, *The Vienna Convention on the Law of Treaties* (Manchester: Manchester University Press, 1984) 137; MK Yasseen, 'L'interprétation des traités d'après la Convention de Vienne sur le droit des traités' (1976) 151 *Recueil des cours de l'Académie de La Haye* 48; Report of the WTO Appellate Body, 4 October 1996, *Japan – Taxes on Alcoholic Beverages*, WT/DS8/AB/R, WT/DS10/AB/R, WT/DS11/AB/R, p 13.

[58] The Warsaw Convention, signed in 1933, no longer applies to countries that have ratified the 1999 Montreal Convention, but it continues to apply to others.

[59] M Rimaboschi, *L'unification du droit maritime. Contribution à la construction d'un ordre juridique maritime* (Marseille: PUAM, 2006) 163–85 ('procédure et méthodes d'interprétation des traités').

[60] ILC, *The Draft Conclusions on the Determination of Customary International Law* (A/73/10, 2018), specifically conclusion 6 on forms of practice and conclusion 10 on 'forms of proof of acceptance as law (opinio juris)'.

[61] P Merkouris, 'Interpreting the Customary Rules on Interpretation' (2017) 19 *International Community Law Review* 126.

[62] J Ellis, 'General Principles and Comparative Law' (2011) 22 *European Journal of International Law* 949.

judge. Indeed, even if the 1993 resolution of the Institut de droit international (IDI) on 'the activity of the domestic judge and the international relations of the State' invites the former to 'discover' general principles of international law, only the international judge enjoys a sufficiently overarching position, due in particular to the translation of the diversity of legal orders in the composition of international jurisdictions, to identify from the various national legal orders a principle that is to be transposed into the international order.[63] Yet, assuming that the domestic judge also has opportunities to identify a general principle within the meaning of Article 38 of the Court's Statute, foreign law would not belong to the 'law as knowledge' realm, but rather to that of the 'law as power', since it would be taken into account as a result of a rule of identification of international law. Once again, the detour via foreign law to establish a general principle of law is imposed by international law itself through its rules of recognition.

2. Comparative International Law as a Mere Convenience of Language

Far from the realm of the 'law as knowledge' that characterises comparative law, domestic judges are constrained as to the use they must make of foreign law in their consideration of international sources. Therefore, the references made by the domestic judge to foreign law in dealing with international law do not reflect a totally optional, open-ended approach. At best, it is international law compared 'within' and not 'against', to use Mathias Forteau's intuitive formula to speak of the comparative work inherent in the very existence of the International Law Commission: the comparison is internal to the process of identifying a norm of international law and is not the result of an effort to open up to other systems,[64] or at least these other systems are integrated into international law in some way. In other words, by intervening in the operation of characterising legal facts contained in the rules of recognition of international law, foreign law is merely an element of fact captured by international law. This is why the term 'comparative international law' is hardly appropriate to describe this practice,[65] unless we consider it to be a mere linguistic convenience and thus give up providing it with any scientific or disciplinary consistency.

Comparative international law appears in this case as a linguistic convenience used to describe a practice which is inherent to the international legal reasoning and which is as such devoid of any scientific or disciplinary consistency. There

[63] N Jain, 'Comparative International Law at the ICTY: The General Principles Experiment' (2015) 109 *American Journal of International Law* 486.

[64] M Forteau, 'Comparative International Law within, Not against, International Law: Lessons from the International Law Commission' (2015) 109 *American Journal of International Law* 498.

[65] S El Boudouhi, 'L'utilisation du droit étranger dans l'appréhension des sources internationales par le juge interne: quel droit comparé?' in Marie and Tranchant (n 54) 201.

is perhaps as little scientific basis, mutatis mutandis, for speaking in this sense of comparative international law before domestic courts as before the European Court of Human Rights (ECtHR) or the Court of Justice of the European Union (CJEUI): the use by these courts of what is commonly referred to, for the sake of convenience, as comparative law, to designate the taking into account of the law of Member States,[66] is not 'law as knowledge', which could simply enrich or inspire the practice of the European judge, but rather 'law as power', imposed, implicitly or explicitly, by the applicable international law, European law in this case. It is indeed questionable that the comparative examination of national legal orders by the ECtHR is, strictly speaking, comparative law, even though eminent comparatist scholars consider that 'the progress of European integration tends to give … a new lustre to the comparative approach in Europe',[67] thereby linking the phenomenon occurring before the European judge and comparative law.

Indeed, just as we identified above the bases for recourse to foreign law in the consideration of international law, we can identify bases in the law of the EU or in the law of the European Convention on Human Rights for the judge's consideration of the law of Member States and its comparative examination. In the case of the ECtHR, we can take the example of the concept of European consensus, which triggers the benefit – for the defending state – of the doctrine of the national margin when examining the necessity of a given restrictive measure. It is thus within the necessity test that the Court engages in the comparative exercise.[68] Admittedly, the Convention does not refer directly or indirectly to the laws of Member States, but it does contain the criterion of necessity, which has been interpreted by the Court as requiring the search for a European consensus, and the assessment of the European consensus can only be made by reference to national laws. The law of the Member States then comes into play at the level of the legal characterisation of the European consensus, ie, taking into account the different 'facts' constituted by the laws of the Member States and ultimately subsuming them under the necessity criterion. The taking into consideration of Member States' laws is thus called for by the applicable law. With regard to EU law, in a comparative study of the practices of the European Court of Justice and the US Supreme Court,

[66] However, the situation is radically different when a European judge steps outside their own system and refers to the case law of a third country or to that of another regional court. In this case, we are faced with genuine comparative law arguments in the sense of 'law as knowledge'. For an example of this type of study, see JF Flauss, 'La présence de la jurisprudence de la Cour suprême des Etats-Unis d'Amérique dans le contentieux européen des droits de l'homme' (2005) *Revue trimestrielle des droits de l'homme* 313.

[67] H Muir Watt, 'Droit comparé' *Encyclopédie Universalis*, available at www.universalis.fr/index/droit-compare (own translation).

[68] JT Theilen, *European Consensus between Strategy and Principle: The Uses of Vertically Comparative Legal Reasoning in Regional Human Rights Adjudication* (Baden Baden: Nomos, 2021); AM Lecis Cocco Ortu, 'La comparaison en tant que méthode de détermination du standard de protection des droits dans le système CEDH' (2011) *Rivista Associazione Italiana dei Costituzionalisti*, www.rivistaaic.it/images/rivista/pdf/Lecis%20Cocco%20Ortu.pdf.

Lenaertz and Gutman have themselves identified 'general and specific legal bases in the treaties authorizing the Union courts to use the comparative law method'.[69] According to them, these bases fall into three broad categories: the discovery and development of general principles of the EU, the interpretation of EU concepts and rules, and the control of compatibility. This makes it, at first sight, difficult to draw comparisons with the US Supreme Court's use of foreign law, since the latter really does use foreign law as 'knowledge' which has no basis in law, except when it comes to applying conflict-of-laws rules or considering international sources. The authors acknowledge this difference, stating that comparative law is perceived as 'external' before the US Supreme Court, whereas it is 'internal to the legal order of the European Union' before the Luxembourg Court,[70] thus echoing the comparison 'within' referred to by Forteau.[71] This might be enough to stop the transatlantic comparison exercise dead in its tracks, given that what is referred to as 'comparative law' does not occupy the same place in legal reasoning in both cases, unless it is limited solely to the European judge's reference to the foreign law of third countries. But it has to be admitted that the comparative appeal is powerful. Comparative law, far from the disciplinary specificity that characterises its origins, thus becomes a catch-all covering any exercise involving intertwining or comparing several legal orders, whatever their logical position in legal reasoning, or in the legal syllogism if one recalls the benefits of some degree of formalism.[72] It is at least understandable that the US Supreme Court's recourse to foreign law should provoke more controversy and stronger political reactions than references by the Court of Justice or the ECtHR to the domestic legal systems of their Member States:[73] the latter do not look outside their own legal system when resorting to other legal systems, whereas the US Supreme Court may look outside its own legal system for a source of inspiration, in exactly the same way as it would draw on studies in sociology, anthropology or economics to legally characterise (ie, subsume under a legal concept) a given factual situation.

And yet, today, no one disputes that these two regional tribunals make use of 'comparative law', themselves enshrining the status of the latter both in the drafting of their rulings and in the organisation of their departments. This is a sign that

[69] K Lenaertz and K Gutman, 'The Comparative Law Method and the European Court of Justice: Echoes across the Atlantic' (2016) 64 *American Journal of Comparative Law* 844.

[70] ibid.

[71] Forteau (n 64).

[72] See more generally d'Aspremont on the uses of formalism in the sources'doctrine: J d'Aspremont, *Formalism and the Sources of International Law: A Theory of the Ascertainment of Legal Rules* (Oxford: Oxford University Press, 2011).

[73] For a presentation of the main arguments before the US Supreme Court regarding the use of comparative law, see N Dorsen, 'The Relevance of Foreign Legal Materials in US Constitutional Cases: A Conversation between Justice Antonin Scalia and Justice Stephen Breyer' (2005) 3 *International Journal of Constitutional Law* 519.

comparative law for these courts, like comparative international law for others, is more often than not a linguistic convenience.[74] It is perhaps also the sign of a certain disciplinary imperialism on the part of a comparativist scholarship which has succeeded in infusing comparative law 'everywhere', even where formally, and from the point of view of legal logic, we are not faced with comparative law, but with an exercise in legal characterisation or legal interpretation according to rules that require the consideration of other legal systems. The expansion of the field of comparative law towards international law is perceptible in the literature. In addition to the advocates of the 'comparative international law' movement who have distinguished themselves in recent years, some comparatists also tend to see (albeit in passing) only general principles of law as fertile ground, since in their view, their identification 'can only be conducted on the basis of comparative law',[75] thus totally blurring the definition of the latter. On the other hand, more in-depth analyses of general principles of law by international law experts, for example, are careful not to use the expression 'comparative law';[76] comparative law is scarcely mentioned at all, the more neutral expression 'comparative method' being favoured instead.[77]

Leaving aside the use of the term for the sake of convenience, we can hardly claim that the link with comparative law is justified by the object under analysis, that is, the taking into account by the domestic judge of foreign law in the consideration of international sources. It remains to be seen whether there is any justification, or at least any significance, for this expansion of comparative law towards international law. Indeed, it may well be a methodological interest that could explain why the use of the term 'comparative law' extends beyond the use of 'law as knowledge' to include cases of 'law as power' when foreign law is used in the consideration of international sources. The international law norms that require foreign law to be taken into consideration are so vaguely formulated that they leave national and international judges alike a wide margin of discretion, which calls for comparative practice to be approached with caution. Even if the methodology of comparative law remains for the most part widely debated,[78] it appears that it

[74] Once again, we exclude from the analysis the situation where the ECtHR and the CJEU refer to the law of a third country, which is a matter of comparative law in the scientific sense of the term and is more than a linguistic convenience.

[75] R David, C Jauffret-Spinosi and M Gore, *Les grands systèmes de droit contemporains* (Paris: Dalloz 2016) 7–8.

[76] See, eg, G Gaja, 'General Principles of Law' in R Wolfrum (ed), *Max Planck Encyclopedia of Public International Law* (Oxford: Oxford University Press, 2013) 370.

[77] B Cheng, *General Principles of Law As Applied by International Courts and Tribunals* (London: Stevens, 1953) 392.

[78] B Jaluzot, 'Méthodologie du droit comparé: bilan et prospective' (2005) 57 *Revue internationale de droit comparé* 29; see also G Samuel, 'Dépasser le fonctionnalisme' in P Legrand (ed), *Comparer les droits, résolument* (Paris: PUF, 2009) 405.

is even more important for judges than for academic comparatists to 'take the criteria of comparison seriously'.[79]

D. Comparative International Law as a Quest for Methodology: The Methodological Value of Applying the Language of Comparative Law to International Law

While it may seem scientifically inaccurate to speak of comparative international law when referring to the use that domestic judges make of foreign law in establishing or interpreting international law, the fact remains that domestic judges mobilise foreign law as a factual element that they assess quite freely,[80] even for the purposes of legal characterisation with regard to international norms that leave a margin of appreciation.[81] In practice, therefore, and despite the formalist analysis provided above, we are closer to 'law as knowledge' than to 'law as power', hence the possible relevance of comparative law and its methods. Indeed, the main consequence of asserting that the consideration of foreign law in the examination of the sources of international law is commanded by international law itself is the withdrawal of this activity from the critical scrutiny inherent in the examination of the mobilisation of comparative law as 'law as knowledge'. In other words, that is the consequence of a strictly formalist analysis which tends overall to shield the choices made in legal reasoning from scrutiny. Formalism thus appears to be at the service of the judge's discretion to freely characterise the foreign law under examination. And it is for the purposes of countering this formalism, in a way, that comparative law can prove useful, understood – perhaps in an idealistic manner – as an essentially critical discipline. The main interest in using comparative law language to examine the domestic judge's use of foreign law lies in the emphasis (essentially critical in nature) on the freedom of choice available to the domestic judge, even when the consideration of foreign law is dictated by international law (see section D.1). However, this methodological interest appears limited by the irreducible difference in nature between comparative law, a genuine 'law as knowledge', and foreign law in the consideration of international sources, which remains, from a formal and logical point of view, 'law as power' (see section D.2). Thus, if some degree of de-formalisation appears necessary for critical analysis purposes, formalism can explain the specificity of the comparative analysis of international law.

[79] Ponthoreau (n 38) 19; see also Sauvé (n 49).

[80] In that regard, it may be useful to distinguish between situations where foreign law is taken into account as a matter of law – ie, in conflict-of-laws cases – and those where foreign law is only a factual element.

[81] See above the case of the use of 'comparative law' by the ECtHR or the CJEU.

1. The Value of Borrowing Comparative Law Methods for a Critical Approach to International Law

Today, the permeability between disciplines and legal systems means that methodological concerns in international law are on the rise more than ever before. This is evidenced by the choice of topics made by the International Law Commission in recent years: after the 1969 Convention on the Law of Treaties, the determination of the rules of international law scarcely attracted its attention for decades, until a genuine methodological surge resulted in the successive inclusion on its agenda of the determination, understood as methodological principles, of customary international law in 2011, general principles of law in 2018 and auxiliary means of determining the rules of international law from 2022 onwards.

These concerns are also emerging under the influence of comparatist impulses of all kinds, which Muir Watt describes as 'the revenge of the comparatist'.[82] Moreover, comparative law itself has evolved, taking a resolutely methodological turn and moving away from mere knowledge of foreign law, towards 'an awareness on the part of the comparatist of what [s]he is doing when [s]he compares', in the words of Legrand, who himself made a considerable contribution to this evolution.[83] According to Muir Watt, it is today 'epistemological requirements that give [comparative law] its scientific legitimacy'.[84] Comparative law has thus become a more reflexive discipline than it was in the past, when foreign sources were more difficult to access and the bulk of the comparatist's work consisted of researching and classifying them. Today, comparative law can 'subvert the great positivist [formalist] machine by placing grains of sand in its cogs'.[85] Comparative law thus appears as a 'subversive discipline'.[86] This methodological shift, marking a retreat from classical formalist approaches, can also be found in international law, where it sometimes takes a historicist form,[87] sometimes a comparative one, when it does not turn to empirical analyses[88] or resolutely critical ones. Indeed, a convergence of turning points can be observed when members of international law scholarship who are the proponents of a critical theory of international law are the first ones to take an interest in what comparative law could contribute to international

[82] H Muir Watt, 'La fonction subversive du droit comparé' (2000) 52 *Revue internationale de droit comparé* 503, 526.
[83] P Legrand, *Le droit comparé* (Paris: PUF, 1999) 13.
[84] Muir Watt (n 67).
[85] P Legrand, 'Sur l'analyse différentielle des juriscultures' (1999) 51 *Revue internationale de droit comparé* 1061.
[86] GP Fletcher, 'Comparative Law as a Subversive Discipline' (1998) 46 *American Journal of Comparative Law* 683; see also Muir Watt (n 82).
[87] Among a prolific literature on the historicist turn, see Anne Orford's work, which devotes an entire turn to history: A Orford, *International Law and the Politics of History* (Cambridge: Cambridge University Press, 2021).
[88] G Shaffer and T Ginsburg, 'The Empirical Turn in International Legal Scholarship' (2012) 106 *American Journal of International Law* 1.

law.[89] Thus, when Koskenniemi makes 'the case for comparative international law', taking its meaning to be self-evident, he is not so much concerned with whether or not it constitutes a new discipline; what he ultimately aims at is at developing a critical perspective on international law. In other words, he is not so concerned with the object as with the method. However, it should be noted that 'the comparativist project in international law'[90] does not always adopt this critical approach to comparative law, when focusing on the object and its specificity rather than on the method.

And yet the main problem raised by the use of foreign law in the consideration of international sources, as well as by any comparative studies of international law, is that of a risk of disorder engendered by the absence of method in the treatment of foreign law: like the comparatist for whom all foreign laws may be easily accessible, domestic judges could easily find themselves overwhelmed with information or disoriented when faced with a multitude of foreign laws from which they can draw to apply an international norm. In some legal traditions, such as the French, references to foreign law that do not result from the application of conflict-of-laws rules are very rare, or even non-existent;[91] however, in other systems, where there is room for detailed reasoning, including in references to foreign law, the latter are never sufficiently reasoned or systematic. For the purposes of identification or interpretation of international custom, treaties or general principles of law, the treatment given to foreign law by domestic courts is often criticised for being fragmentary or even random.[92] For example, it is criticised for referring only to familiar legal systems, such as *common law*, whereas this is much less justified for international sources than for *common law* principles. Moreover, national judges are not the only ones to be pointed at for their lack of methodology, as the International Court of Justice is often criticised for the way it treats the national laws that enable it to determine whether or not a new customary norm exists. Pellet has even argued that the practice of the International Court of Justice (and its predecessor, the Permanent Court of International Justice) in this area is precisely not in line with comparative law.[93] The treatment of national laws for the purposes of determining an international norm by investment tribunals has redoubled these fears.[94] Investment tribunals dealing with the status of

[89] Among the earliest writers on comparative law, before the emergence of the 'comparativist project', see in particular Kennedy (n 1) 548; A Peters and H Schwenke, 'Comparative Law beyond Post-modernism' (2000) 49 *International and Comparative Law Quarterly* 800; M Koskenniemi, 'The Case for Comparative International Law' (2010) 10 *Finnish Yearbook of International Law* 1.

[90] D'Aspremont (n 39) 93.

[91] These references are implicit in a study of the use of comparative law arguments by domestic judges: B Markesinis and J Fedke, 'The Judge as Comparatist' (2005) 80 *Tulane Law Review* 11.

[92] Coté (n 54).

[93] A Pellet, 'Article 38' in A Zimmermann (ed), *The Statute of the International Court of Justice: A Commentary*, (Oxford: Oxford University Press, 2006) 677.

[94] Unlike the International Court of Justice, which by virtue of its very composition enjoys a presumption of representativeness of the world's principal legal systems, investment tribunals are more easily open to criticism if national laws are compared too superficially.

the protection of legitimate expectations in international law have been criticised for generalising what remain very strictly delimited special cases in the various domestic laws examined in order to create a new rule in international law from scratch.[95] This is an example where contextualisation as a tool of comparative law could have been useful in terms of encouraging caution. With today's relatively easy access to foreign law, including for the purpose of establishing norms of international law, there is a great risk of a lack of method in a branch of law – international law – in which domestic judges are generally not very specialised. It is easy to see how a critical comparative approach could be useful to the domestic judge in understanding international sources.

The methods of comparative law, at their most discursive, dialectical and critical, can prove useful in helping judges and scholars alike in considering other domestic laws than their own relating to international law. Indeed, while the methodology of comparative law is far from uniform or even unequivocally identifiable,[96] it offers the advantage of being characterised by a long-standing methodological scepticism that can soften the dominant formalism, including in the approach of foreign laws relating to international law, by requiring a dose of critical distance, both with regard to the applicable law, which can thus be better understood, and to the foreign law, which can be approached with the greatest 'caution'.[97] Thus, the type of comparative law that could usefully be invoked for methodological purposes is not the more traditional one, based exclusively on functionalism, according to which law must be stripped of its national or local particularities in order to focus solely on the objectives pursued in an approach that is as finalistic as it is allegedly universalist,[98] but the 'post-modern' one, characterised instead by the contextualism embodied by comparatists such as Pierre Legrand.[99]

In addition, and in keeping with a methodology based on scepticism, thinking about the mobilisation of foreign law before the domestic judge in the consideration of international sources in terms of 'comparative law arguments' (although scientifically questionable, as we have seen above) enables us to take a step to the side and perceive the functions of the mobilisation of this law in the consideration

[95] J Ostransky, 'From a Fortuitous Transplant to a Fundamental Principle of Law: The Doctrine of Legitimate Expectations and the Possibilities of a Different Law' in I Venzke and KJ Heller, *Contingency in International Law: On the Possibility of Different Legal Histories* (Oxford: Oxford University Press, 2021) 426.

[96] M van Hoeke, 'Methodology of Comparative Legal Research' [2015] *Law and Method* 1.

[97] The members of the Sixth Committee of the United Nations General Assembly also stress that 'caution is called for' with regard to auxiliary means of determining the rules of international law (AG/J/3703, 1 November 2023).

[98] R Michaels, 'The Functional Method of Comparative Law' in M Reimann and R Zimmermann (eds), *The Oxford Handbook of Comparative Law* (Oxford: Oxford University Press, 2012) 339.

[99] M Siems, 'New Directions in Comparative Law' in M Reimann and R Zimmermann (eds), *The Oxford Handbook of Comparative Law*, 2nd edn (Oxford: Oxford University Press, 2019) 852. For an internationalist look at this methodological turn in comparative law, see Peters and Schwenke (n 89); see also Kennedy (n 1).

of international sources. These functions may be manifold, but they all seem to point towards a quest to legitimise the solution adopted by the judge.[100] In other words, international law requiring that foreign law be taken into account does not mean that the latter cannot be used as an argument, a factual element like any other, in support of the position adopted by the domestic judge, and that it should not be distrusted or at least questioned. In this respect, it is important not to blind ourselves to the neutrality of the mobilisation of the foreign law argument; this mobilisation, although imposed by the rules of identification of international law, is necessarily an instrumentalisation in the service of the choices made by the judge. As the mobilisation of foreign law is never neutral, even when establishing or interpreting international law, it is necessary to establish a rigorous methodological framework that enables us to place the law we draw on or reject in its social, cultural and even historical context. However, the scepticism has to be two-way, as one must not be blind either to the supposed neutrality of the 'metrics' used in comparative law as methodology. Thus, this should be the future task of critical comparative law as critical comparatists such as Muir Watt already show that decolonial private international law approaches can also learn from more established critical methodologies of public international law.[101] This points to a promising cross-fertilisation of methodologies between public and private international law.

We have attempted to prove that the methodological interest of 'post-modern' comparative law lies in taking into account the context of foreign law. But the question can easily be asked whether such methodological precautions are just as necessary for foreign law used in the consideration of international sources as they can be for foreign law invoked to interpret national norms.

2. Limits to the Use of Comparative Law Methods for International Law Purposes

If one accepts that the purpose of international law in adopting the language of comparative law is above all methodological, and that it is a question of framing – or at least being attentive to – the freedom that the domestic judge may enjoy in examining foreign law, then it remains to be determined whether this purpose is truly justified when it comes to international law.

As regards the relevance of the methodological purpose of recourse to comparative law, we should not underestimate the difference in status in legal reasoning that may exist between foreign law as 'law as knowledge' when it is invoked in support of the application of rules of domestic law, and foreign law as 'law as

[100] For developments and examples of legitimisation through the use of foreign law, see El Boudouhi (n 46).

[101] See Muir Watt, ch 10 in this volume.

power' when it is invoked under international legal norms. The 'methods', in the form of limits or 'safeguards', which appear to be indispensable for recourse to foreign law as 'law as knowledge', are not so indispensable when the foreign law is 'law as power'. If there is discretion or a wide margin of appreciation, it results from international law itself and not from any initiative on the part of the parties or the judge to seek arguments outside the legal system concerned. In other words, the judge who has recourse to foreign law in their application of international law has been empowered by international law to do so. It is not a liberty that they take, as it would be if they were to draw on foreign law to interpret a domestic legal norm. The need for legitimisation by method is therefore much less pressing in the case of foreign law used in the consideration of international sources by the domestic judge. In fact, the reasoning behind comparative law as 'law as knowledge' can be reversed: not only does the domestic judge not have to justify their use of foreign law, but it is, on the contrary, the absence of recourse to foreign law, whether in the form of domestic case law practice or otherwise, that can be criticised, even in legal systems where the tradition is to give lapidary reasons. Thus, while it is understandable that the French judge does not explicitly refer to the foreign law that may have inspired them in a particular interpretation of domestic law,[102] it is less understandable that they do not refer to a foreign case law practice sufficient to establish the existence or contours of an international legal norm.

This irreducible difference in logical position in the reasoning results in a second limit to borrowing the language of comparative law to tackle the consideration of international sources by the domestic judge: if we consider that the method of comparative law as it may be mobilised by the domestic judge – and not practised by the scholarship – translates mainly into methodological recommendations aimed at ensuring that recourse to foreign law does not exceed certain limits,[103] we easily perceive its unsuitability for examining the role of foreign law in the consideration of international sources. Indeed, recourse to comparative law by the domestic judge is generally accompanied by recommendations and warnings noted by comparatist scholars themselves: while the use of comparative law arguments is generally encouraged in a quest for cosmopolitanism and openness to 'the other', but above all as an effort to understand one's own law, it must not give rise to aberrations or a distortion of the applicable law, which is national law. Recourse to comparative law is accompanied by warnings concerning the 'conditions for the acceptability of the argument based on comparison',[104] especially in the case of constitutional norms, the formulation of which is the result of delicate choices and subtle balances between various values specific to the national community. The aim is to avoid 'radical cultural relativism'.[105] But

[102] Markesinis and Fedke (n 91).

[103] M-C Ponthoreau, 'L'argument fondé sur la comparaison dans le raisonnement juridique' in P Legrand, *Comparer les droits, résolument* (Paris: PUF, 2009) 537.

[104] ibid.

[105] ibid.

these warnings have no place when the object of comparative examination is an international legal standard. There is no risk of importing values from another, less legitimate system, since the values reflected in international law are deemed to be shared by all the legal systems in which they are embedded. To say that the use of foreign law by the domestic judge in the consideration of international sources is not comparative law, or even a comparative law argument, is not simply formalism, focusing rigorously on the place of different elements in legal reasoning. It is also about underlining the fundamentally different nature of what is being compared: when resorting to the argument of comparative law in administrative law, for example, the judge must be very careful not to turn away from the applicable (national) law and its spirit, and thus refer to foreign law only with caution, taking care to contextualise it. Conversely, when using foreign case law to determine whether there is a new customary norm in international law concerning the immunity of international organisations, for example, the judge is merely applying international law, which requires them to take foreign case law into account. Even if they were to lack methodological rigour, they would still be engaged in the exercise of legal characterisation, which by its very nature leaves the judge with a great deal of leeway in selecting and assessing the facts.[106]

This is why such a recommendation, based on comparative law methodology, is of limited interest when it comes to interpreting or establishing a norm of international law. In a certain sense, the latter must necessarily result from the encounter between several legal systems taken as factual elements, whether the foreign law is taken into account as a matter of state practice, a constitutive element of custom, of subsequent practice useful for the interpretation of a treaty provision, or of principles shared by 'civilised nations'. Unless we consider that international law is not really 'international',[107] it is precisely 'internationality' that guides the judge; it is also 'internationality' that eliminates the risk of the domestic judge allowing themselves to be unduly influenced by a foreign law, less legitimate than the applicable national law. Indeed, there is a significant coincidence between the emergence of the 'comparative international law' movement in the academic world on the one hand, and a sort of scholarly withdrawal into national approaches to international law on the other, as if the loss of 'internationality' relegated international law to the status of national law, likely to become an object of comparative law like any other.[108]

[106] On the freedom of the judge, whether domestic or international, in the selection and interpretation of facts for the purposes of their legal qualification, *cf* S El Boudouhi, *L'élément factuel dans le contentieux international* (Brussels: Bruylant, 2013) 49.

[107] We refer here to the thesis defended by Roberts (n 40).

[108] For some examples of national approaches to international law, see in particular E Jouannet, 'French and American Perspectives on International Law: Legal Cultures and International Law' (2006) 58 *Maine Law Review* 292; H Ruiz Fabri, 'Nécessité d'une approche européenne du droit international? Ni oui, ni non, ni blanc, ni noir' in SFDI/Société allemande de droit international, *Droit international et diversité des cultures juridiques* (Paris: Pedone, 2008) 223; A Becker Lorca, 'International Law in Latin America or Latin American International Law? Rise, Fall, and Retrieval of a Tradition of Legal Thinking and Political Imagination' (2006) 47 *Harvard International Law Journal* 283; F Messineo, 'Is

The previous developments are reflected in the current practice of international law: the reluctance shown by the International Law Commission, during the current work on the general principles of international law, towards the possible borrowing of comparative law methods should not be overlooked: despite several references by the Special Rapporteur to comparative law,[109] the International Law Commission as a whole does not seem to have been convinced by this terminology, and the report emphasises that 'some have pointed out that it was not necessary to refer … to the methods and techniques of comparative law to be employed for the purposes of the analysis of national legal systems'.[110] The methodological interest (more pragmatic than critical) that the rapprochement with comparative law may present is thus seeping through to the International Law Commission, despite resistance, with some members of the Commission even finding that 'comparative examination' would be more appropriate than 'comparative analysis', which is currently retained in the draft text to be adopted and which perhaps implies a greater degree of comparison and subjectivity.[111] By opting for a more reserved stance, the International Law Commission seems to aim at freeing itself from the influence of comparativism and developing its own methodologies for each of the international sources, insisting in particular on certain criteria such as the 'degree of representativity' for the auxiliary means of determining international law, or geographical diversity for the general principles of law.[112]

This reluctance of the International Law Commission to borrow the methods of comparative law only confirms the hypothesis that this rapprochement only makes sense if one opts for a critical approach to international law, which obviously cannot be the case within this institution whose members, although independent, are appointed and elected by states. The role played by the International Law Commission in the institutional landscape of international law is decisive: if stripped of its critical and subversive dimension, comparative law is of little interest to international law, which is endowed with a body charged precisely with developing a methodology for each of its sources.

There an Italian Conception of International Law?' (2013) 2 *Cambridge Journal of International and Comparative Law* 879; L Mälksoo, *Russian Approaches to International Law* (Oxford: Oxford University Press, 2015).

[109] International Law Commission, Second report on general principles of law, by Mr Vàzquez-Bermúdez, A/CN.4/741.

[110] CDI, Rapport de la Soixante-douzième session, à propos du projet de conclusion 5 relative à l'analyse comparative permettant de déterminer l'existence d'un principe commun aux principaux systèmes juridiques, 2021, A/76/10, § 200.

[111] ibid.

[112] ibid. *cf* Draft conclusion 5(3), which states that 'the comparative analysis must be broad and representative: it must encompass different legal families and regions of the world'.

E. Conclusion

Adopting a restrictive approach, the analysis has focused on two manifestations of comparative international law. The first one is the comparative study of the different ways in which the rules of international law are applied in national legal orders. This is the manifestation that resembles most of conventional comparative law, with the caveat that what is being compared is not international law, as is suggested by the phrase 'comparative international law', but the national reception of international law, ie, national laws of foreign relations. The more accurate denomination of this strand of comparative international law could thus be 'comparative law of foreign relations'. The second manifestation that has been dealt with was the use by domestic judges of foreign law in their engagement with international law, which was found to be more of a linguistic convenience than actual analyses of comparative law. This practice is certainly based on the cognitive process of comparison, but it is not of the same nature as that of the constitutional judge or the criminal judge who would venture out of their legal system, since it is based not on the science of comparative law, but on the rules of international law themselves. However, it has been thoroughly examined to show how the role that is played by the so-called comparative law therein is part of the DNA of international law as it flows from the sources doctrine. Despite the discrepancy between the two components of what has been identified above as comparative international law, it has appeared that there is a unifying theme running across these manifestations: the need for more methodology in borrowing from other legal systems. However, such a need for methodology does not unfold in the same way, depending on whether we are talking about comparative studies or, rather, about comparative law arguments.

9

Comparative International Law

What's Next?

UGO MATTEI AND AVI SINGH

A. Introduction

It is difficult to write a re-appraisal of an article on 'Comparative International Law' by Boris Mamlyuk and Ugo Mattei, published some 14 years ago.[1] Mamlyuk and Mattei wrote this article when a process of convergence between international and comparative law was clearly present in Western academia.[2] That convergence had resulted from economic globalisation, Western-centrism and US hegemony,[3] and the original article, benefiting from direct access to Russian sources, had tried to counteract a strategy of historical cancellation of beneficial Cold War dynamics that became part of the mainstream vision after the fall of the Soviet Union. Soviet international law, it argued, was an intellectually strong and sophisticated alternative model that, despite some platitudes and reciprocal mocking, generated, through the 'long Cold War' (1918–89), materials for genuine and relevant comparison. The original article thus advocated scholarly attention to the benefits of such awareness of alternative visions of international law and to the role played by major figures in the Soviet Union and in the Western Bloc in generating reciprocal knowledge and dialogue.[4]

[1] BN Mamlyuk and U Mattei, 'Comparative International Law' (2011) 36 *Brooklyn Journal of International Law* 386.

[2] See, eg, BG Garth, 'The Globalization of the Law' in GA Caldeira et al (eds), *Oxford Handbook of Law and Politics* (Oxford: Oxford University Press, 2008) 245.

[3] See, for a robust analysis of context at the time, U Mattei and L Nader, *Plunder: When the Rule of Law is Illegal* (London: Wiley-Blackwell, 2008).

[4] See Mamlyuk and Mattei (n 1) 394–409, discussing such authors as Evgeny A Korovin and his US student John Hazard. The article explored the USSR's early charge of even the pre-Second World War system as imperialist and incorporating private property, free trade and 'the organic class system'. It explains that Korovin 'was the first to apply Marxism to international law' (at 399). The article was followed by the treatise A Roberts et al (eds) *Comparative International Law* (Oxford: Oxford University Press, 2018), which does not deal with the article substantially, though it acknowledges, in one essay, that international law is not unitary. On the whole, the book is an academic study of the methodology

Mattei made a similar claim in a subsequent article on the influence of Cold War ideology in the maturation of comparative law in the 1950s.[5] Once again, the perspective taken was that of the 'long Cold War'. Comparison with Soviet legal innovation was influential (though undeclared) in Western progressive law reform,[6] and Soviet law became the third family of the dominant taxonomy of world legal systems.[7] Mattei argued that any foundational comparison generated a peaceful dialogue among scholarly institutions that contributed to *détente* between the two blocs,[8] even if the peace-generating influence that academic dialogue could exercise had been marginalised in the structuralist-functionalist mainstream (from Rabels to Schlesinger to Sacco) that came to maturity in the 1960s.[9]

In the same years, possibly as a reaction to the Vietnam War, the neo-conservative ideology, which emerged from the coming together of disgruntled liberal democrats with right-wing components of the US Republican Party, began to gain traction.[10] After the Iran hostage crisis of 1980, neo-cons hijacked Ronald Reagan's foreign policy and marshalled Republicans in aggressive international relations that included projects of democracy exportation through war and staunch Zionism. That posture included escalation of new wars by almost every US administration: in the Middle East, Latin America, the Balkans and Ukraine.[11]

It is against this new background that this chapter starts in sections B and C with an analysis that connects the position of the original article with current

of determining sources of international law, and the study of case law to determine the validity of the law, and does not seemingly concern itself with the issues raised in the 'Comparative International Law' article or the current study.

[5] See U Mattei, 'The Cold War and Comparative Law: A Reflection on the Politics of Intellectual Discipline' (2017) 65 *American Journal of Comparative Law* 567.

[6] The interaction between Soviet legality and the Western legal evolution is explored in J Quigley, *Soviet Legal Innovation and the Law of the Western World* (Cambridge: Cambridge University Press, 2007).

[7] See, eg, RB Schlesinger, *Comparative Law: Cases and Materials* (Brooklyn: The Foundation Press, 1950). See also R David, *Traité élémentaire de droit civil comparé: introduction à l'étude des droits étrangers et à la méthode comparative* (Paris: R Pichon & R Durand-Auzias, 1950); R David, *Les Grands Systèmes de droit contemporains* (Paris: Dalloz, 1964).

[8] The choice by some leading comparativists to erase Soviet law from their books in editions following 1991 seems arrogant today. Such erasure is evident in editions published after the fall of the Berlin Wall of some foundational works on comparative legal studies, including those by Zweigert and Kötz (decided by Kötz) and by David (decided by Jeuffret-Spinosi). See, respectively, K Zweigert and H Kötz, *Introduction to Comparative Law*, 3rd edn, trans T Weir (Oxford: Oxford University Press, 1998); and R David and C Jauffret-Spinosi, *Les Grands Systèmes de droit contemporains*, 10th edn (Paris: Dalloz, 1992). Perestroika sowed the seeds for a unitary turn in international law by removing the objections to compulsory International Court of Justice under six international human rights agreements, establishing direct links with international economic organisations, and incorporation of international legal standards into domestic legislation. See Mamlyuk and Mattei (n 1) 418–19.

[9] See A Riles (ed), *Rethinking the Masters of Comparative Law* (Oxford: Hart Publishing, 2001).

[10] See F Fukuyama, *After the Neocons: America at the Crossroads* (London: Profile Books, 2006).

[11] See D Vine, *United States of War. A Global History of America's Endless War from Columbus to the Islamic State*, (Oakland: University of California Press, 2020).

events. Subsequently, sections D–G discuss possible futures of comparative international law – first, noting the decline of US hegemony, and then investigating the possibilities of a new multilateral hegemony with the BRICS as a hegemon candidate and a new model of international law potentially emerging from counter-hegemony.

B. Which International and Comparative Law 'at the End of the End of History'?

When 'Comparative International Law' by Mamlyuk and Mattei was presented in various academic venues in the US and Europe, it was a time of extensive fundamental discussions in the discipline of international law. More innovative and progressive scholars, most of them belonging to the so-called liberal left, generated movements such as Third World Approaches to International Law (TWAIL)[12] or New Approaches to International Law (NAIL).[13] A fundamental retooling of international law was the target of these loose academic organisations that in the US echoed critical approaches inaugurated at Harvard by critical legal studies.[14] A similar claim for critique had already generated some excitement around a scholarly conference in Utah, before the end of last century, but did not yield any organisational outcomes.[15]

'Comparative International Law' illustrated that an emancipatory role of international law and a vision of the discipline aware of its crucial geopolitical dimension had already developed in the Soviet Union, and not only at an academic level. We should remember that one of the first moves of the Bolsheviks was to denounce the secrecy of international treatises and publish those entered by the Tsar, a global turning point in the history of the discipline.[16]

Fifteen years ago, the attention of 'Comparative International Law' to the Soviet model was meant as a contribution to a discipline that had moved beyond its state-centric classical tradition, by challenging sovereignty through international human rights, and state subjectivity through the recognition of transnational players, both non-governmental organisations (NGOs) and

[12] See BS Chimni, 'Third World Approaches to International Law: A Manifesto? (2006) 8 *International Community Law Review* 3; MW Mutua, 'What is TWAIL?' (2000) 94 *American Society of International Law Proceedings* 31.

[13] See JM Beneyto and D Kennedy (eds), *New Approaches to International Law: The European and the American Experiences* (The Hague: TMC Asser Press, 2013).

[14] See D Kennedy and M Koskenniemi, *Of Law and the World: Critical Conversations on Power, History, and Political Economy* (Cambridge, MA: Harvard University Press, 2023).

[15] See NV Demleitner, 'Challenge, Opportunity and Risk: An Era of Change in Comparative Law' (1998) 46 *American Journal of Comparative Law* 647.

[16] See Quigley (n 6).

multinational corporations.[17] The feeling was that moving away from its classic vision had been the outcome of geopolitical transformations at the *end of history* in which the US and its allies imposed one global political agenda (the so-called Washington Consensus) rather than the result of a principled evolution based on dialogue and pluralistic choices.[18] US military domination (eg, the North Atlantic Treaty Organization (NATO) strikes in Serbia and Bosnia) needed justification on technical-legal rather than geopolitical grounds: human rights violations were ideally suited for NATO expansionism. This hypocrisy included wilful blindness to the Western-centric ideological biases of most major NGOs and to the corruptive impact of corporate or philanthropic 'donations' on organisations such as the World Health Organization (WHO) or the Food and Agriculture Organization (FAO).[19] It addressed the concern on the technocratic development of international law in Geneva, New York, Brussels or The Hague, without the knowledge or participation of much of the world.[20]

At that time, some of the more critical and sophisticated international scholars (such as Baxi, Chimni, Koskenniemi, Anghie and David Kennedy) seemed in search of balance in the delicate equilibrium between law and politics in international legal studies.[21] Chimni spoke of a 'northern' vocabulary which denied 'southern' approaches, rather than comparing them as independent, as subsidiary or deviant.[22] The article's idea was to look at a phase of more explicit confrontation to understand the conditions necessary for an international legal order to serve the purpose of human civilisation rather than of capital.[23] At 'the end of the end of history', a narrative of emergency and fear was supplanting

[17] See D Kennedy, 'The International Human Rights Movement: Part of the Problem?' (2001) 3 *European Human Rights Law Review* 581.

[18] See S Pahuja, *Decolonising International Law: Development, Economic Growth and the Politics of Universality* (Cambridge: Cambridge University Press, 2011).

[19] See D Kennedy, *The Dark Side of Virtue: Reassessing International Humanitarianism* (Princeton: Princeton University Press, 2004). See also N Maldonado-Torres, 'On the Coloniality of Human Rights' (2017) 114 *Revista Critica de Ciencias Sociais* 117.

[20] Mamlyuk and Mattei (n 1) 421–22.

[21] For a rich variety of perspectives, see J Dunoff and J Tacktman (eds), *Ruling the World? Constitutionalism, International Law and Global Governance* (Cambridge: Cambridge University Press, 2009). See also V Nesiah, 'Decolonial CIL: TWAIL, Feminism, and an Insurgent Jurisprudence' (2018) 112 *AJIL Unbound* 313.

[22] BS Chimni, 'An Outline of a Marxist Course on Public International Law (2004) 17 *Leiden Journal of International Law* 1, 2.

[23] Grotius, considered one of the fathers of international law, was operating in the context of colonialism and the development of large corporations, such as the Dutch East India Company and the British East India Company, followed by the French, wherein corporations were developed as having legal charters to be agents of colonialist imperialism in order to extract value from states outside Europe. The articulation of international law was an essential condition for colonialism. The instruments for colonialism were international treaties, which were perfectly valid, where sovereigns accepted colonialism in treaties which could be enforced, according to the will of the coloniser, if violated by the subject being colonised. Even Indian scholars, according to Chimni, failed to 'capture the intimate relationship between colonialism and international law'. See BS Chimni, 'The Past, Present and Future of International Law: A Critical Third World Approach' (2007) 8 *Melbourne Journal of International Law* 499; BS Chimni, 'A Just World under Law: A View from the South' (2007) 22 *American University International Law Review* 199, 202.

the optimism that followed the destruction of the Berlin Wall. The decline of US hegemony, challenged by self-inflicted wounds of the post-9/11 assault on civil liberties and legality, signalled a turning point.[24] Discussing international law required a new depth of knowledge of the geopolitical foundations of comparative legal families.

In other words, the *end of history* assumed a single point of view, Western legal hegemony, one universal system of international law with international human and property rights, enforced by the international community despite claims of state sovereignty, particularly over economic resources.[25] In 'Comparative International Law', it was claimed that the end of history was over in the first decade of our century, and the TINA (there is no alternative) vision was bound for catastrophic consequences. Geopolitically, this vision translated into Wall Street and the City of London, together with the military industrial complex, feeling entitled to roam the world, because international law was at most facilitative (the World Trade Organization (WTO), the International Centre for Settlement of Investment Disputes (ICSID) and Bilateral Investment Treaties (BITs)) and certainly empty of any principle and capacity to bite.[26] Afghanistan, Iraq, Libya and the collapse of Lehman Brothers were outcomes of the hegemonic model of globalised capitalism incapable of serving any interests other than those of the Anglo-American dominant power.[27]

The system has remained, in essence, extractive and colonial. As Partha Chatterjee wrote, modernity will 'inevitably structure the world according to a pattern that is profoundly colonial' and undemocratic.[28] One of the agents of colonialism has always been the corporation as a juridical person in domestic law, and a subject and object, without any treaty, of international law. For instance, Hauck writes of the United Fruit Company (UFC), incorporated in Boston, US in 1899. The UFC was a key plantation owner, as well as an infrastructure owner, covered by US diplomatic protection in international law, which provided the legal cause for force, if necessary. The protection of the UFC's property rights, which extended to labour suppression, was a US sovereign interest as 'public order'. The power of the UFC has translated into the public imagination of a banana republic, the subservient neo-colonised sovereign as an agent of the UFC.[29] The diplomatic protections to juridical persons with an incorporation in municipal law remains an unchallenged bedrock of international law.

[24] See, eg, B Ackerman, *The Decline and Fall of the American Republic* (Cambridge, MA: Harvard University Press, 2013); D Cole, *Enemy Aliens: Double Standards and Constitutional Freedoms in the War on Terrorism* (New York: New Press, 2003).

[25] See S Marks, 'Four Human Rights Myths' in D Kinley et al (eds), *Human Rights: Old Problems, New Possibilities* (Cheltenham: Edward Elgar, 2013).

[26] U Mattei, 'A Theory of Imperial Law: A Study on US Hegemony and the Latin Resistance' (2003) 10 *Indiana Journal of Global Legal Studies* 383.

[27] See JS Nye Jr, *Bound to Lead: The Changing Nature of American Power* (New York, Basic Books, 1990).

[28] P Chatterjee, 'Beyond the Nation? Or within?' (1998) 56 *Social Text* 57, 68.

[29] SG Hauck, 'Locating the United Fruit Company in the History of International Law' (2024) 61 *Third World Approaches to International Law Review* 1.

The geopolitical conditions 'at the end of the end of history',[30] when 'Comparative International Law' was written, were impossible to be governed through the post-Second World War model of international law based on US hegemony, which included the supremacy and sovereignty of the dollar as an outcome of the demise of the Gold Standard. The search for possible alternatives, models of international legality that were more inclusive and culturally pluralistic, could not be postponed. To be clear, the article did not propose a return to Soviet international law as a global alternative. It was simply claiming that *some* alternative had to emerge given the global geopolitical conditions, and that such an alternative had to be based on dialogue rather than on the iron fist of power. It proposed that such dialogue was necessary if some system of international law were still a desirable alternative to global chaos. Where to look for such an alternative?

Even before the barbarism of the Gaza war that started in 2023, it was clear that international law had morphed into a problem rather than a solution in post-Cold War conditions. It is as if the lack of countervailing powers – that is, of a credible alternative to one-sided global hegemony such as in the *end of history* narrative – was bound to confirm an 'evil technology hypothesis' as a structure of international law,[31] which would determine clashes of civilisation because of the incapacity of the West to live up to its promises of democracy and the rule of law.

The construction of enemies following 9/11, and the use of unilateral instruments for executing the war on terror, consistent with the supposed efficiency of achieving strategic and tactical targets, with almost near-disregard of international law and the continuous one-sided eruptions of US aggressions in the form of wars, strikes, renditions, illegal detentions in Guantanamo Bay, provocations in the form of military exercises and so on, could not have had a different effect. Mattei argued for a 'commons solution' in Palestine to get beyond the untenable ideas of 'two states' and 'one state' solutions.[32] In the same vein, in a recently published chapter with Margot Salomon, Mattei argues for the emergence, from the bottom up, of a 'people's international law' capable of avoiding any temptation of a lazy return to formalism, which would be the final surrender of international law to de facto violence.[33]

Given the geopolitical stakes, this search for *some* alternative cannot be a mere academic exercise. If international law must be imagined as some form

[30] See U Mattei et al, 'IUC Global Legal Standards Research Group, At the End of the End of History: Global Legal Standards Part of the Solution or Part of the Problem?' (2009) 9(3) *Global Jurist* 1334; A Hochuli, G Hoare and P Cunliffe, *The End of the End of History: Politics in the Twenty First Century* (Winchester: Zero Books, 2021).

[31] U Mattei and L Russi, 'The Evil Technology Hypothesis: A Deep Ecological Reading of International Law' (2012) *Cardozo Law Review de novo* 263.

[32] U Mattei, 'Comparative Law, Geopolitics, and the Conflict in Palestine: Disciplined Disengagement and the Commons Solution' (2018) 18(3) *Global Jurist* 1. This article was included in the Special Issue entitled 'International Law: Legitimacy and the State of Israel', with materials from the Cork Conference of 2017.

[33] See U Mattei and M Salomon, 'From Poverty and Development to People's International Law' in R Buchanan et al (eds), *The Oxford Handbook of International Law and Development* (Oxford: Oxford University Press, 2023) 773.

of global constitution, it can function only in the presence of political checks and balances and a broader consensus: not just among sovereign governments at odds with each other and often in consort with multinational corporations, whose only legitimacy in international law is more attenuated than normalised in our imaginations. Such political checks and balances are absent when one hegemon sovereign displays military power with gloves off, or loses – because of such transformation of hegemony into unprincipled domination – any capacity to deploy a credible narrative. The alternative to force and conflict, in myriad engagements across technology, people and states that follow rules, is also international law. This is largely ignored in the dominant discourse of international law, which in itself seems to have run out of steam in managing its contradictions.

The position presented in 'Comparative International Law' was never meant to be unitary, but, as will be seen below, there are now multiple emerging approaches to international law and its understanding, which force a return to a more complex approach to comparative international law and which may be the only means to understand the development of international law. The development will not be in neat lines, though these were also illusory in the United Nations (UN) and Bretton Woods system from the debris of the Second World War,[34] but one which reflects the reality of international relations and the developing customs of engagement, including conflict, that are the reality of our lives, the news and the tragedies that abound.

C. Whither International Law?

In the face of death and destruction by Israel in Gaza the impotence of the UN, paralysed by an obsolete system of Security Council veto power, transforms international law into a caricature.[35] The prima facie finding of the International Court of Justice (ICJ) on the case of genocide initiated by South Africa against Israel, which directs humanitarian and other measures, has been blithely ignored, as has its subsequent judgment on the illegality of the occupation of East Jerusalem, the West Bank and Gaza, and the applicability of the Fourth Geneva Convention (which puts the onus on Israel to administer the territory for the benefit of its population). The occupation continues uninterrupted and with more illegal invasive measures.[36] The ICJ, in continuation of its orders, on

[34] The system was developed while most of the population of the world lived under colonial governments. India was still a colony. China was represented by the Republic of China.

[35] After vetoing three following resolutions asking for immediate ceasefire, on 1 March 2024, the US placed a veto even on the condemnation of the atrocious shooting of hungry Palestinians waiting for food. See N Boeglin, 'Gaza/Israel: en torno al veto indefendible de Estados Unidos en el seno del Consejo de Seguridad' (*Derecho internacional público. Costa Rica*, 22 February 2024), https://derechointernacionalcr.blogspot.com/2024/02/gaza-israel-tercer-veto-de-estados.html.

[36] *Legal Consequences Arising from the Policies and Practices of Israel in the Occupied Palestinian Territory, Including East Jerusalem*, General List No 186, 19 July 2024.

a further application by South Africa that the assault on Gaza was a violation of the Genocide Convention, ordered the Rafah offensive to be halted 'as it may inflict on the Palestinian group in Gaza conditions of life that could bring about its physical destruction in whole or in part'.[37] This was of course also ignored, and international law had no answer.

In parallel, the ICJ also issued an Advisory Opinion on 19 July 2024, that the Israeli occupation of the West Bank was illegal, as it was de facto annexation, and denied the Palestinians the right to self-determination. It also held that the occupation is a violation of the UN Convention on the Elimination of Racial Discrimination. Subsequently, the UN, in a vote of 124 in favour, 14 against and 43 abstaining, endorsed the ICJ's Advisory Opinion.[38]

The post-Second World War international order has been tested and has failed. The findings against Israel are a tragic irony of history, but the enforcement of the decisions of the ICJ represents a 'make or break moment in international law'. The traditional exponents of the international law institutional framework as well as the international rules-based order (RBO) are arranged against it, and those held to not be playing the game by the rules line up for it.[39] On 24 September 2024, the General Assembly voted, *again*, for a ceasefire, and the US voted against it, while the UK abstained; France, China and the Russian Federation voted for the resolution. A headline in an Arabic-speaking newspaper at the end of 2023 against the backdrop of the rubble in Gaza created by Israel's bombing targeted at the civilian population screamed the 'Rubble of International Law'.[40] The scholar Ata R Hindi, taking inspiration from rap artists, particularly American rapper Nas and the history of rap, quipped that: 'International law is dead. So, *we gather here for the dearly departed*.'[41] Among the collateral damage of an assault on an unarmed population by one of the world's most powerful armies is the turning upside down of *truth*. Ultimately, the definitive establishment of a regime of knowledge in which falsity becomes truth and truth becomes lies might be the conclusion of the Gaza laboratory.[42] The establishment seems to be testing how the widespread sense of moral superiority of Western liberalism can be safeguarded within the dismissal of the narrative of *rule of law* and of *international human rights*. *Might makes right* and the *death of law* prelude a return of rampant violence, accompanied by the drone of war propaganda. Critique is not

[37] *South Africa v Israel*, Order 26 January 2024 and Order dated 24 May 2024. Case no 192 'Application of the Convention on the prevention and punishment of the crime of genocide in the Gaza Strip'.

[38] United Nations General Assembly Resolution 24-16675, 13 September 2024.

[39] A Singh, 'For the ICJ to Say it is "Plausible" That Israel is Carrying out Genocide is a Defining Moment' *The Wire* (28 January 2024).

[40] Front page of *Al Hayat Aj-Jadeeja* (1 November 2023).

[41] AR Hindi, 'International Law is Dead, Third World Approaches to International Law' (2023) *Third World Approaches to International Law Review Extra*, https://twailr.com/international-law-is-dead.

[42] Repressive measures by academic authorities against on-campus expressions of solidarity with Palestinians are reposted in Germany, England and the US. Following the global outcry, reported in V Patel and A Betts, 'Campus Crackdowns Have Chilling Effect on Pro-Palestinian Speech' *New York Times* (17 December 2023).

respected as opposition, but rather accused of antisemitism and high treason. The *end of history*, a world governed by the US and its Western allies, within a narrative of democracy and the rule of law,[43] has morphed into mandatory single thought (TINA). Corporate and military control, endowed with smart technology, is a new Western despotism claiming dominion over bodies and minds.[44] Dissent and transparency are either banned or locked into echo chambers – if not, like Julian Assange, behind bars, until he was coerced into accepting a plea deal so that he could go into exile in the country of his birth.[45] As Bisharat writes: 'When [international law] is applied selectively, unfairly and cynically, it is merely an elevated form of propaganda.'[46]

Scholars do not work in vacuums. Today, this almost banal observation has generated a shared sense, at least in the international and comparative law academic community, of the futility of pretending to have a neutral observation point in the face of social dynamics as complex as the geopolitics of law.[47] Years ago, when the blatant violations of international law by the State of Israel were already certified by some 70-plus UN declarations, Ugo Mattei observed in a series of papers[48] that for decades, a reductionist strategy had allowed Western comparative law scholars to treat apartheid systems, like South Africa and Israel,[49] as interesting and advanced mixed legal systems studied and admired in Europe and the US. Such systems, sharing aspects of the civil law and common law traditions, were celebrated as projections of the liberal ethos of Western legality in otherwise obscurantist and undemocratic contexts like Africa and the Middle East. Such crypto-orientalism[50] has been an original sin of the 'country and western tradition' of comparative law,[51] making it more universal (and consequently like international law) than what emerged from its professional self-portrait. Rather than reflecting on how rule of law projects, like the territorial nation-state narratives deployed in contexts of power imbalance such as the Global South,

[43] F Fukuyama, *The End of History and the Last Man* (New York: Free Press, 1992).

[44] See G Sanguinetti, 'Le despotisme occidental' *Le Club de Mediapart* (12 April, 2020), https://blogs.mediapart.fr/sanguinettigianfranco3/blog/120420/le-despotisme-occidental.

[45] See U Mattei, *Il diritto di essere contro. Dissenso e resistenza nella società del controllo* (Milan: Piemme, 2022).

[46] See G Bisharat, Rethinking International Law after Gaza Symposium: Palestine at the ICJ – International Law v the 'Rules Based Order' *Opinio Juris* (7 October 2024), https://opiniojuris.org/2024/10/07/palestine-at-the-icj-international-law-v-the-rules-based-order.

[47] See, generally, Kennedy and Koskenniemi (n 14).

[48] U Mattei, 'Sudafrica' in R Sacco (ed), *Digesto Discipline Privatistiche, Sezione Civile* (Turin: UTET, 1999) 197; Mattei (n 32).

[49] James Baldwin wrote of the Israeli state as a settler state.

[50] See T Ruskola, *Legal Orientalism: China, the United States, and Modern Law* (Cambridge, MA: Harvard University Press, 2013); T Ruskola, 'Beyond Anti-anti-Orientalism, or How Not to Study Chinese Law' (2022) 70 *American Journal of Comparative Law* 858.

[51] See W Twining, 'Comparative Law and Legal Theory: The Country and Western Tradition' in I Edge (ed), *Comparative Law in Global Perspective: Essays in Celebration of the Fiftieth Anniversary of the Founding of the SOAS Law Department* (Ardsley, NY: Transnational, 2000) 21.

morph into colonialist tools of plunder,[52] the international and comparative law community has participated in a Western ideological self-promotion beneficial to Zionist (and post-Afrikaner) projects.[53]

Even law requires the consent of those who are on the periphery of power. The international law doctrines of international humanitarian law, decolonisation and sovereignty (including control of economic interests) were perhaps never meant to be the *real* international law, which must be limited to those issues which are declared breaches of international law. As Hindi puts it, decolonisation is 'cool' until theory becomes practice.[54] Law is always both a system of dominance and resistance, and international law has been critiqued for the former, as a powerful instrument for the status quo. Does its recent abandonment by its architects and greatest benefactors leave it bereft of instrumentality and solely as a critique of power? Gleider Hernandez writes that in recent years, in international law, there has been an emergence of proceedings that articulate resistance, such as the 2019 decolonisation of the Chagos Islands, the ICJ proceedings on climate change, the Rohingya proceedings against Myanmar etc, which rest on the expansion of the *erga omnes* dictum. However, the battle, as Hernandez acknowledges, is 'for the nature of international law itself'.[55]

That is why the case of *South Africa v Israel* acquires an even greater meaning. It took decades and the iconic figure of Nelson Mandela to educate the West about the atrocities of the apartheid system in the 'advanced' mixed legal system of South Africa. Mandela was an ardent supporter of the Palestinian cause and considered himself in solidarity with, and in debt to, the Palestinian leadership for its support of the African National Congress' struggle against apartheid. Apartheid was opposed not by the custodians of international law, but the newly decolonised states, and the 'war on terror' rhetoric was sometimes used to delegitimise the armed struggle of the African National Congress against the apartheid regime in South Africa. These are not in the narrative of international law. How long will it take to reach the same conclusions on Israel and the Zionist project, which some have called a racist constitutional regime incompatible with legality?[56] Will the international legal community be capable of addressing how the State of Israel, just like the Afrikaans state, is structured to maintain, in the interest of Anglo-American power, the political conditions of turmoil necessary for plunder? Can the decision of the highest court of 'classic', state-centred, international law, as the ICJ is, aid us

[52] See R Merino, 'Reinventing Sovereignty. Removing Colonial Legacies, Opening Plurinational Futures' in R Buchanan et al (eds), *The Oxford Handbook of International Law and Development* (Oxford: Oxford University Press, 2023) 789.

[53] See U Mattei and L Pes, 'Civil Law and Common Law. Towards Convergence?' in GA Caldeira et al (eds), *Oxford Handbook of Law and Politics* (Oxford: Oxford University Press, 2008) 267.

[54] Hindi (n 41).

[55] G Hernandez, 'High Politics and the International Court of Justice', Centre for International Law, National University of Singapore, 17 October 2024, https://cil.nus.edu.sg/blogs/high-politics-and-the-international-court-of-justice.

[56] See G Bisharat, J Handmaker, G Karmi and A Tartir, 'Mobilizing International Law in the Palestinian Struggle for Justice' (2018) 18 *Global Jurist* 1.

in the task of building a democratic state for *all* inhabitants of Palestine – Jews, Muslims, Christians, Druze – governed by law rather than by might?

The contradictions in the Israeli position can be seen in the only partly dissenting opinion of the ad hoc Israeli judge, the distinguished jurist Aharon Barak, a retired Chief Justice of the Israel Supreme Court. It has anguish seeping through it. Barak evokes the memory of Lemkin, a Jewish lawyer who grew up in present-day Ukraine, and was the architect of the Genocide Convention, in recalling that he was five years old when the Nazis put him in a ghetto. He admits that the 'idea that Israel is now accused of committing genocide is very hard for me personally', but he still retains what can only be described as a delusion – that 'every Israeli soldier carries with him (or her) in their backpack, the rules of international law'. Such a declaration was, to put it mildly, entirely inconsistent with the images and the stated orders of the war on the civilian population in Gaza. Even Barak voted for humanitarian aid and the direction to stop incitement to genocide. He has since resigned for personal reasons.[57]

All of this seems as far-fetched as the idea of Mandela's presidency following his quarter-century of incarceration. Just as Barghouti remains behind bars in Israel,[58] the mainstream international legal community considered apartheid in South Africa an advanced example of a mixed legal system.[59] Similarly, some may say that it will require years, but that an understanding that 'there is either International Law or the Zionist State'[60] is a necessary step for a future of peace, law and respect in the Middle East.

The degradation of international law, and perhaps an extension of it or perhaps parallel to it, the international RBO, as George Bisharat, writes, is not a post-7 October 2023 phenomenon. He reports 'that in a recent survey rating the compliance of 74 nations with the United Nations Charter going back to 1945, the United States ranked last and Israel second-to-the-last'.[61] According to Bisharat, relying on John Dugard, the RBO is a set of principles that the US has been relying on since 1991.

Law does not stand still, but rarely faces moments of crises such as those described in and encountered during the writing of this chapter. From the first draft until the final draft, the Pre-Trial Chamber of the International Criminal Court (ICC) has issued arrest warrants against the Prime Minister and Defence Minister of Israel 'for crimes against humanity and war crimes committed from

[57] Hindi (n 41).

[58] Mirwain Barghouti, a Fatah politician, member of the Palestinian Legislative Council and a member of the Fatah Central Committee, has been held in Israeli prisons since 2002, and is serving five life sentences. He is often called the 'Palestinian Mandela'. See https://ecfr.eu/special/mapping_palestinian_politics/marwan_barghouti.

[59] See R Zimmermann and D Visser, *Southern Cross: Civil Law and Common Law in South Africa* (Oxford: Clarendon Press, 1996).

[60] In the words of the United Nations General Assembly Resolution 3379, 10 November 1975, 'Zionism is a form of racism and racial discrimination'.

[61] Bisharat (n 46).

at least 8 October 2023 until at least 20 May 2024, the day the Prosecution filed the applications for warrants of arrest'. Pertinently, the warrant is based on international armed conflict existing between Palestine and Israel.[62] President Trump has announced that the US intends to 'take over' Gaza, and Palestinians should leave.[63]

In this context, in the context of its collapse, understanding the reconstruction of *some* system of international law is a dramatic priority. International law is already being reshaped, and continues to function, but the systems of international law and its unitary nature are degraded, irreparably.

D. The Decline of US Hegemony or 'The King is Dead, Long Live Who?'

Comparative legal scholarship on the conditions that make a legal culture dominant has predicted the decline of US hegemony.[64] Prestige plays a key role for a legal culture to become a global factory of production of law, and such prestige follows the recognition by legal professionals worldwide that the dominant culture deserves admiration for its values, its techniques or its 'more advanced' state of development.[65] In the last couple of centuries, the hegemony of French law, due mostly to Napoleonic codification, was followed by the hegemony of German law, thanks to the construction of legal conceptualism and, more recently, for the first time in history, a model belonging to the common law tradition such as the US has reached a level of prestige capable of determining its global legal leadership.[66]

At the beginning of this century, the global prestige of the US was squandered by a sequence of transformations at every level of the legal system. The most admired Supreme Court in the world offered decisions in *Bush v Gore*, *Citizens United* and *Dobbs* that no righteous jurist can possibly admire.[67] Post-9/11 legislation and the war on civil liberties (including the ongoing war on freedom of expression on US university campuses) have eroded perhaps the most important

[62] 'Situation in the State of Palestine: ICC Pre-Trial Chamber I Rejects the State of Israel's Challenges to Jurisdiction and Issues Warrants of Arrest for Benjamin Netanyahu and Yoav Gallant', International Criminal Cour, www.icc-cpi.int/news/situation-state-palestine-icc-pre-trial-chamber-i-rejects-state-israels-challenges.

[63] See https://edition.cnn.com/politics/live-news/trump-netanyahu-gaza-cabinet-tariffs-02-05-25/index.html.

[64] See E Grande, *Imitazione e diritto. Ipotesi sulla circolazione dei modelli* (Turin: Giappichelli, 2000).

[65] The classic remains A Watson, *Legal Transplants: An Approach to Comparative Law*, 2nd edn (Athens, GA: University of Georgia Press, 1993).

[66] See U Mattei, 'Why the Wind Changed. Intellectual Leadership in Western Law' (1994) 42 *American Journal of Comparative Law* 195.

[67] *Bush v Gore* 531 US 98 (2000); *Citizens United v Federal Election Commission* 558 US 310 (2010); *Dobbs v Jackson Women's Health Organization* 597 US 215 (2022).

source of prestige of the US model, the idea of a robust set of rights protected no matter who you are. Despite a less than colour-blind track record, the blind deity has always been the *sine qua non* of 'rule of law' rhetoric.[68]

Another element explaining the decline of US legal hegemony is a legal academia more and more parochial, self-reverential, swayable by corporate money and seemingly incapable of serious critique. This is despite the so-called critical legal studies movement that has always remained globally visible, but locally marginal and rather ineffective.[69] In such conditions, US law is bound to become uninteresting for legal scholars and intellectuals worldwide, following the same path of decline of previous hegemonic legal cultures such as the French and the German, ultimately victims of arrogance and parochialism.

The differential treatment of the war in Ukraine and the permanent war in the Middle East against the Palestinian people has also undercut US legitimacy as a custodian of international law. Although Russia has not been condemned by the institutions of global legal governance, in contrast to Israel, the Russian Federation is an outcast of international law for its violent aggression against Ukraine.[70] Sovereignty is an argument that holds less powerfully when contrasted with the US position and actions of supplying weapons to enable Israeli actions. The argument for rule-based order must retain the very basic coherence required of law.

Mamlyuk and Mattei wrote about Korovin's use of legal indeterminism as a practical tool for the Soviet state to operate in 'a hostile foreign environment'.[71] This, Korovin argued, was to undermine the bourgeois concept of law. In an ironic twist, it is the founders and gatekeepers of international law which have trapped themselves in arguing for legal indeterminism – where every state is able to, in a proto-efficiency argument, 'interpret their [international law] obligations in radically different ways'.[72]

The end of US hegemony is also evident from its retreat from multilateral institutions where it does not control the decision making, many of which were past instruments for its hegemony. The WTO is one such example, where the dispute resolution mechanism, which is problematic in many respects, was hindered by US refusal to cooperate in the appointment to the appellate body,

[68] A comprehensive discussion of the transformations following *Bush v Gore* can be found in Mattei and Nader (n 3) 176.

[69] RM Unger, *The Critical Legal Studies Movement: Another Time, a Greater Risk* (New York: Verso, 2015).

[70] The provisional order of the ICJ directing a halt to Russian military operations in Ukraine was based on a finding that there was no evidence substantiating Russian allegations of a genocide in Ukraine, and that it was unlikely that a potential Ukrainian violation of the Genocide Convention authorised the use of force by another member state. See *Ukraine v Russian Federation*, Allegations of Genocide under the Convention on the Prevention and Punishment of the Crime of Genocide, International Court of Justice, General List No 182, 16 March 2022.

[71] Mamlyuk and Mattei (n 1) 400.

[72] ibid. Even WE Butler rejected 'the righteous Post-WWI policy-oriented jurisprudence that sought to advance a personal conception of the good life against all others'.

thus rendering toothless one of the most effective instruments to enable free trade harmonisation and normalisation, and a powerful instrument of international law.[73]

E. What New Hegemony? A New Multilateral Hegemony?

Since the early part of this century, commentators have cultivated the illusion that the EU legal system, with its innovative and pluralistic technical aspects making it an experiment in *law without state sovereignty*, could be a candidate for a role of new global hegemony in replacement of the US.[74] After all, the European welfare model seemed to produce a new form of Western capitalism tamed by social rights, inclusive and with a human face.[75] Unfortunately, this proved illusory. The inclusive and pluralistic features of EU law were mostly a self-portrait, unveiled by harsh immigration policy and soft labour law. Europe, especially after the Greek crisis and the Ukraine war, has shown not only its staunch neoliberal and austerity-driven approach, but also its general loyalty to the American ally, so that its chances to become the next global leader replacing the US seem slim.

Nevertheless, the very consideration of Europe, which is not a sovereign state, as a possible global legal hegemon shows the success of those questioning the traditional features of the separation of comparative law and international law. More than 20 years ago, in an essay that became a landmark, Mathias Reimann, a German scholar at the University of Michigan Law School, argued for comparative work to be done not only among nation states (as in the tradition), but also among international organisations that should thus become objects of comparison.[76] The comparative international law hypothesis constitutes an extension of that intuition, so that we must be ready to accept that a future hegemonic legal tradition might be emerging within international organisations. This might be a closer reality than

[73] Peter Ungphakorn, Technical Note: Appeals 'into the Void' in WTO Dispute Settlement', *Trade Beta Blog* (13 February 2021), https://tradebetablog.wordpress.com/technical-note-appeals-into-the-void-in-wto-dispute-settlement.

[74] See, eg, MW Hesselink, *The New European Private Law: Essays on the Future of Private Law in Europe* (The Hague: Kluwer Law International, 1995); H Haukkala, 'The European Union as a Regional Normative Hegemon: The Case of European Neighborhood Policy' in RG Whitman (ed), *Normative Power Europe: Empirical and Theoretical Perspectives* (Basingstoke: Palgrave Macmillan, 2011) 45. See, more recently, A Clarkson, 'The EU Stealthy Hegemony and Ambiguous Neighbors' (2021) 120 *Current History* 112; CS Rapatz, *Das Internationale Privatrecht der EU – Vorbild oder Vormacht?* (Tübingen: Mohr Siebeck, 2023).

[75] See J Rifkin, *The European Dream: How Europe's Vision of the Future is Quietly Eclipsing the American Dream* (New York: JP Tarcher/Penguin, 2004).

[76] M Reimann, 'The Progress and Failure of Comparative Law in the Second Half of the Twentieth Century' (2002) 50 *American Journal of Comparative Law* 671, 680–83, 685–95.

we expect, especially when a geopolitical discussion on families of legal systems heralds a deep change.[77]

During the COVID-19 pandemic, China (and others like South Korea) demonstrated an advantage in emergency law. China has been able to deploy invasive surveillance measures, consistent with the Chinese view of the government representing the people absolutely, without being impaired by rhetoric about individual liberties that produces tension within countries of the Western legal tradition like Italy, Canada, Australia or Israel, where similar authoritarian measures were taken (including lockdowns, electronic controls and compulsory injections).[78] Might it be that the Chinese people trust their government more than the Italians trust Pfizer, and the corporate capture of public health might be for other reasons? It is a fact that in many Western countries, the fundamental guarantees of personal liberty have been abridged between impressive protests, without generating the kind of judicial opposition to executive discretion that one might expect, given the dominant rule of law rhetoric.[79] The rhetoric of the judicial model, which became hegemonic after the Second World War under US leadership, simply cannot hold for long when political tensions rise. It took the fall of the Twin Towers to materialise a prediction that George Kennan made more than half a century earlier:

> [W]e have about 50% of the world's wealth but only 6.3% of its population … In this situation, we cannot fail to be the object of envy and resentment. Our real task in the coming period is to devise a pattern of relationships which will permit us to maintain this position of disparity … We should cease to talk about vague and … unreal objectives such as human rights, the raising of the living standards, and democratization. The day is not far off when we are going to have to deal in straight power concepts. The less we are then hampered by idealistic slogans, the better.[80]

Beyond the rhetoric of a rules-based model, the rise of the Leviathan state has always been an exercise of the state of exception. The German legal theorist Carl Schmitt's belief, later adopted by Nazi Germany, that the sovereign alone 'decides on the exception' is not alien to the development of international law in response to the multitudes of crises and war – terror, health and climate.[81]

[77] See U Mattei, 'The Legal Metaverse and Comparative Taxonomy: A Reappraisal' (2024) 71 *American Journal of Comparative Law* 900.

[78] See U Mattei, L Ghanghua and E Ariano, 'The Chinese Advantage in Emergency Law' (2021) 21 *Global Jurist* 1.

[79] See S Thompson and EC Ip, 'Covid 19 Emergency Measures and the Impending Authoritarian Pandemic' (2020) *Journal of Law and Biosciences* 1; Mattei (n 45). However, see E Peluso Neder Meyer, U Levy Silverio dos Reis and B Braga de Castro, 'Courts and Covid 19: An Assessment of Countries Dealing with Democratic Erosion' (2023) 5 *Ius Cogens* 85.

[80] S Everett Gleason et al (eds), 'Foreign Relations of the United States, 1948, General; The United Nations, Volume 1, Part 2, Document 4: Report by the Policy Planning Staff, Review of Current Trends: Top Secret' (1948), https://bit.ly/3TNkaQ6.

[81] J Neoh, 'Kierkegaard and Schmitt on the State of Exception' (2024) 39 *Journal of Law and Religion* 1.

Because hegemony requires acceptance by the subordinated of the new order, it is unlikely that Western lawyers, blinded by legal orientalism,[82] will develop that sense of admiration for the Chinese model of surveillance, even if it might prove more politically legitimate than their corporate dominated one. It is difficult to consider politically more legitimate a surveillance system controlled by a handful of private corporations, such as in the West, than a system deployed by an organised political party and by a legitimate government, such as China. Nevertheless, lawyers admire the 'judicial way',[83] and it may take a while before they finally relinquish rule-of-law narratives and privacy delusions, and begin to imagine a legal system functional to the needs of our dramatic present. In the absence today of a credible legal system candidate for a new global hegemony, it might well be that no single legal system will ever occupy the void left by the decline of US legal prestige. Such an observation does not mean that some alternative to the judicial way of the Western tradition will not emerge someday, somewhere, eventually becoming capable of seducing the world through its prestige, or that numerous systems will grind at each other, with hopefully sporadic conflict. However, the new global leadership might be more technological than legal[84] and might emerge from the dialogue within a bloc of countries rather than a singular political entity. After all, the West has always preached the independence of law from politics, so it is perfectly consistent with the traditional view that a full-fledged legal system could develop outside a single sovereign political power.

It is not that international law has ceased to exist, but a different, less coherent and less ideologically coherent system has emerged. As Mattei and Mamyluk wrote, Korovin postulated Lenin's maxim *gde obshchezhitie – tam parvo*[85] (where there is society there is law), as being applicable to international law. The system may be broken, but disputes and rules persist, and rules and agreements continue to operate. Often, the rules are being sought to be enforced by those considered to be outliers or renegades of international law, such as China seeking to use the free trade dispute resolution mechanism of the WTO and the US shunning it.[86] As the article states with regard to Korovin's advance:

> Read together, *International Law of the Transition Period* and *Comparative Public International Law* describe how, despite being bitter ideological foes, two states modelled

[82] See both works by Ruskola (n 50).

[83] See RA Kagan, *Adversarial Legalism: The American Way of Law*, 2nd edn (Cambridge, MA: Harvard University Press, 2019).

[84] See U Mattei, 'The Death of Law' (2022) 23 *Global Jurist* 1; Mattei (n 77); E Ariano, '"Al di sopra della mischia": diritto e degenerazioni del Politico' (2023) 29(2) *Cardozo Electronic Law Bulletin* 45, 79–87; W Lucy, 'The Death of Law: Another Obituary' (2022) 81 *Cambridge Law Journal* 109.

[85] Mamlyuk and Mattei (n 1) 401.

[86] J Fernandes, 'China Files Complaint with WTO against Donald Trump's Tariffs on Goods, Call US Actions "Malicious"', *Live Mint*, www.livemint.com/economy/china-files-wto-complaint-against-donald-trump-tariffs-on-goods-report-trade-war-us-actions-malicious-world-news-economy-11738650394424.html.

> on radically different economic models could, and would, coexist in parallel universes and cooperate with each other on matters of common concern. This tremendous insight would, of course, go on to form the basis for the doctrine of coexistence and eventually, the doctrine of permanent peaceful coexistence after the Cuban missile crises.[87]

Perhaps the pendulum will return to the mean of peaceful existence between competing systems of international law that Korovin understood.

F. BRICS as a Hegemon Candidate

India, Indonesia, Egypt and the erstwhile Yugoslavia sought to create an alternative to a bipolar world with the *Non-Aligned Movement*, which emphasised sovereignty and cooperation, and had as its members the majority of southern countries. The non-aligned movement was not successful in creating a plurality of international law models. It was met with resistance from the powers of international law and international capital. As Samir Amir writes, the counter-revolution of the West and its refusal to accept the New International Economic Order 'crystallised after Bandung'.[88] In 2006, Chimni had to argue that the term 'Third World' was not anachronistic.[89]

China always had a difficult initial relationship with the Bandung Conference, and the movement that emerged. Its engagement with international law was instrumentalist, while also being aware of the inequality of the international legal system. Although invited by the Indian government to the conference, the 1962 Sino-Indian war was a blow to the legal principles espoused at the conference. India and China, and specifically Nehru and Enlai had agreed on Panchsheel (five principles) in the 1954 Sino-Indian declarations, with mutual respect for sovereignty and territorial integrity, non-aggression, non-interference in internal affairs, equality and mutual benefit, and peaceful co-existence being the five principles.[90]

[87] Mamlyuk and Mattei (n 1) 405.

[88] Chimni (n 22) 4, citing A Samir, 'The Social Movements in the Periphery: An End to National Liberation' in S Amin et al (eds), *Transforming the Revolution: Social Movements and the World-System* (New York: Monthly Review Press, 1990) 96.

[89] ibid.

[90] L Lüthi, 'Sino-Indian Relations, 1954–1962' (2012) 3 *Eurasia Border Review* 93 in a Special Issue on China's Post-Revolutionary Borders, 1940–1960s. Although the ideological commitment of Nehru (non-violence) and Enlai ('Political power grows out of the barrel of a gun') were starkly different, and they faced the longest unmarked border in the world once China had increased its control over Tibet, citing ancient Chinese claims on its sovereignty, the Panchsheel agreement was an attempt to put rules on engagement that became the cornerstone of the Non-Aligned Movement and subsequently TWAIL. India also recognised China's claims on Tibet, and agreed to withdraw Indian presence from the territory, whose governance was considered feudal by Nehru. Although it seems that Nehru was wary of Chinese fealty to these principles, but constrained by a limited choice of options, which were violated in 1959 and 1962 with military campaigns, the Chinese did still insist on fealty to these principles. Even the support for the Communist Party of India by the Chinese leadership was justified as being a furtherance of the 'inevitable course' of world revolution, and thus not inconsistent with the principles of peaceful co-existence. Chinese non-recognition of the McMohan Line, agreed between the

The preparatory conference for Bandung elevated Panchsheel to the guiding principle of the Non-Aligned Movement.

For the time being, and especially from the perspective of comparative international law – that is, of comparing international organisations and/or different political interpretations of the same international organisation – China is by no means alone in challenging a world dominated by the US.[91] It is as if certain countries of the 'rest' (as opposed to the West), including their legal elites, far from admiring the American judicial way, begin to challenge its fundamental hypocrisy when deployed as a rhetoric to justify global aggression and plunder.[92] Consequently, such variegated countries as Brazil, Russia, India and South Africa have joined China in an international organisation, the BRICS, which originally appeared loose and incoherent, but now is rapidly changing.[93] It is now endowed with a common Central Bank, presided over by former Brazilian President Dilma Rousseff, that aims for the construction of a trade system independent from the dollar and the *lex americana* based on a banking system in which the dollar is the default instrument of international banking.[94] Without the dollar being in the central position, the US, for instance, would not be in a position to impose unilateral sanctions, ostensibly for violations of international law. Not only is this a major challenge to US unilateralism, formalised in 1971 by President Nixon's freeing the dollar from the standard of gold conversion, but it is also a return to the Bretton Woods vision of multilateral cooperation among the allied powers (the International Monetary Fund (IMF), the World Bank etc) as foreseen by enlightened leaders before the end of the Second World War and before the Cold War. Since its foundation in 2009, BRICS has maintained a posture of respect for its members' political sovereignty[95] and has developed a methodology of cooperation that thoroughly prepares dossiers of common interest in various matters, not limited to economic or financial, for unanimous decision at the annual meeting at the top political levels.

Such a model of cooperation, envisaging a multipolar world rather than the Western end of history, has generated a degree of confidence and economic interconnection among members that has proved remarkable. After the eruption of the Ukraine war in 2022, for example, no BRICS country implemented economic

British and the Tibetans, was justified due to the colonial nature of the agreement, and the fact that the Tibetans had not ratified the agreement with China, which held traditional rights over Tibet.

[91] See M Ignatieff, 'The Threat to American Hegemony is Real' *Project Syndicate* (5 March 2024) (with tones of Cold War propaganda), www.project-syndicate.org/commentary/us-western-hegemony-vulnerable-to-russian-chinese-coordinated-challenge-by-michael-ignatieff-2024-03.

[92] See R Kumar et al (eds), *Locating BRICS in the Global Order: Perspectives from the Global South* (Abingdon: Routledge, 2022).

[93] See R Cardilli and S Porcelli (eds), *Aspetti giuridici dei BRICS/Legal Aspects of BRICS* (Padua: Cedam, 2015); X Xiujun (ed), *The BRICS Studies: Theories and Issues* (Abingdon: Routledge 2022).

[94] President Donald Trump seemed to recognise the centrality of the American dollar, threatening in his election campaign to punish countries that sought to use an alternative currency.

[95] See L Scaffardi (ed), *BRICS: Paesi emergenti nel prisma del diritto comparato* (Turin: Giappichelli, 2012).

sanctions against Russia, challenging the harsh policy of the US, the EU and other countries of the Western Bloc. Trade between Russia and China surged after the sanctions, filling the gap left by the West.

Beginning in January 2024, BRICS increased membership to include Iran, Egypt, Ethiopia, Saudi Arabia and the United Arab Emirates. Most significant is the joining of powerful states such as Saudi Arabia and Iran, ferociously divided along religious grounds within Islam and now members of the same organisation. Common membership within BRICS will improve the reciprocal relationship among members, which is another important vehicle to develop prestige and possibly hegemony in law.[96]

India's reluctance to engage with international law has numerous explanations. It was not, as stated by Prabhakar Singh, a super-sovereign at the time it gained its independence in 1947.[97] According to Singh, Chimni's conception of TWAIL II 'rejuvenates the opposition to aspects of international law expressed by Third World States and intellectuals' from the 1950s to the 1970s, which is united against an unjust world order.[98] Chimni saw six distinct visions of a just world order from academic and political discourse in India: establishment, left, Dalit, subaltern, anti-modernist and spiritual.[99] These approaches have different perspectives on, inter alia, international law and represent a pluralistic tradition.

China, by contrast, has been developing a coherent, if not practised, system of articulating international law as a tool for the development of modern China. The *Chinese Journal of International Law* is an established journal of international law. As opposed to the people's international law espoused by TWAIL scholars such as Baxi, Gathii, Chimni and Rajagopal, the Chinese view remains state-centric. A new non-Western theory, for instance, of universal human rights based on collective rights is articulated. Economic sovereignty is emphasised.[100]

BRICS is not the only institution with institutions established in China. The Shanghai Cooperation Organisation has its secretariat in China, and although it has been criticised for being ineffectual, the deference to sovereignty is consistent with the Chinese view of international law. Established by the Central Asian republics, China and Russia as an instrument of Russian foreign policy, its power has shifted to China, though India and Pakistan became full members in 2017, and

[96] Since 2013, a peer-reviewed publication (the *BRICS Law Journal*) has been published in English, fostering international dialogue that might be the prelude to the development of a legal model. See, eg, S Mancuso and M Bussani (eds), *The Principles of BRICS Contract Law: A Comparative Study of General Principles Governing International Commercial Contracts in the BRICS Countries* (Cham: Springer, 2022).

[97] P Singh, 'Indian International Law: From a Colonised Apologist to a Subaltern Protagonist' (2010) 23 *Leiden Journal of International Law* 79.

[98] ibid. See also A Imseis, 'Concept Paper: Third World Approaches to International Law and the Persistence of the Question of Palestine' (2008) 15 *Palestine Year Book of International Law* 1.

[99] Chimni (n 22).

[100] Yilin Wang, 'Locating TWAIL Scholarship in China' (2023) 13 *Asian Journal of International Law* 318.

Iran is also a member. Its principles are Panchsheel-esque and it has a secretariat as well as an anti-terrorism centre. Regardless, it is one of the 'least-known and least-analyzed groups'.[101]

Not even in the EU can such a rich variety of radically different legal traditions joining a robust international organisation of economic and political nature be found. Every family of legal systems, no matter which taxonomy one deploys, is present in BRICS, a degree of difference that seems manageable only by a fundamental principle of internal sovereignty. The recent case of *South Africa v Israel* featured many BRICS countries manifesting solidarity with the Palestinian people. The commendable attitude to keep resorting to the highest court of international law, despite the many political humiliations that this High Court suffered and still suffers, illustrates an important belief in international law by BRICS countries.

G. What New Model: International Law Emerging from Counter-hegemony?

What seems to be occurring is an incremental development of a new model of institutional law that is at the same time old.[102] In this model, equal sovereignty is respected as the fundamental classic idea of international law, ranking higher than international human rights and similar universalistic notions. This is not new; it evidences a return to Westphalian foundations.[103] Sovereigns are privileged to deploy their internal standards that, as ugly as they may seem, are part of a political dialectic that must remain local and free from external infiltration, provocation and instrumentalism.

Taking sovereignty seriously as the foundation of a different model of international law that the BRICS might be making requires full respect of sovereign equality among the member states. At a minimum, in a new international law, there must be much more respect for equality among sovereigns than this Westphalian principle of international law was ever able to obtain, tainted by colonialist mentality.[104] In developing a new alliance respectful of international law but uncompromising on sovereignty, BRICS challenge the current dysfunctional UN system. The permanent membership of the Security Council, accompanied by a veto power, has torpedoed the possibility of the UN to be taken seriously. Regardless of the membership of Russia and China, the current Security Council arrangement is a blatant violation of formally equal sovereignty 'justified' by

[101] Center for Security Studies, ETH Zurich, Flexibility by Design: The Shanghai Cooperation Organisation and the future of Eurasian cooperation.

[102] See J von Bernstorff and P Dann (eds), *The Battle for International Law: South-North Perspectives on the Decolonization Era* (Oxford: Oxford University Press, 2019); A Becker Lorca, *Mestizo International Law: A Global Intellectual History 1842–1933* (Cambridge: Cambridge University Press, 2016).

[103] See A Anghie, *Imperialism, Sovereignty and the Making of International Law* (Cambridge: Cambridge University Press, 2005).

[104] See, among many others, P Fitzpatrick, *The Mythology of Modern Law* (London: Routledge, 1992).

the outcome of a conflict that took place 80 years ago. While both the General Assembly and the ICJ have always performed in coherence with the requirements of international law and justice, the Security Council destroyed the credibility of the entire UN.

Any approach of comparative international law must look at two competing notions of sovereignty. Sovereignty, scorned as the last resort of tinpot dictators resisting international human rights and free market nirvana, is the rationale for the maximalist opposition to Russian aggression in Ukraine, and its step-child – the right to self-defence – the justification for the crimes being committed by Israel in the persecution of its air and ground attacks in Gaza, the West Bank and, at the time of writing, Lebanon, Iran and Yemen. The extension of the maximalist theory of sovereignty was of course the pre-emptive self-defence justification by the US for the second Iraq war. Although that justification warrants being discarded simply for being ineffectual at great human and geopolitical cost, its arguments can still be heard in Ukraine and Israel.

Sovereignty was being diminished at the high point of the end of history era, where sovereign economic power was being relocated to international institutions. International law sought to define and privilege a democratic state, with its commitment to the rule of law being defined as voluntarily waiving sovereignty over human rights, monetary policy, investment, trade, technology and policy on private property, which were mutated into rights in international law. The regulation of the market was to similarly internationalise, as was the acceptance of the multinational corporation as both being a creation of national law, entitled to diplomatic protection, as well as a fluid object and subject of the international law, with a juridical personality in all jurisdictions.

The BRICS model for sovereignty, though not articulated, is less incoherent, and includes sovereignty not only from interference in guise of a global responsibility to protect, but also economic sovereignty consistent with General Assembly Resolutions, such as the New International Economic Resolution, 1974.[105] On 29 June 2024, President Xi reiterated a long commitment to the Panchsheel principles in international law. Although more principles than self-acting, it operates on a principle of a more idealised sovereign respect for territorial integrity and internal affairs than the international RBO. Although bilateral relations between China and India are far from the Panchsheel model,[106] with an almost hot border dispute leading to frayed ties, economic trade is still expanding, and cooperation within BRICS, the Shanghai Cooperation Organisation (SCO) and other fora is ongoing.[107]

[105] United Nations General Assembly Resolution 3201 and 3202, May 1974.

[106] Jawaharlal Nehru, *India's Foreign Policy: Selected Speeches, September 1946–April 1961* (New Delhi: Publications Division, Ministry of Information and Broadcasting, Government of India, 1983).

[107] 'Chinese President Xi Lauds Relevance of Panchsheel to End World Conflicts' (*The Tribune*, 29 June 2024), www.tribuneindia.com/news/world/chinese-president-lauds-relevance-of-panchsheel-to-end-world-conflicts-634941.

There has also been a divergence of approaches to international economic law, whether on free trade, debt relief or international investment law. Chimni already put the responsibility for financial crises firmly on the shoulders of the multinational corporation 'class'.[108] An often understudied system of international law is the powerful tools in the Bretton Woods system of sovereign debt management, which conflate contract law with international law, and have emerged as a significant mode of imposition of international *rules* for debt relief, irrespective of the rights of the borrowing sovereign to default. Without a multilateral treaty on sovereign debt or even an adjudicating body, the IMF has played a pivotal role in coordinating with the 'Paris Club' of major creditor countries who delegate the conditionality and mechanism of sovereign debt relief to the IMF.

The rise of China not only as an important trading partner but also a major financial lender requires the study of at least two systems of sovereign debt in international law.[109] Since the mid-2010s, developing countries' average outstanding debts to China are larger than the debts to all 22 Paris Club creditors combined.[110] Chinese lenders do not coordinate sovereign debt management with the IMF, but have a primarily commercial orientation on debt restructuring. They have been reluctant to join the Paris Club as 'membership in this quintessential 'rich countries club' could cast a shadow on China's much cherished identity as a developing country'.[111] The structure of Chinese debt does not depend on the international law obligations of the sovereign, but instead on commercial collateral. The terms of the loan contracts and any debt relief are often confidential. Debt repayments are settled without fanfare on a bilateral basis. The divergence is evident from clauses ensuring that collateral and debt is excluded from Paris Club arrangements.[112] IMF staffers have admitted that the new lenders do not delegate to the IMF. The divergence of creditors can only benefit borrowers of sovereign debt.[113] It can be argued that the convergence in the Paris Club is to the benefit of the creditors rather than the aspired efficacy of the debt relief mechanisms. The 2018 credit extension to Pakistan allowed Pakistan to resist IMF pressure on social programmes or other traditional 'structural adjustment program' conditionalities.

The conflation of contract law and international law and the granting of rights to corporations with contractual claims in countries to pursue their rights

[108] Chimni (n 22).

[109] LL Ferry and AO Zeitz, 'China, the IMF, and Sovereign Debt Crises' (2024) 68(3) *International Studies Quarterly*, https://doi.org/10.1093/isq/sqae119. It is pertinent that as the primacy of the legal obligation to pay past Kerensky and Tsarist debt was a significant point of friction between Western powers and the new USSR, and was flagged as a demonstration of Korovin's earlier indeterminacy theory.

[110] ibid 3.

[111] ibid 4.

[112] ibid.

[113] The argument by Ferry and Zeitz that the efficacy of monopolistic negotiations is efficacious, and thus beneficial for the borrower, is difficult to accept.

in 'arbitration' has created an extremely efficient enforcement mechanism for protection of international capital in international law, with the normative explanation of it being a necessary precondition for international investment. In 2018, a BRICS symposium in Xiamen University investigated a common BRICS approach to international investment law. Brazil has designed a new Cooperation and Facilitation Investment Agreement, in contrast to the model of the US model treaty. China, on the other hand, has expanded investment protection treaties, as it is a source of outbound capital. South Africa has withdrawn from the international treaty system and replaced it with a system that centralises domestic courts. India, too, has since then withdrawn from existing bilateral investment treaties and proposed a new model which does away with the 'umbrella' clause (ie, obligations to observe specific undertakings towards foreign investors) and introduces an exhaustion of domestic remedies clause. Although there is divergence in the approaches of BRICS nations, there is a distinction from traditional approaches of international investment law that warrant a comparative study.

In a new inclusive model of international law based on comparative dialogue, as originally advocated in 'Comparative International Law', the Security Council must either be abrogated or reformed by the abolition of permanent membership. This is the *Grundnorm* of international law that must be re-established. The current practice of *dialogical sovereign equality* within BRICS might be a way to see how a Security Council, legitimised in a different way, with full-fledged participatory means, might work. Technological transformations of tremendous magnitude might be dismantling not only international law but also the law in general. Nevertheless, participatory peer-to-peer technology might also take steps in the making of a 'People's International Law',[114] perhaps a second chamber of the commons (ie, people's participation) aside from the states in the General Assembly. However, the adoption of the 'third world' in international law's existing leadership positions may come too late to save those institutions over new ones. As Zeitz writes, 'important multilateral institutions for governing the global economy were designed without China's input or full participation'.[115] The members of the Paris Club are mostly members of the Organisation for Economic Co-operation and Development (OECD), another multilateral body which is another (often understudied) source of international law and economic governance.

It is merely a matter of time before this new system of international law emerges, like the groundhog from its tunnel. Comparative international law has demonstrated that outside of the ideological parentheses of the end of history (attempting to transform it in a technology), international law remains a deep phenomenon of political interpretation which offers a variety of models to compare. When Mamlyuk and Mattei wrote 'Comparative International Law',

[114] See Mattei and Salomon (n 33).
[115] Ferry and Zeitz (n 109) 2.

they found a lesson in the Cold War experience of academic dialogue for mutual enrichment. Today the same lesson can be learned from the high degree of respect of equal sovereignty that has allowed BRICS to thrive, and the international relations between these often-competing countries which stand in contrast to the accident site of international law governed spaces – Ukraine, Israel etc. BRICS seem to provide the necessary energy for such an ambitious project of reform, perhaps through more strategic use of litigation in the ICJ or even through the possible creation of a BRICS court. Regardless, the divergence of BRICS players from global governance systems and the introduction of different international law principles require a comparative study, using the tools only comparative law offers, to understand what international law is – rather than what is today only the history of international law, the post-Second World War system, with one pillar collapsing in 1991. The potential questions that require answering will perhaps be addressed.

H. Conclusion

> Things fall apart; the centre cannot hold;
>
> Mere anarchy is loosed upon the world,
>
> The blood-dimmed tide is loosed, and everywhere
> The ceremony of innocence is drowned;
>
> The best lack all conviction, while the worst
> Are full of passionate intensity.[116]

The stakes have never been higher and the paths are clouded. Thirteen years ago, Mattei and Mamyluk's article was a canary in the coalmine: a study of non-dominant approaches to international law, and a critique of the unitary postulation of international law. The warning has been prescient, and the argument for a unitary international law seems impossibly naïve in the context of recent developments.

The rift in international politics must necessarily affect the argument for unitary international law, but the argument was never coherent in the first place. The system put in place after the Second World War was in itself comparative, until the concessions and subsequent abandonment of one pillar. The RBO pushed forward after 1991 was perhaps never reliant on unitary international law, but on US power cloaked in self-serving and unilaterally articulated principles, such as the right to pre-emptive self-defence, which were never and did not become principles of international law. The often-unilateral sanctions regime, enlarged without

[116] WB Yeats, 'The Second Coming', verse 1.

any foundation in international law, to unprecedented scales against the Russian Federation after the invasion of Ukraine was another such example.

The war in Gaza perhaps demonstrates the degradation of the power of the RBO consistent with the relative decline in US power. Faced with other bullies in the proverbial schoolyard, the US is not content to lose the game, but wants to take the ball home while declaring victory at the same time. The emergence of alternatives in BRICS etc is not sufficiently coherent, but does reflect a shift in numerous issues, such as sovereign debt, the emphasis on sovereign regulatory power over international human rights and private law etc. There are both benefits and harms in such a comparative view, but the co-existence of different instrumentalities of international law will be needed in order for the international system – in the context of rapid technological advancement and the question of the national and international character of corporations – to become less indeterminant. Comparative international law is the only tool to examine these issues.

10

Decolonising the Comparative Metrics of (Private) International Law

HORATIA MUIR WATT

A. Preliminary Observations: The Metrics of Comparison and Decolonial Critique

The invitation for the conference that formed the basis of this edited collection can be understood as an opportunity to think, diachronically and synchronically, about plural conceptions of (public) international law across time and space, and the role of legal comparison, or rather its associated devices (such as legal transplants), among their modes of production. At first glance, it is somewhat surprising that it can still seriously be asked whether international law is 'really international'.[1] This question may of course be understood in several ways: it could be about the 'sources' or materials from which international law is purported to spring; it might also signal an enquiry as to whether its mode of existence is in any way specific in respect of lesser(?), domestic forms of legality; a further avenue would be to call into doubt the very possibility of any unitary signification of the formally uniform content of international norms; finally, it might – as will be the case here – be taken as an invitation to think of the comparative metrics rooted in the colonial past of European international law, of which the premises are not shared by much of the world it purports to rule.

Whatever the terms of the question of whether international law is really international, several other works in this volume[2] already make it clear that an exercise in measurement or scaling is inherent to international law, whether from the perspective of legal interpretation (the illusory search for meaning in international texts) or in the context of the various critical strands of third world or subaltern (race, gender etc) studies that target the very ideal of 'civilisation' or 'development'. If anything, the very need to revisit the question of international law's inherent comparativism signals the perverse effects of the compartmentalised structure of

[1] A Roberts, *Is International Law International?* (Oxford: Oxford University Press, 2017).
[2] See, eg, Husa, ch 13 and Olaoye, ch 3 in this volume.

our legal knowledge. One might indeed be tempted to paraphrase a snowclone: 'It's the *episteme*,[3] stupid', since both the fugacity of meaning and the risk of structural bias underlying legal thought are problems that apply across the board in all areas of the law.

Nevertheless, decolonial critique[4] has surfaced far more in public international law than in respect of the deeply encoded and frequently exclusionary approaches to alterity that underwrite much legal comparison. This contrast may be due to the fact that the discipline of comparative law was confiscated for some time – significantly, during the half-century that followed its own self-constructed mythical origin in the 1900 Paris Conference[5] – by European private lawyers, who were little inclined to relinquish positivism and universalism for the sake of connecting legal phenomena to the wider political economy or indeed to the wider world. These were often the very scholars (or of the same school and legal tradition) who, during the same era, built the twin narrative of the new paradigmatic emergence of modern private international law (or in the anglophone world, the conflict of laws) in the mid-nineteenth century with von Savigny's great treatise of Roman law. Analogous categories, principles and tropes came to encode both areas.[6]

This chronology suggests that the colonial project carried by 'modern' (meaning here the late nineteenth century) public international law was spectrally present, even if the disciplinary discourse of both private and comparative law was largely devoid of any explicit reference to the looming, broader context. We can take this supposition as a cue to return to the coloniality of comparison from the perspective of the less explored, private dimension of international legality. The particular interest of doing so lies both in the scarcity of critical work from this perspective and the enduring claim that both comparison of legal systems and their coordination are all simply about 'method', disconnected from any governance project (whether imperial, colonial, post-colonial, geopolitical, or other).[7]

[3] On the *episteme*, see M Foucault, *Les Mots et les Choses* (Paris: Gallimard, 2014, reprint). Analogous concepts are: collective imaginaries or belief systems (J d'Aspremont, *After Meaning: The Sovereignty of Forms in International Law* (Cheltenham: Edward Elgar, 2021)), paradigms (GH Samuel, *Rethinking Legal Reasoning* (Cheltenham: Edward Elgar, 2018)) or (legal) consciousness (D Kennedy, 'Three Globalizations of Law and Legal Thought: 1850–2000' in D Trubek and A Santos, (eds) *The New Law and Economic Development* (Cambridge, MA: Harvard University Press, 2010) 19).

[4] 'Decoloniality' is to be understood as distinct from colonialism as a particular regime of appropriation. It is an ontology of asymmetrical power relations (that can of course be found at the very centre of the colonial metropolis) and thus embodies a particular relationship to alterity.

[5] See M Fournier, 'Comparative Law Gets Entitled: The 1900 Paris Congress in Contexts' (LLM thesis, University of Victoria, 2018), http://dspace.library.uvic.ca/bitstream/handle/1828/9984/Fournier_Mireille_LLM_2018.pdf; H Dedek, 'The Tradition of Comparative Law: Comparison and its Colonial Legacies' in M Siems and PJ Yap (eds), *The Cambridge Handbook of Comparative Law* (Cambridge: Cambridge University Press, 2024) 387.

[6] See more generally, with references, H Muir Watt, *Law's Ultimate Frontier: For an Ecological Jurisprudence* (Oxford: Hart Publishing, 2023).

[7] With of course some remarkable exceptions: see PG Monateri, *Geopolitica del diritto. Genesi, governo e dissoluzione dei corpi politici* (Rome: Laterza, 2013).

In other words, decolonising the parameters used in the apparently neutral measurement of the world's various legal systems means uncovering the frames, scales, criteria and devices that still command a large part of legal comparative work and that remain for the most part unquestioned. Comparative (private) international law can therefore be framed as an exercise in unearthing the unacknowledged assumptions of measurement at work in the discipline known as the conflict of laws.[8]

The premise of this chapter, then, is, first, that all comparative exercises across the political humanities rest on sets of metrics that carry (often unacknowledged) assumptions and biases. This is as true of comparative linguistics, history or political ideas as it is of comparative law. A further claim here is that all norms that aspire to some form of unity across legal cultures, whether they are labelled international, global, universal, transnational or uniform, rest in turn (though less visibly) on standards that involve measurement of difference of one kind or another. On this point, it is less usual to uncover the implicit comparative premises that structure private international law as conventionally understood, as opposed to the analogous assumptions underlying its public counterpart. In other words, coloniality is embedded within both of these disciplines, for very similar reasons. However, it remains far less investigated on the private side. Nevertheless, this line of research is beginning to flourish, enriching the analysis through additional insights from critical anthropology (whether legal or otherwise)[9] or, from the perspective of non-modern systems, powerful epistemological or gnoseological critiques form the Global South,[10] with strong resonance moreover in indigenous ontologies resisting extinction in settler states and counting on the resources of inter-legality to survive.[11]

Building on these insights, this chapter goes on to propose a series of considerations on decolonising the legal episteme from the perspective of the

[8] While measurement systems such as those used by the World Bank in its Doing Business reports clearly call for a similar analysis, and have indeed come under continuous fire, including by critical law and development scholars, by reason of the hidden premises on which they rest, it is interesting to see that one of the most critical comparative legal scholars is now proposing the use of quantitative methods in order to enhance the potential of critical comparison in (private) international law: see PG Monateri, 'Comparative Conflict of Laws between Form and Substance' (2024) 37 *International Journal for the Semiotics of Law – Revue internationale de Sémiotique juridique* 1533.

[9] See V Corcodel, *Modern Law and Otherness: The Dynamics of Inclusion and Exclusion in Comparative Legal Thought* (Cheltenham: Edward Elgar, 2019); D Bonilla Maldonaldo, *Legal Barbarians: Identity, Modern Comparative Law and the Global South* (Cambridge: Cambridge University Press, 2021); T Ruskola, *Legal Orientalism. China, the United States, and Modern Law* (Cambridge, MA: Harvard University Press, 2013). Further research has led the exploration into the private international legal sphere, in respect of the ways in which Western or settler courts have approached the coordination between their own and third-world legal systems, where indigenous norms struggle to compete with settler law and epistemologies: see S Brachotte, 'The Conflict of Laws and Non-secular Worldviews: A Proposal for Inclusion' (PhD thesis, Sciencespo Paris, 2022). See also the research project on decoloniality and law led by R Michaels and L Salaymehé at the Max Planck Institute, Hamburg.

[10] AA Diouf, 'Repenser le droit civil en Afrique Noire Francophone' (2022) 74(2) *Revue internationale de droit comparé* 369.

[11] W Mignolo, *The Politics of Decolonial Investigations* (Durham, NC: Duke University Press, 2021).

frequently unacknowledged metrics that underwrite private international law. The point here is to use this lens to argue that a colonial conceptual scheme lurks in unexpected legal sites – those that are ostensibly neutral, tolerant, inclusive or empowering and many of which are deployed as mere 'method' (a central category in both comparative and private international law). The conclusion to be drawn from this argument is that until the question of the Other is raised squarely in the terms of Western, modern law, there is all likelihood that existing legal forms continue along the same paths. From this perspective, the 'branch' or sub-discipline of law in which they are deployed – private, international or comparative – makes little difference.

B. Interlocking Dynamics: Private, International and Comparative

There are some obvious patterns that connect the two seemingly distinct disciplines of comparative and international law and, in respect of the latter, are relevant across the public and private divide. Thus, to a large extent, all these fields are underwritten, at least in the dominant versions thereof, by similar political and epistemological approaches, which emerged simultaneously as projects and technologies of legal ordering in the colonial West and evolved thereafter in sync. They all share the trope of 'youth',[12] rebirth or modernity, as applied to nineteenth-century versions of legality, distancing themselves from a less brilliant past and, as has been noted, inhibiting any impulse to learn from history.[13] The genealogy common to all these versions can be found in patterns of ideas that construct a temporal and moral 'ladder' of greater or lesser proximity to sets of values constructed as core to a certain community and generally associated with the rule of law. Each as it were feeds on the other in a triangular and paradoxical dialectic. Thus, conventional accounts of public international law are inherently comparative, despite the ostensibly universal status of the norms that compose it. But while private international legality is more obviously local or part of municipal law (unless unified by treaty), its retreat into methodological neutrality or techne ensures the broad success of its model, even in sites where, contemporaneously, the first-world colouration of public international law is contested. Conversely, the most widespread versions of comparative law proceed from an implicit programme of world ordering that echoes and consolidates the aspirations of its international legal opposites.

[12] On the misleading narrative of the youth of the discipline, as if 1900 had been a clean break with the past, see Dedek (n 5). This point is also true of many accounts of the history of public international law (as told by lawyers, not historians), which usually start with 1648 and the Peace of Westphalia, then fast forward to the end of the nineteenth century.

[13] Dedek (n 5).

However, as critical comparative legal studies have long shown, the standard twentieth-century representation of schemes of legal 'families' comprising germane cultural traditions is no exception to the ethnocentrism of comparison.[14] Legal systems or traditions were sorted according to their relative proximity to a triad of particular understandings of the rule of law, in which ideas of moral, scientific and economic progress were tightly entangled. Under this classification system, most of the world was relegated to a residual category of the wholly or partly lawless. Much the same can also be said of the premises of international law as it emerged in the latter part of the nineteenth century in its conventional form. The framework unanimously adopted by the European powers rested on assumptions that divided the civilised world from the barbaric rest. While the frontiers were somewhat fuzzy or at least subject to degrees, the concept of civilisation fulfilled a function similar to that of Christianity for an earlier age, and to modernisation or development or progress thereafter. In public international law, this parameter has defined the access to the concert of nations, or international community of states, which excludes diverse forms of failed states or non-state terrorist or indeed indigenous organisations, and accepts that the legally equal sovereigns of the world can nevertheless be ranked according to their score on an economic development grid. In private international law, similar ideas about the values and objectives of society as understood in the terms of a secular, Western, liberal model define the conditions of access to a specific coordinator methodology ('savignism'),[15] or the contours of common values, described in the language of 'public policy' or indeed fundamental rights.

All these elements highlight the implicit comparative metrics of a supposedly uniform or universalising legal regime when confronted with an alien epistemology and accompanying worldview. This point is very familiar in private international law, which is constantly confronted with divergence in national understandings of purportedly unitary norms (whether provisions of international treaties, transnational standards or simply ostensibly similar legal categories). However, such divergence is usually seen as a merely technical anomaly in a context of a world order that is largely premised on shared conceptions of law and its supposedly common denominators across the closed concert of legal systems. Its implications for the wider contemporary political economy are rarely explored. However, more interestingly, it has been shown that the *fin de siècle* surge of studies on 'global law' have not overcome an inherent ethnocentrism, despite their aspirations to transcend earlier configurations of a global law paradigm.[16]

[14] See, among many other of his works, P Legrand, 'Sur l'analyse différentielle des juriscultures' (1999) 51 *Revue internationale de droit comparé* 1053.

[15] An expression used by Pierre Gothot to describe the cult devoted to (and hardly respectful of) the intellectual legacy of Carl von Savigny: see P Lagarde, 'Pierre Gothot (1936–2021)' (2022) 1 *Revue Critique de Droit International Privé* 1.

[16] M Xifaras, 'The Global Turn in Legal Theory' (2016) 29 *Canadian Journal of Law and Jurisprudence* 215.

Genealogies of such projects of global ordering point to their roots within competing narratives as to the origins of the Western tradition.[17]

Showing up the embedded comparative premises of private international legal method as conventionally understood is a seemingly easier task than unearthing analogous assumptions underlying its public counterpart. It is hardly questioned today that nineteenth-century private international law (the conflict of laws) lost its claim to universality – understood as an aptitude to be accepted by all nation-states as the rules of the game or ideal – well before it became similarly evident in a post-colonial world that the legitimacy of public international law was highly contested across the globe and that not all the communities inhabiting the latter were admitted equally within the concert of nations. The First World War marked the decline of *fin de siècle* universalist aspirations of the conflict of laws, which retreated thereafter into a nationalist and relativist shell. Moreover, the remarkably European phase of post-war American legal consciousness and style that had spread worldwide through conquest or prestige,[18] united legal comparison and conflicts under a narrative of alliance or *cousinage* ('families' being a decidedly recurring trope in this context!).

Projected onto various scenes of ambitious unification programs within the Western world (the Paris Conference, the International Institute for the Unification of Private Law (UNIDROIT), the Hague Conference etc), competing representations of comparative law with deep roots in equally debated legal theory supplied either methodologies designed to discover shared ground between the world's legal systems (functionalism), or reasons to doubt the very commensurability of legal cultures. Academic debates focused thereafter on the common history of legal institutions, the feasibility of legal transfers or the best devices for adjustment and coordination of legal differences. In private international law, a transatlantic split widened the gap between the realm of legal realism and that of formal (usually 'civilian') codes. It became difficult thereafter to claim that there was any universality in method or epistemology, even without venturing beyond the narrow confines of the first world. The Cold War excluded any further consideration of the value of Central and Eastern European traditions, while Asia (with the exception of legal transplants to Japan) remained largely exoticised as lawless.[19]

Paradoxically, meanwhile, the more recent rise of powerful post-colonial strands of critique on the public side of international law (third world, *mestizo*, subaltern, political economy, gender, queer, commodities-based or value-chain-based etc) has had very little effect on the conventional account and practice of its private dimension, which was otherwise engaged in engineering the neoliberal turn in the

[17] PG Monateri, *Dominus Mundi, Political Sublime and the World Order* (Oxford: Hart Publishing, 2018).

[18] U Mattei, 'Three Patterns of Law: Taxonomy and Change in the World's Legal Systems' (1997) 45 *American Journal of Comparative Law* 5.

[19] See Ruskola (n 9).

cross-border economy. For the latter purposes, the world legal order is indeed a smooth place, seemingly devoid of the political conflicts that affect the universal vocation of its public counterpart. This may explain why many of its actors have fled over to the private side, joining forces in such sub-fields such as international trade and investment law, or dispute resolution where property and contract still reign as the 'natural' apparatuses of the rule of law, or in the regulation of the internet, where technologies of governance maintain a discourse of neutrality. Indeed, the claim of unity on the public international side covered over chasms that are currently re-appearing in the context of tragic wars outside the traditional centre – this is nothing radically new in the post-colonial era except that these are sufficiently close to create powerful ripples inside it. Conflicts in public international law – over definitions of colonisation, imperialism, genocide, terrorism and aggression – have their counterparts in domestic politics and echo further unsettling struggles as the styles of domestic and regional political regimes are directly affected by broader geopolitical struggles. Moreover, the sites of such wars open themselves up to struggles involving the arms industry, gender politics or ecological politics, foreclosing rather than opening up discussion as to what it means exactly to talk of community, statehood, law, environment etc. One way of questioning the history of the troubled present of our world order is to explore the apparently innocuous encoding of comparative metrics on the private side of international legality.

C. Scales of Progress and Capture of Time

A first line of decolonial critique to which private international and comparative legal insights can usefully contribute concerns the 'development episteme'.[20] The diachronic concept of 'development' presupposes that the various communities of the world (and specifically 'developing' post-independence economies) are located in time within specific stages of progression (economic, cultural or scientific) towards an ideal, largely fashioned according to a Western imaginary (that the reality of Western societies does not necessarily fulfil). From a genealogical perspective, development is an avatar of the idea of 'civilisation' that defined access to the concert of nations. It is a crucial concept within the neoliberal political economy, a political and economic model or ideal towards which the countries of the periphery must strive in order to be accepted within the global economic order. Both include a powerful temporal element, suggesting an aspiration to progress through time – towards the very model that reinforces their state of dependency. Indeed, we also know that the 'gift' of civilisation, supposedly conferred through European colonisation (particularly of the African continent in

[20] C Dekker and E McMahon, *The Idea of Development in Africa: A History* (Cambridge: Cambridge University Press, 2020).

the course of the long nineteenth century), is not only an extraordinarily distorted fantasy of the supposed needs of colonised societies, but actually arrested their development,[21] if the latter is to be understood as a quest for social equality, solidarity, health, education, and cultural and economic autonomy. Development replaces this previous paradigm and serves similarly to justify interventions of various (now usually secular) sorts: investment opportunities for foreign actors (usually first world corporate groups, particularly in the extractive industry) of which there is little or no empirical evidence to show that they benefit the local populations, the national economy or indeed the planet.

The point here is that the discursive construction of 'progress' rests on a certain idea of linear time that is not only specific to Western modernity but also underwrites the comparative metrics that parade under the banner of epistemological neutrality. This temporality of measurement is common to a modern Western episteme, and not specific to a given area such as law, but extends to the ways we think about science and medicine, the humanities and religion etc. Such deeply encoded premises can be contrasted (and is this not what comparative legal studies should be doing?) with the cosmogonies of other non-exotic societies[22] that inhabit the other continents of the world. Not unsurprisingly, anthropology (the 'mother of all comparison'),[23] which also requires decolonising as a discipline and scientific method, uncovers radically different ideas of temporality (as well as far more complex and markedly non-modern ideas about time within Western metaphysical, political and legal thought). The 'catch-22' point here is that these very Others of time become the discursive justification for the disqualification of social or cultural alterities as primitive, unscientific – or even undeveloped. How we perceive time, then, is an important part of the riddle of what is needed for the purposes a decolonial legal enterprise.

Civilisation evokes the exit of a population from a state of barbary or savagery through the abandonment over time of improper and unsophisticated practices and belief systems in favour of the acquisition of 'culture', while development suggests some sort of meritorious striving for 'progress' that similarly involves the relinquishment of the primitive or the rustic in favour of the rational, the managerial and the efficient. In both cases, the strong moral overtones of this temporality of progress are closely linked to an ideal in terms of economic status and the type of social relations it requires. The colonial world fitted into the scheme of the Capitalocene in a specific way. As observed by political theorist Tim Mitchell, the colonial enterprise involved a 'capture of the future'.[24] He writes that the world beyond the European West was 'imagined as the world of places that didn't

[21] ibid.

[22] S Jasanoff, 'Cosmopolitan Visions: Science and Reason in a World of Difference', Gifford Lecture, Edinburgh, 2016.

[23] P Descola, *Par-delà nature et culture* (Paris: Gallimard, 2015).

[24] T Mitchell, 'The Body Politic that Captured the Future' in B Latour et al, *A Book of the Body Politic. Connecting Biology, Politics and Social Theory* (Venice: Fondazione Giorgio Cini, 2017) 49, taking the example of infrastructure (railways) as a techno-political means of colonising the future.

properly have an economy; it was the world that had to be transformed, so it could have economies'.

But of course. this temporal episteme was not the preserve of a world vision in a geographical sense, understood as deliberately reaching beyond the territorial space of the domestic arena. Describing the rise and deployment of an ideology of enclosure in eighteenth-century England, Susan Marks shows how the new order of expanding private property (in a domestic setting) and the correlative expropriation of the commons rested upon the discursive denigration of the past (and those who continue to be locked within it) as backwardness, drudgery and poverty.[25] Backwardness was ascribed to, or measured by, the economic. Unsurprisingly, a similar discourse applied in a colonial context to whole (primitive or savage) populations,[26] undergirded moreover by further fantasies linking the wild to the exotic.[27] Decadent 'quasi-sovereign' China,[28] or the 'veiled protectorate' of Egypt, found their way somewhere in-between, on the road towards assimilation. The backwardness of 'native peoples inhabiting an earlier stage of development' justified the visible helping hand of colonial power (or its agents).[29] Indeed, in the politics of civilisation,[30] democracy could not apply to people that had not achieved a mature stage of collective development.

At the high point of coloniality, law had largely integrated these temporal hierarchies, with help from the new, co-productive disciplines of comparative law and colonial anthropology.[31] Private international law contains multiple legal devices that have participated in the perverse temporal dynamics of the capitalist economy, reaping profits from the capture of the past. Its contribution is particularly significant because the spatial element of the economic order is so crucial. Enclosure is, as Susan Marks reminds us, 'a metonym for all the rest'. That the discipline contributed to the intellectual substratum of the colonial regime on this point is amply shown by various studies that illustrate similar patterns throughout comparative forms of colonialism. Interestingly, private international legal

[25] S Marks, *A False Tree of Liberty, Human Rights in Radical Thought* (Oxford: Oxford University Press, 2019).

[26] A Simpson, 'Subjects of Sovereignty: Indigeneity, The Revenue Rule, and Juridics of Failed Consent' (2018) 71 *Law and Contemporary Problems* 191 emphasises the ways in which 'indigeneity and sovereignty have been conflated with savagery, lawlessness, and "smuggling" in recent history', with an example taken directly from the conflict of laws and the interpretation of the so-called 'revenue rule' (that prevents the application and enforcement of foreign public law).

[27] See J Surkis, *Sex, Law and Sovereignty in French Algeria, 1830–1930* (New York: Cornell University Press, 2019).

[28] Ruskola (n 9).

[29] On the position of JS Mill in favour of the 'iron arm' of the East India company, since the population was 'not ready' to receive direct rule, see T Poole, *Reason of State: Law, Prerogative and Empire* (Cambridge: Cambridge University Press, 2016) 185.

[30] ibid.

[31] Bonilla Maldonaldo (n 9); Corcodel (n 9). Compare the observation by Rachel Seider (Indigenous Peoples, Gender Justice, and Legal Pluralism in the United States, Mexico, and Guatemala: Exploratory Seminar at the Radcliffe Institute for Advanced Study, 8–9 September 2016) that state law is identified by its ideals (progress) and indigenous law by ethnographic findings (static).

technologies serve the colonial economic order through moves that involve not only property (enclosure of land), but its strict severance from family law. The expropriation/expulsion[32] of local communities from their anchorage in land/place borrows from a combination of moves that connect the representation of territory as unoccupied with depictions of backwardness.[33]

For instance, in her study of jurisdictional aspects of British rule in New Zealand,[34] Nan Seuffert describes the ways in which the project of consolidating this society as a white, Christian nation-state was deployed through the drawing of jurisdictional boundaries in marriage cases that excluded Maori marriage laws and practices through associating them with the pre-modern, racialised concepts of concubinage and polygamy. Underlying the idea of nation, the Maori lands were simultaneously considered as unoccupied and therefore subject to the legal title of the new landowners. Another example comes from the legal history of the French colonisation of Algeria. Judith Surkis paints a picture drawn from the archive of the Court of Appeals of Algiers for the century that followed the declaration of French rule in 1830.[35] Similarly, she shows how the notion of indigenous 'personal status' – a concept that has its pedigree in the conflict of laws – was actually used to dissociate the local (or native) religious family law practices from the lands, that, indissociable under the latter, became subject to French civil law and massively transferred to the colonisers.

These regimes had far-reaching deleterious effects, extending long into the present in the form of structural, inter-generational inequalities.[36] The latter are

[32] S Sassen, *Expulsions: Brutality and Complexity in the Global Economy* (Cambridge, MA: Harvard University Press, 2014).

[33] The patterns are similar all around the colonised world (including the far north). The legal doctrine of *terra nullius* displaced indigenous populations around the European-colonised world: the stolen generation in Australia, the Inuits in Greenland ('Arctic-orientalism') or the descendants of the emancipated slave population of Haiti.

[34] N Seuffert, *Jurisprudence of National Identity: Kaleidoscopes of Imperialism and Globalisation from Aotearoa New Zealand* (London: Routledge, 2006), explaining further how territorial jurisdiction contributes to the construction of political subjectivity by tying individuals to the fixed boundaries of the modern nation-state. Additional reading on the 'quiet genocide' of the 'Stolen generation' of Aboriginal children can be found (for example) at https://interactive.aljazeera.com/aje/2017/quite-genocide/index.html. On the idea that racialised humanity is disposable, or parked in barren sacrificial zones, see C Gonzales and A Mutua, 'Mapping Racial Capitalism: Implications for Law' (2022) 2 *Journal of Law and Political Economy* 127.

[35] Surkis (n 27).

[36] This is now acknowledged in contexts of transitional justice and memorial laws in various places around the world. For instance, in the case of Australia's 'Stolen generation' of Aboriginal and Torres Strait Islander children, forcibly removed from their families between 1910 and 1970, Prime Minister Kevin Rudd offered a formal apology on 13 February 2008, on behalf of the Australian Parliament. In France, in respect of the colonisation of Algeria, French President Emmanuel Macron (who had previously, before his election, qualified colonisation as a crime against humanity) proffered a formal apology on 20 September 2021 to Algerians who fought alongside French colonial forces in Algeria's war for independence, and who were then massacred and ostracised as traitors. Such recognition is of course important. However, the downsides are emphasised by N Fraser and R Jaeggi, *Capitalism: A Conversation in Critical Theory* (New York: Polity Press, 2018): we are led to separate our present from the past as if we can compensate for past wrongs and turn the page. Egregious historical wrongs, usually assessed as economic losses and thereby both measurable and commensurable, are not behind

ongoing, but the more they are denied, the more they are likely to resurface from our collective past. Globalisation has undoubtedly enabled, magnified and accelerated the troubling of time, multiplying the places and shapes where conflicts arise and subverting earlier linear representations of universal temporality.[37] Indeed, the subconscious (whether individual or collective) knows no chronological time. The past is embroiled in the present as much as the latter captures the future. This insight has significant consequences for what we understand as 'method' in comparative and private international law, since the deployment of schemes of comparison and devices of coordination is premised on a certain idea of the road to progress and the location in time and space of various legal systems along the way.

D. Comparative Metrics and the Ethics of Method

Comparison is always at work in a unified regime. On the private and comparative side of the international fence, neither the 'translational' nor the 'global' is free from ethnocentrism, exemplifying that (comparative, legal) method is not innocent, nor neutrality is a plausible stance. This has already been amply argued by critical thinkers, so that it may be more interesting to reflect upon the less visible (often unconscious, sometimes unwanted) exclusionary consequences of purportedly inclusive doctrines as illustrated by the conventional wisdom of private international law, in its approach to legal or normative difference. Whatever is perceived as foreign – threatening to social stability or values – gives rise to a hermeneutic of suspicion produced within our late modern legal consciousness.[38] One concept that appears within this context that has powerful overtones in colonial jurisprudence (and scientific thought more generally,

us, but an ongoing mode of capitalist expansion (on the same dismal plane are slavery, land grabbing, apartheid, toxic products, genocide and ecological catastrophes). In the same vein, feminist private international legal scholars Karen Knop and Annelise Riles have analysed 'the saga of the comfort women' (forced prostitution of Korean women by the Japanese army) as the return of repressed historical events. One of the (many) significant points made by these scholars is that the simultaneous appearance of multiple statues of the 'comfort women' in many different sites is emblematic of the haunting presence of the past: K Knop and A Riles, 'Space, Time, and Historical Injustice: A Feminist Conflict-of-Laws Approach to the Comfort Women Agreement' (2017) 102 *Cornell Law Review* 853.

[37] As E Viveiros de Castro observes in *Ends of the World* (New York: Polity Press, 2017) 114, one of the most significant contemporary debates revolves around the speed of history and its variation. It opposes the philosophical (metaphysical, political, aesthetic) current that proposes a political economy of acceleration and the partisans of a political ecology of deceleration (Isabelle Stengers), which unfolds into a set of themes which she shares with Bruno Latour: 'hesitation', 'attention', 'diplomacy' and the need for 'making room for others'. The latter are importantly part of the 'shadow' or alternative mode of existence of the conflict of laws (on this point, see Muir Watt (n 6)).

[38] On the hermeneutic of suspicion as characteristic of our legal consciousness, see D Kennedy, 'A Political Economy of Contemporary Legality' in P Kjaer (ed), *The Law of Political Economy* (Cambridge: Cambridge University Press, 2020) 89.

if we follow the psychiatric work of Frantz Fanon)[39] is 'assimilation'. In private international law, this takes on an apparently mild form: a preference for the legal classifications of the forum and the use thereof to filter alterity. However, the will to assimilate – make the same – foreign forms always involves the institution of a hierarchical relationship between self and other.

The conflict of laws provides many classical examples of the ways in which the use of juridical categories can lead to the exclusion or reduction of foreign institutions or practices that do not fit within the 'systematic structure' of the host legal system – that is, that do not comply with its underlying cultural worldview.[40] Contemporaneous with the institution of comparative law as a discipline, the discovery of difference in the morphology of legal systems[41] led, paradoxically, to the dominance of a methodological approach that required the flattening of difference.[42] Thus, a series of ingenious devices (created by the courts or imagined by jurists) ensures the management and processing of legal misfits from an overarching (a view-from-nowhere) perspective.[43] However, once repressed, differences come back to roost in one way or another. The polygamous (French/Algerian) citizen, the incestuous (Swiss/Russian) uncle and niece or the limping, status-less child (Italy/Ukraine) are all the warped hauntological figures[44] produced by the denial of alterity.

[39] F Fanon, *Peau noire, masques blancs* (Paris: Le Seuil, 1952).

[40] The doctrinal justification for such exclusions is the 'theory of characterisation'. Characterisation applies to the dispute or to specific legal issues. It consists in selecting the appropriate legal category that should house the claim according to the viewpoint of the court (the forum).

[41] Including among those in the close cultural proximity shared by the concert of nations and von Savigny's community of laws.

[42] See the case of the 'poor widow's quarter', claimed before the French colonial court under the *Code Rohan* in force in Malta (Court of Appeals of Algiers, 24 December 1889, *Bartholo*, B Ancel and Y Lequette, *Grands arrêts de la jurisprudence de droit international privé*, 5th edn (Paris: Dalloz, 2006) n° 9)), where unfamiliar imports to the latter from the common law (trusts), strong vestiges of canon law from the Byzantine empire (is a Greek orthodox religious marriage ceremony a legal form or an issue of substance? see the French *Caraslanis* case, Cour de cassation, Civ 1 février 1955, n° de pourvoi: 55-02.067) and, progressively, the arrival before the courts of the metropolis of citizens from the periphery bearing the legacy of colonial cultures led both to the affirmation of the forum as the sole, or Archimedean, reference point and to the need to make foreign law 'fit' into the structure of the host legal system. The problem has in no way disappeared by the apparent smoothing of legal differences. A significant illustration can be found in the (more recent) case of the Hopi masks, in which 70 Katsinam chamanic masks, sacred to an Indian tribe of Arizona, had found their way to a French private collection and were put up for auction in France (see M Cornu, 'About Sacred Cultural Property: The Hopi Masks Case' (2013) 20 *International Journal of Cultural Property* 451). The application for provisional measures was heard and refused by the Paris Court of First Instance (TGI Paris, interim orders of 12 April 2013, RG n°13/25880; 6 December 2013, RG n°13/59110; 27 June 2014, RG n°14/55733). In their pursuit of provisional measures before a French court in order to prevent the dispersal of the collection, the Hopis were denied legal title (and therefore legal standing) on various grounds, including the unenforceability of foreign law at the provisional stage and the unfamiliarity of collective tribal cultural property under French civilian legal categories.

[43] 'Characterisation' was soon to be followed by other devices, such as renvoi, preliminary questions and all sorts of (obsessional) apparatuses that serve to veil the morphology of difference, in the very name of tolerance.

[44] These are all classical tropes of private international law, to be found in most textbooks. They are also the spectral figures of law's 'hauntology'.

Moreover, less perceptible are the underlying fantasies and imaginaries that are relayed simultaneously through the apparently technical structure of the legal system and its categories. Judith Surkis' study of the long nineteenth-century colonial construction of personal status in Algeria (that is, beyond the familiar European community of laws), presented above, shows how orientalist colonial imaginaries were projected onto local indigenous customs and religious institutions, distorting their very meaning and internal balance.[45] Today, similar neo-colonialist imaginaries continue to project fantasies – of rejection and fascination, relating to sexuality (polygamy) or punishment (stoning) – on Muslim communities, whether foreign or domestic.[46] Moreover, the supposed lawlessness of more distant 'archaic' cultures is still considered a feature of underdevelopment (or indeed more mystifying, orientalised queerness). As the question of the status of the Muslim veil shows, legal orientalism takes on many varied, contemporary forms.[47]

Within the conflict of laws, then, the question of our relationship to alterity appears as a central but deflected debate about the proper shape of legal categories.[48] Diversity can indeed be hosted, but only (at least in the conventional account) on the terms (that is, within the categories) designed by the host legal system. Thus, tolerance can produce rejection, purported equality of treatment, hierarchy, and rights deprivation. The important point in each of these cases is to winkle out the stance of superiority, the lure of the instrumentalisation of the Other, lurking under our liberal ideas of openness in respect of alterity, extraneity or foreignness. As Isabelle Stengers writes in her appeal to 'do away with tolerance',[49] the latter slides easily into condescension and the establishment of a hierarchy between self and others. Moreover, as stated by the philosopher of alterity Emmanuel Levinas, reification and depersonalisation are temptations that are inherent to the comparison of norms and laws, and to all those institutions

[45] The fantasies projected onto the Muslim family are illustrated by Judith Surkis' exploration of the judicial archive of the Court of Algiers under French rule. Notably, family matters remained within the orbit of indigenous personal law (often largely reimagined as allowing extraordinary sexual licence), while being separated from the land regime; the latter became subject to the (French) civil, secular and codified law of property (and ensured a massive transfer of title to the colonisers). This example was replicated around the colonial world – in the British colonisation of India, or in New Zealand, as shown by Nan Seuffert's study (n 34).

[46] On the 'Shariah law row' triggered in the UK by the Archbishop of Canterbury Rowan Williams' plea for greater legal pluralism, see www.independent.co.uk/news/uk/home-news/archbishop-ignites-sharia-law-row-779505.html. For egregious 'anti-foreign law' measures in the US around the same time, see www.splcenter.org/hatewatch/2018/02/05/anti-sharia-law-bills-united-states, which relates that since 2010, 201 anti-Sharia law bills have been introduced in 43 States. In 2017 alone, 14 States introduced an anti-Sharia law bill, with Texas and Arkansas enacting the legislation.

[47] On its current forms in the veiling debate, see G Frankenberg, *Comparative Law as Critique* (Cheltenham: Edward Elgar, 2016) 113–62.

[48] 'Deflected' here means that it hides something else. This can be seen in the debates about characterisation; see above.

[49] I Stengers, *Pour en finir avec la tolérance* (Paris: Empêcheurs de Penser en Rond, 1997).

that neutralise subjects in order to make them fit into categories and subject them to rules.[50]

Both these reflections, well known in substance to (critical) comparative lawyers, are significant for understanding private international law's traditional methodologies. The latter can be said to rest, on the one hand, on the idea of tolerance for difference as embodied in foreign law,[51] and, on the other hand, on the processing of the latter through a series of categories that reflect the structure and epistemology of the receiving legal system and serve as entry points or filters.[52] The cunning of tolerance lies, then, in an epistemological and ethical trap – that is, the denial of alterity in the name of equality. Indeed, the smoothing over of difference in an assimilationist mode contains an equally powerful (if less visible) value judgement on legal cultures other than one's own, just as much as the use of alterity to discriminate or disparage.[53]

In comparative legal studies, the heated debate over the premise of commonality (notably, the epistemological assumption of similarity between laws that underlies 'functionalism' as its the dominant comparative method) reveals that an implicit hierarchy between us and them can niche within an ostensibly neutral stance. As Pierre Legrand writes, the quest for commonalities that commands dominant strands of comparative law signifies that 'I'll recognize you if and to the extent that you are like me'.[54] In other words, ironing out differences leaves little place for the acknowledgement and ethical attention due to alterity. Furthermore, any remaining discrepancy becomes an anomaly that leads to exclusion – when it does not lead to an occult or inverted rejection in the form of cultural exoticisation or legal orientalism.[55]

If we turn to 'symmetrical' anthropology (or the ontological turn within the latter), we recall that the 'law of the others' corresponds to their own, equally

[50] For Levinas, the transformation of persons into things (a feature of totalitarianism) is the worst thing that can happen to humanity. See C Pelluchon, *Pour Comprendre Levinas* (Paris: Le Seuil, 2020) 191, observing the analogy with the temptation to manage humanity as 'human resources'. The latter vocabulary belongs of course to that of neoliberal governance.

[51] The idea that the conflict of laws embodies tolerance in respect of foreign law is a trope within the discipline.

[52] As in the process of characterisation (see above); it acts as an epistemological and ethical filter in respect of foreign laws.

[53] On the negation of alterity through the eminently modern 'narcissistic European gesture that aimed at seeing its own image repeated throughout the universe', see S Santiago, *The Space In-between: Essays on Latin American Culture*, trans A Gazzola (Durham, NC: Duke University Press, 2002).

[54] Legrand (n 14).

[55] See Ruskola (n 9), tracing back to Montesquieu and then to the traders of the British Empire the idea that the East is despotic or illiberal, as opposed to the West's concern for the rule of law (noting, however, that prejudices, in the neutral sense used by Gadamer, can only be managed, not eliminated: at 51). Similarly, in his study of 'Black Gaius', questioning the supposed cultural 'purity' of the Roman legal tradition, PG Monateri shows how comparative legal thought in the twentieth century ran along lines already traced by linguistic theory. The cultural (racialised) purity of language was echoed in a genealogical narrative that recounted the Roman Christian origins of the Continental legal system as (imagined) legal community: PG Monateri, 'Black Gaius: A Quest for the Multicultural Origins of the "Western Legal Tradition"' (2000) 51 *Hastings Law Journal* 479.

legitimate, modes of veridiction.[56] This is not an assertion of liberal equality, because all these life forms are incommensurable. However, it is an acknowledgement that each has its own intrinsic value in its distinctive trajectory. It is particularly relevant in the context of colonisation through legal form – in other words, the normative forms that count or are discounted as such in the encounter between the West and the rest of the world. Thus, private international law has become a filter in respect of alternative or alien (non-modern, non-secular) legal forms or categories that are alien to modernity's (archaic?) obsession with the written word, such as ceremonial rituals, oral traditions or 'mosaic' patterns.[57] Even if they are no longer explicitly dismissed as primitive, they do not receive recognition as *nomos*. The supposed lawlessness of the populations inhabiting the *terra nullius* of colonial space is just one epistemological implication of (ethno) centred method, with the deleterious long-lasting structural consequences seen above. Purportedly neutral, such a method dismally fails the requirements of our ethical responsibility to acknowledge the intrinsic and incommensurable value of the law of all others (*les êtres-en-tant-qu'autres*).

E. The Social Construction of Acceptability: Collective Values or 'Ordre Public'

Conflictuality in the encounter with the law of others is inevitable nevertheless. It also raises the quandary of cultural relativism, a spectre often opposed to any attempt to rein in the absolutism of social values. Private international law houses an overtly comparative legal technology which sets the parameter of compatibility of foreign values in respect of those of the court. This is the notoriously disorderly procedural 'exception'[58] known as *ordre public* (lost in translation into 'public policy' or 'public order'), covering a variety of values, principles or mandatory policies. The need for an exception is framed traditionally as the necessary counterpart of the purported neutrality, impartiality or blindness of the choice-of-law rule: its 'leap into the unknown' undeniably requires a safety net. Such a filter involves only too often a negative (or condescending) value judgement. Various

[56] B Latour, *Enquête sur les modes d'existence. Une anthropologie des modernes* (Paris: La Découverte, 2012) 452, emphasising this (pluriversal) point in response to the objection that deep ecology is a form of ecofascism. Each form of life is incommensurable and has intrinsic value on own trajectory.

[57] A Mills, 'The Lifeworlds of Law: On Revitalizing Indigenous Legal Orders Today' (2016) 61 *McGill Law Journal* 847.

[58] *Ordre public* is 'exceptional' both procedurally (because it grounds arguments that are raised in defence to a claim based on the legal rule) and substantively (because it authorises a derogation from the ordinary rule of law that allows in foreign norms). It is often ascribed to some sort of transcendent order (such as natural law, 'universal principles of justice' or fundamental rights). However, at the same time, *ordre public* has obvious family links with other politically potent and equally elusive concepts that evoke police power, such as 'reason of state' or 'state of necessity', that also legitimate the reversal of rule of law and exception.

institutions of foreign family law in particular (polygamy, divorce of all kinds, paternity suits, same-sex marriage, adoption, surrogacy etc) have, from time to time, been subject to a gut civilisational reaction of this kind.

Indeed, just like the requirement of compliance with the shape of legal categories evoked in the preceding section, this particular form of epistemological firewall developed in the context of colonial encounters with alterity. As Silviano Santiago writes of tolerance in such a context, the latter embodies:

> [A]bove all the lack of respect (and not mere intellectual curiosity) in relation to the Other; it is intolerance with the values of the Other. It is the main effect of the narcissistic European gesture that aimed at seeing its own image repeated throughout the universe. In full glory, the so-called universal history begins with European expansionism. The New World is only the occasion for another mirror, and the native is the clay to mould a double, similar figure – and add more violence and destruction.[59]

We know that closely following contemporaneous findings in anthropology, theories of early twentieth-century comparative law divided (and in the case of some textbooks still divide) the world's cultures into 'families', classified according to the intensity of their proximity to the heritage of the (Roman Christian) West. 'Legal barbarians'[60] – that is, those whose 'primitive' modes of access to reality did not fit with a universalised ideal of civilisation were relegated to the periphery of the classificatory system (and similarly disqualified by international law from the concert of nations). In this respect, the exception of public policy or *ordre public* similarly represents a ploy of 'imagined community'.[61] The dual ideas of universality and non-derogability of certain values serve both as the amplifiers of difference and the parameters of exclusion. However, the threshold is uncertain and the triggering factors are the subject of endless debate (individual injustice assessed *in concreto*, intolerable norms envisaged *in abstracto*, additional parameters of proximity, or again, expectations rooted in past histories, situations or practices).[62] Above all, these uncertainties provide a niche for rationalities of exclusion and rejection of alterity.

[59] Santiago (n 53) 13.

[60] Bonilla Maldonaldo (n 9).

[61] B Anderson, *Imagined Communities: Reflections on the Origin and Spread of Nationalism* (New York: Verso, 1983).

[62] Thus, there is a widely shared principle according to which the requirements of public policy – or the limits of the intolerable – must be assessed on the day the court sits. Such a principle only serves to emphasise their inconstancy and relativity, in time and space. The various family law institutions cited above, rejected yesterday and promoted today (or the reverse), are archetypical sites of such axiological variations within Western legal cultures. The assumption here (familiar to constitutional jurisprudence) is that the judiciary has an inherent legitimacy to decide upon the social-legal acceptability of given practices or *mores* (and moreover an innate or intuitive receptivity to the trends of public opinion that dispense with empirical research or indeed technical expertise). Second, once the appropriate standard of acceptability (or, in earlier versions, 'civilisation') is established, a delicate modulation ensues as to the intensity of its requirements according to the spatial distance and specific temporality of individual situations (this is the 'principle of proximity', traced by P Lagarde, 'Le principe de proximité dans le droit international privé contemporain' (1987) 196 *Recueil des Cours de l'Académie de droit international* 9). When the values are enclosed in human, fundamental or constitutional rights,

Beyond the variability of our own social institutions, there are always – as seen above in respect of the shape of our legal categories – further assumptions or fantasies underlying our cultural construction of moral acceptability. The temptation (into which courts and others regularly fall) is to relegate practices that are endowed with entirely diverse meanings in their own cosmological context to the realm of the 'undeveloped' or, in the mode of an anathema, to the primitive or the savage. However, three examples taken from anthropological or culturalist approaches to the comparative moral economies of law (successively from the work of Philippe Descola, Louis Asser-Andieu and Pierre Legrand) can serve to show that what we perceive to be the most abhorrent of 'foreign' practices – cannibalism, incest, excision[63] – may well have a symbolic significance in a context that does not justify their relegation to 'barbarian' status (even if we do not accept them).

It is important to dissipate any misinterpretation that these evidently provocative examples are likely to induce. The point here is in no way to claim that these practices are in any way 'good' in the moral terms of (our) cultural codes or, more importantly, that 'we' should accept them within the bounds of our communities. However, the argument here is that alien cultural practices, which are perceived as primitive (or condemned as savage), may entertain a far more respectful vision of otherness than our Western/naturalist/modernist own.[64] Philippe Descola's classification of the various relationships collectives entertain with alterity brings home the fact that non-modern visions (animism, totemism or analogism) are more attentive than their modern counterparts to the extraordinary interdependence of all forms of beings (sentient and non-sentient, visible and invisible, past and future). We should be aware that many of our own practices appear wasteful and cruel in the eyes of non-modern or non-naturalist communities. Our grabbing of land and natural resources, our cruelty and neglect of other species, and our colonisation of the rest of humanity all appear equally devastating in 'the gaze of the jaguar'.[65]

Indeed, 'naturalism' supports the belief that there are various traits that are a-historical and a-contextual, that is, inherent to human nature and therefore universal (in a world that is unitary and not pluriversal, as seen above). Here,

the assessment of the threshold of intolerability takes on the different form of balancing, or again proportionality, but does not change in substance.

[63] See respectively, Descola (n 23) 544 on cannibalism as 'le moyen paradoxal d'incorporer l'altérité au plus profond, tout en restant fidèles à eux-mêmes'; L Asser-Andrieu, 'Le crépuscule des cultures. L'affaire Pitcairn et l'idéologie des droits humains' (2012) 82 *Droit et société* 763; P Legrand, 'Foreign Law: Understanding Understanding' (2011) 6 *Journal of Comparative Law* 67, referring in fn 388 to RA Shweder, 'What about Female Genital Mutilation? and Why Understanding Culture Matters in the First Place' in RA Shweder, M Minow and HR Markus (eds), *Engaging Cultural Differences* (New York: Sage, 2002) 216.

[64] This point is highlighted with particular clarity by Descola (n 23) 438 in respect of cannibalism as a mode of 'devenir-autre'.

[65] On the 'gaze of the jaguar', see E Viveiros de Castro, 'Cosmological Deixis and Amerindian Perspectivism' (1998) 4 *Journal of the Royal Anthropological Institute* 469.

however, the interdisciplinary cross-fertilisation of a 'thick' description of culture,[66] ethno-psychoanalysis[67] and history suggests a very different take. Anthropological descriptions of the practices, social institutions and belief systems of various communities (and comparative legal studies in their wake) emphasise the extraordinarily varied range of censorship devices (across different communities, in space and time) that divide the acceptable from the inconceivable, the sacred from the profane, and desire from rejection.[68] These differences are reflected at any given time in attitudes towards war and aggression, sexuality and family, shame and honour, and crime and punishment.

In the context of private international law and its obviously comparative metrics here, we see how the exception of public policy highlights these tensions and contradictions within the cultural 'construction of the intolerable'.[69] It points to the extreme variability of values that are proclaimed at any point as universal or fundamental. What is also interesting is that it suggests ways to address these inevitable paradoxes that attend the encounter between embedded belief systems and the ever-changing individual needs of equity in individual cases. In this respect, on the other (tail) side of the (head) coin of public policy or reason of state, the message is that an ethical stance towards alterity does not enjoin one culture to adopt institutions that are abhorrent to it or even to admit them in the form of a foreign law or judgment. However, it does require that these other schemes are acknowledged as alternative modes of access to reality, endowed with equal dignity to our own.

At this point comes the Herculean difficulty of dissolving a hegemonic scheme that has gone far in capturing our entire world – right up to the very idea of the future, as seen above. It also shows very clearly that the only way ahead for law's alternative political ecology lies in the inscription within the law of an ethical responsibility towards the other forms of life and beings that surround us. It is through the appeal of these others, as Latour explains, that ethics are encoded within our very world.[70] But they must be heard *on their own terms* – in other words, decolonising means eradicating the assimilationist comparative metric that lurks within dominant versions of (public and private) international law and

[66] C Geertz, *The Interpretation of Cultures* (New York: Basic Books, 1973).

[67] On the integration of ethnography and social history in the formation of the psyche, repairing history's omission of the collective psyche in the explanation of historical events or social attitudes: see H Mazurel, *L'inconscient ou l'oubli de l'histoire. Profondeurs, métamorphoses et révolutions de la vie affective* (Paris: La Découverte, 2021).

[68] Given the centrality of sexuality and gender in the understanding of cultural difference, a good example is the 'invention' of sexuality in the Western seventeenth century, as analysed by Michel Foucault: this obviously does not mean that sexuality did not exist before modernity (nor that it does not exist outside the West!), but that the latter induced a novel way of thinking about human life, health and intimacy, so that sexuality was not repressed but actually 'produced' by new forms of (bio)power, themselves in turn indissociable from emerging medical science and technologies and above all the new (biopolitical) functions of state in respect of its population.

[69] D Fassin 'L'ordre moral du monde Essai d'anthropologie de l'intolérable' in D Fassin and P Bourdelais (eds), *Les Constructions de l'intolérable. Études d'anthropologie et d'histoire sur les frontières de l'espace moral* (Paris: La Découverte, 2005) 17.

[70] Latour (n 56) 454.

accepting that the legal forms of the Other take place within a radically different episteme. This is the cue to listen to insights from less conventional accounts of private international law.

F. Conclusion: The *Episteme* of the In-between

The main achievement of we 'moderns', as Bruno Latour wryly observes, has been to universalise the (legal) forms that have facilitated the collective cecity and amnesia whereby our 'anthropocentric machine'[71] hurtles on regardless, devastating other lifeworlds in its path and devouring the very resources it needs to survive. Indeed, the political economy[72] of late modernity rests on a radical severance within the *oikos*,[73] whereby the 'economisation' of the ecology signifies a radical lack of accountability of humanity towards the natural world. To connect this with coloniality, this rupture is a further instantiation of the split within humanity itself along social, cultural, racial and geopolitical lines, with a correlative neglect or negation of alterity. How, then, did the economy become our 'secular religion', the 'great dispatcher' of all things?

A broad hypothesis is that one key (among many) lies in the legal dimension of the political economy (whether under colonial capitalism or its later avatars and replications). In other words, legality has always been instrumental in various dislocations – in the disembedding of markets from society, in the dissociation of risk and responsibility, in the severance of calculus from scruple,[74] and in the screening-off of the Mississippi behind Manchester[75] – with disastrous consequences for both humanity itself and the planet. In the background – that is, inside the economic calculus, behind the political model of economic freedom, under the surface of legal entitlements – the natural (and the third or 'developing') world serve both as tap (for precious minerals, energy, petrol, nutrition and, of course, labour) and sink (for refuse and waste of all kinds).[76]

[71] G Agamben, *Open: Man and Animal* (Stanford: Stanford University Press, 2002), taking up Descartes' concept of the 'animal machine'.

[72] K Polanyi, *The Great Transformation: The Political and Economic Origins of Our Time* (New York: Farrar & Rinehart, 1944). On the contemporary political-economic relevance of Polanyi's thought in the translational legal order, see C Joerges and J Fal (eds), *Karl Polanyi, Globalisation and the Potential of Law in Transnational Markets* (Oxford: Hart Publishing, 2011).

[73] See D Leshem, *The Origins of Neoliberalism: Modelling the Economy from Jesus to Foucault* (New York: Columbia University Press, 2016). *Oikonomia* was the law of prudent management of resources ('squeezed between ethics and politics' in the words of M Koskiennemi, 'International Law and raison d'état: Rethinking the Prehistory of International Law' in B Kingsbury and B Straumann (eds), *The Roman Foundation of the Law of Nations: Alberico Gentili and the Justice of Empire* (Oxford: Oxford University Press, 2010) 334).

[74] Latour (n 56) 459.

[75] Fraser and Jaeggi (n 36) 39 et seq.

[76] The sink evokes 'waste colonialism', meaning the exportation-externalisation of waste from North to South, the abode of racialised, disposable populations; see Gonzales and Mutua (n 34).

There is no need to underscore the colonial episteme here. Humanity's ontological privilege over its non-human surroundings is refracted in turn through an analogous prerogative asserted by Western modernity in relation to the rest of the (culturally 'primitive') world and its inhabitants (possibly devoid of soul or fully human nature). This visual ordering of nature endorses coloniality, insofar as there is an evident mirror effect or echo between the legal shape of humanity's relationship to the natural world (whether composed of animals, minerals or things, visible or invisible) and the form it gives to interactions, hierarchies and divisions within the social world. Law's contribution to the ontological distance between the social and the natural also enabled the unrestricted appropriation of the earth's resources and the correlative neglect of alterity in terms of biological and cultural forms of life.

Indeed, legal techniques reflect and reinforce this understanding of the purported order of nature through the axial categories through which it channels our access to the real world, splitting mind from body, persons from things, and agency from environment. Indeed, law was present at the very origin of this severance of nature from society. Gradually detaching its abstract forms from the materiality of life, it shaped modern metaphysics, co-producing the conditions for (Western) humanity's subjugation of its surrounding world. The initial divide between persons and things was mirrored in turn by further epistemological separations between subject and object, self and environment. But following AA Diouf, the African episteme or cosmogony never subscribed to this vision, to which it nevertheless became subjected through colonial rule.[77] Nevertheless, comparative law is also there to highlight a diversity of imaginaries. Diouf has pointed out the need to decolonise knowledge and allow law to reflect the cosmogonies that underwrite African views of the social, and the place of transcendence therein. While the dominant shape and content of Western legality has evolved in cadence with statehood, secularism and capitalism, with its intrinsic colonial dimension and successive trans-formations,[78] it has passed by the alternative schemes that thrived among the societies it purported to civilise and develop.

The relevance of private international law here as a possible counter-model lies in its distinctive status as a frontier discipline. In stark contrast to the 'jurisdictional thinking'[79] that emptied, divided, disenchanted and flattened the world, separating humanity and the planet (us and them; the body politic and its surroundings), there has always been an alternative, shadow scheme haunting the history of the conflict of laws and resonating with an ecological 'jurisprudence of the border'.[80] It understands frontiers not as exclusionary dividing lines, but as

[77] A Aziz Diouf, *Le droit africain à la quête de son identité* (Paris: Harmattan, 2021).

[78] H Brabazon (ed), *Neoliberal Legality: Understanding the Role of Law in the Neoliberal Project* (New York: Routledge, 2016).

[79] S McVeigh, 'Law as (More or Less) Itself: On Some Not Very Reflective Elements of Law' (2014) 4 *UC Irvine Law Review* 471.

[80] Mignolo (n 11).

passing-places, in which existence can 'take place' in a hybrid and intermediating mode.

Borrowing from non-modern cosmological schemes of intelligibility, this alternative legal mode 'dwells' in the interstices of entanglement or indeed on the borderline of law itself. It rests on a decolonial imaginary that weaves in-between[81] different lifeworlds and cultural forms, crossing frontiers, and acknowledging the coexistence on our planet of multifarious universes[82] that are not separate or exclusive, but overlapping and interacting.[83] 'Dwelling'[84] at the threshold of multiple worlds (in 'pluriversal mode[85]), it involves an ability to decentre and adopt the lateral standpoint of the Other – that is, of each of these interlocking cultural and natural ecosystems. As described by Boaventura de Sousa Santos, this Other is an 'abyssal' model,[86] made of (ontological) hybridity or interstitiality and (aesthetic) entwinement and oscillation. A shrouded (or less rationalist) penumbra of entanglement in-between multiple normative worlds.

Importantly, here, the latter signifies a radical reversal of coloniality as an attitude towards alterity. Dwelling in the border is a reaction or resistance to colonial forms of universalism, or, in respect of law, to the 'jurisprudence of jurisdiction' that flattens lifeforms and empties the world of its alterity. It promises an alternative legal shape and ontology, a 'jurisprudence of the border'. Most of the contemporary moves in respect of the law originate in struggles to save and give voice to non-modern lifeworlds in the Global South or to indigenous minorities in Western colonial or settler states. They seek to track the sinuous operation of power and the embedding of hierarchies under the smooth, neutral-seeming surface of our linear, monist and universalising jurisdictional grid.

At the final point of this chapter, the 'dismal swamp', then, comes into its own.[87] Navigating in-between spaces, thresholds of uncertainty, the shadow

[81] The in-between as a critical concept is borrowed from decolonial literary critique: see Santiago (n 53).

[82] See K Eitel and M Meurer, 'Exploring Multifarious Worlds and the Political Within the Ontological Turn(s)' (2021) 84 *Berliner Blätter* 3.

[83] A Escobar, *Pluriversal Politics: The Real and the Possible* (Durham, NC: Duke University Press, 2020) 9 defines this concept as 'a world where many worlds fit'.

[84] The idea of 'dwelling', central in Mignolo's pluriverse, is also a focus of (Western) anthropology in its ontological turn: see T Ingold, 'The Temporality of Landscape' (1992) 2 *World Archaeology* 25. Ingold's 'dwelling perspective' has spread to other disciplines such as landscape architecture: as an attempt 'to reconcile the separation between man and landscape by imagining the landscape as a continually unfolding story. The landscape bears witness to the passing of time; it contains a living memory of all who have lived in it. To perceive the landscape is to carry out an act of remembrance – one is immersed in this unfolding, gathering details and impressions that can be related again': J Abelman, 'Response to Tim Ingold', www.groundcondition.com/essays/the-dwelling-perspective.

[85] For the use of pluriversality in private international law, see the Max Planck Institute research project, 'Decolonial Comparative Law', led by Ralf Michaels and Lena Salaymeh.

[86] B de Sousa Santos, *Demodiversity: Toward Post-abyssal Democracies* (Abingdon: Routledge, 2020).

[87] On the description of private international law as a dismal swamp, see S Symeonides, 'Exploring the "Dismal Swamp": The Revision of Louisiana's Conflicts Law on Successions' (1987) 47 *Louisiana Law Review* 1029. On the aesthetic of the swamp, the work of Brazilian literary critic Silviano Santiago

avatar of the conflict-of-laws proposes two distinctive features of an alternative scheme of legality. These might be described in terms of law's ontology, namely its diplomatic, 'go-between' function and, in terms of legal aesthetics, its interstitial and multi-sided location at the very crossing of borders, opening up different vistas or ways of seeing. On the one hand, instead of dividing up and severing, it reconnects and repairs. On the other hand, it contains an invitation to stand and look back at ourselves, not from law's traditional unitary or monist standpoint, but from the lateral and necessarily plural perspective of the Other. It enjoins us to replace the frenetic and competitive pursuit of gain for an ethos of hospitality towards the foreign or the alien, whether cultural or natural, human or animal. The conflict of laws serves here as a bridge, suggesting that our relationship to otherness in legal form could find expression in what might be termed a law of inter-alterity. However, this horizon[88] is so very faint in our late modern (legal) tradition that it is imperative to return first to the causes, or forces, that prevent us from approaching it. In other words, the starting place has to be the profound chasm that lies at the core of Western law's colonial epistemology, or the collective denial of history[89] in our collective (sub)consciousness. This could be the promise of a critical 'comparative international law'.

(n 53) is particularly interesting, having developed the idea of the swamp as the 'in-between space' (*o entre-lugar* in Portuguese).

[88] The horizon is central in the thought of Emmanuel Levinas, according to whom it is 'split' insofar as it is constituted by alterity. C Pelluchon, *Pour Comprendre Levinas* (Paris: Le Seuil, 2020) 37 observes that in contemporary philosophy, the notion of horizon has replaced the traditional concept of truth.

[89] A Angie, *Imperialism, Sovereignty and the Making of International Law* (Cambridge: Cambridge University Press, 2007) argues that the West forgets its own history. A similar point in a Western context is made by historian-psychoanalyst Mazurel (n 67).

11

Science in Comparative International Law

PETRA MINNEROP

A. Introduction

This chapter investigates how science is used in legal regimes pertaining to the so-called global commons.[1] Employing a functional approach to the comparative analysis, the notion of science is used as *tertium comparationis* to understand how an extra-legal knowledge system advances and shapes legal regimes.[2] While not dealing with a 'legal' transplant *per se*,[3] the chapter analyses how science and law become intertwined in the four regimes that share a functional equivalence in their legal use of science, allowing for a meaningful comparison.[4]

Sufficient similarity for the comparison is rooted in the reliance on science across the life cycle of each of the regimes that cover subject areas of societal importance, at the intersection of environmental protection and distribution of

[1] J Brunnée, 'Common Areas, Common Heritage, and Common Concern' in D Bodansky, J Brunnée and E Hey (eds), *The Oxford Handbook of International Environmental Law* (Oxford: Oxford University Press, 2007) 550, 553; E Molenaar and AG Oude Elferink (eds), *International Regime of Areas Beyond National Jurisdiction: Current and Future Developments* (Leiden: Martinus Nijhoff, 2010) 35.

[2] A Roberts et al, 'Conceptualizing Comparative International Law' in A Roberts et al (eds), *Comparative International Law* (Oxford: Oxford University Press, 2018) 1, 14. This method of comparative law is concerned with identifying the substantive content of international law, as influenced by an extra-legal knowledge system of natural sciences. See also M Forteau, 'Comparative International Law Within, Not Against, International Law: Lessons from the International Law Commission' in A Roberts et al (eds), *Comparative International Law* (Oxford: Oxford University Press, 2018) ch 8.

[3] See Siems, ch 1 in this volume, section D; TS Goldbach, 'Why Legal Transplants?' (2019) 15 *Annual Review of Law and Social Science* 583, 884; JM Miller, 'A Typology of Legal Transplants: Using Sociology, Legal History and Argentine Examples to Explain the Transplant Process' (2003) 51 *American Journal of Comparative Law* 839.

[4] The chapter thereby expands the typology of comparative international law inquiry as envisaged by Roberts et al (n 2) 8. According to Ralf Michaels, there is not only 'the' functional method of comparative law: R Michaels, 'The Functional Method of Comparative Law' in M Raimann and R Zimmermann (eds), *The Oxford Handbook of Comparative Law*, 2nd edn (Oxford: Oxford University Press, 2019) 345, 347, 375. For an overview of this distinction, see M Siems, *Comparative Law*, 3rd edn (Cambridge: Cambridge University Press, 2022) 335–40; for other differentiations, see Roberts et al (eds) (n 2).

benefits in the interests of humankind. Science in these legal regimes promises to connect legal standards with a measure of objectivity, originating from outside the law and therefore providing a unifying rationale beyond states' national interests. Science not only appears to best protect the interests of humankind in areas beyond the jurisdiction of any state, but also to promote legal convergence by following comparable patterns across the global commons' treaty regimes.[5]

Traditionally, the global commons comprise Antarctica, Outer Space, the High Seas and the Atmosphere.[6] Each of these treaties set forth an extensive regulatory regime that integrates extra-legal scientific knowledge and explicitly or impliedly assigns certain functions to science, notably, in relation to goal formation, treaty membership, regime development and treaty implementation.

This chapter demonstrates how the legal language in each of the regimes suggests certainty in and about the science, without constructing criteria to accommodate qualitative distinctions or the evolving nature of scientific research. It has been established that the legal effect of law's reference of, or even deference to, scientific experts, is that one must 'abide' by its results.[7] Scientific knowledge has to appear objective and impartial, if not disinterested, in order to authorise governmental action.[8] Some attention in the literature has been devoted to the interactional potential of co-production where science is used as 'serviceable truth' for social and legal practices.[9] The European Commission has been identified in literature as a facilitative agent of co-production in evidence-informed environmental law making.[10] The consequential risks that decisions can be flawed in judicial settings if necessary engagement with science is absent or inadequate, or where science becomes a proxy for legal reasoning, are well documented.[11]

[5] For an explanation of legal transplants and convergence as phenomena in comparative international law, see Siems (n 4) 290.

[6] R Wolfrum, 'Identifying Community Interests in International Law: Common Spaces and Beyond' in E Benvenisti and G Nolte (eds), *Community Interests across International Law* (Cambridge: Cambridge University Press, 2018) 19, 20; R Wolfrum, *Die Internationalisierung Staatsfreier Raume: Die Entwicklung einer Internationalen Verwaltung fur Antarktis, Weltraum, Hohe See and Meeresboden* (Berlin: Springer, 1984).

[7] *Case Concerning the Temple of Preah Vihear (Cambodia v Thailand)* [1962] ICJ Rep 6 (Separate Opinion Judge Fitzmaurice) at 58–59: 'This is so in all walks of life. A man who consults a lawyer, doctor, architect, or other expert, is held (in the absence of fraud or negligence-not here in question) to accept the possibility that the expert may be mistaken in the advice he gives, or less than perfect in the work he does.'

[8] A Orford, 'Scientific Reason and the Discipline of International Law' (2014) *25 European Journal of International Law* 369, 382.

[9] S Jasanoff, 'Serviceable Truths: Science for Action in Law and Policy' (2015) 93 *Texas Law Review* 1723.

[10] A Čavoški, 'Science and Law in Environmental Law and Policy: The Case of the European Commission' (2020) 9 *Transnational Environmental Law* 263, 264; D Rimkute and M Haverland, 'How Does the European Commission Use Scientific Expertise? Results from a Survey of Scientific Members of the Commission's Expert Committees' (2015) 13 *Comparative European Politics* 430, 435.

[11] LB Chazournes, 'Introduction: Courts and Tribunals and the Treatment of Scientific Issues' (2012) 3 *Journal of International Dispute Settlement* 479; MM Mbengue MM, 'Scientific Fact-Finding by International Courts and Tribunals' (2012) 3 *Journal of International Dispute Settlement* 509; B Simma,

By contrast, little attention has been paid in scholarly writing to the root cause of assigning distinct functions to science in the life cycle of treaties across legal regimes, if these treaties are not fully equipped to fulfil the scientifically guarded objectivity and impartiality promise. This chapter fills that gap and argues that absent legal criteria for the selection of science, the inclusion of reference to 'best available science' in treaty texts mandates evolutive interpretation in light of the latest scientific evidence, including the treaty objectives, and especially where changes in science have been affirmed in authentic means of treaty interpretation such as decisions of conferences of the parties (COP Decisions).[12]

While the chapter undertakes a critical examination of the authority that law assigns to science, no evaluation of science or of the modes and methodologies of generating scientific knowledge is implied. The main conclusion that resonates from the analysis is that not less but more science is needed in the law across the global commons.

The comparative analysis of how science is referenced at the level of treaty regimes is based on three premises that apply to international environmental law generally. First, scientific progress shapes international environmental law's conceptual architecture through an extra-legal impulse for political and legal decision-making. Second, science therefore has a distinct functionality in the comparative analysis of 'units' of international law.[13] It promises some form of remediation of the global common's destiny, be it the 'tragedy' or the 'real tragedy'.[14] Third, autopoiesis can describe and explain how law evolves within each of the individual legal regimes for the global commons. These regimes evolve in accordance with specific treaty- and sub-treaty rules, they are sufficiently distinct from the broader legal environment while remaining cognitively open.[15]

The following demonstrates that the contestation of scientific authority and the role of science begins with the goal formation in the law-making process (section B). The analysis of the sub-treaty rule making focuses on how the objectivity promise of science materialises vis-a-vis the idea of equitable benefit and burden sharing, expressed in the principle of the common heritage of humankind (section C) or, albeit less pronounced, articulated as a common concern

'The International Court of Justice and Scientific Expertise' (2012) 106 *Proceedings of the ASIL Annual Meeting* 230.

[12] This could be the case for the Paris Agreement, depending on the wording of decisions of annual conferences of the parties (COPs); see P Minnerop, 'The Legal Effect of the Paris Rulebook under the Doctrine of Treaty Interpretation' in PD Cameron, Xiaoyi Mu and V Roeben (eds), *The Global Energy Transition* (Oxford: Hart Publishing, 2020) 101, 109.

[13] M Siems, 'The Power of Comparative Law: What Types of Units Can Comparative Law Compare?' (2020) 67 *American Journal of Comparative Law* 861, 877, on 'Methods and Concepts of Comparative Law'.

[14] G Hardin, 'Tragedy of the Commons' (1968) 162 *Science* 1243. Stephen Gardiner argues that Hardin's arguments are deeply flawed and shifts the focus from tragedy to 'real' tragedy: SM Gardiner, 'The Real Tragedy of the Commons' (2001) 30 *Philosophy & Public Affairs* 387, 388.

[15] A D'Amato, 'International Law as an Autopoietic System' in R Wolfrum and V Röben (eds), *Developments of International Law in Treaty Making* (Berlin: Springer, 2005) 336, 350.

of humankind. The text then addresses the function of science in treaty implementation, through the evolving standards of due diligence, as a qualification of international cooperation, and as the emergent property of consensus (section D). The final section (section E) concludes. Turning the assumption that science has a role in the sphere of comparative international law and that the law itself must regulate points of intervention in autopoietic systems over the global commons, into a well-reasoned legal argument, is the purpose of this chapter.

B. Goal Formation and Treaty Membership in Autopoietic Treaties Over the Global Commons

Science in comparative international law extends an already wide-ranging array of principles and concepts into the realm of a discipline that is equally diverse and complex, with a different rationality and its very own set of epistemological rules and criteria.[16] Accordingly, courts have noted when confirming standards for the admissibility of expert scientific testimony,[17] the differences between the 'quest for truth in the courtroom and the quest for truth in the laboratory'.[18]

Science as a knowledge system concerns the natural and physical world;[19] law, including international law, is a social construct,[20] created to organise the relationships between human beings and between human beings and the natural and physical world.[21]

It is not a modern twist of the science *of the law* to place great hope in *science in law*. In 1920, Oliver Wendell Holmes remarked in his speech 'Science in Law and Law in Science':

> [I]t is finally for science to determine, so far as it can, the relative worth of our different social ends … and it is our estimate of the proportion between these, now often blind

[16] M Lachs, 'Views from the Bench: Thoughts on Science, Technology and World Law' (1992) 86 *American Journal of International Law* 673; Y Tanaka, 'Provisional Measures Prescribed by ITLOS and Marine Environmental Protection' (2014) 108 *Proceedings of the ASIL Annual Meeting* 365; K Sulyok, 'Science, Epistemology and Legitimacy in Environmental Disputes: The Epistemically Legitimate Judicial Argumentative Space' (2024) 37 *Leiden Journal of International Law* 139, 165.

[17] S Haack, 'Of Truth, in Science and in Law' (2008) 73 *Brooklyn Law Review* 985, 987.

[18] *Daubert v Merrell Dow Pharm, Inc* 509 US 579, 597 (1993).

[19] PC Ellsworth, 'Legal Reasoning and Scientific Reasoning' (2011) 63 *Alabama Law Review* 895, 897; T Meyer, 'Epistemic Institutions and Epistemic Cooperation in International Environmental Governance' (2013) 2 *Transnational Environmental Law* 15, 20; J Klabbers, 'The Virtues of Expertise' in M Ambrus, K Arts, E Hey and H Raulus (eds), *The Role of 'Experts' in International and European Decision-making* (Cambridge, Cambridge University Press, 2014) 82; C Foster, *Science and the Precautionary Principle in International Courts and Tribunals: Expert Evidence, Burden of Proof and Finality* (Cambridge, Cambridge University Press, 2011) 75.

[20] A Cassese and J Weiler, *Change and Stability in International Law-Making* (Berlin: De Gruyter, 1988) 38; A Čavoški, 'Science and Law in Environmental Law and Policy: The Case of the European Commission' (2020) 9 *Transnational Environmental Law* 263.

[21] P Birnie, A Boyle and C Redgwell, *International Law and the Environment*, 3rd edn (Oxford: Oxford University Press, 2009).

> and unconscious, that leads us to insist upon and to enlarge the sphere of one principle and to allow another gradually to dwindle into atrophy.[22]

Designating the relative worth of different social ends based on confidence in scientific knowledge about the physical world defines the very core of the objectives, design and governance of multilateral environmental agreements. Science has been transplanted into legal systems and serves as common thread in the evolution of the UN Convention on the Law of the Sea, the Outer Space Treaty, the Antarctic Treaty and the international climate change regime. In these autopoietic systems, it helps in identifying community interests and influences the processes of goal formation, sub-treaty rule making and implementation.[23]

1. Goal Formation

As a unifying, common ground, science has been introduced into treaties, often vis-a-vis principles that express the idea of balance,[24] such as the 'common heritage of humankind'[25] or to better govern a common interest or concern of humankind. While areas that constitute common concerns of humankind may not cover the full spectrum of the common heritage principle,[26] the role of science in the creation and the autopoiesis of treaty regimes follows a similar pattern. Science offers a rationale that a new treaty regime is necessary and facilitates compromise in the negotiations.

A prime example is the Antarctic Treaty, concluded during the International Geophysical Year in 1957, symbolising the height of international cooperation in Antarctica.[27] The Antarctic Treaty was the first treaty for a global commons area.[28] Negotiations had been initiated upon the invitation of the US to 12 interested states.[29] The main motivation was to harness the benefits of 'scientific knowledge

[22] O Wendell Holmes, 'Law in Science and Science in Law' (1898–1899) 12 *Harvard Law Review* 443, 462.

[23] D'Amato (n 15) 378 speaks of first-level, second-level and third-level rules.

[24] W Lang, 'UN-Principles and International Environmental Law' (1999) 3 *Max Planck Yearbook of United Nations Law* 157, 159; P-M Dupuy and JE Viñuales, *International Environmental Law*, 2nd edn (Cambridge: Cambridge University Press, 2018) 96, 98.

[25] R Wolfrum, 'Common Heritage of Mankind' in *Max Planck Encyclopedia of Public International Law* (November 2009), para 9, https://opil.ouplaw.com/display/10.1093/law:epil/9780199231690/law-9780199231690-e1149.

[26] R Wolfrum, 'The Principle of the Common Heritage of Mankind' (1983) 43 *Zeitschrift für ausländisches öffentliches Recht und Völkerrecht* 312; F Biermann, '"Common Concern of Humankind": The Emergence of a New Concept of International Environmental Law' in O Kimminich et al (eds) (1996) 34 *Archiv des Völkerrechts* 426.

[27] Antarctic Treaty (adopted 1 December 1959, entered into force 23 June 1961) 402 UNTS 71; J Hanessian, PW Frazier and AF Neidle, 'Antarctica: Current National Interests and Legal Realities' (1958) 52 *Proceedings of the American Society of International Law* 145.

[28] Wolfrum, *Die Internationalisierung Staatsfreier Räume* (n 6) 23.

[29] These were Argentina, Australia, Belgium, Chile, the French Republic, Japan, New Zealand, Norway, South Africa, the UK, the US and the USSR: Final Act, 10, Compilation of Key Documents of the Antarctic Treaty System Third edition (2017).

resulting from international cooperation in scientific investigation', with a view to coordinating existing efforts.[30] With two countries asserting that their activities had established a basis for a claim to sovereignty,[31] the future avoidance of geopolitical tensions and military competition was equally high on the agenda.[32] The Antarctic Treaty designates Antarctica as a 'natural reserve devoted to peace and science'.[33] Even though the objective articulates the importance of scientific capacity building and sharing of results, the treaty does not define 'scientific knowledge' or 'scientific investigation'; it assumes a clarity for which no legal assurance is given.

Disagreement about the role of science, not the definition of science, dominated the treaty-making for Outer Space. In Outer Space, scientific exploration was first pursued in the early 1960s and based on memoranda of understandings. Negotiations on the Outer Space Treaty were initiated through two main drafts, submitted by the US and the then Soviet Union, respectively.[34] Including reference to science was a point of contention.[35] The negotiations point to different views on the functional role and the relevant objects for scientific study, revealing concerns for varying degrees of future capacity to conduct scientific investigations and the willingness to share results.[36]

The proposal of the US, submitted to the General Assembly's Committee on the Peaceful Uses of Outer Space, established a treaty outline with 12 key points.[37] Scientific investigation was a priority.[38]

However, the Soviet Union at that time submitted an alternative draft with significantly less emphasis on the role of science.[39] The Preamble to that draft referred to the desire to 'contribute to broad international co-operation in the scientific as well as the legal aspects of the exploration and use of outer space for peaceful purposes'.[40] The proposed Article I expressed that the 'exploration and use

[30] Antarctic Treaty (n 27), Preamble, Final Act, 21; Hanessian, Frazier and Neidle (n 27) 147.

[31] WR Mansfield, 'Who Has the Right of Exploitation, and the Right to Prevent Exploitation, of the Minerals in Antarctica?' (1985) 79 *Proceedings of the Annual Meeting (American Society of International Law)* 58, 59.

[32] ibid.

[33] Article 2 of the Antarctic Treaty (n 27); see also the Final Act of the Eleventh Antarctic Treaty Special Consultative Meeting, <https://documents.ats.aq/atcm40/ww/ATCM40_ww014_e.pdf> accessed at 10 August 2024, at 31.

[34] 'Memorandum of Understanding between the Italian Space Commission of the National Council of Research and the United States National Aeronautics and Space Administration' and 'Outer Space Cooperation: Space Science Research Program' (1962) 13 UST 2120, 2121.

[35] Treaty on Principles Governing the Activities of States in the Exploration and Use of Outer Space, including the Moon and Other Celestial Bodies (Outer Space Treaty) (adopted 19 December 1966, entered into force on 10 October 1967) 610 UNTS 205, UNGA 2222 (XXI). For the history, see HG Darwin, 'The Outer Space Treaty' (1967) 42 *British Yearbook of International Law* 278, 279.

[36] Circulated as UN Docs A/AC.105/32 (US) and A/6352, both 16 June 1966; Darwin (n 35) 283.

[37] Draft Treaty Governing the Exploration of the Moon and Other Celestial Bodies, A/AC.105/32, 17 June 1966, 1–2.

[38] 'There should be *freedom of scientific investigation, and all countries should co-operate in scientific activities* relating to celestial bodies' (emphasis added).

[39] UN Doc A/6352 (n 36).

[40] ibid 2.

of outer space shall be the province of all mankind', providing for free exploration of outer space, the moon and other celestial bodies, without qualifying that this exploration should serve scientific purposes.[41] Similarly, the obligation of cooperation was reduced to the request that in the exploration and use of Outer Space, parties 'shall be guided by the principle of cooperation'.[42]

The final version of the Outer Space Treaty was adopted by the UN General Assembly in 1966, with a compromise that significantly weakened the link between the freedom of exploration and scientific purposes.[43] Only the preamble maintains the objectives to contribute to international cooperation in the scientific as well as the legal aspects of the exploration and use of outer space for peaceful purposes. This had been an important factor for the US in starting the negotiations, in anticipation of the 'substantial contributions of scientific knowledge which will flow from international cooperation in the scientific investigation of celestial bodies'.[44]

A few years later, the Agreement Governing the Activities of States on the Moon and Other Celestial Bodies (hereinafter 'Moon Treaty') ushered in not only the common heritage principle[45] but also brought back a slightly stronger focus on the role of science in building a regulatory regime.[46] The Moon Treaty returned to the language on scientific purposes of investigation in stressing that 'there shall be freedom of scientific investigation on the moon' for all states parties.[47] Article 7 mandates reporting obligations for states parties that have a special scientific interest concerning areas of the moon.[48]

Further sub-treaty legal developments through the UN Committee on the Peaceful Uses of Outer Space (COPUOS)[49] and the UN Office for Outer Space Affairs[50] have shaped the terminology about science, but have not clarified the criteria to identify the relevant science that underpins the treaties' goals. The General Assembly, on the occasion of the fiftieth anniversary of the first United Nations (UN) Conference on the Exploration and Peaceful Uses for Outer Space, ushered in the phrase of 'Space as a Driver of Sustainable Development'.[51] The 'Space2030' agenda, adopted in October 2021, frequently references the term 'space science' and envisions space science as a driver of sustainable development in the four overarching objectives.[52]

[41] ibid Art II.
[42] ibid Art VIII.
[43] UN GA Resolution 2222 (XXI).
[44] UN Doc A/AC.105/32 (n 37) 4, Preamble.
[45] Agreement Governing the Activities of States on the Moon and Other Celestial Bodies (adopted on 5 December 1979, entered into force 11 July 1984) 1362 UNTS 3, Art. 11(1).
[46] ibid Art 6; Art 7(3); Art 11(6).
[47] ibid Art 5(1).
[48] ibid Art 7(3).
[49] The Committee was established in 1959 to govern the exploration and the use of space for the benefit of all humanity: peace, security and development, the United Nations Office for Outer Space Affairs <https://www.unoosa.org/oosa/index.html> accessed 13 August 2025.
[50] ibid.
[51] UN Doc A/RES/73/6.
[52] UN Doc A/RES/76/3, Overarching objective 4, para 4.10.

A clearer description of the purpose of scientific research is provided by the UN Convention on the Law of the Sea (UNCLOS), concluded in 1982.[53] UNCLOS guarantees the freedom of scientific research as one of the six freedoms of the high seas[54] and it requests that the research must serve the conservation of living resources.[55] In particular, this applies to the sharing of scientific information, catch and fishing effort statistics.[56]

An elaborate role is assigned to science in the area of the protection of the atmosphere, addressed primarily through the International Climate Change Regime and the Ozone Regime.[57] The goal to protect the atmosphere was formed, on the basis of scientific evidence,[58] when the UN General Assembly noted in Resolution 43/53 of 6 December 1988 that 'climate change is a common concern of [human]kind'.[59] The General Assembly acknowledged that there was emerging evidence that continued growth in atmospheric concentrations of greenhouse gases could produce global warming and eventually lead to sea level rise, with disastrous consequences for humanity.[60] At the same time, the World Meteorological Organisation (WMO) and the UN Environment Programme (UNEP) established the Intergovernmental Panel on Climate Change (IPCC) to provide 'internationally coordinated scientific assessments of the magnitude, timing and potential environmental and socio-economic impact of climate change realistic response strategies'.[61]

The corroboration of scientific evidence around the causes and the effects of climate change led to the adoption of the UN Framework Convention on Climate Change (UNFCCC) in 1992[62] and the Kyoto Protocol in 1997,[63] followed by

[53] United Nations Convention on the Law of the Sea (adopted 10 December 1982, entered into force 1 November 1994) 1833 UNTS 397.

[54] ibid Art 87(1)(f). Article 87(2) provides that these freedoms shall be exercised with due regard for the interests of other states and with due regard for the rights under this Convention with respect to activities in the Area.

[55] ibid Art 119.

[56] ibid Art 119(2).

[57] AE Boyle, 'International law and the Protection of the global Atmosphere: Concepts, Categories and Principles' in R Churchill and D Freestone (eds), *International Law and Global Climate Change* (The Hague: Martinus Nijhoff, 1991) 7–19.

[58] The Resolution specifically mentions 'that the emerging evidence indicates that continued growth in atmospheric concentrations of "greenhouse" gases could produce global warming with an eventual rise in sea levels, the effects of which could be disastrous for [human]kind if timely steps are not taken at all levels'.

[59] UN Doc GA Resolution 43/53 Protection of global climate for present and future generations of [human]kind of 6 December 1988.

[60] ibid.

[61] ibid.

[62] The UN Conference on the Environment and Development was convened in light of the global character of environmental problems, including the desire of states to protect the atmosphere by combating climate change: UN GA 44/228 United Nations Conference on Environment and Development, 22 December 1989. United Nations Framework Convention on Climate Change (adopted 29 May 1992, entered into force 21 March 1994) 1771 UNTS 107.

[63] Kyoto Protocol to the UNFCCC (adopted 11 December 1997, entered into force 16 February 2005) 2303 UNTS 162.

the Paris Agreement in 2015.[64] The UN International Law Commission (UN ILC)[65] included work on draft guidelines on the protection of the atmosphere in its work programme in 2013.[66] It adopted a set of draft guidelines on the protection of the atmosphere in 2021.[67] In deciding about the ILC's foray into new areas of international law, some states had raised concerns in respect of the feasibility of the topic owing to its highly technical – that is, scientific – issues.[68] Nevertheless, the ILC decided early on in the process that it was necessary to formulate an appropriate 'legal definition that reasonably corresponds to the scientific definition'.[69]

The work of the ILC provides an interesting case study to illustrate the extent to which science advanced the Commission's work in respect of the codification of international law. The tasks to define the term 'atmosphere' and to establish what constitutes 'pollution' and 'degradation' challenged the ILC's legal imagination. The Commission also faced a legal vacuum since existing international legal instruments provided no explanation for these critical terms and it decided to fill this gap by developing a definition that was consistent with 'the approach of scientists'.[70] It acknowledged that scientists define the atmosphere as the envelop of gases surrounding Earth, extending upwards from the Earth's surface, divided vertically into four spheres,[71] distinguished based on temperature characteristics.[72] The Special Rapporteur suggested in the first report that the definition would need to address both the substantive (that is, the scientific aspect of the atmosphere) and the functional dimension as a medium for transport.[73] The

[64] Paris Agreement (adopted 12 December 2015, entered into force 4 November 2016) 3156 UNTS 79.

[65] The International Law Commission was established in 1947 by the General Assembly. It has the mandate under Art 13(1)(a) of the Charter of the United Nations to 'initiate studies and make recommendations for the purpose of … encouraging the progressive development of international law and its codification'. See https://legal.un.org/ilc.

[66] The original proposal of the US for the treaty, submitted to the Committee on the Peaceful Uses of Outer Space of the General Assembly, established an outline for the treaty with 12 key points.

[67] Draft guidelines on the protection of the atmosphere, with commentaries thereto, 2021. Adopted by the International Law Commission at its Seventy-Second Session, in 2021, and submitted to the General Assembly as a part of the Commission's report covering the work of that session (A/76/10). The report, which also contains commentaries to the draft guidelines (para 40), will appear in *Yearbook of the International Law Commission, 2021*, vol II, pt II, https://legal.un.org/ilc/publications/yearbooks/2020_2029.shtml.

[68] Official Records of the General Assembly, Sixty-Sixth Session, Sixth Committee, 20th meeting (A/C.6/66/SR.20), para 48 (France). A similar concern was expressed by the Netherlands, which stated that the 'question of protection of the atmosphere seemed more suited for discussion among specialists' (Official Records of the General Assembly, Sixty-Sixth Session, Sixth Committee, 28th meeting (A/C.6/66/SR.28), para 64.

[69] First Report on the Protection of the Atmosphere, UN Doc A/CN.4/667, para 69.

[70] UN ILC Draft Guidelines (n 67) Guideline 1, Commentary, para 3.

[71] See JM Wallace and PV Hobbs, *Atmospheric Science: An Introductory Survey* (Boston: Elsevier Academic Press, 2006) 10. The American Meteorological Society defines the lower and the upper atmosphere, at http://glossary.ametsoc.org/wiki/Lower_atmosphere and http://glossary.ametsoc.org/wiki/Upper_atmosphere.

[72] Wallace and Hobbs (n 71) (ie, the troposphere, stratosphere, mesosphere and thermosphere).

[73] ibid para 70.

final guidelines follow the scientific definition of the IPCC exclusively and simply define atmosphere as the 'envelope of gases surrounding the Earth',[74] reducing the consideration of the atmosphere's functions to an explanatory note in the commentary.[75]

However, the approach of the ILC towards science appears selective. The Commission was less inclined to take science on board in respect of the differentiation between pollution and degradation. It preferred to eliminate from the term 'atmospheric pollution' global issues such as ozone depletion and climate change,[76] and covered these within the meaning of 'atmospheric degradation',[77] thereby accepting that the operation of established principles such as the 'polluter pays' and the 'no harm rule' in the context of degradation would be less certain if not excluded. It is also interesting that, in attempting a definition, no reference was made to the relevant IPCC reports, but to the 1985 Vienna Convention for the Protection of the Ozone Layer[78] and the UNFCCC, respectively. Yet these two treaties shed no light on the meaning of atmospheric degradation or pollution; indeed, these terms are not even mentioned. Equally, an elaboration of the UNFCCC terminology on 'adverse effects', and how it relates to the differentiation between degradation and pollution, is missing.

If treaties set out to incorporate science starting with the goal formation, the expectation is that a consistent and continuous integration of evidence will be ensured and safeguarded by treaty-based mechanisms. In the absence of such mechanisms, systemic consideration of latest or best available scientific evidence remains illusory. For example, the UNFCCC does not have the objective to stop climate change altogether, but to stabilise greenhouse gas concentrations 'at a level that would prevent dangerous anthropogenic (human induced) interference with the climate system'.[79] The meaning of 'dangerous' is open to further clarification and, as our understanding of climate change evolves, the threshold of what counts as 'dangerous' and as an 'interference' changes. Latest scientific analysis shows that the reliance on sinks to achieve a 'net' balance between emissions and sequestration in the global carbon cycle may be ill-founded.[80] This progression in scientific understanding is not reflected in the legal perception of what constitutes a 'dangerous interference'. Notwithstanding these challenges, the UNFCCC envisages a

[74] UN ILC Draft Guidelines (n 67) Guideline 1, Use of Terms, (a).

[75] ibid Preamble, Commentary, para 2.

[76] ibid para 6.

[77] ibid para 12.

[78] Vienna Convention for the Protection of the Ozone Layer (adopted on 22 March 1985, entered into force 22 September 1988) 1513 UNTS 26164.

[79] UNFCCC (n 62) Art 2.

[80] M O'Sullivan et al, 'Process-Oriented Analysis of Dominant Sources of Uncertainty in the Land Carbon Sink' (2022) 13 *Nature Communications* 4781, 1, 3, https://doi.org/10.1038/s41467-022-32416-8. See also the latest study that reveals the shrinking capacity of carbon sinks: P Ke et al, 'Low Latency Carbon Budget Analysis Reveals a Large Decline of the Land Carbon Sink in 2023' (2024), <https://arxiv.org/pdf/2407.12447v1> accessed 13 August 2025.

timeline for balancing the global carbon cycle which can only be achieved with a direct and continuous engagement with the latest science.[81]

The Paris Agreement demonstrates that in line with solidifying science, a temperature threshold for the protection of the atmosphere became agreeable as a long-term goal in the 2015 Paris Agreement. The target emerged from an early EU proposal,[82] even before the IPCC in its Fourth Assessment Report of 2007 stated that climate change was unequivocal and anthropogenic, and that it had significant adverse effects.[83] A temperature rise of 2°C above pre-industrial temperature levels was identified as a threshold that would avoid the worst impacts of climate change.[84] While many other issues remained in respect of the legal architecture of the new Agreement, contributing to the deeply discordant political context for the negotiations,[85] a strong consensus on the scientific evidence meant that this temperature limitation turned into the indisputable long-term goal.[86] At the same time, while the Paris Agreement establishes a regular review and stock taking of collective progress towards the long-term goal, it lacks a specific legal mechanism that could safeguard the goal's adjustment in line with the evaluation and quantification of climate risks.

2. Science and Treaty Membership

The capacity to undertake scientific research has been employed as a prerequisite for treaty membership, to strengthen existing collaborations between certain states. The Antarctic Treaty furnishes an illustrative example, where scientific research is a necessary condition for membership.[87] The treaty was signed in 1959 by 12 countries[88] whose scientists had been active in and around Antarctica.[89] These founding parties participate in the Antarctic Consultative Meetings (ATCMs),

[81] Article 2 UNFCCC (n 62) sets the objective to 'allow ecosystems to adapt naturally to climate change, to ensure that food production is not threatened, and to enable economic development to proceed in a sustainable manner'.

[82] EU Council of Ministers, Community Strategy on Climate Change – Council Conclusions, 25 June 1996, Luxembourg; see further Yun Gao, Xiang Gao and Xiaohua Zhang, 'The 2°C Global Temperature Target and the Evolution of the Long-Term Goal of Addressing Climate Change: From the United Nations Framework Convention on Climate Change to the Paris Agreement' (2017) 3 *Engineering* 272, 274.

[83] IPCC, *Climate Change 2007: Synthesis Report. A Contribution of Working Groups I, II, and III to the Fourth Assessment Report of the Intergovernmental Panel on Climate Change* (Cambridge: Cambridge University Press, 2007) 30.

[84] JI Allen et al, 'Making the Paris Agreement: Historical Processes and the Drivers of Institutional Design' (2023) 71(3) *Political Studies* 914, 923.

[85] L Rajamani, 'The 2015 Paris Agreement: Interplay between Hard, Soft and Non-obligations' (2016) 28 *Journal of Environmental Law* 337, 338.

[86] Gao, Gao and Zhang (n 82) 278.

[87] Antarctic Treaty (n 27).

[88] The governments of Argentina, Australia, Belgium, Chile, the French Republic, Japan, New Zealand, Norway, the Union of South Africa, the Union of Soviet Socialist Republics, the United Kingdom of Great Britain and Northern Ireland, and the United States of America.

[89] Secretariat of the Antarctic Treaty <https://www.ats.aq/index_e.html> accessed 3 September 2025.

according to Article IX of the Treaty. Since 1959, 45 countries have acceded to the treaty, and they have the right to participate in the ATCMs insofar as they can demonstrate an interest in Antarctica by 'conducting substantial research activity'.[90] Only 19 parties have had their activities recognised, and the remaining 28 have been invited to attend the meetings, but without a role in the decision making.[91]

Active membership, including rights in the ATCM's decision making, is reserved for countries that acceded to the Treaty under Article XIII, and exists only for the time during which they can demonstrate their scientific interest in Antarctica. The relevant interest can only be demonstrated by conducting substantial scientific research activity or expedition.[92] This is the only example of a treaty for the global commons that weaves in a science-based requirement for full membership.

Scientific research as a condition for membership to the Antarctic Treaty is not without its challenges, given the well-recognised difficulties in defining and applying legal criteria that succinctly identify research programmes and activities for the purposes of scientific research.[93] Nevertheless, the perceived objectivity and the authority of scientific knowledge are relied upon as a crucial resource to settle a political decision.

C. Sub-treaty Rule Making and Treaty Development

What role does science play in influencing sub-treaty rule making and, in particular, how does it support the implementation of principles that reflect the idea of balance in regimes across the global commons? How does the law ensure that science in this vertical perspective can support a more equitable distribution of the research benefits and the resources that are shared by all? The principle of common heritage of humankind first appeared in relation to the law of the sea,[94] and it is most prominently mentioned in Article 136 UNCLOS (it is also mentioned in the Preamble and other provisions – for example, Article 125 and provisions referring to Article 136). Article 136 UNCLOS refers to the Area, a zone established by UNCLOS, as the seabed and ocean floor and subsoil thereof, beyond the national jurisdiction of any state.[95] The rights in the resources of the

[90] For full ratification status, see https://treaties.un.org/pages/showDetails.aspx?objid=0800000280136dbc.

[91] Secretariat of the Antarctic Treaty, 'Saudi Arabia Accedes to the Antarctic Treaty' (17 July 2024) <https://www.ats.aq/devph/en/news/267> accessed 3 September 2025.

[92] Specifically, in Art IX(2) of the Antarctic Treaty (n 27).

[93] *Whaling in the Antarctic (Australia v Japan: New Zealand Intervening)*, Judgment [2014] ICJ Rep 226, 293, para. 227.

[94] United Nations, *A Quiet Revolution: The UN Convention on the Law of the Sea* (New York: UN Department of Public Information, 1984) 4; Zou Keyuan, 'The Common Heritage of Mankind and the Antarctic Treaty System' (1991) 38 *Netherlands International Law Review* 173, 174.

[95] UNCLOS (n 53) Art 1(1)(1).

area are vested in humankind as a whole and the International Seabed Authority is expected to represent and protect the interests of humankind – that is, it must administer the area and its resources accordingly,[96] such as polymetallic modules and polymetallic sulphides.[97]

1. Science and Treaty Development for the Benefit of Humankind in Relation to the Common Heritage Principle

UNCLOS stipulates that the seabed and the ocean floor and their resources are the common heritage of humankind.[98] No state shall claim or exercise sovereignty or sovereign rights, nor can these areas be subject of appropriation. The function of science in that regard is to protect the environment through 'best environmental practices' and to aid in the distribution of benefits derived from the exploitation of the deep seabed.

The General Assembly decided in December 2017 to convene an Intergovernmental Conference, under the auspices of the UN, to consider elements and to elaborate the text of a legally binding instrument under UNCLOS on the conservation and sustainable use of marine biological diversity of areas beyond national jurisdiction.[99] Specifically, the decision was to develop an implementing instrument that would address:

> [T]he conservation and sustainable use of marine biological diversity of areas beyond national jurisdiction, in particular, together and as a whole, marine genetic resources, including questions on the sharing of benefits, measures such as area-based management tools, including marine protected areas.[100]

This mandate underscores the close nexus between the sharing of benefits and the conservation of resources, and the objective role of science for both. A new treaty was adopted in June 2023 on the conservation and sustainable use of marine biological diversity of areas beyond national jurisdiction, in short, the UN Agreement on Biodiversity Beyond National Jurisdiction (BBNJ).[101] It outlines general principles and approaches, including the polluter-pays principle and the principle of the common heritage of humankind, in conjunction with an emphasis on the freedom of marine scientific research. To achieve the objectives of the Agreement, parties shall be guided by the 'use of best available science and

[96] ibid Art 136(1).
[97] ibid Art 1(1)(2), Arts 56–158.
[98] ibid Art 136(1), www.un.org/depts/los/convention_agreements/texts/unclos/unclos_e.pdf.
[99] UN Doc A/RES/72/249.
[100] ibid para 2.
[101] Agreement under the United Nations Convention on the Law of the Sea on the conservation and sustainable use of marine biological diversity of areas beyond national jurisdiction (BBNJ), A/CONF.232/2023/4*.

scientific information'.[102] The importance of 'best available science' is referenced throughout the operational provisions and prominently articulated in the context of project proposals,[103] monitoring of impacts,[104] emergency measures[105] and the environmental impact assessment.[106] For example, Article 19(3) demands that:

> Proposals shall be formulated on the basis of the best available science and scientific information and, where available, relevant traditional knowledge of Indigenous Peoples and local communities, taking into account the precautionary approach and an ecosystem approach.

Furthermore, in situations of natural or human-caused disasters that have caused or are likely to cause serious or irreversible harm to marine biological diversity, emergency measures shall be adopted by the Conference of the Parties, based on best available science.[107] Likewise, the Conference of the Parties is mandated to take decisions or recommendations on the implementation of area-based management tools, on the basis of the best available science.[108]

The process of environmental impact assessments (EIAs) provides a key area for the consideration of best available science. Parties undertaking scoping for the EIA are required to define the scope using best available science, including for the assessment of impacts.[109] Best available science must also be used for the monitoring of impacts once activities have been authorised.[110] Only certain qualified concerns can be raised, both within and after the EIA, and a party must provide the science that meets the criteria of best available science.[111] However, it is not specified how the validity of concerns will be assessed by the Scientific and Technical Body, other than that this will proceed based on the evidence provided by parties.[112] Parties have the right to register their views on the potential impacts of planned activities, based on the best available science and scientific information.[113]

The Antarctic Treaty also acknowledges that cooperation between parties must serve the interests of science and the progress of all humankind:

> Convinced that the establishment of a firm foundation for the continuation and development of such cooperation on the basis of freedom of scientific investigation

[102] ibid Art 7(i).
[103] ibid Art 19.
[104] ibid Arts 26, 35 and 37.
[105] ibid Art 24.
[106] ibid Arts 31 and 39.
[107] ibid Art 24(1)–(3).
[108] ibid Art 26(5).
[109] ibid Art 31(1)(c).
[110] ibid Art 35.
[111] ibid Art 31(1)(a)(ii).
[112] ibid Art 31(1)(a)(iv).
[113] ibid Art 31(1)(a)(ii).

in Antarctica as applied during the International Geophysical Year accords with the interests of science and the progress of all [human]kind.

Reference to the principle of common heritage was only introduced into the Antarctic Regime in 1991, when the Protocol on Environmental Protection (the so-called Madrid Protocol) to the Antarctic Treaty was signed.[114] This specific agreement on environmental protection was concluded to complement and strengthen the Antarctic Treaty' regime in the interest of humankind as a whole,[115] establishing the Committee for Environmental Protection with the function of applying and implementing EIA procedures.[116] It followed the failure of the Convention on the Regulation of Antarctic Mineral Resource Activities (CRAMRA).[117] The Madrid Protocol designates the Antarctic environment and the dependent and associated ecosystems as a natural reserve, devoted to peace and science.[118]

The Madrid Protocol establishes a clear mandate to only conduct activities covered by the Antarctic Treaty on the basis of information sufficient to allow prior assessments of, and informed judgements about, their possible impacts on the Antarctic environment and dependent and associate ecosystems and on the value of Antarctica for the conduct of scientific research.[119] The Protocol has six integral annexes[120] and prohibits any activities relating to mineral resources, other than scientific research. It points out that human activity, in the absence of scientific evidence that indicates the benefits of the respective undertakings, risks contradicting the interest of humankind. Activities must be planned so as to 'accord priority to scientific research and to preserve the value of Antarctica as an area for the conduct of such research'.[121]

In Outer Space, human activities unguarded by scientific evidence, and scientific exploration unrestricted by law, have already led to significant environmental challenges, not least due to the accumulation of space debris in the congested Earth orbit.[122] The Preamble to the Outer Space Treaty[123] refers to the common

[114] The Protocol on Environmental Protection to the Antarctic Treaty (Madrid Protocol) (adopted on 4 October 1991, entered into force on 14 January 1998) 2941 UNTS A-5778.

[115] ibid Preamble.

[116] The Committee for Environmental Protection is established under Art 11 of the Madrid Protocol, Committee for Environmental Protection, 25 Years of the Protocol on Environmental Protection to the Antarctic Treaty, Secretariat of the Antarctic Treaty, 2016, 12.

[117] ibid 7.

[118] ibid Art 2.

[119] ibid Art 3(2)(c).

[120] Annex I: Environmental Impact Assessment; Annex II: Conservation of Antarctic Fauna and Flora; Annex III: Waste Disposal and Waste Management; Annex IV: Prevention of Marine Pollution; Annex V: Management of Protected Areas; Annex VI: Liability for Environmental Emergencies.

[121] Madrid Protocol (n 114) Art 3(3).

[122] PJ Blount, 'Technically Speaking: UNCOPUOS and the Technical Governance of Space' (2023) 1 *Indian Review of Air and Space Law* 1, 24.

[123] Outer Space Treaty (n 35), for the history of the Treaty see Darwin (n 35).

interest of all humankind in the progress of the exploration and use of outer space for peaceful purposes.[124] In the operational part, Article 1(1) determines that:

> The exploration and use of outer space, including the moon and other celestial bodies, shall be carried out for the benefit and in the interests of all countries, irrespective of their degree of economic or scientific development, and shall be the province of all [humankind].

The Liability Convention, concluded in 1971, elaborates on the provision contained in Article 7 of the Outer Space Treaty[125] and re-affirms the role of the common interest of all humankind in furthering the exploration of Outer Space.[126] Science in the Outer Space Treaty is incorporated primarily to ensure that a country's progress in scientific development is without prejudice to its space activities.[127] The distributive function of the common heritage principle is reaffirmed in the Moon Agreement.[128] Article 11 assigns the moon and its natural resources the quality of resources of the common heritage of humankind, 'which finds its expression in the provisions of this Agreement, in particular in paragraph 5 of this article'.[129] Parties are required to inform the scientific community of any natural resources they may discover,[130] yet like the notion of scientific research, the term 'scientific community' lacks a definition.

Science in these regimes promises to provide an objective benchmark for the managing of resources, in the interest of the common heritage principle. The law places trust in the scientific assurance, but abstains from establishing criteria for the notion of science itself, thereby leaving considerable uncertainty for the management of the shared resources and the distribution of benefits, including those from scientific exploration, in the interests of humankind.

2. Science in the Management of a Common Concern

The UNFCCC and the Paris Agreement abstain from mentioning the common heritage principle and retain the language of 'common concern of humankind'

[124] ibid Outer Space Treaty, second preambular.

[125] Convention on the International Liability for Damage Caused by Space Objects (adopted 29 March 1992, entered into force 1 September 1972) 961 UNTS 187, UN GA 2777 (XXVI), www.unoosa.org/oosa/en/ourwork/spacelaw/treaties/liability-convention.html.

[126] ibid Preamble.

[127] ibid Art I(1).

[128] Moon Agreement (n 45).

[129] ibid Art 11(1).

[130] This comes with the limitation that such information is only required 'to the greatest extent feasible and practicable': ibid Art 11(6).

and the pivoting role of science in addressing this concern,[131] referencing intergenerational equity by emphasising that the climate system's protection is for the 'benefit of present and future generations of humankind'.[132]

The UNFCCC uses the phrase 'best available' in relation to science in two places. Article 4(2)(c) provides that calculations of emissions by sources and removals by sinks should take the best available scientific knowledge into account. The second mention is in respect of the Conference of Parties (COP) to review the adequacy of national policies and corresponding measures on the mitigation of climate change (Article 4(2)(b) and (c)). 'Best available' implies that science is qualitatively distinguishable, and that quality and availability may be a constraint. Both quality and availability are also temporally diffuse: data may become more widely available, and better data may be generated in the future. There is an inherent acknowledgement that science reflects a status quo of research and that availability of scientific data is variable.

The 2015 Paris Agreement reiterates that climate change is a common concern of humankind.[133] It expands on the terminology of the UNFCCC through notions such as 'best available scientific knowledge'[134] or 'best available science' in addressing climate change,[135] and it underscores the evolutive nature with reference to the 'strengthening scientific knowledge' on the climate.[136] Collective progress through the global stocktake is measured through a central, facilitative mechanism 'in light of equity and the best available science'.[137]

Endorsing a scientifically supported temperature threshold of limiting global warming to 'well below 2°C' in the Paris Agreement, suggests that this reflects the best available science.[138] Yet since 2015, scientists have increasingly produced evidence that underpins limiting warming to no more than 1.5°C, that is, the lower benchmark of the temperature range of Article 2(1)(a), with the latest research pointing out that even 1°C would be too high for fragile ice sheets, with severe implications for inevitable sea-level rise.[139]

Despite the Paris Agreement's articulated intent to remain aligned with, or at least consider, the best scientific evidence, it still remains to be seen if the continuation of the periodic review (as agreed at COP29) and the Global Stocktake can provide the necessary legal processes that ensure a timely response to the evolution of science. Decisions taken during the yearly COPs have shown since the 26th Conference of Parties (COP26), an increasing awareness of states

[131] ibid.
[132] UNFCCC (n 62) Art 3(1).
[133] Paris Agreement (n 64) Preamble.
[134] ibid.
[135] ibid Art 4(1); Art 7(5).
[136] ibid Art 7(7)(c).
[137] ibid Art 14(1); Decision 19/CMA.1, paras 1, 2, FCCC/PA/CMA/2018/3/Add. 2.
[138] Gao, Gao and Zhang (n 82) 278.
[139] CR Stokes et al, 'On the Reconstruction of Palaeo-Ice Sheets: Recent Advances and Future Challenges' (2015) 125 *Quaternary Science Reviews* 15.

that 1.5°C should indeed be the yardstick for their actions.[140] In particular, the outcome of the Global Stocktake as the central and collective oversight mechanism underpins the international agreement that 'impacts of climate change will be much lower at the temperature increase of 1.5°C compared with 2°C' and that parties will resolve 'to pursue efforts to limit the temperature increase to 1.5°C'.[141] While this emerging focus on the scientific necessity to maintain the lower threshold of the Paris Agreement is well documented in parties' decisions that, arguably, constitute subsequent agreements of the parties on the interpretation of the treaty,[142] these are not regularly afforded the interpretative and legal force that they deserve in international law making.[143] The legal reality of the Paris Agreement thus spells out the desire of parties to observe best available science, but it does not provide coherent criteria for it, leaving courts to determine the explanatory and interpretative value of COP Decisions.[144] The result is that science is at risk to remain an insufficiently integrated transplant from a different knowledge system, with an objectivity promise that is assumed but not assured.

The Paris Agreement Rulebook, adopted as a set of decisions by parties in 2018,[145] is the only legally relevant text among the four regimes of the global commons that makes an attempt to define the meaning of the term 'best available science'. Decision 19/CMA.1 provides that the output of the components of the global stocktake should summarise opportunities and challenges for enhancing action and support in light of equity and the best available science,[146] and that this science should be derived from a dialogue between IPCC experts and parties to enable a 'focused scientific and technical exchange of information on the findings of the IPCC'.[147]

[140] Glasgow Climate Pact, Decision 1/CP.26 paras 15–17; Sharm El-Sheikh Implementation Plan, Decision 1/CP.27, paras 4, 11.

[141] Outcome of the First Global Stocktake, FCCC/PA/CMA/2023/16/Add.1, Decision 1/CMA.5 para 4.

[142] Minnerop (n 12).

[143] J Brunnée, 'COPing with Consent: Law-Making under Multilateral Environmental Agreements' (2002) 15 *Leiden Journal of International Law* 1, 21; Minnerop (n 12) 116.

[144] For example, the German Federal Constitutional Court acknowledged that modelling a national carbon budget to 'well below 2°C' may be regarded as politically too unambitious but not unlawful in light of the evidence and paras 162, 163 of the Paris Agreement. For the interpretative value of these COP Decisions, see VerfG, Order of the First Senate of the Court (Beschluss des Ersten Senats), 24 March 2021, 1 BvR 2656/18, published on 29 April 2021. The full German version is available at www.bundesverfassungsgericht.de/SharedDocs/Entscheidungen/DE/2021/03/rs20210324_1bvr265618.html; a shorter English version is available at www.bundesverfassungsgericht.de/e/rs20210324_1bvr265618en.html.

[145] FCCC/PA/CMA/2018/3/Add.1 and FCCC/PA/CMA/2018/3/Add.2.

[146] FCCC/PA/CMA/2018/3/Add.2, Decision 19/CMA.1, paras 13, 27.

[147] ibid para 29.

The Montreal Protocol on Substances that Deplete the Ozone Layer,[148] adopted under the Vienna Convention for the Protection of the Ozone Layer,[149] complements the legal framework on the atmosphere by providing specifically for the reduction and consumption of controlled ozone-depleting substances.[150] Since the adoption of the Kigali Amendment, the Protocol also covers the phase-down of hydrofluorocarbons (HFCs) that were originally not included, but were used to replace ozone-depleting substances, only to be found to possess strong radiative forcing properties and thereby threatening to offset efforts under the UNFCCC.[151] In a unique manner, the Montreal Protocol lays down a procedure for an assessment and review mechanism of control measures on the basis of new and emerging scientific information, including a concrete legal process through which adjustments to the list of measures and substances can be agreed.[152]

D. Treaty Implementation

International adjudication suggests that although disputed in courts and often inadequately reflected in the judicial assessment,[153] the scientific nature of a dispute can nevertheless lead to clarification in respect of the legal standards for treaty implementation, especially in respect of due diligence, and it can be employed to instruct states to extend their cooperation in the field of science.[154] Scientific fact-finding thereby, qualifies and directs international collaboration, be it to implement a judicial decision or to find an extra-judicial solution, predicated on the objectivity promise of a scientific consensus.[155]

[148] Montreal Protocol on Substances that Deplete the Ozone Layer, Montreal (adopted 16 September 1987, entered into force on 1 January 1989) 1522 UNTS I-26369, 3.

[149] Vienna Convention on the Protection of the Ozone Layer (n 78).

[150] The Kigali Amendment (2016): The amendment to the Montreal Protocol agreed by the Twenty-Eighth Meeting of the Parties (Kigali, 10–15 October 2016), 3287 UNTS A-26369.

[151] See https://ozone.unep.org/treaties/montreal-protocol/amendments/kigali-amendment-2016-amendment-montreal-protocol-agreed; P Minnerop, 'Climate Protection Agreements' *MPIL Encyclopaedia of Public International Law* (2018), para. 17, https://opil.ouplaw.com/display/10.1093/law-epil/9780199231690/law-9780199231690-e2207.

[152] See Art 2(9), Art 6 and Art 7.

[153] K Sulyok, *Science and Judicial Reasoning* (Cambridge: Cambridge University Press, 2021) 82, 83; A Riddell, 'Scientific Evidence in the International Court of Justice: Problems and Possibilities' (2009) 20 *Finnish Yearbook of International Law* 229.

[154] See, eg, *Gabcikovo-Nagymaros Project (Hungary/Slovakia)*, Judgment [1997] ICJ Rep 7, where the Court considered at para 140 that both parties 'should look afresh at the effects on the environment of the operation of the Gabcikovo power plant'. *Southern Bluefin Tuna (New Zealand v Japan; Australia v Japan)*, Provisional Measures, Order of 27 August 1999, ITLOS Reports 1999, 280, 298–300; see further the Joint Declaration of Vice-President Wolfrum and Judges Caminos, Marotta Rangel, Yankov, Anderson and Eiriksson (at 302), stressing the lack of cooperation at scientific and governmental levels.

[155] *Gabcikovo-Nagymaros Project* (n 154).

1. The Evolving Standards of Due Diligence and the Precautionary Approach

Using the 'best available science' at the point of treaty implementation is conceptually linked to the evolving standard of due diligence obligations. Due diligence is a variable concept[156] and is to be distinguished from the notion of due regard.[157] The ICJ posited in *Pulp Mills on the River Uruguay* that due diligence is 'an obligation which entails not only the adoption of appropriate rules and measures, but also a certain level of vigilance in their enforcement and the exercise of administrative control applicable to public and private operators, such as the monitoring of activities undertaken'.[158] At the same time, the ICJ has been criticised for not leveraging a 'golden opportunity' to demonstrate its ability to approach scientifically complex disputes in a state-of-the-art manner.[159]

While both concepts – that is, the best available science and the ensuing standard for due diligence – remain each indeterminate and under-defined, some clarity can be derived from their inter-dependence. The Seabed Disputes Chamber in *Responsibility and Obligations of States with Respect to Activities in the Area* acknowledged that measures 'considered sufficiently diligent at a certain moment may become not diligent enough in light, for instance, of new scientific or technological knowledge'.[160] The Seabed Disputes Chamber found that states have the obligation, among other things, to 'apply best environmental practices'.[161] These best practices are fundamentally shaped by evolving science. Thus, higher regulatory standards for 'best environmental practices' must correspond to the advancement in scientific knowledge.[162] Science is therefore defining what is an objectively reasonable practice and it limits the discretion of states who must consider 'objectively, the relevant options in a manner that is reasonable, relevant and conducive to the benefit of [human]kind as a whole'.[163] In a co-evolutive manner, best environmental practices shape the standard and limit the options that are reasonable.[164]

It may also be recalled that the Chamber found that the applicable regulations for the Area (in respect of nodules and sulphides) turned the precautionary

[156] *Responsibilities and Obligations of States with Respect to Activities in the Area*, Advisory Opinion, 1 February 2011, ITLOS Reports 2011, 10, at para 117.

[157] C Foster, 'Due Regard for Future Generations? The No Harm Rule and Sovereignty in the Advisory Opinions on Climate Change' (2024) 13 *Transnational Environmental Law* 588, 599.

[158] *Pulp Mills on the River Uruguay (Argentina v Uruguay)*, Judgment [2010] ICJ Rep 14, 79, para 197.

[159] *Pulp Mills on the River Uruguay, (Argentina v Uruguay)*, Dissenting Opinion, Judges Al-Khasawneh and Simma at para 28; Riddell (n 153) 231.

[160] ibid.

[161] *Responsibilities and Obligations of States with Respect to Activities in the Area* (n 156) paras 122, 133, 136.

[162] ibid para 136.

[163] ibid para 230.

[164] ibid.

approach into a binding obligation for states. In referencing Principle 15 of the 1992 Rio Declaration on Environment and Development,[165] the Chamber held that 'the provisions of the aforementioned Regulations transform this non-binding statement of the precautionary approach in the Rio Declaration into a binding obligation'.[166] This is an example that illustrates how law is capable of not only integrating a general mandate to observe the evolving nature of scientific evidence, but can even succeed in concretely reducing the risk that remaining scientific uncertainty is used to lower the due diligence standard, at least in respect of the specific activities or prospecting and exploring.[167] Such a result can only be achieved if the law provides a rule for uncertainty treatment, as was the case for the nodule regulations in the Area. There are other examples where treaty law exists that specifically oblige states to take preventive measures in the absence of conclusive causal relationships between the 'inputs and the effects'.[168]

2. Science as a Horizontally Integrating Functional Unit

As science evolves and especially where it is endorsed by states within the mechanisms of international law making, ie, through IPCC reports that are mandated and approved by states, the relevant science obtains an additional function as a horizontally integrating functional unit. The Advisory Opinion of the International Tribunal for the Law of the Sea (ITLOS) on climate change provides an illustrative example. The Tribunal devoted an entire section to 'scientific aspects' and engaged in detail with the reports of the IPCC in the context of UNCLOS.[169] It recognised that 'best available science informs that anthropogenic GHG emissions pose a high risk in terms of foreseeability and severity of harm to the marine environment'.[170] The Tribunal signalled an acute awareness of the

[165] In order to protect the environment, the precautionary approach shall be widely applied by states according to their capabilities. Where there are threats of serious or irreversible damage, lack of full scientific certainty shall not be used as a reason for postponing cost-effective measures to prevent environmental degradation.

[166] *Responsibilities and Obligations of States with Respect to Activities in the Area* (n 156) para 127.

[167] ibid para 130.

[168] See, eg, Convention for the protection of the marine environment of the North-East Atlantic, 2354 UNTS 67, Art 2(1)(a): 'the precautionary principle, by virtue of which preventive measures are to be taken when there are reasonable grounds for concern that substances or energy introduced, directly or indirectly, into the marine environment may bring about hazards to human health, harm living resources and marine ecosystems, damage amenities or interfere with other legitimate uses of the sea, even when there is no conclusive evidence of a causal relationship between the inputs and the effects'.

[169] *Request for an Advisory Opinion Submitted by the Commission of Small Island States on Climate Change and International Law*, 21 May 2024, https://itlos.org/fileadmin/itlos/documents/cases/31/Advisory_Opinion/C31_Adv_Op_21.05.2024_corr.pdf, II. A.

[170] ibid paras 62, 241.

latest scientific evidence that underpins the lower temperature threshold of the Paris Agreement when it stated that:

> There is also broad agreement within the scientific community that if global temperature increases exceed 1.5°C, severe consequences for the marine environment would ensue. In light of such information, the Tribunal considers that the standard of due diligence States must exercise in relation to marine pollution from anthropogenic GHG emissions needs to be stringent.[171]

The Tribunal based its findings on two crucial elements: first, it referenced 'best available science'; and, second, it measured the broad agreement among scientists with the notion of 'scientific community. ITLOS articulated concrete requirements for a state to put in place in fulfilling the due diligence obligations under Article 194 UNCLOS, 'including legislation, administrative procedures and an enforcement mechanism necessary to regulate the activities in question, and to exercise adequate vigilance to make such a system function efficiently'.[172] While these measures are obligations of conduct, the Tribunal added a clear objective to deliver the result 'to make such a system function efficiently, with a view to achieving the intended objective'.[173]

The applicable standard of due diligence is therefore not discretionary, but must be determined objectively, and science helps in defining the necessary standard which can be even more stringent when taking into account relevant factors, such as the 'nature of transboundary pollution'[174] in cases involving high risks of serious and irreversible harm to the marine environment from climate change impacts and ocean acidification[175] if the pollution could 'spread'.[176]

3. Science as a Qualifier for International Cooperation and Compromise

The implementation of international environmental law depends on the duty to cooperate;[177] it is indeed 'a fundamental principle in the prevention of pollution' and applies to the marine environment, but equally to general international law.[178] International cooperation in environmental matters implies an important shift in the general orientation of the international legal order because it ensures

[171] ibid para 241.
[172] ibid para 235.
[173] ibid para 238.
[174] ibid paras 257, 258, 279.
[175] ibid para 234, Answer to question (b), lit (c) at 151.
[176] ibid para 248.
[177] *MOX Plant (Ireland v United Kingdom)*, Order of 13 November 2001, ITLOS Reports 2001, p 89; Separate Opinion Wolfrum, ibid, at 134, 135.
[178] *MOX Plant*, ibid. (n 177) para 82.

that community interests are taken into account vis-a-vis individualistic state interests.[179]

Across international environmental law and the legal systems for the global commons, science qualifies the purpose of this international cooperation.[180] For example, the Antarctic Treaty specifies not only the goal of the treaty to advance scientific knowledge, but also provides that parties agree to exchange 'to the greatest extent feasible and practicable' relevant information on scientific programmes in Antarctica.[181] The pursuit of scientific research qualifies not only the cooperation between contracting parties, but also extends to the 'exchange on a regular basis, through competent international organizations, of available scientific information'.[182]

International adjudication suggests that regardless of how science is disputed in the courtroom, it nevertheless gives rise to the expectation that it may have a unifying and compromise inducing function in contentious cases. It is not unusual for international courts and tribunals to defer to the generation of additional scientific knowledge through international collaboration.[183] Faced with conflicting interpretations of scientific data, ITLOS has been reluctant to decide what constitutes 'best science' and instead hinted that improved scientific knowledge may induce agreement between Parties outside the court.[184] In the *Southern Bluefin Tuna* cases, the Arbitral Tribunal was confronted with contradicting interpretations of scientific data in respect of the disputed recovery of fish stocks.[185] It admitted that 'although [it] cannot conclusively assess the scientific evidence presented by the parties', the conservation measures should be taken as a matter of urgency.[186] Deciding on provisional measures, the Tribunal took recourse to the legal safety of a precautionary approach and ordered parties to resume negotiations with 'a view to reaching agreement on measures for the conservation and management of southern bluefin tuna'.[187] Similarly, ITLOS ordered in *Mox Plant* that Ireland and the UK should enter into consultations to exchange information and monitor the risks of the operation of the Mox Plant for the Irish Sea.[188] In the Advisory Opinion on climate change, ITLOS held that the

[179] Wolfrum (n 177); AN Craik, 'The Duty to Cooperate in International Environmental Law: Constraining State Discretion through Due Respect' (2019) 30(1) *Yearbook of International Environmental Law* 1, 22.

[180] The ICJ stressed that states have a 'duty to co-operate with the IWC and the Scientific Committee': *Whaling in the Antarctic* (n 93) 257, para 83.

[181] Antarctic Treaty (n 87) Art III(1)(a).

[182] *Request for Advisory Opinion Submitted by the Sub-Regional Fisheries Commission*, Advisory Opinion, 2 April 2015, ITLOS Reports 2015, 4, at 59 para 209(ii).

[183] ibid; *Gabcikovo-Nagymaros Project* (n 154).

[184] *Gabcikovo-Nagymaros Project* (n 154).

[185] *Southern Bluefin Tuna Cases (New Zealand v Japan; Australia v Japan)*, Reports of International Arbitral Awards, vol XXIII, 1–57. The decision was rendered by the Arbitral Tribunal constituted under Annex VII of the UNCLOS.

[186] *Southern Bluefin Tuna Cases* (n 185) para 80.

[187] ibid para 90.

[188] *MOX Plant* (n 177) 111.

duty to cooperate 'is given concrete form in a wide range of specific obligations of States Parties, which are central to countering marine pollution from anthropogenic GHG emissions at the global level'.[189]

In 2018, the ICJ awarded for the first time in its history compensation for environmental damage in *Certain Activities in the Border Area*. Confronted with two different approaches for the calculation of damages, the Court found that since both were used in international practice, neither of these were devoid of the calculation in the concrete case. However, given that these were not the only methods that could be applied, the Court found itself unable to choose between them or use either of them exclusively.[190]

4. Scientific Consensus and the Scientific Community

As has been discussed, the treaty regimes for the global commons assign specific functions to the best available science, without making an attempt to define how the relevant science should be qualitatively ascertained. This is equally true for the notions of 'scientific consensus' and 'scientific community', and states sharing a 'special scientific interest'.[191] There is neither an all-encompassing nor a treaty-specific agreement on the definition of scientific research or a scientific community, either internationally or nationally, that produces the relevant evidence to assist parties in implementing the treaties across the global commons. So far, the mechanisms of general international law determine which 'best available science' will be deemed reliable in international settings. This will be the validation of science through state consent, as is the case for the IPCC. The ITLOS Advisory Opinion is an illustrative example, it determines the legal standard of due diligence in light of the IPCC reports. Whether or not it is epistemically the only approach to identify best science by harking back to state consent, it appears to be a realistic option for the judiciary to secure the support of states upon which the acceptance of international jurisdiction hinges.

In the absence of scientific certainty, the continuation of good faith negotiations may be necessary and ordered by courts. Legal disputes turning on the consensus among scientists face well-documented challenges concerning the standard of review, judicial reasoning techniques and judicial engagement with scientific assessments and uncertainties.[192] Treaty language that requires concrete implementing measures for the conservation of shared fish stocks, based on the

[189] *Request for an Advisory Opinion* (n 169) para 297.

[190] *Certain Activities Carried out by Nicaragua in the Border Area (Costa Rica v Nicaragua)*, Compensation, Judgment [2018] ICJ Rep 15, para 52.

[191] The latter term is uniquely used in the Moon Treaty (n 45), Art 7(3).

[192] It has long been acknowledged that 'General scientific acceptance' in domestic law is not a criterion, or not the only one, for the admissibility of scientific evidence. See, S Brewer, 'Scientific Expert Testimony and Intellectual Due Process' (1998) 107 *Yale Law Journal* 1535, 1681.

'best scientific evidence' available, prepares the ground for contradicting scientific findings.[193]

The often-assumed scientific consensus may not exist, and the objectivity of science may be flawed for a number of reasons, yet the law does not provide criteria that would make it possible to distinguish between science, best science or best available science, or, indeed, the composition of the scientific community. For example, the Paris Agreement Rulebook refers to the 'scientific community',[194] and the role of scientists among other stakeholders,[195] even mentions universities.[196]

The ICJ in *Gabcikovo Nagymoros* identified 'some scientific circles',[197] but has historically found it challenging to determine 'which of those points of view' are scientifically better founded.[198] However, the Court has made important statements about how the legal and the scientific system are inter-related, providing some insights that could be used to procedurally strengthen legal criteria for incorporating science. The Court stated that the interference with the environment must consider 'new scientific insights and the growing awareness of the risks for [human]kind – for present and future generations … new norms and standards have been developed, set forth in a great number of instruments during the last two decades'.[199] It has also acknowledged that 'the state of scientific knowledge' is not static, but that it undergoes significant development.[200]

This view implies that 'best available' science is and must remain closely tied to the evolving nature of research, where best science is understood to include the most recent findings. However, it is possible that most recent science challenges an existing, solidified position. For example, at the time of the conclusion of the Paris Agreement, the temperature target of 'well below 2°C' had become undisputed. However, since then, science has developed and the IPCC Special Report on Global Warming, as well as AR6, indicate that 1.5°C is the threshold that would avert the worst impacts of climate change. This most recent science is not only no longer reflected at the level of treaty law.

E. Conclusion

Science has a functional equivalence for the treaty regimes of the global commons,[201] it promises objectivity and coherence. The knowledge system of

[193] *Advisory Opinion Submitted by the Sub-Regional Fisheries Commission* (n 182) para 208.
[194] FCCC/PA/CMA/2018/3/Add.2, Decision 15/CMA.1 para 20(d).
[195] ibid Decision 17/CMA.1 Preamble; para 10.
[196] ibid para 10.
[197] *Gabcikovo-Nagymaros Project* (n 154) para 31.
[198] ibid para 55.
[199] ibid para 140.
[200] ibid para 57.
[201] For the comparative function of the *tertium comparationis*, *cf* Michaels (n 4) 372.

science and the legal regimes that protect the global commons are co-evolving, and there are several points of intervention through which science influences the law. Yet this permeability of the law for science is not reciprocal, as the law remains reluctant to impose substantive criteria for selecting 'best available' science for legal purposes. Similarly, procedural avenues for scientific intervention in recursive legal processes and corresponding modes to assess legal concepts in relation to the progressive nature of scientific knowledge are absent from the legal systems of the global commons. Unless the legal regimes orchestrate their own continuous engagement with science and clarify criteria that redeem the objectivity promise, courts will face the challenge to decide whose science should prevail. Rules and processes are necessary to ensure that recourse is taken to what the law defines as best and latest scientific evidence. However, the law can be imagined collocating an orderly irritation of its autopoietic fabric through interpretation.

Autopoiesis indeed supports the argument that once a treaty regime has defined its goal on the basis of science, then continuity of the irritation placed within the legal system must be defined by legal norms, including those directing interpretation. Defining the relative social value through co-production between the legal and the science systems at the point of goal formation makes the law permanently dependent on subsequent production of expert evidence. Too often, the law is content with accepting an epistemic subsidiarity that undermines the objectivity and impartiality of the 'scientification' promise in sub-treaty rule making, treaty development and implementation. Recalibrating the role of the science of law for the sake of the science in law is a continued challenge for the law to master.

The IPCC reports provide illustrative examples of how legal authority for science intervention can be ascertained. It resonates from the analysis that IPCC reports, as scientific knowledge generated in accordance with international law's mechanisms (eg, involvement of states), provide extra-legal evidence that constitutes an emergent property for the autopoiesis of treaty regimes. In particular, the ITLOS Advisory Opinion on climate change underpins how legally assured science permeates the law beyond the scope of the specific treaty regime for which the specific evidence was originally intended. ITLOS seized an opportunity and reiterated the solidified scientific consensus in respect of the causes and impacts of climate change, both in relation to the atmosphere but also in relation to the marine environment. It found that greenhouse gas emissions released into the atmosphere and absorbed by the oceans are a form of marine pollution.[202]

This finding of the Tribunal cannot be under-estimated in its legal dimension, especially when compared with the approach of the UN ILC in the Draft Guidelines on the Protection of the Atmosphere. As has been discussed in this

[202] *Request for an Advisory Opinion* (n 169) para 179: 'Tribunal concludes that anthropogenic GHG emissions into the atmosphere constitute pollution of the marine environment within the meaning of article 1, paragraph 1, subparagraph 4, of the Convention.'

chapter, for the ILC, climate change was a matter of atmospheric degradation and accordingly, releasing greenhouse gas emissions did not qualify as atmospheric pollution. In light of the Advisory Opinion, this may now change; it is otherwise difficult to reconcile that oceans are polluted by absorbing greenhouse gas emissions when releasing these emissions into the atmosphere does not constitute a form of pollution. Therefore, the Advisory Opinion, in using *best available science as identified by law's own normative standards*, should spark further developments that transcend the law of the sea and affect legal concepts as they also apply to the protection of the atmosphere. The evolutionary nature of the best available science in this case has advanced the concept of pollution of the marine environment *and* of the atmosphere.

Notwithstanding this positive example and the many benefits of law's intersection with science, the comparative analysis in this chapter has demonstrated that reliance on science in treaty regimes without a normative framing, including for continuous interaction between law and science, can place treaty development and implementation on a fragile ground. The absence of criteria for scientific inputs can conceal political trade-offs, and limit the co-evolutive potential that depends on an interdisciplinary learning to capture what scientists 'really mean'. The law–science interaction cannot be static; instead, the law must evolve in accordance with the evolution of scientific evidence, through recursive legal processes. The best available scientific evidence can be superseded by even better knowledge. How to chart the road for best protection of the global commons is a normative question.

12

Quantitative International Comparisons

A Tale of Missed Encounters

MARTA INFANTINO

A. Introduction

In the last 50 years or so, the iterative production of quantitative comparative exercises (often called indicators) to describe and control social phenomena has spread globally as a new technology of governance. The emergence of indicators could (and perhaps should) have been of interest for international and comparative lawyers alike.[1] Yet it went almost unnoticed by experts of both disciplines. Similarly, the rise of global indicators has yet to attract the attention of recent studies on 'comparative international law', which have so far being exclusively focused on similarities and differences in the understanding and application of international law by different legal systems.[2] In order to understand this missed opportunity, and its research potential, this chapter takes as a case study one particular instance of the current indicatorisation turn – the production by international organisations of global legal indicators.[3] The choice of case study is justified by the fact that global legal indicators produced by international organisations offer the best case for exploring the grey area between international and comparative law, and for testing current limitations and prospective

[1] Speaking of 'international law' and 'comparative law' as monolithic disciplines is quite naive, considering the variety of sub-fields and approaches in both sectors. For the purposes of this chapter, and only for reasons of simplification, I would in general equate 'international law' as the body of law created through the interactions between states (and the study thereof), and 'comparative law' as the practice of performing qualitative comparison of two or more legal systems.

[2] See A Roberts et al (eds), *Comparative International Law* (Oxford: Oxford University Press, 2018) (in which indicators are never mentioned); and A Roberts, *Is International Law Really International?* (Oxford: Oxford University Press, 2017) (where the only reference to indicators concerns the reforms undertaken by Russia to modify the university system under the pressure of international university rankings: see ibid 95). Given the youth of global legal indicators, they obviously remained invisible to the earlier studies on comparative international law explored in ch 2.

[3] Global legal indicators may be tentatively defined as repeated exercises of quantitative comparisons focusing on the world's legal systems. For an attempt to provide a more precise definition, see sections B and C below.

trends for both disciplines (including recent research proposals about 'comparative international law'). As exercises of quantitative legal comparison carried out by international organisations, international organisations-made global legal indicators should in principle be relevant for international, comparative and comparative international lawyers. However, as the following pages will show, global legal indicators have remained largely ignored by such scholars. This chapter argues that this was due to global legal indicators involving regulatory actors and processes that are not included in the circle of the state-related items that are considered legally relevant in these fields. The chapter claims that mainstream views of international and comparative law, including current approaches to comparative international law, are trapped within intellectual boundaries that could be violated, and perhaps should be. As we will see, experts in both disciplines have much to learn from turning their attention to global legal indicators and calling into question the intellectual boundaries of their own fields.

To support this claim, the chapter will develop as follows. Sections B and C will respectively explain what global legal indicators are (section B) and provide a few illustrations of their successful realisation by selected international organisations (section C), namely, the World Bank and the United Nations (UN). Section D will note how legal scholars adhering to unconventional schools of thought (such as those revolving around the idea of global legal pluralism, transnational law and transnational legal orders) attempted to frame the development of global legal indicators. Against such a framework, section E will review the limited ways in which mainstream international and comparative lawyers, but also recent studies on comparative international law, have so far looked at global legal indicators, and highlight some ingrained assumptions that are shared by experts of all these disciplines. In addition, this section argues that global legal indicators could (and perhaps should) matter for both perspectives. Section F will try to show what international lawyers and their comparative law colleagues could achieve if they broaden the horizons and frontiers of their respective disciplines. Finally, section G will try to sum up what options are left to international and comparative lawyers, and why these options are worth pursuing with regard to global legal indicators and beyond.

B. What Global Legal Indicators are

Fuelled by a general paradigm shift towards quantification in the social sciences and management practices throughout the twentieth century, and by technological advancements in the collection and treatment of mass data, indicators have come to the fore in a variety of fields during the last 50 years.[4] Nowadays, a

[4] On this history, see M Infantino, 'Global Indicators' in S Cassese (ed), *Research Handbook on Global Administrative Law* (Cheltenham: Edward Elgar, 2016) 347, 349–52.

plethora of international, hybrid and non-governmental organisations (NGOs), but also national agencies, corporations, advocacy groups, scholarly networks and committed individuals publish global, regional and local indicators on virtually every conceivable social issue – from healthcare to quality of education, from water sanitation to the ease of doing business, from companies' social responsibility to countries' democratic fragility and rates of corruption.[5]

What exactly are indicators? According to the most commonly accepted definition, an indicator is:

> [A] named collection of rank-ordered data that purports to represent the past or projected performance of different units. The data are generated through a process that simplifies raw data about a complex social phenomenon. The data, in this simplified and processed form, are capable of being used to compare particular units of analysis (such as countries or institutions or corporations), synchronically or over time, and to evaluate their performance by reference to one or more standards ... Indicators often take the form of, or can readily be transformed into, numerical data.[6]

In other words, indicators are quantitative comparisons of qualitative social features that are not easily amenable to quantification.

In recent times, indicators have emerged as an important technology for global and local governance insofar as they are distinctively able to combine apparently impartial descriptions with invisible yet powerful prescriptions.[7] By mapping and counting social data, indicators transform complex information into numbers and allow a simplified approach to the social phenomena concerned. In spite of the many fragilities affecting their design and construction,[8] indicators

[5] See, among many others, R Urueña, 'Quantitative Forms of Legal Governance' in M Siems and PJ Yap (eds), *The Cambridge Handbook of Comparative Law* (Cambridge: Cambridge University Press, 2024) 594; M Siems and D Nelken, 'Global Social Indicators and Their Legitimacy in Transnational Law' in P Zumbansen (ed), *The Oxford Handbook of Transnational Law* (Oxford: Oxford University Press, 2021) 953; JG Kelley and BA Simmons, 'Introduction' in JG Kelley and BA Simmons (eds), *The Power of Global Performance Indicators* (Cambridge: Cambridge University Press, 2020) 1.

[6] KE Davis, B Kingsbury and S Engle Merry, 'Introduction: Global Governance by Indicators' in KE Davis et al (eds), *Governance by Indicators: Global Power through Quantification and Rankings* (Oxford: Oxford University Press, 2012) 3, 6.

[7] Kelley and Simmons (n 5); N Bhuta, DV Malito and G Umbach, 'Introduction: Of Numbers and Narratives: Indicators in Global Governance and the Rise of a Reflexive Indicator Culture' in DV Malito, G Umbach and N Bhuta (eds), *The Palgrave Handbook of Indicators in Global Governance* (London: Palgrave Macmillan, 2018) 1; A Broome and J Quirk, 'Governing the World at a Distance: The Practice of Global Benchmarking' (2015) 41 *Review of International Studies* 819; A Cooley, 'The Emerging Politics of International Rankings and Ratings: A Framework for Analysis' in A Cooley and J Snyder (eds), *Ranking the World: Grading States as a Tool of Global Governance* (Cambridge: Cambridge University Press, 2015) 1; S Engle Merry, *The Seductions of Quantification: Measuring Human Rights, Gender Violence, and Sex Trafficking* (Chicago: Chicago University Press, 2015); Davis, Kingsbury and Engle Merry (n 6).

[8] Indicators typically rely on over-simplified, heterogeneous and decontextualised data, and are affected by the biases of their designers, who may under-estimate or neglect relevant features that do not fit their assumptions. Additional problems arise out from the (limited or non-existent transparency of the) many discretionary choices required in constructing an indicator, such as the selection of data providers and the techniques devised for gap-filling. See D Restrepo Amariles and J McLachlan, 'Legal Indicators in Transnational Law Practice: A Methodological Assessment' (2018) 58 *Jurimetrics*

are usually considered to be helpful in singling out problems and patterns for corrective action and in streamlining policy makers' decision-making processes. Further, by converting complex information into simplified data, indicators have an aura of scientificity that, combined with their user-friendly formats and proneness to mediatisation, allow them to easily enter public debates, replace other forms of judgement on social realities and validate specific visions about problems. Thanks to the repetition of measurements over time, indicators are therefore good not only in terms of identifying quantifiable goals, monitoring progress and singling out best performers, but also in pressuring their users and the general public to re-orient their agendas and to conform to the behavioural models expressly or impliedly conveyed by the indicators themselves. Indicators may thus favour the diffusion and spontaneous internalisation of harmonised standards of behaviour bypassing political processes and conventional procedures and achieving results more effectively than traditional legal tools.[9] However, this mode of regulatory intervention is also well known to spur those who are targeted by the indicators into adopting rank-seeking and gaming strategies – that is, techniques for manipulating data and improving results in ways that are unconnected to, or even undermine, the motivation underlying the quantitative exercise.[10]

One of the many beauties of indicators is that anyone can build one. It has been clearly demonstrated that the success of indicators is quite unrelated from the authority, the legitimacy and even the expertise of their producers.[11] Yet to make things simple, the rest of this chapter will consider a specific kind of indicator only: global legal indicators made up by international organisations. Global legal indicators have been defined as 'measures, standards and rankings of the quality of law and legal institutions across the entire world, particular regions, or selected jurisdictions',[12] and as quantitative worldwide initiatives that 'collect variables that purport to measure a range of aspects of a country's legal

Journal 163; Engle Merry (n 7) 27–43, 212–16; Broome and Quirk (n 7); M Jerven, *Poor Numbers: How We are Misled by African Development Statistics and What to Do about it* (Ithaca, NY: Cornell University Press, 2013).

[9] GA Sarfaty, 'Corporate Actors as Translators in Transnational Lawmaking' (2021) 115 *American Journal of International Law* 278, 281–82; A Broome, A Homolar and M Kranke, 'Bad Science: International Organizations and the Indirect Power of Global Benchmarking' (2018) 24 *European Journal of International Relations* 514; JG Kelley, *Scorecard Diplomacy: Grading States to Influence their Reputation and Behavior* (Cambridge: Cambridge University Press, 2017); M Siems and D Nelken, 'Global Social Indicators and the Concept of Legitimacy' (2017) 13 *International Journal of Law in Context* 436, 443; L Fioramonti, *The Politics of Numbers, and How Numbers Rule the World* (London: Zed Books, 2014); WN Espeland and M Sauder, 'Rankings and Reactivity: How Public Measures Recreate Social Worlds' (2007) 113 *American Journal of Sociology* 1.

[10] Espeland and Sauder (n 9).

[11] M Infantino, *Numera et impera. Gli indicatori giuridici globali e il diritto comparato* (Milan: FrancoAngeli, 2019) 66; S Sunn Bush, 'The Politics of Rating Freedom: Ideological Affinity, Private Authority, and the Freedom in the World Ratings' (2017) 15 *Perspectives on Politics* 711.

[12] D Restrepo Amariles, 'Supping with the Devil? Indicators and the Rise of Managerial Rationality in Law' (2017) 13 *International Journal of Law in Context* 465, 466.

institutions or even specific aspects of a jurisdiction's legislative and regulatory environment'.[13] As such, global legal indicators may be exclusively concerned with the measurement of the law or look at a number of social features, including legal ones; they may also be realised by a variety of actors and directed against a variety of targets – international governmental organisations and NGOs, states, regions, cities, corporations, and so on and so forth. The following pages will only deal with global legal indicators made by international organisations and targeting states. However, it is useful to keep in mind that much of the reasoning and conclusions developed therein may well apply to other forms of indicators.

C. Selected Illustrations

To fully understand what global legal indicators are and why they matter in the perspective of both international and comparative law, it is useful to explore some examples of how they are made, for what purposes and with what consequences. This section will provide two main sets of illustrations, among many other possible ones. Section C.1 will shed light on some of the many quantitative measurements licensed by the World Bank since the 1970s in the economic field. Section C.2 will deal with a few indicators promoted, from the 1990s onwards, by a variety of UN bodies and agencies to pursue compliance with human rights and global development. As we will see, many differences exist between the two sets of initiatives, which clearly bear the imprint of more general institutional, organisational and cultural variances between the two international organisations.

1. The World Bank and Global Legal Indicators

With its impressive financial and scientific resources, the World Bank has long experimented with measurements of countries' economic, political and legal frameworks. Such experiments have included the structural adjustment programmes and the so-called Country Policy and Institutional Assessments that the Bank has developed since the 1970s as instruments for supporting and assessing its aid allocation strategies.[14] Another example are the Worldwide Governance Indicators (WGIs), launched in 1995 by a team of neo-institutional

[13] T Krever, 'Quantifying Law: Legal Indicator Projects and the Reproduction of Neoliberal Common Sense' (2013) 34 *Third World Quarterly* 131, 132.

[14] *cf* MA Prada Uribe, 'The Quest for Measuring Development: The Role of the Indicator Bank' in S Engle Merry, KE Davis and B Kingsbury (eds), *The Quiet Power of Indicators. Measuring Governance, Corruption, and Rule of Law* (Cambridge: Cambridge University Press, 2015) 133, 143–55; A Santos, 'The World Bank's Uses of the "Rule of Law" Promise in Economic Development' in DM Trubek and A Santos (eds), *The New Law and Economic Development. A Critical Appraisal* (Cambridge: Cambridge University Press, 2006) 253.

economists affiliated to the World Bank Institute under the directorship of the Chilean economist Daniel Kaufmann.[15] Still today, the WGIs annually measure six dimensions of governance in every country of the world in order to study to what extent a solid institutional infrastructure is correlated with economic growth.[16] But the most (in)famous among the World Bank indicators is (the now withdrawn) Doing Business, an annual report that was inspired by the 'legal origins' theory developed in the mid-1990s by a group of neo-institutional economists, known as LLSV.[17] From its first report in 2003 to its last one in 2020, Doing Business ranked countries according to the business-friendliness quality of their regulatory environment, on the assumption that 'good' laws are conducive to economic growth.[18]

The Doing Business reports were based on the answers to a questionnaire drafted by the Doing Business team at the Washington DC headquarters of the World Bank and distributed every year to approximately 15,000 lawyers and government officials around the world.[19] The questionnaire investigated what would have happened to a medium-sized local enterprise based in the country's largest business city in a series of circumstances that, in the last edition of the report, were articulated along 12 dimensions. Responses were evaluated, assembled, weighted and transformed into numbers by the Doing Business team, producing the ranking of every country in each dimension. Ten of the 12 dimensions that were measured were further aggregated to create the final 'Ease of Doing Business' score, which ranked countries from the most to the least business-friendly.[20]

The limits of Doing Business are well known. The reports were intensely criticised for the fragility of the 'legal origins' theory and the US-centred bias of the questionnaire,[21] the unreliability and unrepresentativeness of expert

[15] See www.worldbank.org/en/publication/worldwide-governance-indicators#home.

[16] WGIs are routinely cited by the academe and the media, and are used by both the World Bank and big donors to assess the eligibility of countries for development aid. For a critical review of WGIs, *cf* Krever (n 13) 137–40; NK Dutta, 'Accountability in the Generation of Governance Indicators' (2010) 22 *Florida Journal of International Law* 401, 427–29.

[17] Referring to the initials of R La Porta, FC Lopez de Silanes, A Shleifer and RW Vishny.

[18] See www.worldbank.org/en/programs/business-enabling-environment/doing-business-legacy.

[19] World Bank, *Doing Business Report 2020: Comparing Business Regulation in 190 Economies* (2019), https://openknowledge.worldbank.org/bitstream/handle/10986/32436/9781464814402.pdf, at 23.

[20] Two dimensions were left out from the aggregate score: 'employing workers' and 'contracting with the government'. While the latter was only introduced in the last edition of the report, the former was present since the beginning, and originally used as a component of the final 'Ease of Doing Business' ranking. However, the Doing Business team stopped including it in the calculation for the final score in 2009, following the harsh criticism by the International Trade Union Confederation and the ILO of the slippery slope towards deregulation that the sub-index favoured. On this story, *cf* H Gött, 'The ILO's Model under Pressure: The World Bank's Employing Workers Indicator', in H Gött (ed), *The Law of Interactions Between International Organizations. A Framework for Multi-institutional Labour Governance* (Cham: Springer, 2020) 67–95; Krever (n 13) 140–41.

[21] See, among others, T Besley, 'Law, Regulation, and the Business Climate: The Nature and Influence of the World Bank Doing Business Project' (2015) 29 *Journal of Economic Perspectives* 99; N Garoupa and C Gomez Liguerre, 'The Syndrome of the Efficiency of the Common Law' (2011) 29 *Boston*

opinions,[22] and the naivety of many assumptions on which the project was based, such as that less regulation is always good, rules can be easily transplanted and there is one 'right' solution to every business legal problem.[23] Notwithstanding these and the many other criticisms that were raised against Doing Business, the World Bank estimated that since the first edition, more than 10,000 articles using Doing Business data were published online and in peer-reviewed journals,[24] more than 60 countries established government offices devoted to improving their performances in them[25] and more than 3,800 legal reforms were carried out worldwide along the lines suggested by the reports.[26]

In 2020, after a scandal about irregularities in the reporting of data, the 2021 edition of the Doing Business report was withdrawn and in 2021 the entire project was discontinued.[27] But the legacy of Doing Business remains. Through its lifespan, Doing Business has given rise to several other experiments with indicators,[28] some of which, such as 'Women, Business and Law' (WBL), are still active.[29]

University International Law Journal 287, 304–31; R Michaels, 'Comparative Law by Numbers? Legal Origins Thesis, Doing Business Reports, and the Silence of Traditional Comparative Law' (2009) 57 *American Journal of Comparative Law* 765, 786–87; B Fauvarque-Cosson and A-J Kerhuel, 'Is Law an Economic Contest? French Reactions to the Doing Business World Bank Reports and Economic Analysis of the Law' (2009) 57 *American Journal of Comparative Law* 811, 821–23; Association Henri Capitant des Amis de la Culture Juridique Française, *Les droits de tradition civiliste en question. A propos des rapports Doing Business*, 2 vols (Paris: Société de législation comparée, 2006). On this point, see also the authors cited in nn 92 and 94 below.

[22] See, eg, S Voigt, 'How (Not) to Measure Institutions' (2013) 9 *Journal of Institutional Economics* 1, 19–20; Michaels (n 21) 778.

[23] Broome, Homolar and Kranke (n 9) 523; Krever (n 13) 132; Garoupa and Liguerre (n 21) 304–05; Fauvarque-Cosson and Kerhuel (n 21) 823; Michaels (n 21) 788–89; Santos (n 14) 294. See also the authors cited in nn 91 and 95.

[24] World Bank (n 19) 27.

[25] World Bank, *Doing Business 2018: Reforming to Create Jobs* (2017), https://openknowledge.worldbank.org/handle/10986/28608a, at v.

[26] World Bank (n 19) 7.

[27] ibid 25.

[28] Spin-offs of the Doing Business reports include the World Bank's 'Investing Across Borders' Index, published once in 2010 to measure countries' openness to foreign direct investments (https://openknowledge.worldbank.org/handle/10986/27883), the 'Global Indicators of Regulatory Governance', released once in 2016 to explore how governments interact with the public opinion when shaping regulations that affect their business community (https://rulemaking.worldbank.org/en/about-us), and the 'Women, Business and Law', established in 2010 with the aim of getting data and scores on women in the economy (https://wbl.worldbank.org/en/wbl). The shock provoked by the first editions of the Doing Business reports (according to which French and French-inspired laws were inefficient) gave rise to the publication, for two editions only, of the French *Index de la sécurité juridique*. See B Deffains and C Kessedjian (eds), *Index de la sécurité juridique. Rapport pour la Fondation pour le droit continental* (2015), https://fondation-droitcontinental.org/fr/wp-content/uploads/2015/04/Rapport-ISJ-Juin-2015.pdf; B Deffains and M Séjean (eds), *L'index de la sécurité juridique ISJ – The Index of Legal Certainty ILC* (Paris: Dalloz, 2018). For some critical remarks on this project, see J Knetsch, 'Measuring Legal Certainty? Critical Feedback about the Development of an Index of Legal Certainty' in M Fenwick, M Siems and S Wrbka (eds), *The Shifting Meaning of Legal Certainty in Comparative and Transnational Law* (Oxford: Hart Publishing, 2017) 177.

[29] The WBL index is used in the formula of the US aid agency Millennium Challenge Corporation to check whether a country deserves financing: C Powell, 'Gender Indicators as Global Governance: Not Your Father's World Bank' (2016) 17 *Georgetown Journal of Gender and Law* 777, 779.

Moreover, the World Bank has now developed a new project – the Business-Ready (B-Ready) project – to take up the legacy of Doing Business in order 'to measure the business enabling environment in economies worldwide'.[30] The first B-Ready report, investigating the commercial legal infrastructure in 50 economies around the world, was launched in October 2024.[31] However, in spite of the claims of novelty, it seems that continuity prevails, meaning that both the methodology and the substance of the B-Ready project are nothing more than a replica of the Doing Business Reports.[32]

2. Global Legal Indicators in the UN System

Since the 1990s, and more intensely from the 2000s onwards, several UN bodies and agencies with competences in the fields of human rights and development have started joining the general turn to indicators. As was hinted at earlier, the UN approach to indicators has diverged remarkably from that adopted by the World Bank. This is of little surprise, as the two international organisations possess different structures and missions, and work under different political and economic constraints. In particular, the engagement of the UN with global legal indicators has taken two different routes.

On the one hand, and in line with the long-time mandate of the UN Statistical Commission of setting common statistical standards,[33] many UN bodies have devoted substantial energy towards building a shared methodology for the measurement of social phenomena, thus developing a number of guidelines for whoever (states, NGOs, donors or scientists) is interested in constructing an indicator. For instance, the International Labour Organization (ILO) published a protocol to produce indicators for human trafficking in 2009 and another on indicators on forced labour in 2012.[34] In the same year, after multiple requests by UN human rights treaty bodies,[35] the Office of the United Nations High Commissioner for Human Rights (OHCHR) published a guide for the

[30] See www.worldbank.org/en/businessready.

[31] See World Bank, *Business Ready 2024* (2024), https://openknowledge.worldbank.org/server/api/core/bitstreams/08942fab-9080-4f37-b7be-ef61c9f9aed9/content.

[32] Fernanda G Nicola, *Mis-uses of Comparative Law in International Development* (New York: Cambridge University Press, 2025); G Chieco, 'L'armonizzazione soft del diritto privato e commerciale: dai Doing Business reports al B-Ready' (2024) 29 *Ianus* 123; A Somma, 'Dai Rapporti "doing business" a "business ready". La Banca Mondiale, la comparazione quantitativa e la valenza normativa degli indicatori' (2024) 55 *Politica del diritto* 507.

[33] See https://unstats.un.org/unsd/statcom.

[34] See respectively ILO, *Operational Indicators of Trafficking in Human Beings* (2009), www.ilo.org/sites/default/files/wcmsp5/groups/public/@ed_norm/@declaration/documents/publication/wcms_105023.pdf; ILO, *ILO Indicators of Forced Labour* (2012), www.ilo.org/global/topics/forced-labour/publications/WCMS_203832/lang--en/index.htm.

[35] Since the 1990s, several UN human rights bodies have requested states to prepare indicators showing their performances against human rights standards: AJ Rosga and ML Satterthwaite, 'The Trust in Indicators: Measuring Human Rights' (2009) 27 *Berkeley Journal of International Law* 253, 257–79.

preparation of human rights indicators.[36] All these guidelines do not provide any quantitative comparison; rather, they are meant to standardise the way in which other people and entities may gather numerical data and build their own indicators. Such efforts also foster the participation of states, of civil society and of other concerned actors in the production of indicators, thus promoting bottom-up and contextually aware initiatives and at the same time gently socialising participants in the fight for important causes.[37]

On the other hand, some UN bodies have directly engaged in building indicators in the fields of human rights and development. But even when they have done so, they have often involved in the construction of their indicators other subjects – including the targeted states – so as to guarantee adequate consideration for local contexts and to promote a climate of collaboration and a culture of compliance with international norms and international organisations' requests.[38] In line with this idea of avoiding measurements that may frustrate states' willingness to participate in the game, UN human rights and development indicators characteristically avoid producing rankings and tend to refuse any form of cross-country comparison.[39] A good case in point is the 'Media Development Indicators' released by the United Nations Educational Scientific and Cultural Organization (UNESCO) since 2008.[40] But perhaps the most notable initiatives in this regard are the (now ended) 'Millennium Development Goals' (MDGs) indicators and the (currently ongoing) 'Sustainable Development Goals' (SDGs) indicators.[41]

To cut a long story short, in 2001 the UN General Assembly adopted the so-called 'Millennium Declaration', identifying the development goals for the year 2015.[42] The realisation of such goals was to be monitored and pursued via

[36] OHCHR, *Human Rights Indicators: A Guide to Measurement and Implementation* (2012), www.ohchr.org/en/instruments-and-mechanisms/human-rights-indicators. The guide has not enjoyed the expected success among UN treaty bodies: see D McGrogan, 'Human Rights Indicators and the Sovereignty of Technique' (2016), 27 *European Journal of International Law* 385, 390; Engle Merry (n 7) 163–206.

[37] M Infantino, 'Human Rights Indicators across Institutional Regimes' (2015) 12 *International Organization Law Review* 146, 160–62.

[38] O de Schutter, *International Human Rights Law: Cases, Materials, Commentary* (Cambridge: Cambridge University Press, 2014) 544–62; Rosga and Satterthwaite (n 35) 280–81; S Engle Merry, 'Measuring the World: Indicators, Human Rights, and Global Governance' (2011) 52 *Current Anthropology* 83, 88.

[39] Infantino (n 37) 163–66.

[40] See https://en.unesco.org/programme/ipdc/initiatives/mdis.

[41] It is worth noting that such an initiative was preceded by the launch by the United Nations Development Programme of several other indicators, such as the 'Human Development Index' (HDI) created under the lead of Mahbub Ul Haq in 1990 (https://hdr.undp.org/en/content/human-development-index-hdi) and its twin gendered-version, the 'Gender Development Index' (GDI), measuring since 1995 gender gaps in human development achievements (https://hdr.undp.org/en/content/gender-development-index-gdi). On both the HDI and the GDI, see S Engle Merry, 'Global Legal Pluralism and the Temporality of Soft Law' (2014) 46 *Journal of Legal Pluralism & Unofficial Law* 108, 110–19.

[42] United Nations General Assembly, *United Nations Millennium Declaration* (18 September 2000), A/RES/55/2, https://mdgs.un.org/unsd/mdg/Resources/Static/Products/GAResolutions/55_2/a_res55_2e.pdf.

the 21 dimensions captured by the MDGs indicators.[43] In 2015, the Millennium Declaration and the MDGs were replaced by the '2030 Agenda for Sustainable Development'[44] and the connected SDGs.[45] The SDGs are a grid of more than 230 indicators aiming to test the realisation of development objectives for the year 2030. To perform the monumental task of gathering uniform national data on the SDGs, the UN has mobilised a complex network of global and local actors. In particular, for each of the SDGs indicators, a focal point was established and charged with the task of coordinating the data collection process. Focal points are often specialised UN institutions (such as the ILO, the OHCHR and UNESCO), but other international organisations are also involved, such as the World Bank, the International Monetary Fund and the Organisation for Economic Co-operation and Development (OECD).[46] As in the case of their predecessors, the SDGs have been poignantly criticised for their heavy and naive reliance on indicators as the main tool for fostering global development.[47] However, critical voices have been largely overshadowed by the mobilisation of a large variety of actors – from other international organisations to states, from NGOs to multinationals, from celebrities to civil society – as well as the massive investments, big enthusiasm and high energy with which these actors have endorsed, and continue to endorse, the initiative.[48]

D. Seeing Global Legal Indicators: Global Legal Pluralism

Could the above developments be framed in legal terms? As we will see in section E, mainstream international and comparative lawyers would largely

[43] See https://mdgs.un.org/unsd/mdg/default.aspx. There is a substantial body of critical literature on the MDGs: *cf* S Fukuda-Parr, *Millennium Development Goals: Ideas, Interests and Influence* (Abingdon: Routledge, 2017); S Fukuda-Parr and A Ely Yamin (eds), *The MDGs, Capabilities and Human Rights: The Power of Numbers to Shape Agendas* (Abingdon: Routledge, 2015); IT Winkler, ML Satterthwaite and C de Albuquerque, 'Treasuring What We Measure and Measuring What We Treasure: Post-2015 Monitoring for the Promotion of Equality in the Water, Sanitation, and Hygiene Sector' (2014) 32 *Wisconsin International Law Journal* 547.

[44] United Nations General Assembly, *Transforming Our World: The 2030 Agenda for Sustainable Development* (21 October 2015), A/RES/70/1, www.refworld.org/legal/resolution/unga/2015/en/111816.

[45] See https://unstats.un.org/sdgs; S Fukuda-Parr, 'Sustainable Development Goals' in TG Weiss and S Daws (eds), *The Oxford Handbook of the United Nations*, 2nd edn (Oxford: Oxford University Press, 2018) 764.

[46] See the list of focal points at https://unstats.un.org/sdgs/dataContacts.

[47] *cf* J Lyytimäki et al, 'Risks of Producing and Using Indicators of Sustainable Development Goals' (2020) 28 *Sustainable Development* 1528; S Murthy, 'Translating Legal Norms into Quantitative Indicators: Lessons from the Global Water, Sanitation, and Hygiene Sector' (2018) 42 *William & Mary Environmental Law & Policy Review* 385.

[48] S Peter de Souza, *Designing Indicators for a Plural Legal World* (Cambridge: Cambridge University Press, 2022) 99–103.

answer this question negatively, although with some notable exceptions. Before exploring that negative answer, it is useful to present the opinion of those who have looked at global legal indicators from other perspectives and would by contrast reply to the above question in the affirmative.[49]

Legal scholars who think that global legal indicators matter have different methodological and substantial backgrounds, but all subscribe to themes, theories and frameworks that are close to the perspectives of global legal pluralism, transnational legal theory and transnational legal orders.[50] Under this view, the emergence, propagation, contestation, resistance, settlement, institutionalisation, imitation, competition, success and failure of global legal indicators are relentless, non-linear processes that occur within, across and beyond states and international organisations, and involve a variety of actors in different places and positions.

According to this perspective, international organisations-made global legal indicators do not only propagate standards, best practices and ideals of behaviour from international organisations to states, but also favour the development of new competences and approaches, and spread vocabularies, visions, assumptions, expectations and practices across a plethora of actors, including states, other international organisations, NGOs, international donors, investors, journalists and scholars. The uses and misuses of indicators by all these actors shape and co-produce the power of quantitative measurements. Through similar interactions, global legal indicators slowly come to define reality, frame problems and solutions, solidify perceptions about what is normal, fair and just, and propagate 'unconventional transnational norms'[51] and 'new forms of regulation'[52] that may be perceived as legitimate and binding. The de facto regulatory power of global legal indicators is thus independent from their (lack of) official authority, and instead stems from the soft mechanism of continuous quantitative monitoring, by peer pressure and threats to reputational capital, and by the voluntary adherence

[49] See Siems and Nelken (n 5) 953–69; Restrepo Amariles and McLachlan (n 8) 163–209; A van Waeyenberge, 'Préface' (2018) 59 *Cahiers de Droit* 3; A Perry-Kessaris, 'The Re-co-construction of Legitimacy of/through the Doing Business Indicators' (2017) 13 *International Journal of Law in Context* 498; M Infantino, 'Comparative Law in the Global Context: Exploring the Pluralism of Human Rights Indicators' (2015) 2 *European Journal of Comparative Law and Governance* 97; B Frydman and W Twining, 'Preface. A Symposium on Global Law, Legal Pluralism and Legal Indicators' (2015) 57 *Journal of Legal Pluralism & Unofficial Law* 1; D Restrepo Amariles, 'Legal Indicators, Global Law and Legal Pluralism: An Introduction' (2015) 47 *Journal of Legal Pluralism & Unofficial Law* 9.

[50] On global legal pluralism, see P Schiff Berman, *Oxford Handbook of Global Legal Pluralism* (Oxford: Oxford University Press, 2020); W Twining, 'Normative and Legal Pluralism: A Global Perspective' (2010) 20 *Duke Journal of Comparative and International Law* 473, especially 511–15. As to transnational law, see Zumbansen (n 5); R Cotterell, 'What is Transnational Law?' (2012) 37 *Law and Social Inquiry* 500. As to the transnational legal orders paradigm, see TC Halliday and GC Shaffer (eds), *Transnational Legal Orders* (Cambridge: Cambridge University Press, 2015); GC Shaffer (ed), *Transnational Legal Ordering and State Change* (Cambridge: Cambridge University Press, 2013).

[51] Restrepo Amariles (n 49) 17.

[52] Frydman and Twining (n 49) 5.

to the system by people and entities who in theory would be free to ignore it, and yet participate in it.[53]

Global legal indicators entail complex relationships with the existing official international (and national) law. They may support the compliance with binding international norms, as in case of the guidelines published by the ILO.[54] They may even side with one national official legal model over others: think of how the Doing Business reports have sustained US leadership in the regulatory competition of company and corporate law.[55] Global legal indicators may specify or modify existing international law, such as when, by defining what should be measured, guidelines on human rights indicators specify the contents of the rather vague provisions of human rights treaties.[56] They may also fill gaps in international law, proposing their own models where official rules are missing: for instance, the WGIs and the SDGs are promoting a 'governance' and 'sustainable development' ideal, respectively, in the absence of any binding international law framework in this regard.[57] Global legal indicators may even conflict with existing official laws; this happened with the dimension 'employing workers' in Doing Business. By rewarding countries where it was easier to fire workers, the dimension promoted a standard for labour regulation that was an alternative to, and clearly inconsistent with, the one stemming from ILO's labour conventions.[58]

E. The Invisibility of Global Legal Indicators in Mainstream Narratives

Whether one agrees or not with the above viewpoints, they make it clear why it is fair to say that international organisations-made global legal indicators live in a grey area that could be of interest for both international and comparative lawyers.

As a by-product of international organisations and as a tool through which the latter manage their relationships with states and nudge compliance with international commitments, global legal indicators clearly belong to the domain of international law. At the same time, being based on repeated, quantitative cross-country comparisons finalised to foster regulatory competition and harmonisation, global legal indicators also resemble comparative legal research. Yet in

[53] See Restrepo Amariles (n 49) 17–19; Sarfaty (n 9) 281–282; Engle Merry (n 41) 109.
[54] See n 34 above.
[55] See n 21 above and also n 94 below.
[56] See n 36 above.
[57] For the WGIs, see nn 15–16 above; for the SDGs, see, nn 45–48 above.
[58] See the literature quoted in n 20.

spite of these features, the majority of international and comparative lawyers have not noticed their emergence and multiplication.

The following sub-sections will try to summarise how global legal indicators are currently (not) taken into account by mainstream international and comparative law literature (sections E.1 and E.2 respectively). Section F will then explore the occasions that both disciplines so far have missed.

1. Viewing Global Legal Indicators from International Law

International lawyers seem not to care about global legal indicators (or indicators in general). Indicators are not mentioned by manuals and textbooks, where at most one or two pages speak of the increasing array of 'soft law' instruments outside treaties, customs, general principles of law and international case law – that is, outside the list of legal sources mentioned by Article 38(1) of the Statute of the International Court of Justice.[59] Recent studies on comparative international law, albeit revolutionary, have also devoted no attention to global legal indicators.[60] However, there are exceptions. Indicators have been observed and studied by a few scholars specialising in international human rights law,[61] law and development,[62] and international institutional law.[63]

---

[59] There is no mention to indicators in the main public international law textbooks and handbooks; see, for instance, M Deyra, *Droit international public*, 10th edn (Paris: Lextenso, 2023); D Alland, *Manuel de droit international public*, 10th edn (Paris: Presses Universitaires de France, 2023); A Orakhelashvili, *Akehurst's Modern Introduction to International Law*, 9th edn (Abingdon: Routledge, 2022); M Shaw, *International Law*, 9th edn (Cambridge: Cambridge University Press, 2021); J Klabbers, *International Law* (Cambridge: Cambridge University Press, 2020); W Mansell and K Openshaw, *International Law: A Critical Introduction*, 2nd edn (Oxford: Hart Publishing, 2019).

[60] See the literature quoted in n 2.

[61] Murthy (n 47); BA Andreassen, 'Comparative Analyses of Human Rights Performance' in BA Andreassen, H-O Sano and S McInerney-Lankford (eds), *Research Methods in Human Rights. A Handbook* (Cheltenham: Edward Elgar, 2017) 222; McGrogan (n 36); de Schutter (n 38) 544–62; Rosga and Satterthwaite (n 35).

[62] Prada Uribe (n 14) 133–55; Krever (n 13) 131–50; A Perry-Kessaris, 'Prepare Your Indicators: Economics Imperialism on the Shores of Law and Development' (2011) 7 *International Journal of Law in Context* 401; S Pahuya, *Decolonising International Law: Development, Economic Growth and the Politics of Universality* (Cambridge: Cambridge University Press, 2011) 224, 231–36, 247–48; L Clegg, 'Our Dream is a World Full of Poverty Indicators: The US, the World Bank, and the Power of Numbers' (2010) 15 *New Political Economy* 473; Santos (n 14) 253–300.

[63] *cf* M Riegner, *Informationsverwaltungsrecht internationaler Institutionen: Dargestellt am Entwicklungsverwaltungsrecht der Weltbank und Vereinten Nationen* (Tübingen: Mohr Siebeck, 2018); RF Urueña, 'Indicators as Political Spaces: Law, International Organizations, and the Quantitative Challenge in Global Governance' (2015) 12 *International Organization Law Review* 1, 3–5; M Riegner, 'Towards an International Institutional Law of Information' (2015) 12 *International Organization Law Review* 50; B Kingsbury, 'Indicadores y derecho' (2014) 25 *International Law. Revista Colombiana de Derecho Internacional* 9; A von Bogdandy and M Goldmann, 'Taming and Framing Indicators: A Legal Reconstruction of the OECD's Programme for International Student Assessment (PISA)' in Davis et al (eds) (n 6) 52.

While law and development experts have mostly looked at indicators as instruments perpetuating neo-colonialism,[64] those focusing on general public international law have investigated, under the lens of international institutional law, the legal foundations of international organisations' power to subject member states to indicators. Such works ask, for example, whether international organisations can produce indicators relying on their implied powers or should that capacity be mentioned in their charters?[65] Or, in addition, to what extent is that capacity covered by the Articles of Agreement of the World Bank that contain an authorisation to 'publish reports'[66] or by the provision in the ILO's Constitution that empowers ILO's Office to pursue 'the collection and distribution of information on all subjects relating to the international adjustment of conditions of industrial life and labour'?[67] A further question that has arisen concerns the legal value of the internal acts and documents through which international organisations make indicators, such as the questionnaires used for collecting information[68] and the decisions by executive boards approving the publication of indicators.[69] Some have even wondered about which human rights obligations, if any, should apply to international organisations producing indicators.[70]

Along similar lines, international human rights lawyers have scrutinised the basis on which UN bodies can ask states to participate in the production of indicators or to submit their own indicators. Some have looked for textual references to indicators within human rights treaties.[71] Are indicators covered by the provisions of the International Covenant on Economic, Social and Cultural Rights and of the Convention on the Elimination of All Forms of Discrimination against Women requiring states to ensure (and therefore give evidence of), respectively, 'the reduction of the stillbirth-rate and of infant mortality'[72] and

[64] See the authors cited in n 62 above.

[65] On this, see Riegner, *Informationsverwaltungsrecht* (n 63) 193–97; von Bogdandy and Goldmann (n 63) 57; Santos (n 14) 269.

[66] *cf* Art V, s 13 of the IBRD's Articles of Agreement (Bretton Woods, 22 July 1944), www.worldbank.org/en/about/articles-of-agreement/ibrd-articles-of-agreement; Art IV, s 11 of the International Finance Corporation's Articles of Agreement (Washington DC, 25 May 1955), www.ifc.org/wps/wcm/connect/CORP_EXT_Content/IFC_External_Corporate_Site/About+IFC_New/IFC+Governance/Articles; Art VI, sec 11 of the IDA's Articles of Agreement (Washington DC, 24 September 1960), https://thedocs.worldbank.org/en/doc/341581541440486864-0330022018/original/IDAArticlesofAgreementEnglish.pdf.

[67] Article 10 of the ILO Constitution (Versailles, 28 June 1919), www.ilo.org/dyn/normlex/en/f?p=1000:62:0::NO:62:P62_LIST_ENTRIE_ID:2453907:NO#A10.

[68] See Riegner, 'Towards' (n 63) 71.

[69] von Bogdandy and Goldmann (n 63) 57.

[70] Riegner, *Informationsverwaltungsrecht* (n 63) 198–200.

[71] De Schutter (n 38) 546–47.

[72] Article 12(2), lit (a) of the International Covenant on Economic, Social and Cultural Rights (New York, 16 December 1966), www.ohchr.org/en/instruments-mechanisms/instruments/international-covenant-economic-social-and-cultural-rights.

'the reduction of the female student dropout rates'?[73] Are indicators functional to the obligation of states parties under the Convention on the Rights of Persons with Disabilities 'to collect appropriate information, including statistical and research data, to enable them to formulate and implement policies to give effect to the present Convention'?[74] Does the obligation of states, under several human rights treaties, to take steps towards the realisation of certain goals imply, at a minimum, an obligation to devise indicators for monitoring progress monitoring?[75] In this regard, several commentators have noted how, in recent years, UN treaty bodies have multiplied states' obligations of numerical reporting, thus shifting the focus of their work from monitoring states' compliance with international obligations to monitoring of states' own monitoring activities.[76]

These scholars tend to agree that 'legal indicators function as implicit or even explicit standards'.[77] Yet the majority of them also agree that although 'closely connected with legal-type norms or processes, indicators are not usually framed as laws'[78] and 'are not legal instruments as such, but rather informal tools of data collection, knowledge production and information governance'.[79] Only a minority call indicators a manifestation of 'soft law'.[80] This confirms what was noted at the beginning of this section. Even when they are made or mandated by international organisations, indicators come in a form that does not fit the traditional vocabulary and framework of international law. It is no wonder that international lawyers, including those who recognise the significance of international organisations-made global legal indicators, have failed to acknowledge the role played in transnational governance by indicators made by other actors, such as NGOs, national agencies and scholarly networks.

[73] Article 10, lit (f), of the Convention on the Elimination of All Forms of Discrimination against Women (New York, 18 December 1979), www.un.org/womenwatch/daw/cedaw/text/econvention.htm#article10.

[74] Article 31 of the Convention on the Rights of Persons with Disabilities (New York, 13 December 2006), www.un.org/development/desa/disabilities/convention-on-the-rights-of-persons-with-disabilities/convention-on-the-rights-of-persons-with-disabilities-2.html.

[75] This seems to be the interpretation embraced in particular by the United Nations Economic and Social Council (ECOSOC). For a review of the approach by ECOSOC and other UN treaty bodies to indicators, see de Schutter (n 38) 556–58; Rosga and Satterthwaite (n 35) 275–79.

[76] Murthy (n 47) 422; Rosga and Satterthwaite (n 35) 304–15; see also McGrogan (n 36) 389–90, 400–02.

[77] Krever (n 13) 132, 143–46; *cf* Davis et al (n 6) 15; KE Davis, B Kingsbury and S Engle Merry, 'Introduction: The Local-Global Life of Indicators: Law, Power, and Resistance' in Engle Merry, Davis and Kingsbury (eds) (n 14) 1, 18–19.

[78] Davis, Kingsbury and Engle Merry (n 77) 4; see also R Urueña, 'Indicadores, derecho internacional y el surgimiento de nuevos espacios de participación política en gobernanza global' (2014) 25 *International Law, Revista Colombiana de Derecho Internacional* 543, 550.

[79] Riegner, 'Towards' (n 63) 60.

[80] Murthy (n 47) 390; Engle Merry (n 7) 11.

2. The Feud of Comparative Law

Global legal indicators have notoriously been said to be the most outstanding comparative law product of the recent decades,[81] at least if success is defined in terms of media coverage, scientific citations and real-world legal effects. Yet the making of global legal indicators does not claim to be an exercise in comparative law, and nor could it, according to the very few comparative lawyers who have been prepared to acknowledge their existence.[82]

Actually, up to now, most comparative lawyers have plainly ignored indicators,[83] as shown by the fact that the majority of comparative law handbooks and textbooks avoid any reference to them.[84] Several reasons may be stated as the cause for this reluctance, from comparative lawyers' minimal interest in the global and international legal sphere,[85] to their limited knowledge of quantitative methodologies,[86] to practices of scientific protectionism of their own way(s) of doing comparative law against (what are perceived as) counterfeits.[87]

[81] Michaels (n 21) 766; M Siems, 'The End of Comparative Law' (2007) 2 *Journal of Comparative Law* 133, 144.

[82] See, eg, M Bussani and U Mattei, 'Diapositives versus Movies: The Inner Dynamics of the Law and its Comparative Account' in M Bussani and U Mattei (eds), *Cambridge Companion to Comparative Law* (Cambridge: Cambridge University Press, 2012) 3, 5, who, referring to the Doing Business reports, note that 'in our discipline no one would have dared (perhaps since Wigmore's Panorama) to venture a comparison of so many legal systems in so little space knowing so little about any one of them'. See also Association Henri Capitant (n 21) vol I, 17, 31–32.

[83] The same observation is made, among others, by M Siems, 'Comparative Law: Who is the Elephant in the Room? Book Review of *Comparative Law: A Handbook* (Örücü and Nelken, eds)' (2008) 12 *Edinburgh Law Review* 334; Michaels (n 21) 766–67; V Grosswald Curran, 'Comparative Law and the Legal Origins Thesis: "[N]on scholae sed vitae discimus"' (2009) 57 *American Journal of Comparative Law* 863, 865–66.

[84] There is no mention to indicators in J Husa, *An Introduction to Comparative Law*, 2nd edn (Oxford: Hart Publishing, 2023); V Zeno-Zencovich, *Comparative Legal Systems: A Short Introduction*, 2nd edn (Rome: Roma Tre Press, 2019); G Samuel, *An Introduction to Comparative Law Theory and Method* (Oxford: Hart Publishing, 2014); M Rosenfeld and A Sajó (eds), *The Oxford Handbook of Comparative Constitutional Law* (Oxford: Oxford University Press, 2012); Bussani and Mattei (eds) (n 82) (except for a critical remark in the introduction: at 5). For some exceptions to this trend, see also nn 89 and 97 below.

[85] *cf* J Husa, 'Merging International Law and Comparative Law: Balancing between Normative and Non-Normative' (2021) 85 *Rabels Zeitschrift* 745, 747; M Siems, 'New Directions in Comparative Law' in MW Reimann and R Zimmermann (eds), *The Oxford Handbook of Comparative Law*, 2nd edn (Oxford: Oxford University Press, 2019) 852, 866–69; R Scarciglia, *Metodi e comparazione giuridica*, 3rd edn (Padua: Cedam, 2021) 161–76; Roberts (n 2) 19–21.

[86] See R Hirschl, *Comparative Matters: The Renaissance of Comparative Constitutional Law* (Oxford: Oxford University Press, 2014) 186; A Meuwese and M Versteeg, 'Quantitative Methods for Comparative Constitutional Law' in M Adams and J Bomhoff (eds), *Practice and Theory in Comparative Law* (Cambridge: Cambridge University Press, 2012) 230, 231.

[87] M Infantino, 'Quantitative Legal Comparisons: Narratives, Self-Representations and Sunset Boulevards' (2019) 6 *Journal of International and Comparative Law* 287.

The only initiative that comparative lawyers have noticed[88] and that is seldom included in textbooks[89] has been the World Bank's Doing Business, insofar as it was based on the 'legal origins' theory. In other words, what triggered the attention of comparative lawyers was not the World Bank's indicators per se, but rather the methodology and theoretical constructs underlying the research on the 'legal origins', perhaps because these studies were packaged in an academic format that comparative scholars were more familiar with, and more prone to recognise as similar to their own.[90] Many comparative lawyers have therefore focused on challenging the simplistic use by the 'legal origins' group of many core concepts of comparative law, such as systemology, legal traditions, legal transplants and legal change,[91] the superiority attributed by the group to the common law tradition vis-a-vis the civil law tradition,[92] and the emphasis placed on statutory rules and on selected institutions and variables.[93] Comparative lawyers have equally attacked the economic and American bias underlying 'legal origins' studies,[94] as well as the naivety of their quest for an optimal and universal solution for any legal problem.[95] Some comparative lawyers, particularly those specialising

[88] Besides the contributions to special issues on the legal origins theory in (2009) 57(4) *American Journal of Comparative Law* 765, (2009) 59(2) *University of Toronto Law Journal* 179, (2009) 6 *Brigham Young University Law Review* 1413, (2010) 166 *Journal of Institutional and Theoretical Economics* 1 and (2012) 11 *Annuario di diritto comparato* 7, *cf* M Pargendler, 'The Role of the State in Contract Law: The Common-Civil Law Divide' (2018) 43 *Yale Journal of International Law* 143; N Garoupa, C Gómez Ligüerre and L Mélon, *Legal Origins and the Efficiency Dilemma* (Abingdon: Routledge, 2017); M Siems, 'Comparative Legal Certainty: Legal Families and Forms of Measurement' in Fenwick, Siems and Wrbka (n 28) 115–34; S Deakin et al, 'Legal Institutionalism: Capitalism and the Constitutive Role of Law' (2017) 45 *Journal of Comparative Economics* 188; H Spamann, 'Empirical Comparative Law' (2015) 11 *Annual Review of Law and Social Science* 131; G Xu, *Does Law Matter for Economic Growth? A Re-examination of the 'Legal Origin' Hypothesis* (Cambridge: Intersentia, 2014); M Schmiegelow and H Schmiegelow (eds), *Institutional Competition between Common Law and Civil Law* (Cham: Springer 2014); Garoupa and Liguerre (n 21) 287–335; S Bollée, Y-M Laithier and C Pérès (eds), *L'efficacité économique en droit* (Paris: Economica, 2010); M Siems, 'Numerical Comparative Law: Do We Need Statistical Evidence in Law in Order to Reduce Complexity?' (2005) 13 *Cardozo Journal of International and Comparative Law* 521; Association Henri Capitant (n 21) vol I.

[89] *cf* U Kischel, *Comparative Law* (Oxford: Oxford University Press, 2019) 134–43; Reimann and Zimmermann (n 85) (with the exception of the chapter by Siems (n 85) 871–73); A Somma, *Introduzione al diritto comparato*, 3rd edn (Turin: Giappichelli, 2019) 171–77, 224–34.

[90] Pargendler (n 88) 186–87; Michaels (n 21) 776.

[91] Garoupa, Gómez Ligüerre and Mélon (n 88) 90–110; Deakin et al (n 88) 194–198; CJ Milhaupt, 'Rethinking Law's Relationship to the Economy: Implications for Policy' (2009) 57 *American Journal of Comparative Law* 831, 833–35, 842–43; Fauvarque-Cosson and Kerhuel (n 21) 828.

[92] See Garoupa, Gómez Ligüerre and Mélon (n 88) 59–90; Xu (n 88) 29–39; Garoupa and Liguerre (n 21) 290–305; Association Henri Capitant (n 21), vol I, 35–69.

[93] Deakin et al (n 88) 198; Milhaupt (n 91) 840; M Siems, 'Legal Origins: Reconciling Law & Finance and Comparative Law' (2007) 52 *McGill Law Journal* 55, 67–69.

[94] Kischel (n 89) 138; Deakin et al (n 88) 188–200; Garoupa, Gómez Ligüerre and Mélon (n 88) 538; Garoupa and Liguerre (n 21) 287–335; Grosswald Curran (n 83) 869; Milhaupt (n 91) 843–44; Fauvarque-Cosson and Kerhuel (n 21) 812, 821–22; Michaels (n 21) 786–91; Association Henri Capitant (n 21) vol I, 21–34.

[95] Deakin et al (n 88) 189; Milhaupt (n 91) 836, 841; Michaels (n 21) 778–79, 788; Association Henri Capitant (n 21) vol I, 21–34; Siems, 'Numerical Comparative Law' (n 88) 532–33.

in sectors more prone to quantitative analysis, have even formed their critiques through reworking the 'legal origins' data or by providing alternative numerical measurements of legal infrastructures worldwide.[96]

However, the point remains that besides denouncing the limitations of the 'legal origins' theory (and, to a much lesser extent, of Doing Business), comparative lawyers have largely failed to appreciate the existence of global legal indicators in general. Only very few comparativists have realised that Doing Business was nothing more than one instance of a broader trend to produce and use quantitative comparative analysis as a tool for knowledge and governance.[97] These few authors have also stressed that what global legal indicators do is not that different from what many traditional comparative law scholars do – after all, they both investigate legal architectures in different settings with a (more or less clearly stated) harmonisation agenda in mind.[98] But this conclusion is anathema for the vast majority of my colleagues.

F. Missed Occasions

Against such a state of the art, the question arises as to whether international and comparative lawyers could take a different position on global legal indicators, and what could be the reasons for them to do so.

The argument of the following sub-sections is that experts in both disciplines would have much to gain from turning their attention to global legal indicators, regardless of whether they are made by international organisations or not. Noticing the existence and significance of global legal indicators would not only allow both international and comparative lawyers to better describe and intervene in the social world, but would also provide them with an occasion (among the many others available) to call into question the intellectual boundaries and the main tenets of their own fields, starting from the centrality of states as the main actors and providers of legal norms.

[96] *cf* H Spamann, 'Legal Origin, Civil Procedure, and the Quality of Contract Enforcement' (2010) 166 *Journal of Institutional and Theoretical Economics* 146, 149–65; H Spamann, 'Contemporary Legal Transplants: Legal Families and the Diffusion of (Corporate) Law' (2009) 6 *Brigham Young University Law Review* 1813; Siems (n 93) 74–80; however, see also the website https://repository.cam.ac.uk/handle/1810/256566 and the three CBR Leximetric Datasets stored therein. The experiment made by the Fondation pour le droit continental (n 28) should also be recalled.

[97] As to comparative law manuals, see Urueña (5); R Scarciglia, *Methods and Legal Comparison. Challenges for Methodological Pluralism* (Cheltenham: Edward Elgar, 2023) 118–20; M Siems, 'Empirical Methods' in Siems and Yap (n 5) 157; M Siems, *Comparative Law*, 3rd edn (Cambridge: Cambridge University Press, 2022) 207–53; Scarciglia (n 85) 125–28; Hirschl (n 86) 16, 192–93, 288; in general, see also Infantino (n 87) 287–306; Siems (n 93) 55–81; Michaels (n 21).

[98] See the authors cited in the preceding note.

1. For International Lawyers

There is little doubt that taking international organisations-made global legal indicators more seriously would shed new light on the place occupied by international organisations in international and global governance.

As the examples provided in section C above show, global legal indicators are both an expression and a tool of authority of international organisations vis-a-vis their Member States.[99] Global legal indicators help international organisations strengthen their competence and legitimacy, perform their functions and define their role in the ecology of their own field.[100] As such, global legal indicators are one of the many means (besides binding external acts, treaties and courts' judgments, material incentives, strategies of stigma, ostracisation and conditionality, and operational practices) at the disposal of international organisations for expressing and exercising their authority. However, unlike other forms of international organisations' law making, global legal indicators have the twofold advantage that they are (relatively) cheap to build and (relatively) easy to agree upon and enforce, given their de-politicised nature and scientific appearance.[101] Through global legal indicators, international organisations may not only tap into existing norms, redefine their contents and verify states' compliance with them, but also fill regulatory gaps without the need of political approval, and even enact standards that may override officially binding legal rules[102] (as done by the World Bank with the 'employing workers' dimension in Doing Business).[103]

Besides their being a law-making tool, global legal indicators (and indicators in general) matter for international organisations insofar as their proliferation has spurred substantial changes in the ways in which international organisations work. As noted in section C.2, the demand for indicators by UN treaty bodies have changed both the core functions attributed to these bodies and their relationships with the monitored states.[104] More generally, the increased production of, and

[99] See, among others, Murthy (n 47) 422; Broome, Homolar and Kranke (n 9) 529, 533; Riegner, 'Towards' (n 63) 52–60; von Bogdandy and Goldmann (n 63) 53, 80.

[100] *cf* Murthy (n 47) 445; Broome, Homolar and Kranke (n 9) 516, 529, 533; Riegner, *Informationsverwaltungsrecht* (n 63) 30–166; Urueña, 'Indicators' (n 63) 3–5; OJ Sending and JH Sande Lie, 'The limits of global authority: World Bank benchmarks in Ethiopia and Malawi' (2015) 41 *Revue of International Studies* 993, 1007, 1009; TC Halliday, 'Legal Yardsticks: International Financial Institutions as Diagnosticians and Designers of the Laws of Nations' in Davis et al (n 6) 180; Clegg (n 62) 477. More specifically, for the claim that the World Bank slowly accompanied (or replaced) conditionality strategies with indicators, *cf* S Schueth, 'Assembling International Competitiveness: The Republic of Georgia, USAID, and the Doing Business Project' (2010) 87 *Economic Geography* 51, 57 (2010); Krever (n 13) 136, 143; Merry (n 38) 90.

[101] cf A Broome and J Quirk, 'The Politics of Numbers: The Normative Agendas of Global Benchmarking' (2015) 41 *Review of International Studies* 813, 816; Broome and Quirk (n 6) 823.

[102] Bhuta, Malito and Umbach (n 7) 10; Murthy (n 47) 393, 445; Kelley (n 9) 17; Urueña (n 63) 5; Kingsbury (n 64) 12–16; Davis, Kingsbury and Engle Merry (n 77) 19; Halliday (n 100) 214–215.

[103] See section C.1, n 20 and section D, text before n 58 above.

[104] See section E.1, text corresponding to nn 75–76.

reliance on, indicators have led many international organisations in recent years to develop competences, build up offices, hire new personnel and restructure their core activities and agendas for satisfying the growing needs of collecting, monitoring and managing quantitative data. From this point of view, indicators have contributed to transforming the ways in which many international organisations perform their daily missions.[105]

This is not all. By focusing on global legal indicators made by international organisations only, this chapter has not considered a number of other kinds of indicators. However, it would be enough to broaden the spectrum of the initiatives under review to realise that indicators made by actors other than international organisations may nevertheless produce international legal effects. Among the global legal indicators targeting states, but released by NGOs, think, for instance, of the 'Freedom in the World' reports launched in 1993 by the New York-based NGO Freedom House[106] and the Corruption Perceptions Index published since 1995 by the Berlin-based NGO Transparency International.[107] The Freedom in the World reports have not only provided the basis for thousands of academic studies testing theories about democracy, development and economic growth, but are also used by international organisations, such as the World Bank, as one of the criteria to determine and evaluate aid distribution.[108] The Corruption Perceptions Index is credited with having cemented the international consensus in the fight against corruption, paving the way for the adoption of many anti-bribery international conventions, such as the OECD Convention on Combating Bribery of Foreign Public Officials in International Business Transactions of 1997 and the UN Convention against Corruption in 2003.[109] The study of these and other initiatives would help show that the international realm is inhabited by actors other than states and international organisations, and that international law-making can occur through instruments that do not fit in the traditional list of treaties, customs, general principles of law and case law.

Yet seeing this would require accepting that international regimes are heavily shaped by actors that are devoid of international legal personality. These actors may exert considerable power and even influence international law making by

[105] ML Satterthwaite, 'Rights-Based Humanitarian Indicators in Post-Earthquake Haiti' in Davis et al (n 6) 365, especially 368–74.

[106] Freedom House publishes many other companion indicators, including 'Freedom in the Net' and 'Nations in Transit'. See freedomhouse.org.

[107] See www.transparency.org/en/cpi. Transparency International also publishes the so-called 'Global Corruption Barometer' (GCB); see transparency.org/en/research.

[108] Sunn Bush (n 11) 718–22; Dutta (n 16) 429–30.

[109] See respectively www.oecd.org/corruption/oecdantibriberyconvention.htm and www.unodc.org/unodc/en/treaties/CAC. For the influence of the Corruption Perceptions Index in the adoption of both international treaties, see A Cooley, 'How International Rankings Constitute and Limit Our Understanding of Global Governance Challenges: The Case of Corruption' in Malito, Umbach and Bhuta (n 7) 49, 51; M Bukovansky, 'Corruption Rankings: Constructing and Contesting the Global Anticorruption Agenda' in Cooley and Snyder (n 7) 60, 73.

means that, although not captured by standard sources of international norms, may prove deeply effective.[110]

2. For Comparative Lawyers

Similar observations apply as far as comparative lawyers are concerned.

Rather than limiting themselves to the critique of the methodological fallacies and naiveties affecting global legal indicators,[111] comparative lawyers may first of all be interested in actively contributing to their production. There is indeed little doubt that, as large-scale, quantitative legal comparisons, global legal indicators engage the know-how of trained comparativists and would benefit from the latter's participation in their making. Comparativists could take their knowledge about legal traditions, transplants and harmonisation to indicators' tables, pinpointing possible improvements and facilitating the understanding of multiple cultures and legal change.[112]

But the potential of global legal indicators for comparative lawyers goes beyond that. Comparativists could take indicators as an 'extraordinary place'[113] for study. They could explore the varied world of global legal indicators, investigating the features that are distinctive and those that are shared among different initiatives. As was shown in section C, as well as in the previous section, global legal indicators may take multiple forms, whose concrete size and shape is influenced not only by economic constraints but also by the network of actors who establish and work on the indicator, by the mission the latter see themselves entrusted with and by the agendas they want to pursue. This gives rise to the following questions: what are the factors underlying such variety, and how do they matter in the role that global legal indicators end up playing in their own field? What are the reasons determining the success of some global legal indicators and the failure of others? Through which processes – mutual inter-connections, links, institutional isomorphism or competition – do some

[110] The need to be more sensitive to the role of non-state actors and to unconventional forms of law making is shared by many international lawyers as well: *cf*, among many others, Roberts et al (n 2); KN Scott et al (eds), *Changing Actors in International Law* (Leiden: Brill, 2021); M Noortmann, A Reinisch and C Ryngaert (eds), *Non-state Actors in International Law* (Oxford: Hart Publishing, 2015); J Pauwelyn, 'Informal International Lawmaking: Framing the Concept and Research Questions' in J Pauwelyn, R Wessel and J Wouters (eds), *Informal International Lawmaking* (Oxford: Oxford University Press, 2012) 13, 19–21; A Peters et al (eds), *Non-state Actors as Standard Setters* (Cambridge: Cambridge University Press, 2009).

[111] See section E.2 above.

[112] *cf* Infantino (n 49) 100–01; Meuwese and Versteeg (n 86) 256. So far, the majority of global legal indicators have been made by economists, political scientists and statisticians: see Infantino (n 87) 299–300.

[113] E Örücü, 'Comparatists and Extraordinary Places' in P Legrand and R Munday (eds), *Comparative Legal Studies: Traditions and Transitions* (Cambridge: Cambridge University Press, 2003) 467, 468–71.

global legal indicators reproduce themselves in new initiatives?[114] Trying to answer these and similar questions would require comparativists to engage in the comparative study of international regimes, checking how different international organisations-made initiatives are made, live, propagate and sometimes die.[115] Such research may also include global legal indicators produced by actors other than international organisations.

Whether made by international organisations or not, global legal indicators favour imitative processes that go beyond the relationship between different indicators. As was seen in section C, successful global legal indicators also stimulate the transplant of legal rules, approaches and terminology from the international to the national context, pressuring states to abide by the regulatory 'ideal' promoted by the indicators themselves. Legal transplants and legal harmonisation are the bread and butter of comparative lawyers; therefore, it would be quite reasonable to expect comparativists to study how global legal indicators work as legal harmonisation tools. This would imply researching how the models promoted by these indicators are received in national legal systems, which reactions (of acceptance, rejection, adjustment or resistance) they give rise to, and whether the changes they bring about are deep or superficial, long-lasting or short-lived.[116] One may, for instance, compare the ways in which different countries reacted to Doing Business or are reacting to the SDGs, which reforms were or are being adopted in order to comply with these indicators, and how effective and beneficial the transplants inspired by them have been or will be.

One might even go further and imagine comparativists studying how global legal indicators may work as (what the late Rodolfo Sacco would have called) 'cryptotypes'[117] – that is, invisible factors subtly affecting the way in which the law is conceived and applied. It is quite clear, for instance, that global legal indicators silently give collateral support to a specific approach to legal issues – an approach that is managerial, data-driven and performance-oriented, and therefore quite different from the one that most lawyers are used to.[118] How is this managerial turn happening and what consequences is it producing?

[114] For similar observations about the need of engaging in this research (although not necessarily through comparative law methodology), *cf* Siems and Nelken (n 9) 444–46; Engle Merry (n 7) 35; Davis, Kingsbury and Engle Merry (n 6) 6; WN Espeland and M Sauder, 'The Dynamism of Indicators' in Davis et al ((n 6) 86, 108; S Cassese and L Casini, 'Public Regulation of Global Indicators' in Davis et al (n 6) 465, 466; Engle Merry (n 38) 88.

[115] This of course would imply accepting that the space for comparative international law goes beyond 'identifying, analyzing, and explaining similarities and differences in how actors in different legal systems understand, interpret, apply, and approach international law', as stated by A Roberts et al, 'Conceptualising Comparative International Law' in Roberts et al (n 2) 3, 6.

[116] See Infantino (n 49) 100–01, 123; Michaels (n 21) 766–68, 776–77, 787–88; see also Espeland and Sauder (n 114) 86, 108–09.

[117] R Sacco, 'Legal Formants: A Dynamic Approach to Comparative Law (Installment II of II)' (1991) 39 *American Journal of Comparative Law* 343, 384–87.

[118] Infantino (n 49) 100–01, 123; see also M Infantino and M Bussani, 'Rule by Metrics' (2024) 11 *European Journal of Comparative Law and Governance* 187; M Bussani, S Cassese and M Infantino, 'Quantification of Performance as a Regulatory Technique: A Comparative Appraisal' in M Bussani,

For the time being, all these questions have no answer. As noted by many, in spite of the insistence of comparative legal literature on the significance of legal cultures and sources of law that do not emanate from official institutions, comparative law studies usually take the form of state-to-state comparisons and fail to acknowledge the wide range of legal layers that determine the daily life of law.[119] As long as comparativists see their ideal research domain as confined to state-to-state comparisons of official laws, they are unlikely to ask themselves the above questions.

G. Conclusions: Of Old Boundaries and New Frontiers

The above survey has aimed to demonstrate that nothing prevents international and comparative lawyers from taking an interest in global legal indicators; quite the contrary. One may even claim, as section F attempted to show, that global legal indicators are a promising field of research under both the international and comparative perspective, and a prospective area of interest for research on comparative international law going beyond the mere comparison of local approaches to international law. And yet, global legal indicators have so far gone almost undetected.

The main reason for this seems to be related to some shared (and largely cryptotypical, in Sacco's terms) views that both international and comparative lawyers have of their own fields. After all, contemporary international and comparative laws were both born out of the nineteenth-century rise of European (legal) nationalism and quest for universal and national 'civilisation'.[120] It should therefore be no surprise that they still have in common a perspective that is state-centric and 'lego-centric'.[121] Under the state-centric lens, what matters are states: nations and their associations for international lawyers and national legal systems for comparative lawyers. State-centrism also affects the preferred locus of research, and what is considered to be 'law', under both disciplines: treaties by states and international organisations, states' customs, general principles of the law and case law by international courts for international lawyers, and national official law (constitutions, codes and statutes, and precedents) for comparative

S Cassese and M Infantino (eds), *Comparative Legal Metrics: Quantification as Regulatory Technique* (Leiden: Brill, 2023) 323–64.

[119] For a critique of this state of the art, see M Bussani, 'Strangers in the Law: Lawyers' Law and the Other Legal Dimensions' (2019) 40 *Cardozo Law Review* 3127, especially 3137–43; G Frankenberg, 'Critical Comparisons: Re-thinking Comparative Law' (1985) 26 *Harvard International Law Journal* 411, 445–48.

[120] M Koskenniemi and V Kari, 'A More Elevated Patriotism: The Emergence of International and Comparative Law (Nineteenth Century)' in H Pihlajamäki, MD Dubber and M Godfrey (eds), *The Oxford Handbook of European Legal History* (Oxford: Oxford University Press, 2018) 974.

[121] Along the same lines, see the authors cited in nn 110 and 119.

lawyers. International and comparative lawyers alike are thus mostly interested in the official law stemming from the states – that is, they are 'lego-centric'. Similar considerations apply to current studies on comparative international law, in which the focus on the interpretations and applications of international law adopted at the local level shares the same state-centric and lego-centric view just mentioned.

As demonstrated by the impact of the international organisations-made global legal indicators analysed in this chapter, the sources of power, governance and law in our pluralistic and complex world go well beyond the state. This holds even more true when one considers that this chapter dealt only with (a few) global legal indicators produced by international organisations and targeting Member States. However, there are many other global legal indicators that are produced by and measure non-state actors.[122] How should these indicators be framed, considering that they are made by private actors and yet they inform the public and technical debate, prompt national and international regulations, contribute to the framing of legal expectations as well as ideas about what is good and what is bad, and how to tell the difference?

The above developments are invisible to mainstream international and comparative lawyers. They also remain outside the scope of attention of current studies on comparative international law. Against this state of the art, the chapter claims that global legal indicators matter as a new form of international law making and harmonisation through quantitative comparisons. Until international, comparative and comparative international lawyers open up the range of 'actors' and 'objects' they conceive as legally relevant, global legal indicators will remain invisible – and therefore unaccountable, as well as difficult to contain and to tame.

[122] See the illustrations offered in nn 106–09 above.

13

Global Law and Comparative International Law

JAAKKO HUSA

A. Introduction

Globalisation has been a buzzword of the past two decades, and law is no exception, even though its glamour has perhaps faded in recent years. Even though the heyday of globalisation may be behind us, there is much literature on globalisation, and law and globalisation. Unfortunately, perhaps, no uniform understanding of legal globalisation has emerged. We are constantly faced with the difficulty of defining globalisation in the context of law.[1] For instance, comparative legal scholars, legal historians, international lawyers and commercial lawyers all appear to have their own context-related understandings of what legal globalisation is about. Nevertheless, what seems to be clear is that experts in different legal fields acknowledge that societies, businesses and people of the 2020s are governed by a plurality of normative orders, which are inter-related and not organised into a single body of rules. Importantly, the role of the state as the sole source of legal norms has diminished as other actors have gained a foothold in norm production. This transformation also influences legal disciplines as their objects of study are on the move.

More generally, it can be claimed that both practising lawyers and legal scholars have at least implicitly accepted that the globalisation of law is not a narrow and specialised set of legal phenomena set into the globe. Instead of one globalisation, there are multiple forms of globalisation, giving support to the idea of global legal pluralism.[2] The so-called Westphalian world of sovereign states holding the monopoly of force within their mutually recognised territories has certainly not disappeared, yet its foundation based on the separation of the domestic and

[1] See J-B Auby, *Globalisation, Law and the State* (Oxford: Hart Publishing, 2017) 1–14. See also W Twining, 'Implications of "Globalisation" for Law as a Discipline' in A Halpin and V Roeben (eds), *Theorising the Global Legal Order* (Oxford: Hart Publishing, 2009) 39.

[2] PS Berman, *Global Legal Pluralism: A Jurisprudence beyond Borders* (Cambridge: Cambridge University Press, 2012).

international spheres has been eroded.[3] Alongside states and international organisations the global world of law is filled with new actors – the European Union, Amazon, the World Bank, Coca-Cola and the World Trade Organization – that are no longer Westphalian.[4] Unavoidably, this development influences law and legal professionals. The problem for legal scholars is the sheer scale of globalisation as it necessarily blurs the vision of laws (or normativities having de facto the effect of law). It is virtually impossible to have an overall view as there are so many fields where the Westphalian system has transformed and, in some places, lost its grip. Hence, international law is said to be in a state of crisis as the nation-state paradigm and the United Nations systems fail to meet global challenges.[5] Importantly, as noted by Koh, 'law and globalization has redefined the role of international law and lawyers in a globalized world'.[6] As a result, internationally oriented legal scholars need to redefine their fields of knowledge and themselves as legal scholars because of the changes.

The objective of this chapter is to discuss critically the relation between global law and comparative international law. My argument is that the way in which we understand global law is crucial for the relationship between these legal fields. In short, a narrow lawyerly definition of global law leads to difficulties caused by the very nature of globalisation, whereas recent comparative international law is better equipped to meet the numerous challenges that are caused by the change of the Westphalian world in the form of growing diversity. Even if comparative international law may not be an answer to the problems, it nonetheless addresses relevant issues having to do with the change of the underlying Westphalian assumptions.

This chapter proceeds as follows. Section B discusses what globalisation means for the law and what is meant by globalising law. Section C addresses the notion of global law and two competing ways to conceive of it: as a field of law; and as a process that cannot be contained in any particular field of law. Section D moves on to analyse the rising field of comparative international law that brings nuances to the discussion of globalisation of law, as it abandons the normative universalism of international law by evoking a pluralistic and non-normative view on international law. Section E highlights how global law, if understood narrowly as a new field of law, is difficult to combine with comparative international law, which has relinquished normative universalism of international law. The concluding section summarises the argument of the chapter and discusses the implications of the conclusions for the relationship between global law and

[3] See, eg, JE Alvarez, 'State Sovereignty is Not Withering Away: A Few Lessons for the Future' in A Cassese (ed), *Realizing Utopia: The Future of International Law* (Oxford: Oxford University Press, 2012) 26.

[4] *cf* PG Monateri, *Dominus Mundi: Political Sublime and the World Order* (Oxford: Hart Publishing, 2020) 5.

[5] See, eg, R Domingo, 'The Crisis of International Law' (2009) 42 *Vanderbilt Law Review* 1543.

[6] H Hongju Koh, 'Transnational Legal Process and the "New" New Haven School of International Law' in JL Dunoff and MA Pollack (eds), *International Legal Theory: Foundations and Frontiers* (Cambridge: Cambridge University Press, 2022) 101, 129.

comparative international law. As a caveat, it should be noted that this chapter is written from the point of view of comparative law, which influences how global law and international law are conceived and depicted.

B. Globalising Law?

The fact that law is globalising does not change the basic truths about law and humanity. Law is a human construct and it changes when the surrounding human environment changes. For instance, civil law codifications of the nineteenth and twentieth centuries would not have been possible before modernity. The context of law always plays a vital role and globalisation is no exception in this regard. Quintessentially, discussion of global law – no matter how it is understood – stems from a certain kind of uncertainty caused by global alterations. As Frankopan notes: 'The world is changing around us. As we move into an era where the political, military and economic dominance of the west is coming under pressure, the sense of uncertainty is unsettling.'[7] Against this backdrop, discussion of global law is a discussion of the impact of globalisation on law and lawyers. In essence, global law is an attempt to face the quagmires of the transforming world. Yet, before discussing globalisation of law in a more detailed manner, one should have at least some understanding of what globalisation of law is about. Undoubtedly, seeking to achieve this comprehension is a tall order.

A key observation is that globalisation is not only a recent phenomenon as different waves of globalisation have been taking place virtually throughout the history of humankind.[8] Importantly, there is no single globalisation as there are several overlapping and sometimes conflicting developments leading to varied forms of globalisation.[9] One possible way of defining globalisation of law is to say that it is about overlapping processes by which laws (broadly understood) become increasingly inter-connected and inter-dependent, crossing the traditional borders of states, inter-governmental organisations and non-governmental organisations (NGOs).[10] No doubt, the scope of globalisation of law is immense and goes well beyond the grasp of the Westphalian international law. The result is something that can be labelled as 'inter-legality', which refers to situations where actors are confronted by a multiplicity of norms originating from a variety of legal orders of which all are, at least in principle, potentially valid and applicable.[11]

[7] P Frankopan, *The Silk Roads: A New History of the World* (London: Waterstones, 2016) 521.

[8] See generally, AG Hopkins (ed), *Globalization in World History* (New York: Norton 2002); and J Michie, *Advanced Introduction to Globalisation* (Cheltenham: Edward Elgar, 2017).

[9] See, eg, PL Berger and SP Huntington (eds), *Many Globalizations: Cultural Diversity in Contemporary World* (Oxford: Oxford University Press, 2002).

[10] J Husa, *Advanced Introduction to Law and Globalisation* (Cheltenham: Edward Elgar, 2018) 5.

[11] J Klabbers and G Palombella, 'Introduction: Situating Inter-legality' in J Klabbers and G Palombella, *The Challenge of Inter-legality* (Cambridge: Cambridge University Press, 2019) 1, 9–10.

Because of the scale and lack of clear hierarchy between norms, it is difficult to deduce what is going on at the level of the big picture. This raises a question of how legal scholars know that law is globalising or what it is that they are discussing against the backdrop of globalisation. Addressing the phenomenon reveals what is at stake for our attempt to grasp globalisation from the viewpoint of law. Ramifications go deeper than the mere professional practice of law by international lawyers. At what point did Westphalian assumptions start to dwindle?

Globalising law became a central topic in law and social sciences already in the 1980s; in this century, its topicality has certainly not faded. Looking at the legal scholarship, one indication of legal globalisation is that issues such as global governance, the global rule of law, constitutionalism, *lex mercatoria* and human rights are discussed today in non-national settings.[12] Somehow, it seems that non-national laws are spilling out of their old Westphalian boundaries, as transnational law or global law is taking shape.[13] This transformation is difficult to pinpoint, but what appears evident is that the change creates at least two kinds of needs.

First, there is a need to grapple with national, international, European or transnational laws when legal professionals apply multiple laws (understood in a broad sense). In short, legal scholars hope to epistemically control law that is growing out of its earlier boundaries. Second, there is a need to cope with the practicalities of non-national law by seeking to plot the way across the terrain of the globalised legal environment and accompanying diversity. Admittedly, it would be a mistake to assume that legal scholars would struggle to cover different dimensions concerning the globalisation of law, as globalising law is something that has a fundamental impact on legal scholarship. Lots of ink – real or digital – has been spilled on the subject of law and globalisation. It is no surprise, then, that the rich literature on the subject complicates our ability to have a full grasp of what is going on. An over-abundance of scholarly takes is not helping.

At least six key thematic areas are identifiable when it comes to scholarly takes. Obviously, this list is not exhaustive, but it does offer an overall view that is sufficient for the present discussion. First, an area of law coined as global law or transnational law is built on the foundations of international law.[14] Second, also building on the basis of international law, is an area of scholarship focusing on so-called global governance.[15] Third, one active field of discussion concerns

[12] See, eg, BG Garth, 'The Globalization of the Law' in G Caldeira, R Kelemen and K Whittington (eds), *The Oxford Handbook of Law and Politics* (Oxford: Oxford University Press, 2008) 245.

[13] On the relationship between global law and transnational law, see Husa (n 10) 33–34.

[14] For a critical discussion on international law as Western-made law, see B-V Ikejiaku, 'International Law is Western Made Global Law: The Perception of Third-World Category' (2013) 6 *African Journal of Legal Studies* 337.

[15] This form of scholarship focuses on things like environmental challenges, global warming, human rights, health issues, discriminations, demographic growth, sustainable development and global mechanisms to govern these issues. See, eg, A Harrington, *International Law and Global Governance: Treaty Regimes and Sustainable Development Goals Implementation* (Abingdon: Routledge, 2021).

future legal education in a world where the Westphalian assumptions about law have lost some of their earlier potency.[16] Fourth, there is scholarship that seeks to highlight theoretical dimensions of law and globalisation.[17] Fifth, in the field of comparative law, there are attempts to re-orient comparative law towards a more global direction and away from the Westphalian world that placed the focus on the state.[18] The sixth area of global law concerns legal history, which has grown in the wake of global and/or transnational law.[19] On the whole, it is safe to say that there are multiple views, analyses and discussions as there is no exhaustive view on the globalisation of law. Plurality is to be found in law, but also in the disciplines that seek to understand what is going on in the world of law.

Nevertheless, there is a need to be mindful not to generalise too much and assume that globalisation would be an overwhelming development burying everything else under it. Much of this has to do with our ways of thinking about law. Every era has its fads and follies, and it would be a mistake to imagine that legal scholars would not be influenced by the zeitgeist. For instance, international development that puts pressure on the traditional role of states is not exclusively global. In practice, global issues are never exclusively global because the actions of local, national and regional actors are important. There are also movements against globalisation.[20] As Monateri notes, the 'models of global legal thought produce sharp contrasts and strong reactions and resistance'.[21] Where there is movement, there also tends to be counter-movement. Furthermore, globalisation can also be associated with the growing role of local governments and other forms of decentralised governance.[22] One example is the growing role of big cities, as they have developed into internationally relevant actors.[23]

Nevertheless, it makes sense to point out that in all the various dimensions of law, the role of the state is still essential. In other words, even though globalisation is a phenomenon that concerns the whole globe, it actually takes place at local, national and regional levels.[24] In this context, globalisation is a series

[16] B Garth and G Shaffer, 'The Globalization of Legal Education: A Critical Perspective' in G Bryant and G Shaffer (eds), *The Globalization of Legal Education: A Critical Perspective* (Oxford: Oxford University Press, 2022) 3.

[17] One of the earlier takes is W Twining, *Globalisation and Legal Theory* (Cambridge: Cambridge University Press, 2000), who made a case for a revival of general jurisprudence as a response to the challenges caused by globalisation.

[18] See J Husa, 'Globalisation, Comparison, and Legal Scholarship: Are We All Comparatists Now? (2021) 16 *Journal of Comparative Law* 458 (introductory piece of a thematic issue).

[19] See T Duve, 'What is Global Legal History?' (2020) 8 *Comparative Legal History* 73.

[20] See, eg, JE Stigliz, *Globalization and the its Discontents Revisited* (New York: Norton, 2017).

[21] PG Monateri, *Advanced Introduction to Comparative Legal Methods* (Cheltenham: Edward Elgar, 2021) 85.

[22] *cf* M Siems, *Comparative Law*, 3rd edn (Cambridge: Cambridge University Press, 2022) 43.

[23] See HP Aust and JE Nijman, 'The Emerging Roles of Cities in International Law' in HP Aust and JE Nijman (eds), *Research Handbook on International Law and Cities* (Cheltenham: Edward Elgar, 2021) 1.

[24] There is discussion of the Westphalian world order of sovereign states transforming into a regional world order in Siems (n 22) 323.

of simultaneous and overlapping happenings, not a single grand cosmopolitan event.[25] It is more about muddling through than about any grand global design. In short, there is no unstoppable march towards a unified global legal order. Instead of legal unity, globalisation produces legal fragmentation.[26] This situation, of course, also concerns the globalisation of law and the way in which global law is understood and defined, even though some international law scholars still dream about cosmopolitan law. This, in turn, has an impact on the relationship between global law and comparative international law, as we shall see in what follows.

C. Global Law: Field of Law or Something Else?

When it comes to law, there seems to be some kind of an instinctive propensity to liken globalisation to the notion of global law and its offshoots,[27] as if these two were mirror images of each other. This is not necessarily the case. Pertaining to the way of conceptualising globalising law, there are at least two opposing ways to approach the issue. For the discussion on global law and comparative law, the difference between these two opposing ways is relevant or perhaps even decisive. Building on the notion of global law as a *field of law* leads to a hugely different direction than building on the notion of law and globalisation – that is, globalising law perceived as *overlapping processes* without a pre-destined direction of development. The first notion is normative as to its essential nature, whereas the second allows room for non-normative elements and localised subtleties. I will make the case for the second notion, as it allows more plurality and flexibility than the first one.

As already explained above, pinpointing law and globalisation is not an easy task as there are so many moving parts that are also intersecting in various respects. Westphalian entities of law are mixing with new kinds of border-crossing normative beings. It has been said that the pursuit for 'global law has in recent years become the new holy grail of a global legal expertise'.[28] There is much truth in this statement. Accordingly, any attempt to define global law ends up being merely one possible take. As pointed out by Walker, global law is an ambiguous and open-ended conceptualisation.[29] Following Walker's view,

[25] See J Husa, 'Globalization' in J Smits et al (eds), *Elgar Encyclopedia of Comparative Law*, 3rd edn (Cheltenham: Edward Elgar, 2023) 176.

[26] On the fragmentation of international law, see, eg, A Peters, 'The Refinement of International law: From Fragmentation to Regime Interaction and Politicization' (2017) 15 *International Journal of Constitutional Law* 671, 672–78.

[27] R Mushkat, 'Belatedly But Fruitfully, Law Comes to Grips with the Analytical Challenge of Globalisation' (2019) 49 *Hong Kong Law Journal* 1141, 1148.

[28] J-S Bergé and G Helleringer, *Operating Law in a Global Context* (Cheltenham: Edward Elgar, 2017) 12.

[29] N Walker, *Intimations of Global Law* (Cambridge: Cambridge University Press, 2015) 2–3.

global law is about diverse ways of imagining a global aspect of law in a legally diverse world.[30] However, Walker's pluralism-friendly way to grasp global law is not the only way to grasp it. For many others, global law is, first and foremost, a field of law, which means that global law is conceived as something inherently normative. This understanding grows from a particular legal background: the rule-based legal order crossing the borders of states that took shape in post-Second World War international law, building mostly on Westphalian assumptions.[31] In this reading, international law scholars consider global law as a way to reconceptualise international law and remould their field to something that could be called global governance or alternatively global law. In essence, this kind of global law has two key qualities: first, it is a remedy that can allegedly cure the complexities of international law through the reforged idea of non-state constitutionalism;[32] and, second, as a corollary, global law becomes an attempt to relabel international law, as classic international law is considered incapable of providing solutions for the quandaries of a globalised world.[33]

In a sense, when global law is perceived as something that grows out of the shadows of traditional international law, it is about a new field of law. As a result, global law becomes something like 'international law plus'.[34] From the viewpoint of comparative law, the field-of-law-thinking is not an unknown phenomenon, as it is based on how the legal mind works. In particular, the civilian legal mind tends to regard new thematic areas as new fields of law: when they identify a new area, they have tendency to build up a new field with accompanying doctrinal scholarship.[35] This is why we have things like sports law, elder law, child law etc. Yet it would be a mistake to assume that the emerging field of global law would be a unified area of law, as it is, even as a field of law, open to various interpretations of what it is fundamentally about. Global law, whatever it is, is still very much in the making. This is a problem for legal scholarship as much as it is a problem for the practice of law.

[30] N Walker, 'Epilogue: Rethinking Aloud' in M Maduro, K Tuori and S Sankari (eds), *Transnational Law* (Cambridge: Cambridge University Press, 2014) 381, 386.

[31] See E Fahey, *Introduction to Law and Global Governance* (Cheltenham: Edward Elgar, 2018) 27–30.

[32] Klabbers and Palombella (n 11) 4: 'For in a globalizing world without overarching political authority something was needed to sell the idea – and that something could be constitutionalization', adding that: 'Indeed, the election of Donald Trump in the United States and the Brexit decision in the United Kingdom may well be signs that the salesmen have stopped their work: globalization meets with resistance because it is not met with a partner discourse to legitimize it beyond the unsubstantiated claim that globalization makes us all better off, that "a rising tide lifts all boats," neglecting the awkward circumstance that some boats are lifted far higher than others.' Peters (n 26) 702 points out that 'the perception of fragmentation as a problem for international law grew out of a misguided assumption that international law must be fully coherent to be effective and legitimate'.

[33] *cf* N Krisch, 'The Decay of Consent: International Law in an Age of Global Public Goods' (2014) 108 *American Journal of International Law* 1.

[34] Variants of transnational and/or global law; see Siems (n 22) 352–55.

[35] *cf* G Samuel, *An Introduction to Comparative Law Theory and Method* (Oxford: Hart Publishing, 2014) 122.

Now, there is nothing wrong as such with novel fields of law when they reflect societal changes and fill gaps in law and legal scholarship. The fact that law evolves in interaction with its surroundings is not, of course, an issue. Legal history furnishes countless stories about changing law. As noted above, law is always law *in context*. Accordingly, for instance, outlining global law as a contribution to common good of all humanity free from previous hegemonic interests is certainly one way to advance global law as a field of law.[36] Yet the epistemic tendency to put thematically similar things into newly named fields of law has consequences because a field of law has need of its own concepts, doctrines and theories. As a result, global law ends up being a field of law based on normative universalism, having its own bodies of rules, principles and actors. This kind of global law stands in opposition to global legal pluralism, as it grows from a doctrinal tradition inherently hostile to pluralism.

Normative universalism that emanates from traditional international law implies simply that global laws, such as human rights, are not limited in their scope, but have (or *must* have) a universal application. In essence, normative universalism calls for the unification of law on a global scale. To that end, global law understood as a field of law is normative and has substantive rules because it is a field of law enhancing global governance for the benefit of humanity. For comparative law scholarship, this kind of way to understand global law is problematic, even though its noble motives are legitimate as such. Moreover, as pointed out by Orford, claiming to 'speak on behalf of humanity and to articulate its law is not a politically innocent claim, but is instead a claim that serves to found the jurisdiction, power, and authority of particular transnational elites'.[37] In other words, the claim to 'globality' is also a claim to authority over other competing claims and an attempt to establish a hegemony. For instance, it is easy to see that China's ideas of global (legal) order are different from those of the European Union or those of the United States.[38] Who gets to define what global law means exerts power over other attempts at definition.

If one does not conceptualise globalising law in the form of a legal field, what is the alternative? Is there a way to escape the narrow normative point of view but still retain a legal perspective? One conceivable way to grasp global law is to see it more as a *process* which cannot be situated in any field of law as it flows not only over the Westphalian borders but also over the boundaries of fields of law and legal disciplines. In effect, this would deal a blow to equating legally relevant globalisation with global law. Moreover, this would entail accepting that the world of law is a messy world of inter-legalities. As a result, one would need to abandon the idea according to which international law is understood as 'the law of

[36] See, eg, R Domingo, *The New Global Law* (Cambridge: Cambridge University Press, 2011).

[37] A Orford, 'A Global Rule of Law' in J Meierhenrich and M Loughlin (eds), *The Cambridge Companion to the Rule of Law* (Cambridge: Cambridge University Press, 2021) 538, 563.

[38] See, eg, B Ahl, 'Chinese Positions on Global Constitutionalism, Community of Common Destiny for Mankind, and the Future of International Law' (2021) 9 *Chinese Journal of Comparative Law* 304.

globalisation'.[39] Indeed, why should the power to define global law be vested in international law scholars only?

Conceiving of globalised law as different from the state law seems unavoidable if one abandons the reading of international law that seeks to grasp global law as an expanded post-Westphalian form of international law. Globalised laws are different from state laws as they contain all sorts of 'legalities' that range from state law to oral traditions of an indigenous people, or from international human rights instruments to spontaneously elaborated customary rules of international trade.[40] As a result, it is difficult to place globalised laws under the banner of conventional law, as there are different actors in globalisation ranging from states and international organisations to NGOs, global law firms, financial markets, multinational corporations and religious traditions. Importantly, globalised laws are inter-connected and inter-dependent. Instead of a system of law, there seems to be a network of laws – sometimes colliding and sometimes interacting. This makes it difficult to understand global law as 'international law plus' because it transcends conventional boundaries of international law, as the very notion of law (in the context of 'global') expands beyond the traditional definition. For instance, Western secular liberalism has met religious law, which it thought it had left in the past, as the example of Islamic finance demonstrates.[41] For all these reasons, conceptualising global law as a field of law seems questionable. Accordingly, arguing that global law is not a field of law, but a more fluid multi-part process of globalising inter-legalities seems to make more sense.[42]

In essence, legal globalisation is a moving train and captivating its impact on law into a field of law seems too ambitious. So, '[t]he exploration of the interplay between law and globalisation is still "work in progress"', as Mushkat notes.[43] Moreover, we can sharpen this claim by arguing that due to globalisation's nature, it may always be work in progress that never reaches its imagined end point. This is most likely problematic for Kantian views on cosmopolitanism and international law, but it would nevertheless be a realistic way forward in our attempt to tackle globalisation(s) of law.[44]

In conclusion, if global law is seen as law-and-globalisation instead of a field of law, it requires abandoning normative universalism and embracing epistemic universalism. This kind of non-normative universalism assumes the existence of non-state-based legalities, in the sense that the borders of legal systems are

[39] See Siems (n 22) 332.

[40] See SP Donlan and L Heckendorn Urscheler, 'Concepts of Law: An Introduction' in SP Donlan and L Heckendorn Urscheler (eds), *Concepts of Law* (Aldershot: Ashgate, 2014) 1, 2–4.

[41] See, eg, J Ercanbrack, 'The Standardization of Islamic Financial Law: Lawmaking in Modern Financial Markets' (2019) 67 *American Journal of Comparative Law* 825.

[42] See Husa (n 10) 5–9.

[43] Mushkat (n 27) 1165.

[44] For a more detailed discussion on Kant and international law, see W Wouter and G Gordon, 'Kant, Cosmopolitanism, and International Law' in A Orford and F Hoffmann (eds), *The Oxford Handbook of the Theory of International Law* (Oxford: Oxford University Press, 2016) 505.

not the borders of research, and lawyers are able to operate and learn over the borders. The rising new field of comparative international law brings subtleties to the discussion on global law and comparative law as it abandons normative universalism, but accepts epistemic universalism without – as far as I can tell – losing much of its character as international law scholarship. Importantly, comparative international law inherently evokes a pluralistic or localised view of international law that may be able to methodologically embrace the inherent and unavoidable messiness of globalising law. Taken together, what has been said above suggests that there is a difference between styles of scholarship growing from traditional international law vis-a-vis international law that takes its influences from comparative law. Admittedly, adding global law into the equation muddies the waters further.

D. Comparative International Law: The Best of the Both Worlds?

At the outset, it needs to be said that comparative international law is not an established field, which means that there is no accepted view of what it is and what it is not.[45] Broadly speaking, it seems to be connected to the attempts to read international law more contextually, as, for example, the so-called historiographical turn seeks to do.[46] In this sense, it is about pushing the scholarly boundaries of international law further away from universalist assumptions that draw much of their legal force from Westphalian formalism. Nevertheless, what is clear is that it is about international law scholarship's ambitious attempt to draw inspiration from the modern comparative study of law. In my estimation, recent comparative international law does this in a specific manner. Regardless, there are opposing views that conceive of comparative law as a technique that has but one function: to help legal practice. However, there are more helpful views that conceive of comparative law as a diversity embracing field of legal scholarship. Here the traditional view of comparative law as a means to an end – that is, an assistant of international law and servant of international courts – is left out of the discussion and the focus is on recent scholarly comparative international law.[47]

[45] This section draws from J Husa, 'Merging International Law and Comparative Law: Balancing between Normative and Non-Normative' (2021) 85 *Rabels Zeitschrift für ausländisches und internationales Privatrecht* 745.

[46] This turn has been strongly influenced by Martti Koskenniemi's seminal book *The Gentle Civilizer of Nations: The Rise and Fall of International Law 1870–1960* (Cambridge: Cambridge University Press, 2001). For a discussion of Koskenniemi's book, see GR Bandeira Galindo, 'Martti Koskenniemi and the Historiographical Turn in International Law' (2005) 16(3) *European Journal of International Law* 539,.

[47] See Husa (n 18) 758–68, who discusses search of general principles and international courts, EU law and the European Court of Justice, European Convention on Human Rights (ECHR) law and migration law.

It is useful to understand that the earlier versions of comparative international law were not, for obvious reasons, compatible with the modern pluralist comparative law. However, this does not mean that there would not have been earlier scholarly contacts between comparative law and international law. A good example is one of the great international law scholars, Lauterpacht, who at first tried to develop international law based on comparative private law.[48] But Lauterpacht was certainly not the first one to make this connection.

In fact, the term 'comparative international law' is an old one, as it has been traced back to the mid-nineteenth-century French scholar Lerminier.[49] Later in the twentieth century, the point of contact between international law and comparative law was typically conceived of through the prism of Article 38(1)(c) of the Statute of the International Court of Justice. In practice, however, Article 38(1) has not brought about much comparative law scholarship within the discipline of international law.[50] Yet Article 38(1) has provided at least minor comparative law elements for international law scholarship.[51] Moreover, that article has also provided inspiration for older comparative law scholarship, as can be seen in the common core project that sought to show which principles of law concerning formation of contract reached beyond their home legal systems.[52] A more recent example of comparative international law is Butler's scholarship that anticipated today's comparative international law. Butler was one of the first scholars to fully appreciate the kinship of international and comparative law. Regardless, at first Butler spoke of 'comparative approaches to international law' instead of comparative international law.[53] For the purposes of the present discussion, it is beneficial to focus on more recent attempts to establish modern comparative international

[48] See H Lauterpacht, *Private Law Sources and Analogies of International Law* (London: Longmans, Green, 1927). See also R Michaels, 'Private Lawyer in Disguise? On the Absence of Private Law and Private International Law in Martti Koskenniemi's Work' (2013) 27 *Temple International and Comparative Law Journal* 499, 502–04.

[49] WE Butler, 'Comparative International Law' in Smits et al (n 25) 326.

[50] J Ellis, 'General Principles and Comparative Law (2011) 22 *European Journal of International Law* 949; and I Sanders, *General Principles as a Source of International Law* (Oxford: Hart Publishing, 2021) 223–24.

[51] Nevertheless, some argue that comparative law 'has played an important role in the reasoning of international courts', referring to the International Court of Justice: J Ziller, 'Public Law' in J Smits (ed), *Elgar Encyclopedia of Comparative Law*, 2nd edn (Cheltenham: Edward Elgar, 2012) 744. Also, comparative law scholars have regarded comparative law as indispensable for the interpretation of international law; see E Örücü, 'Developing Comparative Law' in E Örücü and D Nelken (eds), *Comparative Law: A Handbook* (Oxford: Hart Publishing, 2007) 43, 55.

[52] See *Formation of Contracts: A Study of the Common Core of Legal Systems*, gen ed RB Schlesinger (Dobbs Ferry, NY: Oceana Publications, 1968). See also RB Schlesinger, 'Research on the General Principles of Law Recognized by Civilized Nations' (1957) 51 *American Journal of International Law* 734. The ramifications of the common core project can be seen in later comparative law-inspired projects like the UNIDROIT Principles on International Commercial Contracts, as well as the European Principles of Contract Law. See O Lando, 'Principles of European Contract Law and UNIDROIT Principles: Moving from Harmonisation to Unification?' (2003) 8 *Uniform Law Review* 123.

[53] For a useful (self-)analysis, see WE Butler, 'Comparative International Law' (2015) 10 *Journal of Comparative Law* 2.

law, even though the pre-globalisation roots from the 1970s and 1980s should not be forgotten.

A recent group of key scholars have proposed a provisional definition of comparative international law according to which it 'entails identifying, analyzing, and explaining similarities and differences in how actors in different legal systems understand, interpret, apply, and approach international law'.[54]

Like modern comparative law, comparative international law focuses on differences and similarities.[55] Then, as a next step, it seeks to explain what reasons are causing the differences and similarities. Crucially, this kind of comparative law-friendly definition abandons the normative universalism of classical international law. One matter that needs to be emphasised here is that if comparative international law is defined in this manner, it has a crucial consequence for the relationship this budding field has with global law. Instead of being a normatively understood field of law, it has a descriptive and even explanatory nature. What does this kind of pluralism-friendly international law scholarship bring about? There are, it is argued, three possible areas in which the comparative approach is regarded as useful.

First, approaches provided by comparative law may help to identify the substantive content of international law. This is not far from a quite traditional approach to international law as it may mean, in practice, an attempt to identify general principles of international law by using a comparative approach. Second, comparative law approaches make it possible to identify, analyse and explain differences and similarities in the application and interpretation of international law. This can simply mean that, through comparison, one can demonstrate how the same treaty provisions are interpreted by national, regional and international courts. Even though this comes close to traditional normative international law, there is one important exception: studying differences and similarities between different actors means that the idea of international law as a universal law forming at least in principle a unified body of rules is partially abandoned. Third, comparative law may provide a path to understanding and explaining different approaches to international law. In practice, this may mean things like revealing states' fundamental ideological commitments through their particular ways of interpreting human rights or sovereignty.[56] Even though these are quite recent ideas, they do not fall far from the earlier ideas, although the scholarly framings are different.

To be sure, Roberts and colleagues were certainly not the first ones to deploy comparative law as a means to bring pluralism into international law scholarship. For example, already in 1984, McWhinney (alongside the above-mentioned Butler)

[54] A Roberts et al, 'Conceptualising Comparative International Law' in A Roberts et al (eds), *Comparative International Law* (Oxford: Oxford University Press, 2018) 3, 6.

[55] See J Husa, *Introduction to Comparative Law*, 2nd edn (Oxford: Hart Publishing, 2023); Siems (n 22); and Samuel (n 35).

[56] Roberts et al (n 54) 7–8.

addressed comparative international law as a move towards a more pluralistic global view.[57] There is an important link here. Even the contemporary comparative international law of Roberts and colleagues is clearly a criticism of the alleged blind universality and formalism of international law. Despite the attempts to safeguard the universality of international law, subversive ideas have grown under the surface of universality stemming from the need to recognise multiculturalism and pluralism.[58] Recent ideas incorporating a comparative approach to international law may be seen to be based on a legal realist take on international law instead of formalism underlining the universality.[59] This kind of realism comes, in fact, close to that of comparative law.[60]

What the above means for international law as a form of legal scholarship is that it endeavours to avoid normative universalism and the narrow 'field of law' framework, as it invokes a pluralistic view of international law. The underlying idea is that a pluralistic non-normative view should motivate international law scholars to use non-unifying comparative approaches when they study their subject matter. As a result, comparative international law invites scholars to pose fundamental questions about theory and methodology as they seek to develop the field of international law. Importantly, this is done not in order to change international law into comparative law, but to gain a deeper understanding of international law itself.[61] In other words, the goal is not to transform international law to comparative law, but to expand the *epistemic scope* of international law with the help of up-to-date comparative approach(es).

One may ponder what intellectual reasons lead to the recent scholarly construction of comparative international law, yet it seems reasonably plausible that this has to do with the difficulties of international law. In my view, these are the same difficulties that have led many international law scholars to turn away from traditional international law toward areas such as global law and global governance. One of the key factors is abandoning normative universalism and acknowledging that the community of international law scholars is not uniform, but a divided band composed of various national or regional communities of lawyers. The underlying pluralistic and non-normative insight is that even though international law scholars are ethically animated by universalism, they build 'their understandings of international law in ways that belie the field's claim to universality'.[62] From there it follows that international law is not a monolith,

[57] E McWhinney, 'Comparative International Law: Regional or Sectorial Inter-Systemic Approaches to Contemporary International Law' in R-J Dupuy (ed), *L'Avenir du droit international dans un monde multiculturel; The Future of International Law in a Multicultural World* (Leiden: Martinus Nijhoff Publishers, 1984) 221, 227.

[58] *cf* AK Zouapet, 'Not a Threat, an Opportunity: Regional Approaches and the Future of International Law' (2023) 48 *South African Yearbook of International Law*, doi: 10.25159/2521-2583/10750.

[59] R Mitchell, 'Sovereignty and Normative Conflict: International Legal Realism as a Theory of Uncertainty' (2017) 58 *Harvard International Law Journal* 421, 428.

[60] See, eg, Husa (n 55) 207–13.

[61] Roberts et al (n 54) 31.

[62] A Roberts, *Is International Law International?* (Oxford: Oxford University Press, 2017) 325.

but a field of law that contains numerous partially overlapping areas. As such, comparative international law does not fit well together with global law if global law is understood as a field of law based on normative universalism in a similar fashion as conventionally understood international law.

In many ways, current comparative international law comes close to law and globalisation scholarship as it invites international lawyers to become more humble and reflexive when they engage with international law. When it comes to comparative international law's relation with modern comparative law, it basically has a similar kind of function as comparative law in general in its relation to all sorts of legal scholarship. To that end, comparative approaches to law may aid international lawyers to grasp international law in a novel light and from non-universalistic perspectives.[63] Even though this seems like an onerous task, that is not necessarily the case. For instance, identifying and interpreting international law by doing comparative analyses of diverse international law-related domestic court decisions does not sound like an overly subversive venture.[64] Moreover, comparative international law has been around for quite some time now, buzzing under the surface of mainstream international law scholarship committed to universalism.[65] The globalisation of law has offered a new opening for comparative international law that was lacking in the 1970s and 1980s. Also, no doubt, critical movements such as Third World Approaches to International Law (TWAIL) have expanded scholarly boundaries and made way for pluralism-sensitive approaches.[66]

From the viewpoint of a pluralist understanding of comparative law, comparative international law seems like progressive legal scholarship, as it aspires to break free from the shackles of a normative and universal view of law, and as it opens up research to directions that seek to study international law in diverse ways. This is not far from how globalisation is seen (critically) from a comparative law viewpoint, as a narrative that professes to uphold a worldwide view that is, in practice, 'only partially shared by the very world it aims to include'.[67] Nevertheless, as noted by Siems, the globalisation of law is of natural interest for the comparatist.[68] Essentially, both comparative law and comparative international law are methodologically and substance-wise pluralist areas of legal studies, not fields of

[63] ibid 325.

[64] A Roberts, 'Comparative International Law? The Role of National Courts in Creating and Enforcing International Law' (2011) 60 *International and Comparative Law Quarterly* 57.

[65] See, eg, WE Butler (ed), *International Law in Comparative Perspective* (Alphen aan den Rijn: Sijthoff & Noordhoff, 1980), focusing on the applicability of comparative approach to international law.

[66] See, eg, JT Gathii, 'TWAIL: A Brief History of its Origins, its Decentralized Network, and a Tentative Bibliography' (2011) 3 *Trade Law & Development* 26; and L Eslava and S Pahuja, 'Beyond the (Post)Colonial: TWAIL and the Everyday Life of International Law' (2012) 45 *Verfassung und Recht in Übersee* 195.

[67] H Muir Watt, 'Globalization and Comparative Law' in M Reimann and R Zimmermann (eds), *The Oxford Handbook of Comparative Law*, 2nd edn (Oxford: Oxford University Press, 2019) 599, 600.

[68] Siems (n 22) 286.

law or obedient servants of an internationalised judiciary.[69] This, in turn, has consequences when it comes to the discussion of the relationship between global law and comparative international law.

E. Global Law and Comparative International Law

Given the above, there seems to be an unavoidable contradiction between global law conceived as a field of law and comparative international law scholarship. To simplify, if global law is based on normative universalism, it is compatible with international law conceived as a normative universalising field of law. However, if global law is perceived as an expansion of normative and universalising international law, it is incompatible with both modern comparative law and comparative international law. This inference seems evident: it is difficult not to regard this as a fundamental contradiction. It is useful to shortly revisit the notions of 'global' and 'globalisation' in order to probe the incongruity a bit further.

Both global law and international law seem to be global in the sense that their reach is supposed to involve the entire world. Both have an overly ambitious scope as they seek to cover the whole globe. Yet it is evident that global law has a broader scope, as it is not limited to what is normally meant by international law. Whereas global law contains several overlapping laws (in a broad sense), the rules of international law come from two key sources: international treaties and customary international law. Importantly, both of these sources of international law are created by states.[70] Adding a global dimension to the traditional international law view means a considerable change of perspective, as the globalisation of law clearly exceeds the narrow limits of the international rules, principles and practices that govern relations between states and international organisations. The number of norm-producing actors is simply bigger in today's world than in the past century. Globalisation has brought fragmentation which, in turn, may also be seen to strengthen the effectiveness and the legitimacy of international law, as argued by Peters.[71]

I argue that it is crucial to understand that globalisation concerns more profound legal change than a particular field of law. As Berman points out: 'We live in a world of multiple, overlapping normative communities.'[72] Whereas Westphalian international law is unable to respond to global legal pluralism

[69] On judicial internationalisation, see E Mak, *Judicial Decision-Making in a Globalised World* (Oxford: Hart Publishing, 2015) 2–3.

[70] See, eg, V Lowe, *International Law: A Very Short Introduction* (Oxford: Oxford University Press, 2015) ch 2.

[71] '[T]he plurality of the viewpoints of actors involved in global governance need not only be seen as inevitable, but may even be appreciated as beneficial': Peters (n 26) 703.

[72] Berman (n 2) 3.

described by Berman, comparative international law reacts by considering global legal pluralism through analysis of international law-relevant *localities*. From the comparative law camp, it has been justly pointed out that legal globalisation does not automatically produce similarities, as there will always be local social, political and economic complications.[73] Moreover, focusing on localities suggests that the universalism of normative international law is halfway abandoned. Consequently, this is irksome if one conceives of international law as the law of all humanity. Accordingly, the issue is also about the ethics and the state of mind of the international law scholar.

If we move the discussion away from comparative international law and examine its neighbouring fields, some observations seem to arise. Now, of course, it could be argued that global law and comparative law are both fundamentally universalistic endeavours. Nevertheless, there is one significant difference. Contemporary comparative law's universalism is *epistemic*, whereas global law's universalism is *normative*.[74] In my view, this is an essential difference with far-reaching consequences. The comparatist seeks knowledge over all kinds of borders, whereas the legal globalist wishes to construct a cosmopolitan legal order.[75] In effect, the ambit of modern comparative law is divergent from the attempt to construct a global legal order as envisaged by some global law scholars.[76] Against this backdrop, it is hardly a surprise that globalisation can be seen as a challenge to the modern comparative study of law.[77] Globalisation's challenge to comparative law means that the ways in which comparatists have defined and constructed legal identities is becoming obsolete, as the regulatory landscape is more complex, diversified and fragmented than was the case previously.[78] Diversity and unity are hard to fit in the same field of legal scholarship if the aim is (also) to demarcate the epistemic boundaries between fields of legal knowledge.

Another problem stemming from modern comparative law is that if global law is conceived of as a field of law based on similar normative universalism as international law, it lacks the critical potential that comparative law offers. In short, modern comparative law's one important task is to provide a critical point of view to globalisation's tendency to universalise law at the service of global governance. When comparative international law follows the path provided by modern comparative law, it does not epistemically dominate local cultures and

[73] Husa (n 55) 193.

[74] As Butler (n 53) 245 puts it, 'the domain of comparative law is without limits because there is no domain: the comparative method is of universal application, as appropriate, in all the sciences and spheres of knowledge'.

[75] For a more detailed discussion, see J Husa, *Interdisciplinary Comparative Law: Rubbing Shoulders with the Neighbours or Standing Alone in a Crowd* (Cheltenham: Edward Elgar, 2022) 213–24.

[76] See, eg, G Ziccardi Capaldo, *The Pillars of Global Law* (Abingdon, Routledge, 2008), who builds on the idea of common global values.

[77] M Adams, 'Comparative Law in a Globalizing World' (2012) 17 *Tilburg Foreign Law Review* 263.

[78] *cf* Monateri (n 4) 20; and Husa (n 55) 287.

experiences by seeking to subdue local forms of governance and replace them with delocalised forms of international law.[79] There is no urge to unify. To that end, a comparative approach refuses to envisage global law as a field of law – that is, a body of norms emerging from globalisation – and seeks to identify, understand and explain local differences instead of trying to sweep everything under the notion of global law.[80] That being the case, it is easy to see the difference between a pluralist comparative law view and a view according to which '[t]he building of the legal system of the universal community has begun'.[81] In summary, there is an underlying tension between universalising and localising tendencies that strains relations between the globalist and the diversity-embracing takes on globalising law. Whatever forms comparative international law takes, it needs to find its path in between these extremes.

In my view, it is important for the comparative study of law to maintain a perspective that allows for diversity simply because, as noted by Glenn, globalisation is not a single process consisting of the spread of Western technology, the Western style of human rights and open markets.[82] If we accept Glenn's sound analysis according to which 'the process of globalization represents something more than expanding western influence encountering local and particular forms of resistance', defining global law as a field of law based on normative universalism becomes virtually impossible.[83] There needs to be room for localised views too. In the post-COVID-19 world in which Russia has attacked Ukraine, and China has tense relations with the West, the noble idea of a global legal order seems much more distant than 20 years ago. Globalisation has led to a situation where strong states are able to use their power across their borders, whereas smaller and weaker states have difficulties asserting authority even within their own borders.[84] Already before the crises of the 2020s, Brexit and the Trump presidency had made it difficult to sell the idea of global law even within the Western sphere.[85] Consequently, the idea of global law is sailing against the wind during these troubled times when the post-Second World War international system is in crisis. Yet it is too early to declare reverse globalisation, at least if it is not seen as a linear dynamic without localised subtleties.[86] In essence, comparative international law faces these challenges as it seeks to step out of the old epistemic boundaries without losing its identity and intellectual calling.

[79] *cf* R Michaels, 'Transnationalizing Comparative Law' (2016) 23 *Maastricht Journal of European and Comparative Law* 352.

[80] See also M Graziadei, 'What Does Globalisation Mean for the Comparative Study of Law?' (2021) 16 *Journal of Comparative Law* 511, 535–36.

[81] Ziccardi Capaldo (n 76) 8.

[82] HP Glenn, *Legal Traditions of the World: Sustainable Diversity in Law*, 4th edn (Oxford: Oxford University Press, 2014) 52.

[83] ibid.

[84] *cf* R Cotterrell, *Sociological Jurisprudence: Juristic Thought and Social Inquiry* (Abingdon: Routledge, 2018) 133.

[85] Klabbers and Palombella (n 11) 4.

[86] *cf* Michaels (n 48); Muir Watt (n 67); and Graziadei (n 80).

F. Conclusion

The observations I have made in this chapter give cause to be attentive when it comes to the relationship between global law and comparative international law. On the surface, it may appear that global law and comparative international law are not only compatible but also easy to combine. However, looking deeper under the surface, it turns out that much depends on how global law is perceived. If global law is understood as a kind of a transformed field of international law based on normative universalism, it means that the recent version of comparative international law is difficult to combine with it. Then again, if global law is understood pluralistically as a process that involves various forms of overlapping laws stemming from multiple sources, it is compatible with the present-day scholarly version of comparative international law. Importantly, it is not about how we define global law, but also about how we define comparative international law. To that end, if comparative international law is understood as a means to an end and something that serves the purposes of establishing general principles of international law and supporting the decision making by international courts, then comparative international law fits well with the field-of-law-understanding of global law. However, this view fits poorly with the untidy and multi-dimensional reality of globalisation.

In the end, the issue also concerns how we understand comparative law. It is evident that if international law scholarship is built on the modern pluralist understanding of comparative law, then the non-normative and localising version of comparative international law is the way to proceed when addressing global law and comparative international law. In conclusion, conceiving of global law as a form of scholarship (ie, law and globalisation) or new epistemology means that global law and comparative international may have a fruitful relationship. In turn, conceiving of global law normatively as a transformed Westphalian legacy leads to difficulties regarding its relation to modern comparative international law scholarship. Global law's innate problem is that it builds on old cosmopolitan assumptions, whereas comparative international law is ready to expand its reach beyond the Westphalian epistemic boundaries.

INDEX

www.ingramcontent.com/pod-product-compliance
Ingram Content Group UK Ltd.
Pitfield, Milton Keynes, MK11 3LW, UK
UKHW020235290926
15470UKWH00002B/557

9 781509 972395